PRAISE FOR THE COCKTA

"This book is a toboggan ride through the history of the cocktail every turn. Cheryl has mined some of the leading experts to con Cocktail" DeGroff, *The Craft of the Cocktail* and *The Essential Cockta...*

"Cheryl has demystified the cocktail, and made it what it should always be: fun and approachable! She takes us on an entertaining journey into the world of libations and those who serve them; their histories, stories, and antidotes. In the end, we better understand how we have arrived where we are and leave a more educated and appreciative imbiber!" —Tony Abou-Ganim, *The Modern Mixologist*

"Eureka! Cheryl Charming just made the internet obsolete. The bartending maven once again has done all the digging and delivered the gold on the history of everything bartending, cocktails, and cocktail bars." —Tobin Ellis, BarMagic of Las Vegas

"Cheryl Charming makes facts fun again! In addition to page-turning chapters on drink evolution through the millennia and the backstory of just about every famous cocktail (I particularly enjoyed her revelations about the Cosmopolitan). This book offers thoroughly entertaining sections on cocktails in film, literature, and television. The 'Name Your Poison' list, in which Cheryl cites the favorite drink of celebrities past and present, is alone worth the price of the book." —Jeff "Beachbum" Berry, *Sippin' Safari*; *Beachbum Berry's Intoxica!*; *Beach Bum Berry's Remixed*; *Beach Bum Berry's Grog Log*; and *Beach Bum Berry's Taboo Table*

"Cheryl has compiled a wealth of knowledge and experiences from virtually every corner of cocktail culture, and masterfully collated it all into a fun book that ushers the reader along a grand tour of kaleidoscopic indulgence." —T.A. Breaux, *Absinthe: The Exquisite Elixir*

"You know what would be valuable? A ten-volume encyclopedia of drink. You know what's even more valuable? Ten volumes of information condensed into one. And that's what Cheryl Charming has compiled—a comprehensive resource for both professionals or serious amateurs curious about spirits, cocktails, the history behind them, and how to make 'em." —Wayne Curtis, *And a Bottle of Rum: A History of the New World in Ten Cocktails*

"This book is a comprehensive, thoroughly researched, easy to read compendium of cocktail history. You can open it to any page and find yourself engrossed for the next hour. Buy a copy for your bar, your coffee table, heck, even your bathroom!" —Philip Greene, *To Have and Have Another: A Hemingway Cocktail Companion* and *A Drinkable Feast: A Cocktail Companion to 1920s Paris*

"In her inimitable fashion, Miss Charming, the bartender who is considered by many, myself included, to be the ultimate Queen of the New Orleans Cocktail Scene, has delivered yet another fabulous book, chock-full of all manner of cocktailian splendor. And this one's a doozy! The world of cocktails flows with fascinating trivia, incredible folklore, accurate historical stories, some tall tales, and lots of straight, hard facts. I believe that Cheryl Charming has detailed near-as-darn-it every single one of these pearls of liquid wisdom in this tome. Skim through it for a few minutes, and see how much time passes before you can even dream of putting it down." —gaz regan, author of *The Joy of Mixology*

**THIS BOOK DOES NOT ADVOCATE OR ENCOURAGE THE ABUSE OF ALCOHOLIC BEVERAGES.
PLEASE DRINK RESPONSIBLY AND WITH MODERATION.**

THE
COCKTAIL
COMPANION

A Guide to Cocktail History, Culture, Trivia and Favorite Drinks

CHERYL CHARMING

Mango Publishing

Coral Gables, FL

You know how it is. You pick up a book, flip to the dedication, and find that, once again, the author has dedicated a book to someone else and not to you. Not this time. This one's for you. With you know what, and you probably know why, and with a cocktail in hand.

www.misscharming.com

Contents

FOREWORD

In her inimitable fashion, Miss Charming, the bartender who is considered by many, myself included, to be the ultimate Queen of the New Orleans Cocktail Scene, has delivered yet another fabulous book, chock-full of all manner of cocktailian splendor. And this one's a doozy!

The world of cocktails flows with fascinating trivia, incredible folklore, accurate historical stories, some tall tales, and lots of straight, hard facts. I believe that Cheryl Charming has detailed near-as-darn-it every single one of these pearls of liquid wisdom in this tome. Skim through it for a few minutes and see how much time passes before you can even dream of putting it down.

Who else would describe garnishes as jewelry for cocktails? Nobody. That's who. It's part of Cheryl's unique style, and it's part of what makes her stand out in any crowd of cocktail aficionados.

You'll find, too, that Cheryl goes the whole nine yards when it comes to research. Fancy a Ramos Gin Fizz, for instance? You'll find that a certain Henry Charles "Carl" Ramos invented the drink in 1888 and his bar went through an incredible 5,000 eggs every week to keep up with demand for the drink.

But Cheryl doesn't stop there. Read on and she'll tell you where to get the best Ramos Gin Fizzes in New Orleans today, and I wasn't surprised to see that Bourbon O Bar, where Miss Charming struts her stuff, is one of them. I've had a Ramos Gin Fizz at the Bourbon "O" Bar. It was sublime.

This book will walk you through drinking scenes from movies, books, and television. As you start this literary bar crawl you might want to keep in mind that Cheryl has also provided a guide to historic bars around the world here, so a literal bar crawl could be in your future too. How about starting off in Dublin at the bar where Oscar Wilde once worked? You'll find it in here.

When was the first golden age of the cocktail? Which family has been producing fine apple brandy in New Jersey since the late 1600s? When were cocktails first served on an aircraft? (Far earlier than you're thinking.) Where can you find a cocktail that incorporates crushed Mexican black ants? Which cocktail should be shaken to the rhythm of the Foxtrot?

All this and more will be revealed to you in this great book.

And buyer beware: if you loan this book to a friend, you might never see it again.

gaz regan

1

STEP UP TO THE BAR: AN ALCOHOL TIMELINE

No one knows the exact date when cocktails started, but through archeological findings, it is assumed that humans have been mixing ingredients together to create tasty beverages for themselves for 10,000 years because that is when domestic agriculture began—and if you believe in the Lost Continent then it goes back even further. Mead (made from honey), ale (beer), and wine (made from fruit) are the most common alcoholic drinks found in ancient civilizations, so it is also assumed that these ingredients were mixed together to create honey-flavored beverages. In addition, it is imagined that herbs and spices were thrown in to infuse more flavor, and possibly steeped medicinal herbs were used on occasion. Social drinking has been part of every culture in some form and with time, people began to travel (for various reasons) and needed shelter, so humble inns along their path provided temporary housing, food, and drink—the same basic amenities modern hotels provide today. Public houses (pubs) were built in towns and served as "information hubs" where you learned of current events, gossiped, complained about the weather, flirted, told stories, and, of course, drank. Things pretty much remained the same for hundreds of years.

There have been many theories of where the word "cocktail" came from. Some include an Aztec princess, an Ancient Roman doctor who called a favorite drink cockwine, a New Orleans French egg cup, Cock Ale Punch that was actually made with a whole rooster and ale (ick!), a gingerroot suppository for a non-spirited horse, and a tavern keeper who put rooster tail feathers in soldiers' drinks (cock-tail).

The first known reference to the Asian spirit "arrack" was by traveling merchants in the 1200s. In the 1300s the word "aqua vitae" ("water of life") was coined and Armagnac and Scotch whisky were being produced in the 1400s. But the first record of a spirit (an early rum) being mixed with three other ingredients in bulk was for ill sailors in the 1500s. Between the 1600s and 1800s, communal drinks were served in big bowls—with cups for all. These cups and bowls gave birth to the individual-sized cocktail we know today.

The Top Ten Things to Know about Cocktails

1. No one knows who invented the cocktail, but it is agreed that communal batches served in punch bowls then drank from cups in the 1600s gave birth to the individual cocktail we know today.
2. There have been many theories about the origin of the word "cocktail." As of today, it has been narrowed down to two. One comes from a 1700s word in the horse trade profession, and the other from a fictional character based on a real person, but neither has been confirmed.
3. To date, the first printed form of the word "cocktail" appeared in 1798. The word pertaining to the drink was first printed in 1803 and the first printed definition was in 1806.

4. The first known British drink receipt (recipe) book was published in 1827. The first known American cocktail recipe book was published in 1862.

5. As far as we know, the Mint Julep is America's first cocktail.

6. Before the 1920s, in America, fancy cocktails were drunk by prominent white males in fancy saloons and bars. The average joe drank beer, wine, whiskey, and cider at pubs, while a fancy bar might have a side room for fancy women called the "Ladies' Bar." The only women allowed in the main bar were madams and prostitutes.

7. The first golden age of the cocktail was between 1860 and 1919, and the seed for the second golden age of the cocktail was planted around the millennium.

8. The Martini is the most iconic cocktail and symbol of the cocktail culture.

9. The repeal of the American Prohibition, women's freedom to socialize in most bars, and Hollywood technology (talkies) glamorized cocktails between the 1930s and 1960s.

10. The world's largest cocktail festival, Tales of the Cocktail, has been held in New Orleans each July since 2002.

•••

A COCKTAIL TIMELINE

1500S

If you owned a pub, alehouse, tavern, or inn, you were probably growing your own food for meals and drink to serve guests. In addition to having land for a garden, you needed to tend to animals, provide stables for travelers (we call them parking lots today), have an area to produce alcoholic drink, and be literate enough to keep books, pay bills, manage help, and collect payments. Tavern floors were often made of sand, and it was common to have a portcullis (metal vertical closing gate) around the bar area. To multitask dinner, a kitchen dog was often placed in a turnspit wheel—the dog would walk inside the wheel, which slowly turned meat roasting over a fire.

Names of alehouses, pubs, taverns, and inns included Beverley Arms, Black Lion, Boar's Head, Bull Long Medford, Crown Sarre, King's Head, the Crane Inn, the Devil's Tavern, the George, the Lion, the Prospect of Whitby, the White Horse, and Ye Olde Mitre.

Drinking words heard were "aled up," "befuddled," "bizzled," "drinking deep," "has on a barley cap," "has more than one can hold," "lion drunk," "malt above the meal," "rowdy," "swallowed a tavern token," "shattered," "shaved," "swilled up," "wassailed," and "whittled."

New brands and spirits created in the 1500s included aguardiente de caña (rum), brandy, cachaça, Disarrono, jenever, kummel, mezcal, pisco, and Scotch whiskey.

1500 – Sugarcane is harvested in Hispaniola to be used to make rum.
– Scotland's King James IV grants the production of aqua vitae.

1514 – King Louis XII of France licenses vinegar producers to distill eau-de-vie.

1518 – Spanish ruler Charles V imports 2,000 slaves to Hispaniola to work the sugarcane fields.

1525 – Amaretto Disaronno is produced in Italy.

– A groundbreaking distilling book is published and inspires Holland to produce brandewijn (burnt wine).

1531 – Spanish settlers distill the local fermented drink in Mexico to make mexcalli (mezcal).

1533 – Sugarcane eau-de-vie is created (later known as cachaça).

– Monks in the Italian mountains make liqueurs.

1534 – A book with over seventy vodka-based medicines is published. It is the first time the word "vodka" is documented.

1537 – King Francis I of France grants the production of eau-de-vie.

1538 – Peruvian farmers make what we know today as pisco.

1552 – In the book *Constelijck Distilleer Boek*, Philippus Hermanni refers to a juniper-infused eau-de-vie in his 1568.

1575 – Lucas Bols sets up a distillery in Amsterdam and begins making jenever.

1586 – Aguardiente de caña (basically, rum), *hierba buena* (Cuban herbal plant that belongs to the mint family), limes, and sugar were batched for a ship of sick sailors and its British sea captain, Sir Francis Drake (nicknamed El Draque—Spanish for "the dragon"). All that was needed was an addition of fizzy water and they'd have had themselves a barrel of Mojitos.

1600S

We have a good idea of what taverns and pubs looked like because Dutch painter Jan Steen painted detailed daily life paintings. His paintings related to drinking include *Prince's Day in a Tavern* (1660; he painted himself in the painting), *Tavern Garden* (1660), *In the Tavern* (1660), *The Drinker* (1660), *A Merry Party* (1660), *Peasants Before an Inn* (1653), *Leaving the Tavern* (unknown date), *Merry Company on a Terrace* (1670), and *Tavern Scene* (1670). Things seen in Steen's paintings are jugs, bottles, vessels (some made of glass), sheet music, musical instruments, flirting, fire, food, laughter, games, gambling, animals, children, toys, messes, men grabbing women, smoking, skulls, barrels, and birds in cages. Minus the children and animals, this is pretty much what is seen in modern bars. My personal favorite painting is titled *As the Old Sing, so Pipe the Young* (1668).

In the early 1600s, punch (paunch, a Hindu word that means "five") became popular among English sailors and spice merchants who would travel to India and back. While sailing homeward, they would make big bowls of punch with five ingredients, including spirit, lemon, sugar, water, and spice. Punch spread to Britain's upper class, and it was soon taken to the New World (America). The upper class owned bowls, cups, and ladles made of silver, and records in London's Central Criminal Court documented many incidents of these items being stolen—most times with the punch still in the bowl!

As for Pilgrims who sought a new life in the New World, life was hard carving out an uncharted land while depending on English ships for supplies. For the most part, settlers were in survival mode, but somehow they found the time and resources to open not one but two rum distilleries. Rum is what funded early America.

Some names of alehouses, pubs, taverns, and inns included Bear at Bridge-foot, Bull and Bush, Bull and Gate, Grapes, Green Dragon Tavern, Hatchet Inn, the Anchor, the Plough, the Red Lion, the Seven Stars, Three Nuns, and Trafalgar Tavern.

Drinking words heard in the 1600s included "admiral of the narrow seas," "beastly drunk," "boozed," "bubbled cap-sick," "caught a fox," "D and D" (drunk and disorderly), "dull in the eye," "elevated," "giggled up," "got bread and cheese in one's head," "muddled up," "on a continual drinking merry-go-round," "on the rampage," and "seeing double."

New brands and spirits in the 1600s include Bushmills Irish whiskey, Chartreuse, and Haig Scotch.

Prince's Day in a Tavern, by Jan Steen, 1660, Dutch painting, oil on panel. Prince's Day was a birthday celebration in honor of Prince William III of Orange-Nassau (November 14, 1660). © *Everett Art / Shutterstock*

1608 – Old Bushmills Distillery is established in Ireland. Today it holds the title of the first licensed whiskey distillery in the world.

1620 – The Pilgrims bring brandy and gin with them on the *Mayflower* to the New World on November 9. The 101 brave colonists live aboard the ship in the winter and supplies run low quickly.

1623 – Jenever is mentioned in the English play *The Duke of Milan*.

1625 – Haig becomes the first recognized Scotch whisky.

1635 – Portuguese government prohibits the sale of cachaça. The ban is lifted in 1695.

1637 – Distillery equipment is brought to the island of Barbados.

1644 – Distillery equipment is brought to the island of Martinique.

1657 – A rum distillery is built in Boston.

1664 – A rum distillery is built in New York City.

1650 – To save room, Admiral Robert Blake switches beer rations with brandy.

1655 – Vice Admiral William Penn orders rum be included in daily rations.

1660 – Popular and cocky punch maker Billy "Bully" Dawson says, "The man who sees, does, or thinks of anything else while he is making punch may as well look for the Northwest Passage on Mutton Hill. A man can never make good punch unless he is satisfied, nay positive, that no man breathing can make better."

1668 – In London's Criminal Court, Thomas Carey is found guilty of stealing punch and its bowl.

1674 – Harvard University builds its own brewhouse.

1676 – When visiting India, physician John Fryer mentions punch that the English make with liquor.

1688 – William of Orange imports jenever from Holland and starts producing British gin.

1691 – Nolet begins to distill in Holland. (They later produce Ketel One Vodka.)

1694 – On Christmas Day, English Navy commander Admiral Edward Russell fills a blue-and-white-tiled fountain with punch and throws a party for 6,000 people in the Spanish port of Cadiz. He hires 800 staff and 1 male child in a boat afloat the punch, serving guests.

1695 – DeKuyker opens a distillery in Holland.

1697 – A fancy British punch bowl is created. They call it Monteith.

1698 – In New Jersey, William Laird begins production of Laird's applejack for personal use.

1699 – Kenelm Digby published *The Closet of Sir Kenelm Digby Knight Opened*, which gives many wine and ale recipes. One recipe in particular is called Cock Ale. Digby says, "These are tame days when we have forgotten how to make Cock Ale." This ale takes a month to make and boiling a rooster is involved. This is the first known reference to Cock Ale. It is seen later in a couple of 1700s cooking books.

1700S

Colonial America was settling into its new home. By 1700, the population reached 275,000 (with Boston and New York City having the highest populations). In 1700, there also were over 140 rum distilleries in the colonies. By the end of the century, the population reached 5.3 million, of which 1 million was of African descent.

In this century, the colonists struggled to break free of Britain. Examples of the old country not wanting to let loose include the Molasses Act (taxing the rum), the Wool Act, the Iron Act, the Currency Act, the Sugar Act (taxing the rum), the Stamp Act, the Boston Massacre, and the Boston Tea Party. This all led to the American Revolution (1775–1783). After breaking off from England, a drink called Sling became popular. It was simply made with a spirit of your choice, sugar, and water. Later, a dash or two of bitters was added making it a Bittered Sling, which was considered a good drink for the morning. These are the exact ingredients for an Old-Fashioned.

The signing of the United States Declaration of Independence in 1776 was toasted with Madeira. Benjamin Franklin wrote a drinking dictionary, invented bifocals, and discovered electricity. James Hargreaves invented the spinning wheel. American whiskey distilleries began to pop up, the sandwich was invented, and for fun, the hot air balloon took its first flight in 1782. On the other side of the pond, the Industrial Revolution was leading the race in textile production, steam power, and iron making, but losing the battle on gin addiction. This was also the century absinthe was discovered.

Often postal service sections were set up in taverns starting in the mid-1700s. Some names of alehouses, pubs, taverns, and inns included Beetle and Wedge, Bell in Hand Tavern, City Tavern, Fraunces Tavern, Jean Lafitte's Blacksmith Shop, Jessop's Tavern, the Stag and Hounds, the Eagle, the Lamb, the Dirty Duck, the Green Man, the Crown, the Old Ship, the Publik House, Prospect of Whitby, Wiggin's Tavern, Blue Bell Inn, and O'Malley's Pub.

Drinking words heard in the 1700s are too many to mention because Benjamin Franklin wrote a 1737 book—by candlelight—titled *The Drinker's Dictionary*, which listed over 200 drinking words. Some of these and others include "addled," "been at Barbados," "cockadoodled," "cherry merry," "cracked," "cranked," "clips the King's

English," "dizzy as a coot," "drinking like a fish," "drunk as a wheel barrow," "fears no man," "fuddled up," "full as a goat," "got a snootful," "groggy," "happy juiced," "head full of bees," "in the altitudes," "jacked up," "jolly," "juiced to the gills," "lapping it up," "lost his rudder," "rotten drunk," "screwed and tattooed," "tipsy," and "stewed."

New brands and spirits in the world include absinthe, Admiral Nelson rum, Appleton rum, Cruzan rum, Drambuie, Evan William's whiskey, Gordon's gin, Harvey's Bristol Cream Sherry, Jose Cuervo, Laird's applejack, and Madeira.

1708 – The poem "Old King Cole" describes the king asking for his pipe, bowl (punch bowl), and musicians: "Old King Cole was a merry old soul, and a merry old soul was he; He called for his pipe, and he called for his bowl, and he called for his fiddlers three."

1712 – The first known bitters is created and patented by Richard Staughton.

1717 – The Colt Neck Inn in New Jersey is opened by a William Laird descendant and sells applejack for the first time.

1718 – The French founded New Orleans. Within one hundred years, French-influenced cocktails would be created.

1721 – A quarter of the city of London is used to produce gin.

1726 – London has over 6,000 places to purchase gin.

1727 – Eliza Smith publishes *The Compleat Housewife: Or, Accomplish'd Gentlewoman's Companion* in London. Eighteen editions are produced in fifty years. The book contains hundreds of household receipts (recipes) including many wines, cordials, and a Milk Punch recipe: "To make fine Milk Punch. Take two quarts of water, one quart of milk, half a pint of lemon juice, and one quart of brandy, sugar to your taste; put the milk and water together a little warm, then the sugar, then the lemon juice, stir it well together, then the brandy, stir it again and run it through a flannel bag till 'tis very fine, then bottle it; it will keep a fortnight, or more." Smith also gives a recipe for Cock Ale Punch using an old rooster. The recipe will probably churn even the stomachs of today's flesh-purchasing humans since they are used to the product being wrapped in shiny plastic, so it is not described here, but can be googled if so desired.

1732 – America's first angling club—and the oldest continuous club today—is called "Colony in Schuylkill." (Today it's called Schuylkill Fishing Company of Pennsylvania.) The goal of the club is to socialize, fish, eat, and drink. The famous "Fish House Punch" is created here with a mixture of rum, peach brandy, lemon, sugar, and water. President George Washington is an honoree member.

1734 – On December 4, a mention of arrack punch is mentioned in London's Central Criminal Court: "Mrs. Holcomb came in a Coach to my Door about 2 o'clock in the Morning: I shew'd 'em up two Pair of Stairs, and they had a Bowl—it was but one Bowl—of Arrack Punch, a Bottle of Wine, and three Jellies."

1735 – Arrack punch is mentioned again in London's Central Criminal Court:
> "He asked me to drink a Glass of Punch, and so I went in, and he and I drank four or five Bowls of
> Arrack Punch, which came to 20 s. and three Pints of Wine."
> Court: What! Did you two drink all that?

– There are too many London's Central Criminal Court documents to mention; almost every available alcohol at the time was mentioned. View them online at oldbaileyonline.org. The most shocking and saddest document shows how addicted England was to gin; on February 27, 1734, a mother kills her two-year-old baby girl so she can sell her clothes to buy gin.

1736 – The Gin Act is passed in England to curb the consumption of gin.

1740 – Is grog the first Daiquiri? On August 21, fifty-five-year-old Vice Admiral Edward Vernon of the Royal Navy issues an order that the daily rum ration should be mixed every day with a quart of water, half pint of rum, lime juice, and sugar mixed in a scuttled butt on the deck in the presence of the Lieutenant of the Watch. (Vernon's nickname was "Old Grog" because of the waterproof cloak he would wear on deck, which was made of grogram cloth. The sailors named the drink "Grog.") Well, grog appears to have the same ingredients of a classic Daiquiri—just without the ice. Before you pull out your cell phone and google "scuttled butt," it was equivalent to the modern-day office water cooler but made out of a wooden cask (barrel) that sailors gathered around. A hole was cut on top to allow the grog to be served to each man.

1742 – Eliza Smith publishes the first known American cookery recipe book. It is the fifth edition of *The Compleat Housewife: Or, Accomplish'd Gentlewoman's Companion*

1743 – The Glenmorangie distillery is established in Scotland.

1744 – A man visiting Philadelphia named William Black records in his diary that he was given:
– "Cider and punch for lunch; rum and brandy before dinner; punch, Madeira, port, and sherry at dinner; punch and liqueurs with the ladies; and wine, spirit, and punch till bedtime; all in punch bowls big enough for a goose to swim in."

1745 – Drambuie is produced in Scotland. The most popular modern cocktail made with Drambuie is the Rusty Nail.

1749 – Appleton rum is produced in Jamaica.
– J&B Scotch is produced.

1751 – England passes another Gin Act.
– The first health warning is printed on a bottle of gin.

1755 – The Marie Brizard Company is founded in Bordeaux, France.

1757 – The first U.S. president, George Washington, writes about his personal beer recipe and titles it "To Make Small Beer."

1758 – Admiral Nelson's Premium Rum is produced.
– George Washington campaigns with a barrel of Barbados rum.
– Don Jose Cuervo receives a land grant to cultivate agave plants in Mexico.

1759 – Arthur Guinness signs a 9,000-year lease on an unused brewery at St. James's Gate in Dublin.

1760 – George Washington is introduced to Laird's applejack.

— Cruzan Rum from the Virgin Islands is produced.

1761 — Bombay Gin from England is produced.

1765 — Richard Hennessy founds Hennessy Cognac.

1769 — Gordon's gin is produced. Gordon's gin will be mentioned in the first James Bond novel, 1953's *Casino Royale*, when Bond orders a Vesper.

— The Henriod sisters advertise their elixir d'absinthe.

1771 — Evan Shelby opens the first rye whiskey distillery in Tennessee.

— Discoveries on how to create carbonated water are documented.

1780 — Jacob Beam builds a whiskey distillery in Kentucky.

— John Jameson opens a whiskey distillery in Dublin, Ireland.

— Johann Tobias Lowitz develops charcoal filtration for vodka.

— Elijah Pepper builds a log cabin distillery in Kentucky.

1783 — Evan Williams Bourbon is produced.

1784 — Philadelphia physician and politician Benjamin Rush publishes a pamphlet titled *An Inquiry into the Effects of Spirituous Liquors on the Human Mind and Body*.

1786 — Antonio Carpano invents vermouth in Italy.

1789 — Reverend Elijah Craig ages corn whiskey in charred oak barrels in Kentucky.

— The first temperance society forms in Litchfield County, Connecticut.

1790 — Jean-Jacob Schweppe makes artificial mineral water.

1791 — George Washington imposes a whiskey tax.

1792 — Pernod absinthe is produced.

1795 — Old Jake Beam Sour Mash whiskey is introduced.

1796 — Harvey's Bristol Cream Sherry is produced.

1791 — George Washington becomes a whiskey distiller.

1798 — Anistatia Miller and Jared Brown are credited with finding the most current recording of the word "cocktail." On Friday, March 16, the *Morning Post and Gazette* in London, England, reported that a pub owner won a lottery and erased all his customers' debts:

> A publican, in Downing-street, who had a share of the 20,000 l. prize, rubbed out all his scores, in a transport of joy: This was a humble imitation of his neighbor, who, when he drew the highest prize in the State Lottery, not only rubbed out, but actually broke scores with his old customers, and entirely forgot them.

– Four days later, on Tuesday, March 20, the customer's debts were published in the same newspapers. The word "cocktail" appears:

> "Mr. Pitt, two petit vers of "L'huile de Venus"
>
> Ditto, one of "perfeit amour."
>
> Ditto, "cock-tail." (Vulgarly called ginger.)

– Esteemed spirits and drink historian David Wondrich is of the opinion that the usage of the word "cocktail" (at this time) came from the horse trade. He learned that to make an older horse you were trying to sell look frisky, one would use a chunk of ginger (probably peeled) as a suppository that would cock up the horse's tail.

– The cocktail John Collins is invented in London.

1800S

Cocktails and cocktail making took the stage with a bright white spotlight in the 1800s and American bartenders were the cocktail stars of the whole world. They wore pressed jackets, diamond tiepins, crisp collared shirts; basically, they dressed to the nines. The first recipe books were published, the availability of pond ice (and later, artificial ice) were game changers, and the golden age of the cocktail shone the brightest it has to date. The position of a bartender—even though blue collar—was seen as the aristocracy of the working class. In those days, you had to be a bartender apprentice for several years before you could be a bartender. One celebrity bartender, Jerry Thomas, traveled the world with a set of solid silver bar tools and he published the first known American cocktail recipe book, *Bar-Tender's Guide, How to Mix Drinks, or the Bon-Vivant's Companion* in 1862.

This century began with an American population of around five million and by 1899 unbelievably increased to a staggering seventy million. Much advancement happened during this time that laid the foundation for the next century. This included gas lighting, sewing machines, the telegraph, Morse code, bicycles, typewriters, mail order catalogs, Coca-Cola, matchbooks, and ice delivery. Moreover, like always, only the wealthy were able to enjoy these modern inventions in the beginning.

These times brought on civilized behavior with new technological advances. A prominent white man at a fancy bar could order a cobbler, crusta, flip, grog, Champagne Cocktail, Manhattan, Earthquake, Martinez, Old-Fashioned, Hailstorm, Rob Roy, Tom & Jerry, Snow-Storm, Roffignac, Eye-Opener, Ramos Gin Fizz, Sazerac, Santa Cruz Punch, smash, Stone-Fence, sour, toddy, or Tom Collins.

Some names of alehouses, taverns, saloons, and bars include Bull and Mouth, Bush Tavern, Chapter House, Crystal Palace Saloon, Golden Cross, Grove House Tavern, Hustler's Tavern, Jack's Elixir Bar, Knickerbocker Saloon, Iron Door Saloon, McSorley's Old Ale House, Old Absinthe House, Pete's Tavern, the Bucket of Blood, the Cock Tavern, the Imperial Cabinet, the Stag Saloon, the Village Tavern, Tujague's, Occidental, and White Horse Tavern.

Drinking words heard in the 1800s include "above par," "a bit on," "a couple of chapters into the novel," "a cup too much," "a date with John Barleycorn," "a drop too much," "a little in the suds," "a public mess," "a spur in the head," "at peace with the floor," "been looking through a glass," "banged up on sauce," "can't see a hole in a ladder," "corked," "dead to the world," "doped up," "drunk as Bacchus," "drunk as forty billy goats," "feeling glorious," "fired up," "fog driver," "full to the brim," "ginned," "lifting the little finger," "lushed," "moonshined," "off the deep end," "moistening the clay," "of flip & c," "phlegm-cutter," "piece of bread and cheese in the attic," "polished," "quenching a spark in the throat," "sloshed," "stinking," "soaked," "swazzled," "tanked," "wetting the whistle," "woozy," and "whacked out of one's skull."

New brands and spirits launched include Averna, Black & White Scotch, Beefeater gin, Boodles gin, Canadian Club whisky, Cherry Heering, Don Q rum, Galliano, George Dickel whiskey, Grand Marnier, Johnnie Walker Scotch, Herradura tequila, Pimm's No. 1, Rose's lime juice, Sauza tequila, Seagram's 7 whisky, vermouth, Seagram's VO whiskey, Tanqueray gin, Fundador Spanish brandy, Lillet, Myers's dark rum, and Lemon Hart rum.

1801 – Chivas Regal Scotch is produced.

1803 – On April 28, the first known American recorded use of the word "cocktail" as a beverage appeared in New Hampshire's newspaper the *Farmer's Cabinet*:
– "Drank a glass of cocktail—excellent for the head...Call'd at the Doct's. found Burnham—he looked very wise—drank another glass of cocktail."

1806 – The second American recorded use of the word "cocktail" as a beverage appeared in Hudson, New York's the *Balance and Columbian Repository* (No. 18 Vol. V) on May 6:Rum! Rum! Rum!

> It is conjectured, that the price of this precious liquor will soon rife at Claverack since a certain
> candidate has placed in his account of Loss and Gain, the following items:
> Loss. 720 rum-grogs, 17 brandy do., 32 gin-slings, 411 glasses bitters, 25 do. Cock-tail
> My election.
> Gain. NOTHING.

– There was an election in Claverack, New York, and it was common (in those days) to try to win votes with free booze. The loser published his Loss and Gains in this local newspaper. Translation for 25 do. = $25 and $25 = $600 in 2017.
– Seven days later, the newspaper's twenty-eight-year-old editor, Harry Croswell of Columbia County, New York, publishes the "first definition of cocktail" known to be an alcoholic beverage—to date—on May 13. Croswell rarely publishes anything he says but makes an exception this time to answer a question from a subscriber.
– The subscriber writes:

> To the Editor of the *Balance*:
> Sir,
> I observe in your paper of the 6th instant, in the account of a democratic candidate for a seat
> in the legislature, marked under the head of Loss, 25 do. cock-tail. Will you be so obliging as to
> inform me what is meant by this species of refreshment? Though a stranger to you, I believe, from
> your general character, you will not suppose this request to be impertinent.
> I have heard of a forum, of phlegm-cutter and fog driver, of wetting the whistle, of moistening
> the clay, of a fillip, a spur in the head, quenching a spark in the throat, of flip & c, but never in my
> life, though have lived a good many years, did I hear of cock-tail before. Is it peculiar to a part of
> this country? Or is it a late invention? Is the name expressive of the effect which the drink has on
> a particular part of the body? Or does it signify that the democrats who take the potion are turned
> topsycurvy, and have their heads where their tails should be? I should think the latter to be the
> real solution; but am unwilling to determine finally until I receive all the information in my power.
> At the beginning of the revolution, a physician publicly recommended the moss which grew on
> a tree as a substitute for tea. He found on experiment, that it had more of a stimulating quality
> than he approved; and therefore, he afterward as publicly denounced it. Whatever cock-tail is, it

may be properly administered only at certain times and to certain constitutions. A few years ago, when the democrats were bawling for Jefferson and Clinton, one of the polls was held in the city of New York at a place where ice cream was sold. Their temperament then was remarkably adjust and bilious. Something was necessary to cool them. Now when they are sunk into rigidity, it might be equally necessary, by cock-tail to warm and rouse them. I hope you will construe nothing that I have said as disrespectful. I read your paper with great pleasure and wish it the most extensive circulation. Whether you answer my inquiry or not, I shall still remain,

Yours,

A SUBSCRIBER

– Croswell answers the subscriber's question of wanting to know what is the refreshment called cock-tail, while at the same time making fun of politics:

As I make it a point, never to publish anything (under my editorial head) but which I can explain, I shall not hesitate to gratify the curiosity of my inquisitive correspondent: Cock-tail, then in a stimulating liquor, composed of spirits of any kind, sugar, water, and bitters it is vulgarly called a Bittered Sling, and is supposed to be an excellent electioneering potion inasmuch as it renders the heart stout and bold, at the same time that it fuddles the head. It is said also, to be of great use to a democratic candidate: because, a person having swallowed a glass of it, is ready to swallow anything else.

1809 – Washington Irving writes, "This class of beverages originated in Maryland, whose inhabitants were prone to make merry and get fuddled with mint-julep and apple toddy. They were moreover, great horse-racers and cock-fighters; mighty wrestlers and jumpers, and enormous consumers of hoecake and bacon. They lay claim to be the first inventors of those recondite beverages, cock-tail, stone-fence, and sherry cobbler."

1817 – Elizabeth Hammond publishes *Modern Domestic Cookery, and Useful Receipt Book*, which has some punch recipes.

1820 – La Piña de Plata (the Silver Pineapple) restaurant and bar opens in Havana, Cuba. No one knows what cocktails were served here at that time—yet, but one hundred years later the bar was named Bar la Florida with a nickname of Floridita. It became famous for its frozen Daiquiris and celebrity patrons including Nobel Prize winner Ernest Hemingway.

– The first blended Scotch whisky, Johnnie Walker, is produced.

– The Beefeater gin distillery is built in England.

1821 – Author James Fenimore Cooper writes about a fictional character named Betty Flanagan who invented the cock-tail. The Flanagan character was supposedly based on a real person named Catherine Hustler (1767–1832) who ran Hustler's Tavern in Lewiston, New York, during the War of 1812 and put rooster tail feathers in drinks (cock-tails).

1823 – Pimm's Cup No. 1 is first produced by James Pimm in London.

– The Gin-Twist (gin, hot water, lemon juice, and sugar) is mentioned in the novel *Saint Ronan's Well* by Sir Walter Scott.

– Bourbon County, Kentucky, starts to call their whiskey "bourbon."

1824 – George Smith founds the Glenlivet distillery.

1825 – The first lavish London gin palaces begin to be built. They are decorated with opulent style. Later, in 1836, Charles Dickens said, "perfectly dazzling when contrasted with the darkness and dirt we have just left."
– Sandeman Port is produced.

1827 – Students of Oxford University publish the first known alcoholic drink recipe book, *Oxford Night Caps: A Collection of Receipts for Making Various Beverages at the University.* Basically, college students are credited for taking the time to put together a book of recipes so they can party. They publish several editions for almost one hundred years.
– Ballantine's blended Scotch is produced.

1830 – Talisker Scotch and Tanqueray gin are produced.

1843 – Charles Dickens writes in *Martin Chuzzlewit*, "He could...smoke more tobacco, drink more rum-toddy, mint-julep, gin-sling, and cocktail, than any private gentleman of his acquaintance."
– Courvoisier Cognac is produced.
– The Tom & Jerry hot cocktail is mentioned in the *Symbol and Odd Fellow's Magazine.*

1844 – Dry vermouth produced by the Noilly Company is first introduced in America via New Orleans.

1846 – Dewar's blended Scotch whisky is established.
– Aalborg akvavit is produced in Norway.

1850 – The first known published illustration of a two-piece cocktail shaker is seen in the *London News.*

1851 – Walter and Alfred Gilbey open Gilbey's Gin Distillery.

1852 – Joseph Santini invents the Brandy Crusta in New Orleans.

New Orleans in 1851. New Orleans has created more cocktails than any city in the world and some served during this time include Roffignac, Sazerac, and Brandy Crusta. Other adopted popular cocktails served include Mint Julep, Old-Fashioned, and Milk Punch. For the wealthy, ice from frozen lake and ponds was also available. © *Everett Historical / Shutterstock*

1853 – New York barkeep George Sala talks about barkeeps in Charles Dickens's weekly twenty-four-page journal, *Household Words.* The article describes the barkeep and his assistants as scholarly gentlemen, accomplished artists, skilled acrobats, master magicians, and bottle conjurers as they throw glasses and toss bottles about.

1854 – Canadian Club whisky is produced.

1856 – The word "mixologist" is first coined in the *Knickerbocker* or *New York Monthly Magazine.*
– The London *Weekly Dispatch* quotes the *New York Times* saying, "Every sentence a man utters must be moistened with a julep or cobbler. All the affairs of life are begun and ended with drinks."

1858 – Seagram's VO whisky is produced.

1859 – American bartender Jerry Thomas begins working on his first book, which is published in 1862.

1860 – Campari is introduced by Gaspare Campari.

1862 – Jerry Thomas publishes the first known American cocktail recipe book, *Bar-Tender's Guide, How to Mix Drinks, or the Bon-Vivant's Companion.*
– The cocktail Pink Gin is invented in London when Angostura bitters was exhibited at the Great London Exposition.

1863 – G. E. Roberts publishes *Cups and Their Customs.*

1864 – George Pullman designs railway sleeping cars, dining cars, and lounge cars serving cocktails.

1865 – Alexander Walker, Johnnie Walker's son, develops Old Highland blended Scotch whisky.

1867 – Scotsman Lauchlin Rose introduces sweetened lime juice and names it Rose's Lime Cordial. By 1879, he perfected the packaging.
– George Dickel builds his distillery.
– *Harper's New Monthly* November issue reports that 500 bottles of sherry were opened—in one day—to make Sherry Cobblers priced at one franc at the Exposition Universelle in France. One French franc is equivalent to $13 in 2018 currency.

1868 – Articles on American cocktails and cocktail shakers are published in two British publications: the British periodical *Notes and Queries* and *Meliora: A Quarterly Review of Social Science.*

1869 – Englishman William Terrington publishes *Cooling Cups and Dainty Drinks: Collection of Recipes for "Cups" and Other Compound Drinks and of General Information on Beverages of All Kind.* He goes on to publish a second edition in 1872.
– J. Haney publishes *Haney's Steward and Barkeepers Manual.*
– Mark Twain mentions a Champagne Cocktail in his memoir *Innocents Abroad.*
– American composer Joseph Winner wrote the drinking song "Little Brown Jug." It mentions the spirits gin and rum. Seventy years later, bandleader Glenn Miller recorded it with his swing orchestra.

1872 – Lillet is produced.

1873 – At the World's Exposition held in Vienna, Austria, the American Exhibition has a giant wigwam with Native American bartenders making cocktails behind three circular bars. The Exposition's Rotunda bar introduces something new in their cocktails—straws.

1874 – The Criterion restaurant and theater open in London with an American Bar. The decor consists of mirrors and white marble.
– Fundador Spanish brandy is produced.
– While in the UK, Mark Twain writes a letter to his wife, Livy, to gather four ingredients for his return: Scotch whisky, Angostura bitters, lemons, and crushed sugar. He has been drinking this cocktail before breakfast, dinner, and bed at the suggestion of a surgeon to help digestion.

1875 – H. L. W publishes *American Bar-Tender* or *The Art and Mystery of Making Drinks*.
– The Jack Daniel's Distillery is established.

1878 – L. Engel publishes *American and Other Drinks*.

1879 – O. H. Byron publishes *The Modern Bartender's Guide*.
– J. Kirtion publishes *Intoxicating Drinks: Their History and Mystery*.
– The Grand Hotel Stockholm opens an American Bar.
– Myers's Dark rum is produced.

1880s – The Cocktail à la Louisiane restaurant invents the Cocktail à la Louisiane in New Orleans.

1882 – Harry Johnson publishes *Harry Johnson's Bartender Manual* or *How to Mix Drinks of the Present Style*.
– The first known mention of a Manhattan cocktail appears in the *Sunday Morning Herald* from Olean, New York.

1884 – E. J. Hauck patents a three-piece cocktail shaker.
– The New York G. Winter Brewing Company publishes a list of glassware for first-rate saloons. The bartender guide lists over twenty-five types of glassware needed.

1887 – Jerry Thomas publishes the second edition of *The Bar-Tender's Guide* or *How to Mix All Kinds of Plain and Fancy Drinks*.
– C. Paul publishes *American Drinks*.

1888 – Henry Charles "Carl" Ramos invents the Ramos Gin Fizz in New Orleans.
– H. Lamore publishes *The Bartender* or *How to Mix Drinks*.

1890s – Jules Alciatore invents the Café Brûlot Diabolique (Devilishly Burned Coffee) in New Orleans.

1891 – Henry J. Wehmann publishes *Wehmann's Bartenders Guide*. To date, this book has the second known reference to a Martini recipe.
– William T. Boothby publishes *Cocktail Boothby's American Bartender*.

1892 – "The Only William" Schmidt publishes *The Flowing Bowl—What and When to Drink*. Four years later, he published his second book, *Fancy Drinks and Popular Beverages*. Schmidt's books were different from all other cocktail celebrity books at the time because his recipes called for unusual items such as tonic phosphate, Calisaya (Italian herbal liqueur), crème de roses, and even a garnish that involved stenciling on a nutmeg. He had Christmas cocktails published in the paper, created a $5 cocktail ($140 in 2018 currency), and although not 100 percent confirmed—but highly believed—he was the first known gay celebrity bartender.
– George Kappeler invents the Widow's Kiss at the Holland House Hotel in New York.
– G. F. Heublein produces the first commercial Manhattan and Martini bottled cocktails, with the tagline "A better cocktail at home than is served over any bar in the world."
– Cornelius Dungan patents the double cone jigger.

1895 – C. F. Lawlor publishes *The Mixicologist* or *How to Mix All Kinds of Fancy Drinks*.
– Jack Daniel's begins bottling in its famous square bottle.
– R. C. Miller publishes *American Bar Tender*.

– George J. Kappler publishes *Modern American Drinks: How to Mix and Serve all Kinds of Cups and Drinks.*

1897 – The Rob Roy is introduced at New York's Fifth Avenue Hotel.
– Sir Thomas Dewar and Fredric Glassup release a Dewar's Scotch commercial film in New York City that is projected on a canvas screen in Herald Square at 1321 Broadway. It is the first alcohol commercial to appear on film.

1898 – The Savoy Hotel in London opens an American Bar.
– The Ward 8 cocktail is invented in Boston.

1899 – Sweden opens their first American Bar.

1900S–2000S

The Waldorf-Astoria in New York City had been open for seven years and set the standard for quality cocktails around the world. Drink making was appreciated and bartending was an art form. The hotel bar never published a cocktail book, but newspaperman and barfly Albert Crockett published *The Old Waldorf-Astoria Bar Book* in 1931 and 1935, which gives us a glimpse into that era. In the early 1900s, breweries owned most saloons, barkeeps made $15 a week ($400 in 2018 currency), and Sunday was the busiest day of the week. On January 16, 1920, the American Prohibition started, then ended December 5, 1933. The stock market crashed, media popularized cocktails, many brands were produced, discotheques increased sales, the drinking age changed twice, the AIDS epidemic hit, the stock market crashed again, and strict drinking and driving laws confused imbibers for several years—as a result of all this upheaval, the quality of cocktails sunk to an all-time low.

Hotel Astor, New York

1912 Vintage postcard depicting the Hotel Astoria in Times Square. This hotel set the standard for cocktails around the world. © *Susan Law Cain / Shutterstock*

There were also five significant wars in the 1900s that affected imbibing Americans: World War I, World War II, Korean War, Vietnam War, and the Gulf War. The millennium brought the skankification of women in rap music videos, the increase of Cognac sales, half-dressed female bartenders dancing on bar tops, the Cosmopolitan and the Mojito became the most popular cocktails in the world, embarrassing Martini bars popped up—but—the most important development is that the cocktail culture renaissance seeds were planted.

More technology happened during this time than 10,000 years combined. Some inventions in this century include electricity, the blender, the juicer, refrigeration, air-conditioning, the phonograph, radio, the eight-track player, the cassette tape, the compact disc, the boom box, the Walkman, DVDs, iTunes, the automobile, the airplane, the helicopter, the spaceship, motion picture theaters, talkies, drive-in theaters, television, VCRs, special-effects blockbusters, DVRs, online television, the camera, the video camera, neon lights, the zipper, stainless steel, canned beer, the telephone, the cellular phone, the smartphone, texting, the microwave, the calculator, robots, the ballpoint pen, medical discoveries, the fax machine, the pager, the computer, the internet, Skype, the Hubble space telescope, and social media.

Names of bars, saloons, and clubs in the 1900s–2000s include Fox and Hound, Filthy McNasty's, Fuzz & Firkin, Slug and Lettuce, Snooty Fox, Ciro's, Chez Victor, the Ohio Club, the Ritz, Whiskey A Go-Go, Stork Club, the Tiki Lounge, VooDoo Lounge, the Palace Saloon, Sloppy Joe's, Studio 54, Le Freak, Disco Inferno, Cabaret, Electric Cowboy, the Rainbow Room, the Starlight Room, the Velvet Tango Room, Coyote Ugly, Angel's Share, Absinthe Brassiere & Bar, and Milk & Honey, PDT, Death & Co, Honeycut, Clover Club, Bourbon & Branch, Canon, Revel, Employees Only, the Violet Room, Three Dots and a Dash, and the Dead Rabbit.

Drinking words heard include "acting like a fool," "baked," "bashed," "blasted," "blitzed," "blown away," "bombed," "bonkers," "buzzed," "canned," "creamed," "crocked," "done," "double vision," "fried," "gone," "hammered," "high," "liquored up," "lit," "party animal," "three sheets to the wind," "shitfaced," "slave to drink," "stoned," "tipsy," "toasted," and "wasted."

Brands and spirits launched in the 1900s–2000s are too many to mention, but include Cutty Sark Scotch, Havana Club rum, Jägermeister, Kahlúa, B&B, Crown Royal, Don Julio tequila, Captain Morgan spiced rum, Irish Mist, Yukon Jack, Finlandia vodka, Stoli vodka, Midori melon liqueur, Baileys Irish cream, Zacapa rum, Absolut vodka, Chambord, Peachtree schnapps, Bartles & Jaymes wine coolers, Absolut Peppar, Absolut Citron, Bombay Sapphire, Gentleman Jack, Patrón Tequila, Guinness in cans, Johnnie Walker gold, Crown Royal Reserve, Skyy vodka, Wild Turkey Rare Breed, Grey Goose vodka, Belvedere vodka, Tito's vodka, Redrum, Plymouth gin, Three Olives vodka, Smirnoff Ice, Van Gogh gin, Hendrick's gin, Jack Daniel's Single Barrel, Bulleit Bourbon, and Smirnoff flavored vodkas, Ancho Reyes Chile liqueur, Ford's gin, Chambord vodka, Zucca Amaro, St. Germain Elderflower Liqueur, Stiggins Plantation pineapple rum, and Sipsmith gin.

Early 1900s – The Pisco Sour is invented in Peru.

1900 – Harry Johnson publishes *Harry Johnson's Bartenders' Manual or How to Mix Drinks of the Present Style*.
– William T. Boothby publishes the second edition of *Cocktail Boothby's American Bartender*.

1902 – Louis Eppinger invented the Bamboo Cocktail in Yokohama, Japan.

1903 – Edward Spencer publishes *The Flowing Bowl*.
– Tim Daly publishes *Daly's Bartenders' Encyclopedia*.

1904 – Frederick J. Drake and Company publishes a vest-pocket recipe book, *Drinks as They Are Mixed*. The recipes were gathered by leading Chicago bartenders.
– John Applegreen publishes *Applegreen's Bar Book*. This book contains a recipe for a Martini Cocktail.
– Paris Ritz bartender Frank P. Newman publishes *American-Bar Recettes des Boissons Anglaises et Américaine*.

1905 – Johnnie Solon invents the Bronx cocktail at the Waldorf-Astoria Hotel.
– Charles S. Mahoney publishes *The Hoffman House Bartender's Guide*.

1906 – Louis Muckensturm publishes *Louis' Mixed Drinks*. This is the first book in English calling for gin and vermouth for the Dry Martini recipe.
– George J. Kappeler publishes *Modern American Drinks: How to Mix and Serve All Kinds of Cups and Drinks*.

1908 – Hon. Wm. Boothby publishes *The World's Drinks and How to Mix Them Standard Authority*.

1910 – First in-flight cocktails are served to paying passengers on a scheduled airliner, on the Zeppelin flying over Germany.

1911 – Sir Thomas Dewar erects the world's largest mechanical sign (sixty-eight feet) advertising Dewar's Scotch whisky on the Thames River embankment.

1912 – Charles S. Mahoney publishes *The Hoffman House Bartender's Guide*.
– The Bartenders Association of America publishes *Bartenders' Manual*.

1914 – Jacques Straub publishes *Drinks*.

1915 – The El Presidente cocktail is invented at Bar la Florida (Floridita) in Havana, Cuba.

1916 – The first recorded cocktail party is hosted by Mrs. Julius S. Walsh Jr. from St. Louis, Missouri, and published in the *St. Paul Pioneer Press* newspaper mentioning cocktails: Clover Leafs, Highballs, Gin Fizzes, Bronxes, Martinis, and Manhattans.
– Hugo R. Ensslin publishes *Recipes for Mixed Drinks*. The book mentions the first Aviation cocktail.

1917 – Even though African Americans had been tending bar since the 1700s, Tom Bullock is the first to publish a cocktail recipe book, *The Ideal Bartender*.

1919 – Harry MacElhone publishes *Harry's ABC of Mixing Cocktails*. One of the most popular cocktails is the White Lady.
– American tourists love Italy's Torino-Milano cocktail, so the name was changed to Americano.
– The Grasshopper is believed to be invented at Tujague's in New Orleans.

1920 – Americans flock to Cuba, Mexico, and Canada to drink legal cocktails.
– Bertha E. L. Stockbridge publishes *What to Drink*.
– The book *This Side of Paradise* by F. Scott Fitzgerald has the first known literary mention of the Daiquiri.

1922 – Patrick McGarry invents the Buck's Fizz at the Buck's Club in London.
– Harry MacElhone invents the Brandy Alexander at Ciro's in London.
– The Blood and Sand cocktail is created after Rudolph Valentino from the film of the same name.
– It is believed that Fosco Scarselli creates the Negroni.

1923 – Harry MacElhone invents the Monkey Gland at the New York Bar in Paris.
– Bartender Frank Meier invents the Mimosa at the Ritz Hotel in Paris, France

1924 – Harry MacElhone and O. O. McIntyre create the International Bar Flies at the New York Bar in Paris.

1927 – Harry MacElhone publishes *Barflies and Cocktails* in Paris.

1928 – Jerry Thomas's book is republished (Thomas died in 1885) with the title *The Bon Vivants Companion or How to Mix Drinks*.

1930 – Harry Craddock publishes *Savoy Cocktail Book*.

– Greta Garbo stars in her first "talkie," *Anna Christie*, and her first words are "Gimme a whiskey, ginger ale on the side."

1932 – The Napier Company produces a cocktail shaker with engraved recipes called the Tells-You-How Mixer.
– Davide Campari packages Campari and soda water in cone-shaped bottles.

1934 – Walter Bergeron invents the Vieux Carré cocktail at the Carousel Bar in New Orleans.
– Don the Beachcomber invents the Zombie in Hollywood, California.
– The first *Thin Man* film is released starring William Powell and Myrna Loy. Cocktails seen include Martini, Bronx, and Knickerbocker. Powell says his famous line when showing the bartenders how to shake a cocktail: "The important thing is the rhythm. Always have rhythm in your shaking. Now, a Manhattan you shake to foxtrot time; a Bronx, to two-step time; a dry Martini you always shake to waltz time."
– Jazz Bandleader and singer Cab Calloway releases the song "The Call of the Jitterbug." The first line of the song is "If you'd like to be a jitterbug, first thing you must do is get a jug, put whiskey, wine, and gin within and shake it all up and then begin."

Jazz singer, songwriter, and bandleader Cab Calloway. © *Photofest*

1936 – The Bacardi Cocktail is the first and only cocktail to date to win a court case making it illegal to serve this cocktail without using Bacardi rum.
– Kahlúa Mexican coffee liqueur is introduced.

1937 – Constantino Ribaliagua Vert invents the Hemingway Special (Papa Dobl) at Bar la Florida (Floridita) in Havana, Cuba.

1939 – The Zombie is served at the 1939 New York World's Fair.
– Crown Royal is introduced. It was created for Queen Elizabeth's visit to Canada.

1940s – The Moscow Mule is invented.

1942 – Pat O'Brien invents the Hurricane in New Orleans.
– Joseph Sheridan invents the Irish Coffee at Foynes Airbase in Limerick, Ireland.
– It is believed that the Rusty Nail is invented in Hawaii.
– The film *Casablanca* is popular and many cocktails are seen in Rick's Bar.

1944 – Trader Vic invents the Mai Tai in Oakland, California.

1945 – The Andrews Sisters release the song "Rum and Coca-Cola" and it becomes the #1 song in America. Radio stations ban the song, which makes it even more popular.
– Giuseppe Cipriani invents the Bellini at Harry's Bar in Venice, Italy, but does not name it until 1948.
– Victor Bergeron publishes *Trader Vic's Bartender's Guide*.

1948 – The Margarita becomes the official drink of Mexico.
– A small group of California bartenders—who were overseas members of the United Kingdom Bartenders' Guild—start a California branch of that organization in the Los Angeles area.

– Gustave Tops invents the Black Russian at the Hotel Metropole in Brussels.

– The first known mention of a cocktail on a radio show is heard. Guests at a party order Stingers from the butler on *The Whistler* radio drama show, "Guilty Conscience". Several references are made to their intoxicating strength.

1952 – Stanton Delaplane brings the Irish Coffee to the Buena Vista Cafe in San Francisco. Today they sell over 2,000 a day.

1953 – Ian Fleming writes about a fictional character named James Bond. In chapter seven, Bond orders a Dry Martini served in a deep champagne goblet with three measures of Gordon's gin, one of Gordon's vodka, and half a measure of Lillet dry vermouth, then shaken very well until ice-cold, and topped with a garnish of lemon peel. This is the first reference to combining both vodka and gin in a Martini. It is named Vesper.

1954 – The Piña Colada is invented at the Caribe Hilton's Beachcomber Bar in San Juan, Puerto Rico.

1955 – The Rat Pack, headed by Frank Sinatra, glamorizes cocktails by holding them on stage and during TV performances.

Singer and actor Frank Sinatra on the 1950s. © *Photofest*

1957 – Harry Yee invents the Blue Hawaii at the Hawaiian Village on the Island of O'ahu.

1957 – The Piña Colada becomes Puerto Rico's official drink by winning a global award.

1951 – The International Bartenders Association (IBA) is started.

1960 – The first Playboy Club opens at 116 East Walton in Chicago and becomes the busiest bar in the world, often serving 1,400 guests a day. Cocktails cost $1.50 ($13 in 2018 currency).

1962 – The first James Bond film, *Dr. No*, shows Sean Connery making a Smirnoff Martini in his hotel room and ordering Vodka Martinis shaken not stirred. In today's terminology—it went viral.

1965 – Alan Stillman opens a New York City bar and grill as the first public cocktail party hang and names it TGI Friday's (Thank God It's Friday). *Lifetime* magazine credited Friday's with ushering in the Singles Era and within six months of opening, Stillman was written up in *Time*, *Newsweek*, and the *Saturday Evening Post*. Before then, there was not a place for twenty- and thirty-somethings to meet except for cocktail parties held around the city in homes and apartments. Stillman painted the building blue, put up red-and-white-striped awnings, bought the staff red-and-white-striped shirts, threw sawdust on the floor, hung up some Tiffany lamps, and added brass railings. Many creative, fun, and party cocktails were birthed in TGI Friday's.

1966 – India's ambassador B. N. Chakravarty says, "Americans are a funny lot. They drink whiskey to keep warm; then they put some ice in to make it cool. They put sugar in to make it sweet; and then they put a slice of lemon in it to make it sour. Then they say, 'Here's to you' and drink it themselves."

1969 – Bobby Lozoff invents the Tequila Sunrise in Sausalito, California, while tending bar at The Trident.

1972 – Robert "Rosebud" Butt in Long Island, New York, invents the Long Island Iced Tea while tending bar at Oak Beach Inn.

– Stolichnaya vodka is introduced.

– The TV show *M*A*S*H* debuts. The lead doctor characters, Hawkeye and Trapper John, drink Martinis from the still they built in their quarters.

1973 – After the Vietnam War, TGI Friday's begins franchising all over the world and actually stays a fresh bar until the late 1970s. TGI Friday's set a standard when it came to training staff. They had a reputation for the most challenging training programs for any chain restaurant/bar in the world. They created the first bartender gods since the beginning of Prohibition. TGI Friday's bartenders also started flair bartending, which led to the 1988 Tom Cruise film *Cocktail*.

– Jose Cuervo puts the recipe for a Tequila Sunrise on the back of their bottle, then three months later the Eagles release their hit song "Tequila Sunrise."

1974 – Baileys Irish cream is introduced and new drinks created include the Mississippi Mudslide and B-52.

1975 – In the fall, Neal Murray creates the first known Cosmopolitan.

1977 – Jimmy Buffett releases the song "Margaritaville," making the Margarita the most popular drink of the year—and it has stayed in the top ten since.

– Stan Jones publishes the Jones' Complete Barguide.

– The first known newspaper mention of a Kamikaze was in the February 1 issue of the Minneapolis Star.

1978 – Midori melon liqueur is launched to create the Melon Ball for the wrap party of *Saturday Night Fever* at Studio 54. Midori Sours become popular.

1979 – The Piña Colada is popular due to Rupert Holmes's Piña Colada song, "Escape."

– Absolut vodka is introduced.

– Ray Foley publishes *Bartender Magazine*.

1981 – Neal Murray (1975 inventor of the Cosmopolitan) introduces San Francisco to the Cosmopolitan at the Elite Café (2049 Fillmore Street).

1982 – Schumann's Cocktail Bar opens in Munich, Germany.

1984 – Peachtree schnapps and Captain Morgan spiced rum are introduced.

– The Fuzzy Navel becomes popular.

– Earl Bernhardt and Pam Fortner invent the Hand Grenade® for the 1984 Louisiana World Exposition.

– The Sex on the Beach cocktail becomes popular.

– Heywood Gould releases the novel *Cocktail*.

1985 – General Manager of the Fog City Diner in San Francisco, Doug "Bix" Biederbeck, hires Neal Murray as a bartender where he makes his Cosmopolitan making the cocktail even more popular.

– Balladeer and researcher Tayler Vrooman was fascinated with songs from the 1600s and 1700s and released his album *Baroque Bacchanalian*. On the album, there are songs about drinking with titles that include "Come Let Us Drink About," "Good Claret," "The Delights of the Bottle," and "The Thirsty Toper."

1986 – Chef Paul Prudhomme invents the Cajun Martini in New Orleans.

– TGI Friday's makes a bartender video of company bartenders John "JB" Bandy, John Mescall, and "Magic" Mike Werner. Later in the year, the company holds the first flair bartending competition in Woodland Hills, California, and calls it Bar Olympics. John "JB" Bandy wins.

– Absolut launches their first flavored vodka, Absolut Peppar.

1987 – After Touchstone Productions interviews thirty-four bartenders, they chose John "JB" Bandy to be the flair instructor for Tom Cruise and Bryan Brown for the 1988 film *Cocktail*.

– In October, bartender Patrick "Paddy" Mitten brings the Cosmopolitan cocktail to New York City from San Francisco and begins serving it at the Life Café (343 E 10th Street B).

The first flair bartending video (VHS) in 1989 by the first flair bartending competition winner, John "JB" Bandy. JB taught Tom Cruise and Bryan Brown flair bartending for the 1988 film *Cocktail*. © John "JB" Bandy

1988 – *Cocktail*, the film starring Tom Cruise as a bartender, ignites flair bartending around the world.

– Absolut Citron, Bombay Sapphire, Gentleman Jack, and Guinness in cans are introduced.

– Dale "King Cocktail" DeGroff begins a gourmet approach to cocktails at the Rainbow Room in New York City.

1989 – Unaware of any other cocktail called a Cosmopolitan, Cheryl Cook creates her Cosmopolitan in March 1989.

– Kathy Casey from Seattle, Washington, pioneers the bar chef movement.

– The world's longest bar is installed at the Beer Barrel Saloon in South Bass Island, Ohio.

– The bar has 160 barstools and is 405' and 10" long (that's 45' and 10" longer than a football field).

– Melissa Huffsmith brings the Cosmopolitan cocktail to The Odeon from the Life Cafe (New York City). With a selection of higher quality ingredients to choose from she revamps the Cosmopolitan cocktail using Absolut Citron, Cointreau, fresh lime juice, and cranberry.

1990 – The first Portland, Oregon, fresh classic bar, Zefiro, opens.

1991 – Gary Regan publishes *The Bartender's Bible*.

– Wild Turkey Rare Breed is introduced.

– Charles Schumann publishes Schumann's American Bar Book.

1992 – Cocktail godfather Paul Harrington is recognized in San Francisco for making classic cocktails.

– Absolut Kurrant, Johnnie Walker Gold, and Crown Royal Reserve are introduced.

1993 – The first known cocktail recipe book to list the Cosmopolitan cocktail is *The Complete Book of Mixed Drinks* by Anthony Dias Blue. Blue credits Julie's Supper Club in San Francisco for the recipe.

– *Straight Up or On the Rocks* is published by William Grimes.

1994 – Scotland celebrates 500 years of whisky production.

– On Wednesday, November 16 in *The Central New Jersey Home News* (New Brunswick, New Jersey) the first known recipe for a Cosmopolitan is published in a newspaper. The recipe was contributed by Dale DeGroff.

1995 – The first World Wide Web cocktail-related sites are launched: barmedia.com, bartender.com, cocktail.com (defunct), cocktailtime.com (defunct), martiniplace.com (defunct), and webtender.com.

– Bacardi Limon rum is introduced.

– Steve Olson begins teaching "Gin Cocktail Clinics" helping consumers make fresh and classic cocktails in their homes.

1996 – Sammy Hagar's Cabo Wabo Tequila and the first organic vodka, Rain, are introduced.

– Paulius Nasvytis opens the classic cocktail bar the Velvet Tango Room in Cleveland, Ohio.

– The Corona Limona becomes popular (a shot of Bacardi Limon rum in a Corona beer).

– The film *Swingers* shows characters drinking classic cocktails and quality booze, which helps set the tone for the germinating craft cocktail movement.

1997 – *Quench*, on the Food Network, brings cocktails to TV.

– Simon Difford's Class Magazine is launched.

– Grey Goose vodka and Chopin vodka are introduced.

– Jared Brown and Anistatia Miller publish *Shaken Not Stirred: A Celebration of the Martini*.

– Gary Regan publishes *New Classic Cocktails*.

Paul Harrington and Laura Moorhead, authors of the ground-breaking 1998 cocktail book, *Cocktail: The Drinks Bible for the 21st Century*. © Paul Harrington

1998 – Paul Harrington and Laura Moorhead publish the game-changing *Cocktail: The Drinks Bible for the 21st Century*.

– On April 9, the first known Cosmopolitan cocktail seen and mentioned on a television show was written into the show *ER* by Linda Gase. The season 4 episode 17 is called "A Bloody Mess."

– Patrick Sullivan opens B-Side Lounge, which is considered Boston's first fresh classic cocktail bar.

– Tony Abou-Ganim is hired to bring classic fresh cocktails to all twenty-three bars at Bellagio in Las Vegas.

– The first known videogame to mention a cocktail is Metal Gear Solid when Nastasha Romanenko says that a Stinger is her favorite cocktail.

– On July 19, season one, episode seven "The Monogamists," the Cosmopolitan cocktail was first mentioned on the HBO show *Sex and the City*. The voice-over of the character Carrie Bradshaw read: "That afternoon I dragged my poor, tortured soul out to lunch with Stanford Blach and attempted to stun it senseless with Cosmopolitans."

1999 – Smirnoff Ice, Absolut Mandarin, Van Gogh gin, Hendrick's gin, and Jack Daniel's Single Barrel are introduced.

– Tommy's Mexican Restaurant in San Francisco becomes the number-one tequila bar in America.

– David Wondrich begins to update the online version of Esquire's 1949 *Handbook for Hosts*.

– Ted A. Breaux becomes the first to analyze vintage absinthe using modern science, the results sparking a paradigm shift in our understanding of the infamous spirit.

– Sasha Petraske opens Milk & Honey on New Year's Eve in New York City.

– In the second season of the HBO TV show Sex and the City, the Cosmopolitan becomes the new worldwide hottest cocktail due to being seen in ten episodes and verbally mentioned in three episodes. It pairs nicely with the flavored Martini craze and Martini bars found in all major cities that offered 200+ flavored Martinis on their menus.

2000 – The film *Coyote Ugly* shows scantily clad cowgirl bartenders slinging whiskey and dancing on the bar top.

– Tanqueray 10, Alizé, Tequiza, Smirnoff Twist flavored vodkas, and Wild Turkey Russell's Reserve are introduced.

– The Beekman Arms of Rhinebeck in New York is the oldest continuously operating tavern in America.

2001 – Hpnotiq plans to launch on September 11, but America is attacked, so the launch takes place months later.

– Gary Regan begins conducting a series of two-day bartender workshops called Cocktails in the Country.

2002 – After forty years, James Bond makes another cocktail popular around the world. Pierce Brosnan (Bond) holds a Mojito in Cuba and then hands it to orange bikini–clad Halle Berry—overnight, it revives the classic Mojito and is still one of the most ordered cocktails in the world today. Bartenders are bombarded with drink requests and 99 percent of them do not have one mint leaf behind the bar.

– Dekuyper Sour Apple Pucker is introduced.

– Dale "King Cocktail" DeGroff publishes the book that officially kicks off the craft cocktail movement, *The Craft of the Cocktail: Everything You Need to Know to Be a Master Bartender*.

– The Appletini becomes popular.

– The first cocktail festival, Tales of the Cocktail is launched in New Orleans.

– William Grimes publishes Straight Up or On the Rocks: The Story of the American Cocktail.

– Jeff "Beachbum" Berry publishes *Intoxica*.

– Kevin Brauch hosts the drinking travel series TV show *The Thirsty Traveler*.

– The first known film to show and mention a Cosmopolitan cocktail is *Juwanna Mann*.

Country music star Alan Jackson in 2003. © *Photofest*

2003 – Julie Reiner opens Flatiron Lounge, the first high-volume craft cocktail bar in New York City.

– Colin Peter Field publishes *The Cocktails of Ritz Paris*.

– Alan Jackson and Jimmy Buffett release the song "It's Five O'clock Somewhere." The chorus starts with, "Pour me somethin' tall an' strong, make it a Hurricane before I go insane." The flair bartender in the music video is Rob Husted who runs flairbar.com.

– Absolut vanilla and Blavod black vodka are introduced.

– Gary Regan publishes *The Joy of Mixology*.

– The first known song to mention a Cosmopolitan cocktail is "Cosmopolitans" written and performed by Erin McKeown.

2004 – The Museum of the American Cocktail is founded in New Orleans by Dale and Jill DeGroff, Chris and Laura McMillian, Ted Haigh, Robert Hess, Phil Greene, and Jared Brown and Anistatia Miller.
– Absolut Raspberri is introduced.
– Ted Haigh publishes Vintage Spirits and Forgotten Cocktails.
– The award-winning bar Employees Only opens in New York City.
– Jeff "Beachbum" Berry publishes *Taboo Table*.

2005 – Sasha Petraske opens Little Branch in New York City.
– Captain Morgan Tattoo, Absolut Peach, Starbuck's coffee liqueur, Barsol pisco, Cognac Toulouse-Lautrec XO, Baileys Caramel, Baileys Chocolate Mint, and NAVAN are introduced.
– In September, University of Pennsylvania archaeochemist Patrick McGovern announces the discovery of 5,000-year-old Mesopotamian earthenware from the banks of the Tigris between Iran and Iraq that contain traces of honey, barley, tartaric acid, and apple juice. McGovern described this cocktail as "grog."
– Audrey Saunders opens Pegu Club in New York City.
– Heavy Water vodka from Anistatia Miller and Jared Brown is introduced.
– David Wondrich publishes *Killer Cocktails.*

2006 – CMT airs a reality show called *Inside the Real Coyote Ugly.* Ten women are chosen out of one thousand to learn how to bartend *Coyote Ugly*–style.
– Karen Foley publishes the award-winning drinks magazine Imbibe.
– Oprah Winfrey and Rachael Ray make a Lemon Drop Martini and a Pomegranate Martini on the Oprah Winfrey Show. Bartenders all over America are asked for these cocktails.
– The Jäger Bomb becomes popular.
– Sasha Petraske, Christy Pope, and Chad Solomon start Cuffs & Buttons—a beverage consultant and catering company.
– X-Rated Fusion, 10 Cane rum, Gran Patrón Platinum 100 percent Agave Tequila, Michael Collins Irish single malt, Rhum Clément Very Superior Old Pale (VSOP) rum, Rittenhouse 21, Skyy 90, Yamazaki 18, and Domaine Charbay Pomegranate vodka are introduced.
– Jamie Boudreau opens the craft bar Vessel in Seattle, Washington.
– Wayne Curtis publishes And a Bottle of Rum: A History of the New World in Ten Cocktails.
– Camper English pioneers "directional freezing" to make perfectly clear ice.
– San Francisco Cocktail Week starts its first year.
– Jared Brown and Anistatia Miller publish Mixologist: The Journal of the American Cocktail Vol. 1.
– Dale "King Cocktail" DeGroff, Steven Olson, Doug Frost, Paul Pacult, David Wondrich, and Andy Seymour open Beverage Alcohol Resource (BAR) in New York City.
– The bartenders of Absinthe Brassiere & Bar publish Art of the Bar.
– Dave Kaplan and Alex Day open Death + Co. on New Year's Eve in New York City.

2007 – Lucid absinthe becomes the first wormwood absinthe allowed back into the United States after being banned for ninety-five years.
– Sean Combs launches Ciroc vodka.

- Tony Abou-Ganim publishes *Modern Mixology*.
- The TV show Mad Men debuts and sparks a worldwide interest in classic cocktails.
- Jim Meehan opens PDT in New York City, and the telephone booth entrance creates headlines.
- Eric Seed brings crème de violette back into America after being unavailable for almost ninety years.
- St. Germain Elderflower Liqueur, Chivas Regal 25, Absolut New Orleans, Kubler absinthe, Appleton Estate Reserve, 360 vodka, Grey Goose Le Poire, and Tanqueray Rangspur are introduced.
- Greg Boehm begins to reproduce and publish vintage cocktail books.
- Don Lee invents fat washing by infusing bacon with Bourbon and creates the Benton's Old-Fashioned at PDT in New York City.
- Donald Trump introduces Trump vodka (and he does not drink).
- Colin Kimball launches the Small Screen Network bringing professional online bartending videos to the cocktail community.
- Derek Brown opens the first stand-alone craft cocktail bar in DC, the Gibson, with Eric Hilton, one of the founding members of Thievery Corporation.
- CeeLo Green introduces Ty Ku Sake.
- David Wondrich publishes the James Beard Award-winning *Imbibe!*
- Jared Brown and Anistatia Miller publish *Mixologist: The Journal of the American Cocktail Vol. 2.*
- Tobin Ellis is selected as the number-one bartender in America to compete against Bobby Flay in his TV show *Throwdown! with Bobby Flay*, making Ellis the first successful award-winning flair bartender to cross over to the craft cocktail world.

2008 – The Sazerac becomes the official cocktail of New Orleans through Bill No. 6.
- Julie Reiner opens Clover Club in Brooklyn, New York.
- *Indiana Jones and the Kingdom of the Crystal Skull debuts and* Dan Aykroyd introduces Crystal Head vodka which comes in a glass skull head. Coincidence?
- LXTV associated with NBC hosts a TV show sponsored by Absolut vodka titled *On the Rocks: The Search for America's Top Bartender*. The intro of the show says that there are more than 500,000 bartenders in America.
- Sasha Petraske opens White Star absinthe bar in New York City.
- Jeff "Beachbum" Berry publishes *Sippin' Safari*.
- Cocktail Kingdom is launched, selling high-quality master mixology bar tools.
- Robert Hess publishes *The Essential Bartender's Guide*.
- Prairie organic vodka, Tru2 organic gin, Compass Box Hedonism Maximus Scotch, Cape North vodka, Jett vodka, Canadian Club 30, (ri)1 Kentucky Straight rye, Maestro Dobel Diamond tequila, Siembra Azul tequila, and 1800 Silver Select tequila are introduced.
- Scott Beattie publishes *Artisanal Cocktails*.
- Bridget Albert publishes *Market Fresh Mixology*.
- Dale "King Cocktail" DeGroff publishes his second book, *The Essential Cocktail*.
- Natalie Bovis publishes the first nonalcoholic craft mocktail book, *Preggatinis: Mixology for the Mom-to-Be.*

2009 – The Ritz-Carlton launches a new global "Bar Experience" that features an edible bar menu with a fresh twist on solid and traditional cocktails.
- Sasha Petraske opens Los Angeles's first craft bar, the Varnish, with Eric Alperin. One year later, Alperin teaches actor Ryan Gosling how to make an Old-Fashioned for the 2011 film *Crazy, Stupid, Love*, which combined with

the popularity of the *Mad Men* Old-Fashioned sparks a new interest for a new generation and becomes the number-one most ordered cocktail of the year.

– The Mai Tai becomes the official cocktail of Oakland, California.

– Justin Timberlake introduces 9:01 Tequila. He names it 9:01 because he says that is the time when things start happening at night.

– Absolut airs a bartender mixology TV show special called *On the Rocks*.

– Tobin Ellis starts the world's first pop-up speakeasy series called Social Mixology.

– Sasha Petraske opens Dutch Kills in Long Island City, New York.

– Dry Fly vodka, Stolichnaya Elit vodka, Charbay tequila, Evan Williams single barrel, Beefeater 24, Appleton 30, Double Cross vodka, Bluecoat gin, Vieux Carré absinthe, Bulldog gin, Citadelle Reserve, and Fruitlab organic liqueurs are introduced.

– Ted Haigh publishes the second edition of *Vintage Spirits and Forgotten Cocktails: From the Alamagoozlum to the Zombie 100 Rediscovered Recipes and the Stories Behind Them.*

– Rap star Ludacris introduces Conjure Cognac.

– On November 6—to celebrate their fifteenth anniversary—Consejo Regulador del Tequila wins a Guinness World Record for the largest display of tequila at Hospicio Cabañas, Guadalajara, Mexico. They display 1,201 bottles of tequila from all the states in Mexico.

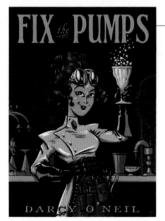

Darcy O'Neil's award-winning 2010 book, *Fix the Pumps*. © *Paul Mitchell*

2010 – David Wondrich publishes *Punch: The Delights (and Dangers) of the Flowing Bowl.*

– Jeffrey Morgenthaler ages a barrel of Negronis and kick-starts the barrel-aged cocktail movement.

– Delta Airlines adds simple fresh cocktails on their flights.

– Darcy O'Neil publishes the award-winning book *Fix the Pumps.*

– Chambord vodka, Zucca Amaro, Solerno blood orange liqueur, Maker's 46, Evan Williams Cherry Reserve Kentucky, ZU Zubrowka Bison Grass vodka, Ransom Old Tom gin, Glenfiddich 40, Bacardi Reserva Limitada rum, Avión tequila, Dulce Vida tequila, Eades Small Batch Speyside whisky, Conjure Cognac, Cognac Frapin Domaine Château de Fontpinot XO, Etude XO Alambic brandy, Bottega Sambuca d'Anice Stellato, Rökk vodka, and Purity vodka are introduced.

– Virgin America Airlines offers a few classic cocktails to passengers.

– Zane Lamprey hosts an alcohol travel show, *Three Sheets.*

– Tony Abou-Ganim publishes *The Modern Mixologist.*

– New trends include slow cocktails (growing your own herbs at home and at the bar), barrel-aged cocktails, pre-Prohibition-style classic cocktails, cold maceration, molecular mixology, mezcal and tequila forward cocktails, punches, moonshine, genever, ginger beer, coconut water, almond milk, shrubs, honeycomb, gourmet bitters, organic products, quality vermouth, tiki bars, all types of ice, soda fountain equipment, siphons, Red Rover Bartenders (celebrity bartenders swapping/traveling to bartend at other bars), flair bartenders crossing over to mixology, spirit and cocktail classes, craft dive bars, cocktails on tap, regular bars with skilled bartenders and good drinks, food and cocktail pairings, and cocktail networking through social media.

– YouTuber turned Cooking Channel star—who also explores cocktails—hosts the TV show *Nadia G's Bitchin' Kitchen.*

– The owners of the award-winning New York City bar Employees Only publish *Speakeasy: The Employees Only Guide to Classic Cocktails Reimagined.*

– The Dry Martini Bar in Barcelona sells their one millionth Martini on June 30. The cocktail bar has had a giant digital counter since 1978 that has been tracking the classic Martinis made with gin or vodka.

Jamie Boudreau at Canon in Seattle, Washington. © *Jamie Boudreau*

2011 – Ryan Gosling makes an Old-Fashioned in the film *Crazy, Stupid, Love*, which results in the cocktail being ordered more than ever.

– The cocktail competition Speed Rack is launched by Lynnette Morrero and Ivy Mix.

– On March 30, TGI Friday's in the UK celebrate their twenty-fifth anniversary by breaking a world record. They had the most people cocktail flairing simultaneously for two minutes. The event was held outdoors at the Covent Garden Piazza in London with 101 flair bartenders wearing all black-and-red-and-white-striped ties.

– Bacardi Oakheart, Angel's Envy bourbon, Johnnie Walker Double Black, Drambuie 15, St. George gin, Hakushu Japanese whisky, Pierre-Ferrand 1840, Brugal 1888, Art in the Age Rhuby, Bols Barrel-Aged Genever, Grand Marnier Quintessence, High West double rye, High West Silver OMG Pure rye, No. 3 London dry, Knob Creek single barrel, and Ron De Jeremy rum (named after the porn star) are introduced.

– Jim Meehan publishes *The PDT Cocktail Book: The Complete Bartender's Guide from the Celebrated Speakeasy.*

– Colin Peter Field publishes *Le Ritz Paris—Une Histoire de Cocktails*, which has a preface written by celebrity Kate Moss.

– On February 11, the New World Trading Company hosts the world's largest gin-tasting event with 796 participants across nine venues in London.

– Jamie Boudreau opens his award-winning bar, Canon in Seattle, Washington.

2012 – Tony Conigliaro publishes the award-winning book *Drinks.*

– Sammy Hagar introduces Sammy Hagar's Beach Bar rum.

– On July 13, Nick Nicora makes the world's largest Margarita, taking the title away from Margaritaville in Las Vegas. Nicora makes it at the California State Fair; the drink is 10,499 gallons. It is made in a large cocktail shaker and sponsored by Jose Cuervo and Cointreau.

– Ford's gin, Templeton rye, High West Whiskey Campfire, L'Essence de Courvoisier, Western Son Texas vodka, Imbue Petal & Thorn vermouth, Amsterdam gin, Leopold Brothers Fernet, and Waha.k.a. Madre Cuishe mezcal are introduced.

– Philip Greene publishes *To Have and Have Another: A Hemingway Cocktail Companion.*

2013 – Tony Conigliaro's award-winning 2012 book, *Drinks*, is reprinted and titled *The Cocktail Lab: Unveiling the Mysteries of Flavor and Aroma in Drink, with Recipes.*

– Kenny Chesney introduces Blue Chair Bay rum.

– Amy Stewart publishes the award-winning book *The Drunken Botanist.*

– Jim Beam Devil's Cut, Montelobos mezcal, Penny Blue XO rum, Art in the Age Snap, Four Roses Single Barrel 2013, Woody Creek Colorado vodka, Kirk and Sweeney rum, St. George Dry Rye Reposado gin, Papa's Pilar blonde rum, Pow-Wow botanical rye, New Columbia Distillers Green Hat Distilled gin, and George T. Stagg 2013 are introduced.

Award-winning drink writers and historians Anistatia Miller and Jared Brown; 2017.
© *Anistatia Miller and Jared Brown*

– Award-winning bartender Charles Joly introduces a line of bottled cocktails called Crafthouse Cocktails Southside.

– Jeff "Beachbum" Berry publishes *Beachbum Berry's Potions of the Caribbean.*

– George Clooney introduces Casamigos Tequila.

– Diageo hosts the world's largest cocktail-making class on September 18 in Barcelona with 1774 participants. It was run by global ambassador Kenji Jesse.

– After sixteen years, Anistatia Miller and Jared Brown publish a second edition of *Shaken Not Stirred: A Celebration of the Martini.*

2014 – Kate Gerwin becomes the first winner (and first woman) to be crowned Bols Bartending World Champion.

– *Death & Co: Modern Classic Cocktails* is published by Dave Kaplan and Nick Fauchald.

– Ancho Reyes Chile liqueur, Mister Katz rock and rye, Green Spot Irish whiskey, Sapling Maple Bourbon, Roca Patrón Añejo tequila, Anchor Old Tom gin, St. George California Reserve Agricole rum, High West A Midwinter Night's Dram, A Smith Bowman Abraham Bowman Bourbon, Elijah Craig 23, and Tanqueray Old Tom gin are introduced.

– The Smithsonian TV show *The United States of Drinking* is hosted by award-winning food writer Josh Ozersky.

– On April 27, the 4-Jack's Bar and Bistro in Punta Cana, Dominican Republic, makes the world's largest Mojito with the Dominican rum Punta Cana. It takes forty people one hour and thirty-five minutes and contains 185 gallons of rum.

– Jeffrey Morgenthaler publishes *The Bar Book: Elements of Cocktail Technique.*

– The Savoy celebrates its 125th birthday on August 6.

– In March, bartender Sheldon Wiley becomes the world's fastest bartender by breaking the Guinness World Record for making the most cocktails in one hour. It is sponsored by Stoli vodka and the official rules are: each cocktail requires a minimum of three ingredients and no cocktail can be duplicated. He makes 1905 cocktails. The event is held at New York's Bounce Sporting Club.

2015 – Salvatore "The Maestro" Calabrese publishes a second edition of *Classic Cocktails.*

– *Cocktails & Classics* is hosted by Michael Urie and celebrity friends who watch and critique classic films while sipping cocktails.

– David Wondrich publishes the second edition of *Imbibe! Updated and Revised Edition: From Absinthe Cocktail to Whiskey Smash, a Salute in Stories and Drinks to "Professor" Jerry Thomas, Pioneer of the American Bar.*

– Crown Royal rye, Amaro di Angostura, La Caravedo pisco, Tanqueray Bloomsbury, Cynar 70, Encanto pisco, Rieger & Co. Midwestern Dry gin, Rieger & Co. Kansas City whiskey, Highspire pure rye, Grey Goose VX, Sipsmith gin, Redemption Rye Barrel Proof, Stiggins Plantation pineapple rum, Fernet Francisco, Caña Brava rum, Balsam

American Amaro, Mr. Lyan Bottled Cocktails, Bacardi tangerine rum, Portobello gin, and Small Hand Foods Yeoman tonic syrups are introduced.

– The owners of the award-winning New York City bar Dead Rabbit publish *The Dead Rabbit Drinks Manual: Secret Recipes and Barroom Tales from Two Belfast Boys Who Conquered the Cocktail World.*

– Philip Greene publishes an updated version of *To Have and Have Another: A Hemingway Cocktail Companion.*

– Chris McMillian and his wife, Laura open their first bar, Revel Café & Bar in New Orleans.

2016 – Jamie Boudreau, owner of the award-winning Seattle bar Canon, publishes *The Canon Cocktail Book: Recipes from the Award-Winning Bar.*

– Jack Daniel's 150th Anniversary; Three Olives pink grapefruit, pineapple, and pear vodka; Cockspur old gold rum; Life of Reilley Disco Lemonade; Clayton Bourbon; Bird Dog chocolate whiskey; Old Home maple whiskey; Don Q 151 rum; Jameson Cooper's Croze; Mount Gay XO; Brooklyn gin; Crown Royal honey; Yukon Jack Wicked Hot; E. J. peach brandy; Pau Maui pineapple vodka; Uncle Bob's root beer whiskey, Laphroig 15, and Jack Daniel's Single Barrel rye are introduced.

– Robert Simonson publishes *A Proper Drink.*

– Owners of the award-winning San Francisco bar Smuggler's Cove, Martin and Rebecca Cate, publish *Smuggler's Cove: Exotic Cocktails, Rum, and the Cult of Tiki.*

– Billy Gibbons from the band ZZ Top introduces Pura Vida tequila.

– Chris McMillian and Elizabeth M. Williams publish *Lift Your Spirits: A Celebratory History of Cocktail Culture in New Orleans.*

– Sasha Petraske's *Regarding Cocktails* is published by his widow, Georgette.

$$\bullet\ \bullet\ \bullet$$

THE COCKTAIL WORLD TODAY—AND BEYOND

Between 2000 and 2010, the craft cocktail movement was in its infancy stage. Bar owners replicated the decor, style, fashion, and ambiance from either of two—significant—previous cocktail time periods: the first golden age of cocktails (1860–1919) or American Prohibition (1920–1933). Around 2010, bar owners had a light bulb moment and thought, "Hey! I don't have to look like an 1800s saloon or a speakeasy to produce fresh quality cocktails because that's the way cocktails should be made anyway." That self-realization (the message pioneers were trying to communicate all along) was the spark needed for millennials to create fresh cocktails for all other types of bars. In 2005, there were only around thirty fresh craft bars in all of America, and in 2018, there are over 500. The craft cocktail pioneers should be very proud of this achievement.

What does the crystal ice ball predict for the future toddler, teenage, and adult stages of the second golden age of cocktails? Will robots replace bartenders? Will future bartenders become eco-conscious exploring ways to recycle the massive amounts of straws, cups, pics, and bottles dumped in landfills every day? Can bartenders cease stoking the embers of their wannabe-famous egos and simply live balanced lives, be good at their jobs, and understand the bottom line of hospitality? Will bars with fresh crafted cocktails be commonplace for the masses? Well, as for robots, probably not, because humans are social beings. Even high-tech futuristic fantasy shows such as *Star Trek,* which have the technological advances to build robot bartenders, choose not to. As millennials take over the cocktail wheel, it is safe to assume that they will follow their bartender ancestors' example—and boldly go where no one has gone before.

2

FROM ANTIQUITY TO AMERICA: THE HISTORY OF ALCOHOL

As far as we know, beer was first made in 8000 BCE, wine in 6000 BCE, and spirits for consumption in 1192. However, they are believed to have been consumed many years before.

Medicinal alcohol distillation was first discovered in 900 CE, and the first known word for a consumable distilled spirit was "aqua vitae" (AH-qua VEE-tee or sometimes pronounced VEE-tai), which translates from Latin to "water of life." Arnaud de Ville-Neuve coined the word in 1310 after he distilled wine with an alembic still. The French translation is eau-de-vie (o-duh-VEE).

Vintage engraving of distillation. © *Morphart Creation / Shutterstock*

According to esteemed alcohol and cocktail historians Anistatia Miller and Jared Brown, thirty-three-year-old French explorer and missionary William de Rubruquis, a.k.a. William of Rubruck (1220–1293), was the first to mention a spirit called arrack (uh-RACK). In 1292, Marco Polo commented about arrack in his travel memoir *Il Millione*, and it is recorded that Genoese merchants brought arrack to Russia a century before. Arrack is distilled from molasses and water using dried cakes of red rice and botanicals containing yeast and other fungi spores that trigger the fermentation process. It was produced on the island of Java, Batavia, and the technique can be traced back thousands of years to China—and even predates the birth of distillation. The island went through many name changes throughout history, but today is named Ja.k.a.rta (or Dja.k.a.rta) and is located in Indonesia. Slowly through the years the distilled spirits vodka, gin, whisk(e)y, rum, tequila, and liqueurs each made a commercial appearance.

The Top Ten Things to Know about Alcohol

1. The first alcohol known to humankind is beer, then wine, and then spirits.
2. There are several types of alcohol, but ethyl alcohol (ethanol) is the only potable one.
3. Distilled spirits were first used as medicine.
4. Vodka, gin, and rum are allowed to be produced anywhere in the world. However, tequila must be produced in Mexico, Scotch whisky in Scotland, Irish whiskey in Ireland, Canadian whisky in Canada, Bourbon in America (and so on with the whiskeys), pisco in Peru and Chile, and cachaça in Brazil.

5. One twelve-ounce beer has as much alcohol as a five-ounce glass of wine and one-and-a-half ounces of a spirit.

6. Grain makes whisky and beer; fruit makes wine and brandy; grapes grown in the Cognac region of France makes Cognac; grapes grown in the Champagne region of France makes champagne; honey makes mead; sugarcane makes rum; agave makes tequila; Brazilian sugarcane makes cachaça; the discarded leftovers from Chilean and Peruvian wine making makes pisco; and anything can make vodka.

7. When you take a drink of alcohol, it passes through the walls of your stomach and small intestine into the bloodstream. Your blood then takes the alcohol to your brain, and then the liver filters out the alcohol from your blood.

8. The discovery of distillation provided convenience, portability, and preservation. No longer did one need to worry about spoilage (like with beer and wine), and traveling with a bottle of brandy—or port, sherry, and Madeira—was much easier than lugging a barrel of it.

9. Most spirits range around 80 proof (40 percent). The highest legal limit for spirit proof is 190 (95 percent), but who would want to drink that is up for debate.

10. The most popular alcoholic cocktails in the world today include Martini, Margarita, Mojito, Manhattan, Old-Fashioned, Daiquiri, Bloody Mary, Mint Julep, Piña Colada, Cosmopolitan, Whiskey Sour, Sazerac, Tom Collins, Caipirinha, and Negroni.

• • •

DISTILLED ALCOHOL TIMELINE

776 – At age thirty-nine, Persian alchemist and chemist Al-Jabir (Abu Musa Jabir ibn Hayyan) invents the al-ambiq still as part of his laboratory equipment.

830 – Muslim Arab philosopher, physician, and polymath Al-Kindi (801–873) distills a digestible elixir from an alembic still.

900 – Persian polymath, philosopher, and physician Al-Razi (854–925) discovers many compounds and chemicals in his medicinal experimentations—and one of them is alcohol.

1000 – The Moors (the name given to a large population of Arabs, Berber North Africans, and Muslim Europeans) introduce alembic distillation methods in France and Spain.

1144 – Englishman and Arabic translator Robert of Chester translates the written works of distillation from Al-Jabir, Al-Kindi, and Al-Razi from Arab to Latin.

1192 – Genoese merchants bring an India spirit called arrack to Russia.

1250 – German friar and Catholic bishop Albertus Magnus (also known as Saint Albert the Great) documents his experiments in making aqua vitae.

1253 – King Louis IX of France sends William de Rubruquis to convert the Tartars to Christianity. During his journey, he becomes the first European traveler to mention koumis (distilled female horse milk) and arrack.

1269 – German poet Jacob van Maerlant publishes twenty books in his lifetime and *Der Naturen Bloeme* mentions juniper-based tonics and medicines.

1280 – English philosopher and Franciscan friar Roger Bacon translates Al-Razi's distillation process into Latin.

1292 – While traveling home from Beijing to Italy, Venetian merchant Marco Polo discovers a spirit indigenous to Samara in Indonesia called "arrack," which is made with sugar palm juice. He records the spirit in the second volume of *The Travels of Marco Polo* (*Il Milione* in Italian).

1297 – Philosopher and writer Ramon Llull explains the secrets of distillation to Britain's King Edward II.

1310 – Physician Arnaud de Ville-Neuve distills wine with an alembic still and coins the term "aqua vitae."

1320 – In 2008, *The Red Book of Ossory* (published in 1320) becomes the first book to be digitalized at the RCB Library in Dublin, Ireland—aqua vitae is documented in the book.

1404 – A grain-based aqua vitae that is produced throughout Poland is mentioned in Poland's Sandomierz Court Registry.

1411 – Armagnac goes into full-scale production in France.

1414 – Armagnac is registered as a commercial product in Saint-Sever, France.

1426 – Geneose merchants pass through Russia and give the Grand Prince of Moscow a bottle of their arrack. It's believed that within a few years, monasteries are ordered to produce a grain-based version called bread wine.

1455 – Austrian-born and Viennese-trained physician Michael Puff von Schrick writes *A Very Useful Book on Distillations*, which describes eighty-two herbal liquors. In 1466, it is printed and published. Even though Schrick dies in 1473, the book goes through thirty-eight editions from 1476–1601.

1478 – Arnaud de Ville-Neuve's *Liber de Vinis* ("Book of Wines") is translated into English, printed, and published. The book is filled with recipes on how to make therapeutic wine using herbs, spices, metal compounds, syrups, and flavored spirits.

1493 – A German physician in Nuremburg writes about kirshwasser, a cherry eau-de-vie made from Black Forest morello cherries: "In view of the fact that everyone at present has got into the habit of drinking aqua vitae it is necessary to remember the quantity that one can permit oneself to drink and learn to drink it according to one's capacities, if one wishes to behave like a gentleman."

1495 – The first recorded mention of Scotch whisky is from a June 1 entry in the Exchequer Rolls of Scotland (accounting records). The entry says, "To Friar John Cor, by order of the King James IV, to make aqua vitae VIII bolls of malt." Four years later, the Lord High Treasurer's account recorded payment: "To the barbour that brought aqua vitae to the King in Dundee."

1500 – German surgeon and alchemist Hieronymous Brunschwig publishes *Liber de arte distillandi: Das buch der rechten kunst zu distillieren* ("The Book of the Art of Distillation") in Strasbourg. It is a groundbreaking book that inspires numerous Holland distilling houses to begin producing brandewijn (burnt wine) from malted grain.

1501 – Others had tried, including Christopher Columbus, but Pedro de Atienza is the first to successfully import sugarcane seedlings to Hispaniola. He harvests his first crop four years later.

1505 – Scotland's King James IV grants a monopoly to the Guild of Surgeons and Barbers to produce aqua vitae.

1514 – One year before he dies, King Louis XII of France licenses vinegar producers to distill eau-de-vie.

1531 – In Santiago de Tequila, Mexico, Spanish settlers construct alquitaras (stills) and distill pulque—a local fermented beverage made from the agave plant. They call the result mexcalli (mezcal).

1533 – Martim Afonso de Sousa and four partners set up three confectioneries and they make a sugarcane wine into aguardiente de caña (sugarcane eau-de-vie)—which is later known as cachaça.

– Fourteen-year-old Italian Caterina de' Medici marries fourteen-year-old Henry, the second son of King Francis I of France. She brings bottles of Tuscany Liquore Mediceo, Fraticello, and Elixir Stomatico di Lunga Vita, which are made by monks in the mountains surrounding Florence.

1534 – Polish pharmacist Stefan Falimirz publishes the lavishly illustrated book of medical treatments *O Ziolach / O Mocy Ich* ("On Herbs and Their Potency"), which is one of the first to document the word "vodka" and details the preparation of over seventy vodka-based medicines.

1537 – King Francis I of France grants wholesale grocers a license to produce eau-de-vie.

1538 – Spanish settlers in Peru begin to harvest and export wine, and the non-suitable harvests are given away to farmers who make what we know of today as pisco.

1552 – In the book *Constelijck Distilleer Boek*, Philippus Hermanni refers to a juniper-infused eau-de-vie.

1575 – Lucas Bulsius moves to Amsterdam and sets up his own distillery. He changes his family name to Bols and begins making jenever. Twenty-five years later, Bols becomes a preferred supplier to the Seventeen Gentlemen, the inner circle of the powerful Dutch East India Company, which means he gets first rights on cargos of herbs and spices, giving him an advantage.

1598 – Spanish settlers begin distilling aguardiente de caña (rum) from molasses.

1620 – The Pilgrims bring brandy and gin with them to America on the *Mayflower*. In 1657, they begin to import molasses from the Caribbean to open the first American distillery in Boston. In addition, by 1664, they build a second rum distillery in New York City.

FUN ALCOHOL FACTS

- Slang terms for distilled alcohol include "aqua vitae," "ardent spirits," "belt," "booze," "firewater," "giggle juice," "grog," "hard stuff," "hooch" (refers to it being homemade), "John Barleycorn," "liquid courage," "moonshine" (made by the light of the moon), "nightcap," "sauce," "snort," "swill," "swish," "tipple," "toddy," and "tot".

- In the United Kingdom, it is legal for children to drink at home with their parents from age six and up. They can be in a pub if accompanied by a parent and, at age sixteen, drink beer or wine in a pub with their parents.

- Dr. David Kimball, lead historian at Independence Hall in Philadelphia, found a 1787 farewell party bar tab for George Washington in 1985. The bar tab showed that fifty-five attendees drank sixty bottles of claret, fifty-four bottles of Madeira, eight bottles of whiskey, twenty-two bottles of porter, eight bottles of hard cider, twelve bottles of beer, and seven bowls of alcoholic punch.

- According to Wikipedia, the country that drinks the most alcohol in the world is the Republic of Belarus, which is bordered by Russia, Poland, Ukraine, Latvia, and Lithuania. The country that drinks the most spirits is Haiti.

- The youngest drinking age in the world is sixteen and the oldest is twenty-five. There are twenty-three countries whose drinking age is sixteen years old (a couple include Cuba and Switzerland), and there are seven states in India where the drinking age is twenty-five. Alcohol is illegal in thirteen countries.

- The alcohol drinking habits of vervet monkeys were studied on St. Kitts island (where the monkeys stole drinks from sunbathing tourists). They learned that the monkeys' drinking behaviors were similar to humans': teetotaler, social drinker (the majority, who only drink with other monkeys), regular drinker, and binge drinkers that will drink themselves into a coma or death.

- Whiteclay, Nebraska, has a population of fourteen. They also have four liquor stores and their yearly beer sales are $3 million (the county next to them is dry).

- All Playboy bunnies working at Playboy Clubs were required to know 143 brands of liquor.

- Make your own flexible ice packs to keep in the freezer with your choice of plain vodka, gin, rum, tequila, or whiskey. Simply pour a cup of water and a cup of spirit into a freezer plastic bag, squeeze out the air, then seal. Seal that bag into another bag, then place in the freezer. Since the spirit will not freeze solid, it will create a flexible, slushy consistency.

- Finding the proof of a spirit dates back to the 1500s. They discovered if you soak a pellet of gunpowder in the spirit and the gunpowder could still burn, the spirits were rated above proof. In the 1800s, the gunpowder test was replaced by a specific-gravity test.

3

THE 18TH AMENDMENT: ALL ABOUT PROHIBITION, BOOTLEGGING, AND SPEAKEASIES

...
A BRIEF HISTORY OF AMERICAN PROHIBITION

The nutshell version of the American Prohibition starts with American citizens in the late 1700s who fell into two groups: those who felt drinking alcohol was a sin (religious groups) and families weary of men spending money at saloons drinking while women and children were left at home penniless and starving. They believed that alcohol was a contributing factor in the rise in crime, health issues, relationship issues, and extreme poverty. Thus, the temperance movement was born.

For America, Prohibition officially started at one minute past midnight on January 17, 1920. However, Prohibition can be compared to a hurricane today in that you have plenty of warning before it hits, so large amounts of alcohol had previously been hoarded for years. When the supply ran out, alcohol was smuggled from Canada and Mexico, and bootleggers began making moonshine. People also took booze cruises twelve miles out (the legal distance) to international waters. Hidden secret bars called speakeasies opened, often hiding in a room behind a legal storefront business, or entrances were in alleys or in basements. It is believed that in New York City alone, there were over 100,000 speakeasies.

All of this created a booming business for bootleggers, but it also created a booming business for a new dark world of organized crime called the Mafia, which spread to all the large cities with many gangs and gangsters. The Mafia made and sold "bathtub gin" to speakeasies (and to whoever wanted it) by purchasing moonshine from bootleggers, or legally through medical suppliers by infusing it with juniper berries and other herbs in an effort to get the smell and taste of pre-ban gin. (They used large containers such as barrels—not bathtubs.) After bottling, they would cut the moonshine with water by placing the bottles and jugs under bathtub faucets. (The bottles would not fit under a sink faucet.) Around 1,000 people would die yearly because it is said that sometimes they would obtain cheap (and poisonous) industrial alcohol, which was used for fuels, polishes, etc., and use that in the cutting process as well.

As for cocktails, more mixers and ingredients were added to the Mafia's bathtub gin to mask the nasty burn, such as the Bee's Knees, made with lots of lemon juice and honey. Cocktails made with smuggled rum, whiskey, and brandy included the Twelve Mile Limit, Mary Pickford, and Between the Sheets. But the average middle-to-lower-class Americans just mixed—any booze they could get—at home with ingredients as simple as plain juices, herbs, and homemade syrups. These recipes will always remain a mystery.

The Top Ten Things to Know About Prohibition

1. Prohibition (the noble experiment) did not outlaw the drinking of alcohol—it outlawed the manufacture, sale, and transportation of alcohol.

2. Prohibition did not only occur in America. It has happened at different times all over the world and still exists in some countries (and U.S. counties) today.

3. To date, the American Constitution has twenty-seven amendments. The Eighteenth Amendment is when American Prohibition began (Tuesday, January 20, 1920) and the Twenty-First Amendment is when Prohibition ended (Tuesday, December 5, 1933) for a total of thirteen years, ten months, and fifteen days.

4. The Eighteenth Amendment did not happen in one fell swoop. Many states banned alcohol before, starting in 1851. It was the same for the Twenty-First Amendment; many states did not lift the ban for years and, today, there are still counties that have alcohol bans resulting in "dry" counties. The Twenty-First Amendment left the decision up to the states.

5. The fight for nationwide American Prohibition was not something that happened in a few years. It began in the late 1700s with the Temperance Movement (a movement to subdue the widespread drunkenness in America).

6. Legal alcohol during Prohibition included sacramental wine for churches; patented medicines; use in scientific research; industrial development of fuel, dye, and other things industries might need; and use in hospitals for cleaning. Homemade beer, wine, and cider, and pre-banned alcohol could be drunk in the privacy of one's own home.

7. Up until the 1920s, the only American women allowed into the large main rooms of saloons/bars were prostitutes and madams. In nice bars there were small "Ladies' Rooms" where prominent women could drink. The speakeasies from 1920 to 1933 were the first drinking establishments where women could patronize the whole bar.

8. Cocktails and drinks in speakeasies were known to be expensive, so you saved up for a special night on the town, had plenty of money (or were with someone with money), or just partied at home.

9. Out of necessity, Appalachian mountain bootleggers tinkered with their vehicle engines to make them faster than police cars. This led to what we know today as the National Association for Stock Car Auto Racing (NASCAR).

10. If you happen to be traveling through Kansas today, then feel lucky because they win for having the longest alcohol ban (sixty-eight years between 1880 and 1948). The alcohol ban was lifted by a new Kansas state law that was passed in 1965. However, it put all public bars out of business because only private bars were allowed. Twenty-one years later, in 1986, the private bar ban was lifted and within a year, 400 public bars opened. However, there was a stipulation—30 percent of bar sales must be from food. On a side note and to open the crazy Kansas box even more, in the 1970s—unbelievably—5'5" Vern Miller (ex–police officer, deputy sheriff, and county marshal who then went on to graduate law school) was elected as the Kansas attorney general in 1970. His job was to aggressively enforce Kansas's liquor laws. Examples of his hostile assertiveness included raiding Amtrak trains that were passing through Kansas and forcing airlines to stop serving liquor while traveling through Kansas's airspace. Miller made headlines and a book about him was published in 2008.

PROHIBITION WORDS TO KNOW

AMENDMENT

An article added to the Constitution of the United States.

ANTI-SALOON LEAGUE

The number-one leading organization that lobbied for an American Prohibition in the early 1900s.

BATHTUB GIN

A gin-like spirit made by the Mafia with purchased legal and illegal alcohol.

BOOTLEGGER

A person who makes and sells illegal alcohol. The American term came from the 1625 term for hiding a liquor bottle in the leg of one's boot.

CAPONE

Alphonse Gabriel "Al" Capone (1899–1947) was one of the famous American Mafia gangsters during Prohibition. He was the first of nine children born in America to his Italian-immigrant parents and grew up in Brooklyn. He quit Catholic school at age fourteen after hitting a teacher in the face, then became a member of two New York City youth gangs. In his adulthood, Capone became a bouncer and bartender for mobster Frankie Yale in a Coney Island dance hall called the Harvard Inn. It was here that Capone earned his nickname "Scarface" after insulting a woman (her brother cut his face). At age twenty, Capone left New York City and moved to Chicago, where he worked for the biggest Mafia boss, James "Big Jim" Colosimo, as a bouncer at a brothel (where he contracted syphilis). Soon he became a famous gang leader spending his money on custom-made suits, gourmet food and drink, jewelry, the best women money could buy, and Cuban cigars. His seven-year reign as crime boss ended when he was thirty-three years old.

EIGHTEENTH AMENDMENT

This established the Prohibition of alcoholic beverages in America by declaring the production, transport, and sale of alcohol illegal.

FLAPPERS

A twenty-something generation of young women who drank cocktails, wore short skirts, short hair, listened to jazz, frequented speakeasies, wore excessive makeup, smoked, drove automobiles, had casual sex in the time known as the "Roarin' Twenties." These women would have been born between 1890 and 1910.

GANGSTERS

A criminal who is a member of a gang.

JAZZ AGE

A period of music from 1920–1928 that was put on hold for four years due to the Great Depression (1929–1933), and then resumed.

RATIFY

To sign or give formal consent to a treaty, contract, or agreement, making it officially valid.

ROARING TWENTIES

This term and period in time encompasses many things. Briefly, it was a period of economic prosperity in the United States, Canada, and Western Europe, and it spread after World War I in 1919. The spirit of the Roaring Twenties was fueled by people wanting to break away from tradition and who desired to enter into a modern era. Some large-scale examples include the introduction of automobiles, telephones, radio, motion pictures, electricity, and commercial aviation. For the first time, media focused on celebrities (especially sports celebs and moving picture movie stars). Cities built gigantic sports stadiums and Hollywood kept moving forward by introducing "talkies." As for style, art deco was everywhere. Dance clubs popped up and fashion changed dramatically (no more corsets). Female long hair was cut into bobs, skirt hems rose, sleeves were cut, and a sexual revolution began to seep.

RUM RUNNER

A person who is involved in the illegal business of transporting and smuggling illegal alcohol. It mostly relates to ships smuggling rum.

SPEAKEASY

An illegal establishment that sold alcoholic beverages (also nicknamed "blind pig" or "blind tiger") that had a password you had to "speak easy" at the entrance door.

TEMPERANCE

Temperance is defined as voluntary self-restraint or moderation in something.

TWENTY-FIRST AMENDMENT

It repealed the Eighteenth Amendment, which mandated a national prohibition on alcohol.

TEETOTALER

A person who chooses to not drink alcohol and in most cases has taken a pledge not to imbibe.

VOLSTEAD ACT

The act that carried out the intent of the Eighteenth Amendment, which established the American Prohibition.

•••
AN AMERICAN PROHIBITION TIMELINE

1784 – A founding father and Philadelphia physician and politician, Benjamin Rush, publishes a pamphlet titled *An Inquiry into the Effects of Spirituous Liquors on the Human Mind and Body.*

1789 – The first known American temperance society is formed in Litchfield County, Connecticut, by leading business owners who feel alcohol hinders the conduct of their businesses.

1813 – The Massachusetts Society for the Suppression of Intemperance is founded.
– The Connecticut Society for the Reformation of Morals is founded.

1826 – Boston ministers found the American Temperance Society (ATS) and by 1831, they are 170,000 members strong.

1833 – The American Temperance Union is founded and a year later, they have one million members.

1838 – Massachusetts prohibits the sale of alcohol in amounts less than fifteen gallons, but repeals the law two years later.

1840 – The short-lived Washington Temperance Society is founded in Baltimore, Maryland (it was named after President George Washington) and becomes known as the Washingtonian movement. This society is likened to Alcohol Anonymous today. Members consist of reformed heavy drinkers who meet together, give testimonials, support one another, and take a pledge to abstain from alcohol. Two years later, they have 600,000 abstinence pledges and by 1843, the society fades away.

1851 – The state of Maine passes a state Prohibition law with the help of Portland mayor Neal Dow (1804–1897). It becomes known as "The Maine Law." Other states that begin to follow suit include Vermont, Kansas, Iowa, North Dakota, and South Dakota.

1869 – The National Prohibition Party is founded in Chicago.

1874 – The Women's Christian Temperance Union is founded.

1876 – The World's Women's Christian Temperance Union is founded.

1880 – Kansas becomes the first state to go completely dry with the help of governor John St. John and the National Women's Christian Temperance Union.

1888 – The Supreme Court strikes down state Prohibition laws if they forbid the sale of alcohol that was transported into the state in its original passage. This means hotels and clubs could sell an unopened bottle of liquor, even if the state bans alcohol sales.

1893 – The American Anti-Saloon League is founded in Ohio. The league is a nonpartisan organization that focuses on Prohibition through the publication of pamphlets, songs, fliers, cartoons, stories, magazines, and newspapers. They are active until 1933.

1899 – Six-foot-tall, fifty-three-year-old Carry Nation begins walking into Kansas saloons with a hatchet destroying everything she can. This goes on for ten years, and she is arrested and fined thirty-two times.

1901 – Prince Edward Island in Canada starts Prohibition. It is lifted in 1948.

1908 – Massachusetts bans alcohol in 249 towns and 18 cities.

– Mississippi bans alcohol on December 31 (kind of mean to do on New Year's Eve), and does not lift their ban until August 5, 1966. The Broadwater Beach Resort in Biloxi (today it's called President Casino Broadwater Resort) is the first to receive an on-premise liquor license and the second—but first liquor store—license goes to the Joe Azar and his brother for Jigger & Jug in Package Store in Greenville, Mississippi (304 US-82). It is still in operation today. On a side note, Joe Azar's son, Steve, grows up to be a Nashville country music star with his biggest hit called "I Don't Have to Be Me 'Til Monday" (2002).

– In May of 2010, Austin Evans and Richard Patrick open Cathead Distillery—the state's first distillery (and only so far). The name Cathead is in honor of blues musicians who are nicknamed "catheads." In addition, on July 1, 2013 the last remaining homebrewing law is passed in Mississippi, making homebrewing legal in all fifty states.

1910 – Australia starts Prohibition, then lifts it in the capital city of Canberra in 1928.

1912 – Congress passes a law overturning the Supreme Court's 1888 ruling, which permitted states to forbid all alcohol.

– Absinthe is banned in America.

1914 – The Anti-Saloon League proposes a constitutional amendment to prohibit the sale of alcohol.

– Russia starts Prohibition, then lifts it in 1925.

1915 – Saskatchewan, Canada, starts Prohibition, then lifts it in 1925.

– Iceland starts Prohibition, then lifts it in 1922. Beer 2.25 percent or over is banned until 1989.

1916 – Alberta, Canada, starts Prohibition, then lifts it in 1924.

– Norway starts Prohibition, then lifts it in 1927.

1917 – The U.S. Senate and the House pass the Eighteenth Amendment, then sends it to the American states for ratification.

– Puerto Rico starts Prohibition, then lifts it in 1933.

1918 – Fueled by the temperance movement to vote for Prohibition, the United States ratifies the Nineteenth Amendment, was which allows women to vote for the first time in American history. On a global side note, New Zealand first allowed women to vote in 1893, and Saudi Arabia in 2015.

– Arizona, Delaware, Florida, Georgia, Kentucky, Louisiana, Mississippi, Maryland, Massachusetts, Montana, North Dakota, South Carolina, South Dakota, Texas, Virginia, ratify the Eighteenth Amendment.

– Connecticut votes against ratification.

1919 – Alabama, Arkansas, California, Colorado, Idaho, Illinois, Indiana, Iowa, Kansas, Maine, Michigan, Minnesota, Missouri, Nebraska, Nevada, New Hampshire, New Mexico, New York, North Carolina, Ohio, Oklahoma, Oregon, Pennsylvania, Tennessee, Utah, Vermont, Washington, West Virginia, Wisconsin, and Wyoming ratify the Eighteenth Amendment.

– Rhode Island votes against ratification.

– Congress passes the Volstead Act, which helps make the Eighteenth Amendment stick. The act states three distinct purposes:

1. To prohibit intoxicating beverages.

2. To regulate the manufacture, sale, or transport of intoxicating liquor (but not consumption).

3. To ensure an ample supply of alcohol and promote its use in scientific research and in the development of fuel, dye, and other lawful industries and practices, such as religious rituals.

– It further stated, "no person shall manufacture, sell, barter, transport, import, export, deliver, or furnish any intoxicating liquor except as authorized by this act."

– Québec, Canada, starts Prohibition, then lifts it in 1920.

– Finland starts Prohibition, then lifts it in 1932.

1920 – Prohibition begins in America on January 17, one minute past midnight.

– The U.S. Virgin Islands start Prohibition, then lift it in 1933.

Customers at a bar in Philadelphia, Pennsylvania, after Prohibition's end in December 1933. © *Everett Historical / Shutterstock*

1933 – The Twenty-First Amendment is passed on December 5 at 3:32 p.m. and the Eighteenth Amendment is repealed.

1934 – In the United States, twenty-one is set as the legal age for drinking, purchasing, and possessing alcohol.

1949 – The American drinking age is set at twenty-one for liquor and eighteen for cereal malt beverages.

1966 – Mississippi is the last state to lift the ban on Prohibition.

FUN PROHIBITION FACTS

› The cocktail dress was invention in the early 1920s by Gabrielle "Coco" Chanel. The black dress was inspired by nuns' habits.

› Carpenters made extra money on the side by designing and building hidden home bars constructed into walls, hollow clocks, furniture, and anyplace else that sparked inspiration.

› During a raid, the 21 Club in New York City had bar levers that, when pulled, dropped the liquor shelves down into the sewer.

4

SHAKEN, NOT STIRRED: VODKA

...

A BRIEF HISTORY OF VODKA

Many drink historians place the origins of vodka anywhere from the 700s to the 1400s. However, most agree that it began somewhere in the "vodka belt." The vodka belt is located in Eastern, Central, and Northern Europe and includes countries such as Russia, Poland, and Ukraine.

Poland wins for finding the word "*wódka*" in court documents in the 1400s, but that word meant it was for medicines. Poland used the word "*gorzeć*" when vodka was for drinking. In 1534, a Polish pharmacist named Stefan Falimirz published *O Ziolach / O Mocy Ich* ("On Herbs and Their Potency"), which is believed to be one of the first documents containing the word "vodka." This luxurious illustrated book gave details for the preparation of over seventy vodka-based medicines.

Every country in the vodka belt had their own words for vodka and they translate into phrases such as "little water," "burnt water," "to burn," "ardent water," and "the water of life."

In 1789, Johann Tobias Lowitz developed charcoal filtration for vodka.

Before this, vodka tended to be infused with various fruits and herbs, so yes, it was flavored. Today, vodka is the number-one best-selling spirit in the world.

The Top Ten Things to Know About Vodka

1. Vodka can be made from any carbohydrate that is fermentable, not just potatoes.
2. Vodka can be made in any country of the world.
3. No one really knows who invented vodka. Most think it was Russia, but Poland seems to have more historical evidence.
4. The word "vodka" translates into "water."
5. Wolfschmidt was the first vodka introduced to America in the late 1800s.
6. The Moscow Mule was the first Smirnoff vodka cocktail marketed to America in the 1940s.
7. Vodka Martinis became extremely popular in America when the first James Bond film, *Dr. No*, was released in 1962.
8. While flavored commercial vodkas in the 1950s–1960s such as lime, grape, mint, and chocolate had some success, it wasn't until the 1980s when flavored vodkas rose to international success with the introduction of Absolut Peppar in 1984 and Absolut Citron in 1988.
9. If American vodka is made from sugarcane, then it must be distilled more than 95 percent abv (alcohol by volume) to be considered a neutral spirit and not rum.
10. Besides drinking, vodka can be used as a cleaning agent.

···
TYPES OF VODKA

There are two categories of vodka: flavored and plain. The plain category can be further categorized by what carbohydrate was used to make the vodka such as corn, wheat, potatoes, etc. The flavored category consists of plain vodka that has been flavored or infused with natural or artificial flavors.

Today, vodka companies like to brag about their water source, how many times their vodka has been distilled, or how many times it has been filtered.

···
POPULAR VODKA BRANDS

ABSOLUT

Produced in Ahus, Sweden, with Swedish water and winter wheat. Absolut introduced the first flavored vodka to America Absolut Peppar) in 1986. In 1988, they introduced Absolut Citron, which lead to the resurrection of the Cosmopolitan. Absolut has also been a prolific leader in the art and advertising world.

CRYSTAL HEAD

Produced in Newfoundland, Canada, with Canadian water and peaches-and-cream corn. It's distilled four times and filtered three times through diamond crystals. The bottle is shaped like a crystal skull head, but the drink is most known for being the brainchild of actor Dan Aykroyd.

GREY GOOSE

Produced in France with soft French winter wheat from Picardy, then shipped to Cognac to be mixed with spring water. Marketing master Sidney Frank created Grey Goose. Frank wanted to introduce the first luxury/super-premium vodka to America. It debuted in 1997.

HANGAR ONE

Produced in Alameda, California, with grains from the America Midwest and California-grown Viognier grapes. It is produced in an upcycled Navy aircraft hangar and distilled four times.

REYKA

Produced in Iceland with glacial Icelandic lava water, barley, and wheat in an eco-friendly distillery. They say that Iceland has the best water in the world.

···
DIFFERENT VODKA INGREDIENTS

The Ocean Organic vodka bottle is angled to emulate the Earth's axis like a globe.
© *Hawaii Sea Spirits Organic Farm & Distillery*

- **Vodka made from corn:** Tito's, Crystal Head, Rain Organic, Pur, Deep Eddy, Prairie Organic and Iceberg.
- **Vodka made from sugarcane:** Firefly, Finlandia Raspberry, Ocean Organic, Cerén Organic, San Francisco Organic Beach, and Amazon Rainforest.
- **Vodka made from wheat:** Absolut, Grey Goose, Effen, Ketel One, Smirnoff, Reyka, Vox, Stoli, and Death's Door.
- **Vodka made from grapes:** Ciroc, Hangar One, Glass, Roth, and DiVine.
- **Vodka made from potatoes:** Chopin, Zodiac, Koenig Idaho, Prince Edward, Famous, and Chuckanut Bay.
- **Vodka made from honey:** Comb, 3 Bees, and Truuli Peak Alaskan.
- **Vodka made from apples:** Ironworks, Tree, and Untamed Irish.
- **Vodka made from barley:** Finlandia, Sipsmith, East Van, Maximus, and Valt Single Malt Scottish.
- **Vodka made from rye:** Belvedere, Shakers, King Peter, and Sobieski.

FUN VODKA FACTS

› The vodka 250,000 Scovilles Naga Chilli is the hottest vodka in the world. It has been infused with Naga Jolokia chillies, then packaged in a heavy glass bottle with industrial-grade sealing wire and a lead security seal, so you will need wire cutters to open it. Their website even suggests that you should not purchase it.

› In 1953, Ian Fleming created a fictional cocktail for James Bond in *Casino Royale* called a Vesper. It was the first cocktail to have both vodka and gin in its recipe.

› Vodka is lighter than water.

› Billionaire vodka is the most expensive vodka in the world. It costs $3.75 million for one bottle. It is filtered through diamonds, and the bottle is adorned with 3,000 diamonds.

› Broadway dancers have been known to soak their socks in vodka, then dry them overnight. The next day, the vodka-soaked socks fight foot fungi.

› In 2005, the *New York Times* did a blind taste test with twenty-one high-end vodkas and for fun threw in Smirnoff vodka. Smirnoff won.

5

MOTHERS RUIN: GIN

•••
A BRIEF HISTORY OF GIN

Gin historians have discovered that juniper-based health tonics were first mentioned in the 1269 Dutch book *Der Naturen Bioemementions* by Jacob van Maerlant te Damme.

In 1575, Lucas Bulsius changed his family name to Bols, moved to Amsterdam, and set up his own jenever distillery. It was a favorite drink among the British troops who were in the Netherlands for the Dutch War of Independence (1567–1609). They gave it a nickname: Dutch Courage. In 1600, Bols had earned a reputation and was a preferred supplier to the powerful Dutch East India Company. This gave him first dibs on spices and herbs to make his jenever. Jenever was mentioned in a 1623 English play called *The Duke of Milan*. Hundreds of small Dutch gin distilleries were in operation by the mid-1600s.

Pietr Blower, a Dutch émigré (self-exiled) made a special recipe of jenever in Barbados. He brought distillery equipment and cane seedlings from Brazil in 1637.

In 1672, William of Orange (from Holland) became the King of England. William heavily influenced the widespread manufacture of gin in England by taxing imported spirits and then allowed anyone to produce gin without a license, which led to distillers using unclean water and toxic, inferior ingredients. Gin was the cheapest drink in town and began to be blamed for a rise in crime, social issues, accidents, and many deaths. London became a slum of crime filled with drunkards. All of this led to the "Gin Craze," "Gin Lane," the "Gin Act of 1736," and the "Gin Act of 1751." In 1721, one-quarter of London is used for the production and sale of gin. Nearly two million gallons are produced.

Between 1825 and 1829, the first lavish London gin palaces opened with opulent style. Charles Dickens wrote about them in 1836, calling them "perfectly dazzling when contrasted with the darkness and dirt we have just left."

Mature juniper berries. © *Bildagentur Zoonar GmbH / Shutterstock*

In 1862, American bartender and author Jerry Thomas published the first known Gin Martini recipe, called Martinez, in the first known cocktail book. The gin listed for the Martini was Old Tom. In 1888, New Orleans bar owner Charles Ramos created the city's most popular gin cocktail, the Ramos Gin Fizz. It also called for Old Tom gin.

During American Prohibition (1920–1933) mobsters made a gin-like hooch by infusing bootlegged moonshine with dried juniper berries, and by the 1940s, gin was revamped into a glamorous spirit with the help of Hollywood movie stars and films.

The Top Ten Things to Know About Gin

1. Gin is English, but was inspired by Holland.
2. Holland made genever (also spelled jenever), and this is what the English tried to replicate.
3. Technically, one can say that gin was the first flavored vodka.
4. Gin was given to Dutch soldiers with the nickname "Dutch Courage."
5. William of Orange brought genever from Holland to England.
6. Many herbs and botanicals are used in gin, but the juniper berry imparts the predominant flavor.
7. England's first commercial gin was called Old Tom. It was a sweet gin much like genever.
8. In the 1700s, the English we're allowed to make gin without a license.
9. Gin can be made anywhere in the world.
10. Gin was the original base spirit used in the Martini. The Martini glass image is the most iconic cocktail culture symbol worldwide. Other popular gin cocktails include Tom Collins, Singapore Sling, Negroni, Ramos Gin Fizz, Gimlet, and Monkey Gland.

• • •

TYPES OF GIN

Gin can be made anywhere in the world, but the prominent countries that produce it include the United States, Japan, France, Spain, Sweden, Canada, Scotland, and Germany, as does the continent of Africa. There are four categories of gin: Genever, London Dry (or just Dry), Plymouth, and New Western.

GENEVER (JENEVER)

Genever was the first invented in Holland. It has a sweet, malty taste. Genevers break down into four more categories: Oude, jonge, korenwijn, and graajenever.

Oude and jonge can only be made and sold in Holland and Belgium.

Old Tom was first created in England, but falls into this category because it is considered a sweet gin.

LONDON DRY (DRY)

Most people think of this when gin is mentioned. Popular brands are Bombay, Beefeater, and Tanqueray. The taste is clean and dry and mixes well in cocktails.

PLYMOUTH

This category is for gins produced in Plymouth, England. Today, the city only produces one gin and its name is Plymouth. It tastes aromatic, earthy, and fruity.

NEW WESTERN

These new gins hit the market around the start of the New Millennium. Most of them would fall into the category of "dry," and the juniper seems to be on the back end instead of the front end. Examples include: Hendrick's, Aviation, and Martin Miller's.

FUN GIN FACTS

> Gin is just vodka after its first distilling. The herbs and botanicals are added during the second distilling. It is fair to say that gin is flavored vodka.

> Almost zero juniper is cultivated; it is mostly picked in the wild.

> Today, the Philippines consumes more gin than any country in the world (25 million annual cases).

> The most famous Martini quote is by American poet and writer Dorothy Parker: "I like to have a Martini, two at the very most; three, I'm under the table, four I'm under my host!"

> The most expensive gin is Watenshi at $2,500 a bottle. The bottles are filled with the evaporation (Angel's Share). It takes one hundred distillations to fill one bottle.

6

YO, HO, HO AND A BOTTLE OF…RUM

...

A BRIEF HISTORY OF RUM

Today, 80 percent of the world's rum is produced in the Caribbean. All spirits start with a plant, and rum starts with a species of grass called sugarcane. But it took sugarcane almost 10,000 years to make it to the Caribbean. And it wasn't until the mid-1800s when it started tasting decent. Up until then, it was harsh.

Here is the short story. We know sugarcane is indigenous to South Asia, and it is believed that the sweet grass was first domesticated on the island of New Guinea around 8000 BCE. India is known to have first extracted and crystallized the sugary plant around 350 CE, and from there trade merchants brought it to Africa and then Spain.

By the 1400s, there was a huge demand for the "sweet salt" (sugar) in Europe, so the Portuguese began planting sugarcane on the Island of Madeira. They soon realized that it was an extremely labor-intensive task in all processes of growing, harvesting, and production. Slaves were therefore imported. In 1493, Christopher Columbus attempted to bring sugarcane seedlings to the Caribbean, but they did not survive the voyage. Spanish conquistador Diego Velázquez was on the ship with Columbus and settled in Hispaniola (Dominican Republic, Haiti, and the tiny islands around them) to be of service to Spanish knight and soldier Nicolás Ovando y Cáceres, who a couple years later became the governor of the Indies.

In the 1501, Pedro de Atienza was the first to successfully import sugarcane seedlings to Hispaniola. He harvested his first crop four years later. In 1511, on behalf of Spain, Diego Velázquez conquered Cuba, bringing Hispaniola sugarcane with him. In 1518, a royal decree from Charles V (ruler of the Spanish and Holy Roman Empire) licensed 2,000 slaves to be imported to Hispaniola to work the sugarcane fields.

1595 engraving with modern watercolor of African slaves processing sugarcane to make rum in Hispaniola. © *Everett Historical / Shutterstock*

And in 1523, another royal decree imported 1,500 slaves to Hispaniola and 2,500 to other Caribbean islands such as Puerto Rico and Jamaica. The Portuguese took their production to Brazil and by the mid-1500s, there were almost 3,000 sugar mills. The Dutch started taking sugarcane seedlings to plant on any Caribbean island they could. Barbados and the islands around the Dominican Republic were among the first. By the 1600s, rum in daily rations was common for the Royal Navy.

In 1758, George Washington campaigned for the Virginia House of Burgess by offering free Barbados rum to voters, and he won. In the 1700s, the Caribbean Islands were losing money on their tobacco and cotton crops due to America growing their own, so switching to sugarcane crops solved this problem. Thus began a mass production of Caribbean rum.

In 1810, the first hospital in Sydney, Australia, was financed by local businessmen in return for a contract that licensed them to import 60,000 gallons of rum to sell. The hospital was called Rum Hospital. In addition, in 1862, Don Facundo Bacardi began filtering his Cuban rum through charcoal.

The Top Ten Things to Know About Rum

1. Early America was funded by rum sales. In 1657, the first rum distillery was built in Boston.
2. In 1664, a rum distillery was built in New York City.
3. The Royal British Navy gave sailors a daily ration of rum from 1731 until 1970.
4. Bacardi's first distillery was in Cuba, not Puerto Rico.
5. No one knows where the word "rum" came from.
6. Eighty percent of rum comes from the Caribbean, but it can be made anywhere in the world.
7. Rum is made from fermented sugarcane juice, sugarcane syrup, or sugarcane molasses, which comes from squeezing, cutting up, and mashing sugarcane stalks. To this day, in many parts of the world, the cane is still crudely harvested by hand with machetes.
8. "Rum and Coca-Cola" by the Andrews Sisters was the number-one song in 1945. The most popular rum cocktails are the Daiquiri, Mojito, Hurricane, Rum Punch, Mai Tai, Dark 'n Stormy, Cuba Libre, Zombie, Planter's Punch, Piña Colada, and Hot Buttered Rum.
9. Barbados Mt. Gay is the oldest rum company in the world. They have held the oldest surviving deed, dating back to 1703.
10. Brazil grows the most sugarcane in the world and has over 2,000 nicknames for rum.

•••

TYPES OF RUM

There are six categories of rum: light (also called white, silver, or platinum), gold (also called amber), dark (also called black), añejo (also called aged or premium), overproof, and flavored.

LIGHT RUM

Some light rum is distilled and then poured directly into the bottle. This light rum (also called fresh rum) is raw. Fresh distilled rum contains trace amounts of hydrogen sulfide gas, which makes the rum taste harsh. This is probably close to the way rum tasted in the 1600s.

Most light rum is aged up to a year in oak barrels previously used for aging American and Canadian whiskey. Aging light rum gives it a better taste for a commercial market.

The most popular light rum in the world is Bacardi. Bacardi's distillery is located in San Juan, Puerto Rico, and produces 100,000 thousand gallons of rum a day. That amount equates to filling an Olympic-size swimming pool in one week!

GOLD RUM

Gold rum is light rum that has been aged in oak barrels until it reaches a golden color. The aging mellows the light rum, resulting in a light-to-medium-bodied rum. It is then filtered and poured into bottles.

DARK RUM

Dark rums are made from the thick black by-product of sugarcane called molasses. After distillation, they are aged in barrels.

AÑEJO RUM

Añejo is the Spanish word for "aged." Añejo rum is light rum that has been aged. There are no guidelines for how long to age rum, so the process ends when the rum master determines it is ready. The result is dark, smooth-sipping rum. Añejo rums are compared to Cognac.

OVERPROOF RUM

Overproof rum is just what it sounds like. To be considered overproof it has to be bottled 100 proof or more, which also means bottled at 50 percent alcohol by volume or more. The number-one overproof rum found in most bars is Bacardi 151.

FLAVORED RUM

Flavored rums are infused with a myriad of flavors. Almost every rum brand has a portfolio of flavored rums.

• • •

OTHER THINGS TO KNOW ABOUT RUM

RHUM VS. RUM

If you find yourself looking at rum labels, every once in a while you will see rum spelled "rhum." Rhum is short for rhum agricole, which just means that the rum in that bottle was made from fresh-squeezed sugarcane juice and not with by-products like molasses.

BRAZILIAN RUM

Brazilian rum is called cachaça (ka-SHAH-suh). It is only made from fresh-squeezed Brazilian sugarcane juice.

NAVY STRENGTH RUM

When you think of Navy strength rum, think overproof gunpowder test. See, the Royal British Navy used to give sailors a daily "tot" of rum. A tot is about eight ounces (one cup). To make sure the rum was not cut with water (its strength weakened) they would put some rum on gunpowder and attempt to ignite it, and if it ignited, the rum was over 114 proof (or over 57 percent alcohol).

FUN FACTS ABOUT RUM

› Rum has gone by many names such as: Barbados water, demon water, grog, kill-devil, Nelson's blood, rhumbooze, rumbowling, rumbullion, rumbustion, and splice the main brace.

› On January 15, 1919, at the U.S. Industrial Alcohol Company in Boston, Massachusetts, a cast-iron tank holding 400,000 gallons of molasses ruptured, creating a sixteen-foot-tall sticky tsunami through the Atlantic railway station, lifting a train off the track, injuring a hundred fifty people, killing twelve horses and twenty-one people, until it finally rested as a lake of molasses in North End Park.

› Bacardi has the largest rum distillery in the world, located in San Juan, Puerto Rico. If you visit by cruise ship, skip the expensive excursion to tour the distillery. Instead, just pay twenty-five cents to ride the ferry. You can see the distillery where the cruise ships dock.

› August is National Rum Month.

› Most rum is produced in the Caribbean and almost every island produces rum.

› Jamaica's Wray & Nephew overproof rum is the world's highest proof rum at 63 percent.

› In 1943, the Disney cartoon character Donald Duck drank cachaça, and in the same theater feature, *Saludos Amigos* (Spanish for "Greetings, Friends") Disney introduced a new character from Brazil named José Carioca.

› The most expensive rum is a 1940 bottle of J. Wray & Nephew. It is valued at $54,000.

7

SOUTH OF THE BORDER: TEQUILA

...

A BRIEF HISTORY OF TEQUILA

The history of tequila is a short one. In the 1300s, the Aztecs used the agave plant to make an alcoholic beverage called pulque. In 1531, Spanish settlers—with knowledge of distillation—distilled the pulque. They called it mexcalli (mezcal).

Farmers loading harvested blue agave for tequila production; 2013 Tequila; Jalisco, Mexico. © *T Photography / Shutterstock*

In 1758, Spain's King Ferdinand VI issued a land grant to Don Jose Antonio de Cuervo to cultivate the blue agave plant in the town of Tequila, Jalisco, Mexico. In 1795, Spain's King Carlos IV granted a permit to produce tequila commercially to his son Jose Guadalupe de Cuervo. (Spanish King Carlos III prohibited alcohol, so it took thirty-seven years to start commercial production). Tequila was known as "mezcal de Tequila" until 1893 and was sold by the barrel. Cuervo's first bottled tequila was sold in 1906. The Cuervo family in modern times is wicked wealthy.

Today there are over 2,000 brands of tequila. Celebrities who have their own tequila brands include George Clooney, Justin Timberlake, Sean Combs, Mario Lopez, Carlos Santana, and Sammy Hagar.

The Top Ten Things to Know About Tequila

1. Tequila is Mexico's national spirit and by law, it can only be produced in five Mexican states and nowhere else in the world.

2. The Margarita is Mexico's national cocktail.

3. Jose Cuervo was the first commercial tequila, and it is still the number-one seller of tequila in the world.

4. There are over 200 varieties of the agave plant, but the blue agave is king.

5. Mezcal (also spelled mescal) is made from many types of agave plants. The marketing ploy of adding an aphrodisiac worm into a bottle of mezcal started in the 1940s and lasted through the 1990s. The worm was actually a moth larva that lives on agave plants in the caterpillar phase of life.

6. The agave plant heart (piña) is used to make tequila. A piña can weigh up to 200 pounds.

7. In the 1950s Herradura tequila—thanks to crooner superstar Bing Crosby—was the first 100 percent blue agave tequila to be introduced in America.

8. Americans tend to drink tequila as shots with salt and lime. Mexicans don't use salt and lime when shooting tequila.

9. Just as it takes a long time and much effort to produce rum from sugarcane, the process of making tequila is also labor-intensive, and is mostly done by hand.

10. The most popular tequila cocktails are the Margarita, Strawberry Margarita, Tequila Sunrise, Bloody Maria, Paloma, and the Prairie Fire shot.

...

TYPES OF TEQUILA

BLANCO

Blanco tequila is also referred to as silver, white, and platinum. Most times, blanco is distilled then poured straight into the bottle. However, blanco is allowed to be stored in stainless-steel tanks for up to sixty days before bottling.

REPOSADO

Reposado means "rested." It's blanco that has been aged between two and twelve months in wood barrels. The color after aging is a light gold.

AÑEJO

Añejo means "old." It is blanco has been aged between one and three years. The color after aging is a dark gold. Añejos will be very smooth, therefore making it a good sipping tequila.

EXTRA AÑEJO

This category was added in 2006. It's blanco that has been aged a minimum of three years.

JOVEN

Joven mean "young." It's blanco that has additives added to it such as coloring (to make it look aged), oak extract, and sugar. Jose Cuervo is a joven.

FUN TEQUILA FACTS

› National Tequila Day is June 24.
› The agave plant is not from the cactus family; it is from the lily family.
› The most expensive tequila is Ultra-Premium Ley .925 Pasion Azteca at $225,000 a bottle. It is expensive because the bottle is made from platinum and white gold. The company also produces another bottle with encrusted diamonds.
› One of the most popular quotes about tequila is: "One tequila, two tequila, three tequila, floor."
› The heart of the agave plant is called piña because it looks like a pineapple.

8

WHICHEVER WAY YOU SPELL IT: A BRIEF HISTORY OF WHISKEY/WHISKY

Scotland and Ireland both have claimed to be the inventor of whiskey since the 1400s. Today, Ireland holds the record for the oldest licensed whiskey distillery in the world—Old Bushmills—established in 1608; however, Scotland first recorded whisky on June 1, 1495 in Scottish accounting records (in the Exchequer Rolls of Scotland), which said, "To Friar John Cor, by order of King James IV, to make aqua vitae VIII bolls of malt." Historians say that VIII equates to around 1,500 bottles, so this shows that making whiskey has been going on for a while. It is believed that the word "whisky" came from the Gaelic word "usquebaugh" (water of life) then shortened to "usque" (usky) and then "whisky."

Whiskey, like many spirits, was birthed out of convenience, portability, and preservation. It is much easier to travel with and store a bottle of whiskey than a keg of beer!

In the 1700s, America began making whiskey. During the Whiskey Rebellion of 1791–1794, grain farmers did not want to pay taxes to the U.S. government. The U.S. government won.

Today, whiskey is made all over the world. Individual countries have their own whiskey regulations, which oversee such things as ingredients having to be home-grown, proofs, and percentages.

The Top Ten Things to Know About Whiskey/Whisky

1. America and Ireland spell whiskey with an "e." Scotland and Canada spell whisky without an "e."
2. Scotland and Ireland still fight today over who first invented whiskey.
3. America produces five whiskeys: Bourbon, rye, blended, corn, and Tennessee.
4. Bourbon whiskey has been the official spirit of the United States since 1964.
5. One can say that whiskey is distilled beer.
6. Popular whisk(e)y cocktails include the Whiskey Sour, Irish Coffee, Old-Fashioned, Manhattan, Rob Roy, Rusty Nail, Mint Julep, Sazerac, Lynchburg Lemonade, and Blood and Sand.
7. Jack Daniel's is a Tennessee whiskey, not Bourbon.
8. Bourbon whiskey can only be produced in America, in any of the fifty states. It must be made with at least 51 percent corn, which must be American. No state except Kentucky can put "Kentucky Whiskey" on its label.
9. Whiskey is made from fermented grains such as corn, rye, wheat, and barley.
10. America's national Capitol Building was built with whiskey. In 1791, President George Washington imposed a whiskey tax to pay for its construction. Thomas Jefferson was opposed to the tax, calling it "big government tactics," then resigned as Secretary of State.

• • •
TYPES OF SCOTCH WHISKY

Scotland produces two types of whisky: single malt and blended. Scotch whisky can only be produced in Scotland, which has six whisky regions: Highlands, Lowlands, Speyside, Campbeltown, Islands, and Islay. Each region's whisky tastes different because of the soil. By law, all Scotch whisky must be aged a minimum of three years.

SINGLE MALT

Single malt means that the whisky comes from a single distillery. Many whisky barrels in a single distillery can be blended together, but that still means it is "single malt."

Another category that comes from a single distillery is called "single barrel." This means the whisky came from only one single barrel.

BLENDED

Blended Scotch whisky is a blend of single malts from several distilleries.

• • •
TYPES OF IRISH WHISKEY

Ireland only has four distilleries that produce single pot still and grain whiskey. By law, all Irish whiskey must be aged a minimum of three years. Currently, there are twelve whiskey distilleries in Ireland.

SINGLE POT STILL

Single pot still Irish whiskey breaks down into two categories: single pot still and single malt. Both must be made at a single distillery in a pot still. The only difference is that single malt must be made from 100 percent malted barley and single pot still is made with a combination of malted and unmalted barley.

GRAIN WHISKEY

Grain whiskey breaks down into two categories: blends and single grain. Grain whiskey is made in a column still, which means it can be made continuously. Single grain Irish whiskey is not common, but some brands make it available. Most of the single grain whiskey is used to make blends and some blends will be blended with single grain and pot stills.

• • •
TYPES OF AMERICAN WHISKEY

Every American should know that America produces five whiskeys: Bourbon, rye, blended, corn, and Tennessee. On May 4, 1964, congress declared Bourbon whiskey to be the official native spirit of the United States.

BOURBON

No one knows who produced the first Bourbon, or when it was produced. Bourbon whiskey can be made in any U.S. state and must be made with at least 51 percent American-grown corn. For the label to say "Kentucky Bourbon Whiskey" the whiskey must be made in Kentucky.

Bourbon Whiskey has two other categories: single barrel and small batch.

Single barrel Bourbon comes from one single barrel. Small batch Bourbon is made in small batches.

RYE

Rye whiskey must be made with at least 51 percent American-grown rye. In 1771, Sapling Grove, Tennessee, becomes the first business on record to make rye whiskey. The owner was a fifty-one-year-old Welsh-American named Evan Shelby.

BLENDED

Blended whiskey can be a blend of many grains; however, 20 percent must be straight (one grain). The two most popular brands are Seagram's 7 and Kessler's.

CORN

Corn whiskey is "moonshine." It is clear and unaged, and 80 percent of the grain must be corn. Today, they are making some high-end corn whiskey with more distillations and extra filtering. A couple of popular brands include Buffalo Trace White Dog and Hudson New York Corn.

TENNESSEE

Tennessee whiskey, as you might have guessed, must be made in Tennessee. From 1875 to 1997 there were only two Tennessee whiskey brands: George Dickel and Jack Daniel's. Jack Daniel's filters its whiskey through sugar maple tree charcoal (while other whiskeys are filtered through oak tree charcoal). Today, there are more brands to choose from that include Benjamin Prichard's Collier and McKeel, Nelson's Green Briar, and TenSouth. There are other brands that are produced in Tennessee, but they cannot be called Tennessee whiskey for multiple reasons, such as they are not aged, made from rye, or not charcoal-filtered.

• • •

TYPES OF CANADIAN WHISKY

For the most part, Canadians make blended whisky. They use several types of grains, and the whiskies produced have the reputation for being smooth. Most of Canada's distilleries are near the border of the United States, which came in handy during the American Prohibition.

Canadian Club Canadian whisky launched a "Hide a Case" ad campaign in 1967. Many cases of the whisky were hidden in places such as Mount Kilimanjaro, Mount St. Helens, and the Swiss Alps. Some have never been found.

• • •

OTHER COUNTRIES THAT MAKE
WHISKEY/WHISKY

Countries that produce whiskey include Australia, India, Japan, New Zealand, South Africa, Spain, Sweden, Taiwan, and Wales.

Currently, Japan houses the world's largest whiskey distillery. It's called Fuji-Gotemba and is located in the foothills of Mount Fuji. The water used comes from melted snow.

FUN WHISKEY/WHISKY FACTS

▸ After serving as the first president of the United States, George Washington started a rye whiskey called Mt. Vernon. It is still in operation today.

▸ In 1874, while in Britain, Mark Twain drank a cocktail made of Scotch whisky, Angostura bitters, lemon juice, and crushed sugar before breakfast, before dinner, and before bed.

▸ One bottle of Glenlivet Winchester Vintage 1964 costs $25,000. The last Glenlivet descendant used American Bourbon oak barrels for aging.

▸ Third generation bartender, Sean Kenyon's favorite spirit is whiskey and he stocks plenty. He owns the award-winning speakeasy bookstore bar, Williams & Graham in Denver, Colorado (3160 Tejon Street). You enter through a secret bookcase.

▸ The steam engine was inspired by whisky distillation.

▸ Whiskey is the military word for the letter "W."

▸ Crown Royal Canadian Whisky was created for Queen Elizabeth's visit in 1939.

▸ The most sought-after American whiskeys are Pappy Van Winkle's twenty-three-year-old Bourbon (you can buy an empty bottle on eBay for $300) and George Washington's straight rye whiskey. Washington's whiskey can only be bought in person at the Shops at Mount Vernon in Mount Vernon, Virginia. Around three times a year a limited supply of small batch spirits are offered. The best thing to do is to get on their notification list at mountvernon.org.

Williams & Graham in Denver, Colorado. © *Greg Feldman / Phylum photography*

9

How Sweet It Is: Liqueurs

The history of liqueurs is brief. From what we know, liqueurs were first used for medicinal purposes. Monks were experimenting with liqueurs in the 1300s. One of the oldest liqueurs is Chartreuse.

Today, there are over 500 commercial liqueurs in the world made with various ingredients such as fruit, herbs, flora, spices, egg yolks, nuts, tea, coffee, honey, and even vegetables.

The Top Ten Things to Know About Liqueurs

1. Liqueurs are highly flavored sugar syrups with a spirit base.

2. Most liqueurs are low proof, but there are also high-proof liqueurs.

3. Cream liqueurs are made with dairy cream and have a shelf life of two years.

4. Crème (French pronunciation is Krem) liqueurs are syrupy and do not contain dairy cream.

5. Malibu rum is considered a liqueur because it is made with coconut flavor and sugar syrup.

6. In America, "schnapps," "cordial," and "crème" often mean the same thing as the word "liqueur." Liqueurs can be drunk on their own or used in cocktails to add a sweet flavor to the drink.

7. Contrary to popular belief, Southern Comfort is a liqueur, not a whiskey.

8. It took the creators of Baileys Irish Cream four years of experimentation to keep the cream from curdling with the whiskey. Baileys debuted in 1974.

9. Liqueurs are not always sweet. Some can fall into the "bitter" category.

10. The most popular cocktails made with liqueurs include Amaretto Sour, Black Russian, White Russian, Aviation, the Last Word, Nutty Irishman, Vieux Carré, Mudslide, Rusty Nail, Fuzzy Navel, Sex on the Beach, Melon Ball, Malibu & Pineapple, Appletini, Godfather, Godmother, Cosmopolitan, Jäger Bomb, Grasshopper, Pink Squirrel, and Harvey Wallbanger.

•••

THE MOST POPULAR AND UNIQUE LIQUEURS FROM AROUND THE WORLD

Bols, Marie Brizard, and DeKuyper are the largest liqueur brands in the world. Each of these companies produces standard crème, cream, and schnapps flavors such as anisette, amaretto, banana, blackberry, blue Curaçao, butterscotch, cacao, cassis, cinnamon, melon menthe, pomegranate, raspberry, sour apple, sloe gin, strawberry, triple sec, and violette.

... POPULAR LIQUEURS

- **Ancho Reyes**: Mexican ancho chili liqueur.
- **Baileys Irish Cream**: made with Irish whiskey, milk from Irish cows, chocolate, and vanilla.
- **Bénédictine**: French herbal liqueur.
- **Canton**: French ginger liqueur.
- **Chambord**: French black raspberry liqueur presented in beautiful sphere-shaped bottles.
- **Chartreuse**: high-proof French herbal liqueur.
- **Cherry Heering**: Dutch cherry liqueur.
- **Cointreau**: French orange liqueur.
- **Disaronno**: Italian almond amaretto liqueur.
- **Drambuie**: high-proof Scotch whiskey-based honey liqueur.
- **Fireball**: high-proof Canadian whisky cinnamon liqueur.
- **Frangelico**: Italian hazelnut liqueur that comes in a unique bottle shape that resembles a monk.
- **Galliano**: Italian anise-vanilla liqueur that comes in a very tall bottle.
- **Grand Marnier**: high-proof French Cognac-based orange liqueur.
- **Jack Daniel's Tennessee Honey**: American whiskey-based honey liqueur.
- **Jägermeister**: high-proof German herbal liqueur.
- **Kahlúa**: rum-based Mexican coffee liqueur.
- **Limoncello**: Italian lemon zest liqueur.
- **Luxardo Maraschino**: Italian Marasca cherry liqueur.
- **PAMA**: American pomegranate liqueur.
- **Pimm's Cup No. 1**: English gin-based herbal liqueur.
- **Southern Comfort**: high-proof American peach spice liqueur.
- **St. Germain**: French elderflower liqueur.
- **Sambuca**: high-proof Italian anise liqueur.
- **Tuaca**: high-proof brandy-based Italian vanilla-lemon liqueur.

... UNIQUE LIQUEURS

- **Advocaat**: brandy-based Dutch liqueur made with eggs and sugar.
- **Akvavit**: high-proof Scandinavian liqueur made with caraway seeds.
- **Amarula**: South African cream liqueur made from the fruit of the marula tree. The fruit is picked in the wild, not cultivated. The marula is also called the elephant tree because elephants will bang against it to knock fruit off the tree.
- **AGWA**: high-proof liqueur made in Amsterdam. It contains herbs and Bolivian coca leaves. The coca leaves are picked in the Andes and then shipped under armed guard.
- **Cynar**: Italian bitter liqueur made with artichokes and herbs.
- **Goldschläger**: high-proof Swiss cinnamon schnapps that contains gold leaf flakes.
- **Killepitsch**: high-proof German liqueur that is made with ninety different fruits.
- **Tequila Rose**: tequila-based Mexican strawberry cream liqueur.

- **Umeshu**: sweet-and-sour Japanese liqueur made from unripe ume fruit. Ume is often nicknamed Chinese plums.
- **Visinata**: Russian liqueur made from sour cherries.

FUN LIQUEUR FACTS

› In 1977, Melon Balls (vodka, Midori melon liqueur, and orange juice) were served at the wrap party for the film *Saturday Night Fever* at Studio 54. This is when Midori was launched in America.

› The shape of a Frangelico hazelnut liqueur bottle is designed to resemble a friar in his habit—it comes with a rope tied around the bottle's waist.

› Goldschläger high-proof Swiss cinnamon schnapps contains fifty cents of real gold flakes in every bottle.

10

Liquid Bread: Beer

...
A BRIEF HISTORY OF BEER

No one knows exactly when or where beer was invented. Some believe that because beer and bread used the same ingredients, they must've happened around the same time.

Archaeologists and scientists have discovered ancient beer recipe tablets, beer residue inside pottery jars, poems mentioning beer, cave drawings depicting beer, beer drinking songs, and more.

From around 8000 BCE to 1000 CE, beer was warm, slightly thick, murky, and probably had particles floating in it. Hops became popular to use when making beer around 800 CE because it added flavor, bitterness, and, most importantly, helped with preservation. Up until the 1400s, beer was something one made at home. By the 1500s the brewing of beer had become commercialized. Beer ingredient laws were passed, lagers were accidently discovered, and beer was stored in cool places underground or in caves. The 1700s brought the Industrial Revolution and beer production soared.

Boilermaker drink: drop a shot of whiskey into a beer. © *Brent Hofacker / Shutterstock*

When the American Prohibition (1920–1933) started, it put 1,300 breweries out of the alcohol business, so they had to sell other products. Some sold ice cream and some used their equipment to make dyes. The large breweries such as Pabst, Schlitz, and Miller sold malt extract (what you needed to make beer at home), but they advertised it as a bread-making product.

In 1979, President Jimmy Carter made it legal to sell beer ingredients for home brewing, which kickstarted the microbrew movement of the 1980s. Today, America has over 4,000 breweries. Almost every big city offers several local beers in all types and styles.

The Top Ten Things to Know About Beer

1. Beer (or ale to be accurate) is the world's first known alcohol on record.
2. The Black Velvet beer-cocktail was invented in honor of Prince Albert in 1861. It was made with stout beer layered on top of champagne.
3. Beer breaks down into two categories: ale and lager. Ale uses top fermenting yeasts and lager uses bottom fermenting yeasts. Ales are ancient and lagers are only a couple hundred years old.

4. Beer uses the most types of glassware/vessels of any alcohol category. The largest is a yard and the smallest a half pint.

5. The most popular beer-cocktail shooters in the world include the Flaming Dr. Pepper, Boilermaker, and the Irish Car Bomb.

6. Beer also wins for using the most types of packaging/storage in various sizes. Examples include cans, glass and aluminum bottles, kegs, and casks.

7. The beer stein was invented in the 1300s and, 200 years later, lids were added to keep flies out of the beer.

8. The Anchor Steam brewery in San Francisco has been using both top and bottom fermenting yeasts in their beer since 1896.

9. The oldest operating brewery in America is Yuengling & Son.

10. A beer-cocktail called Hangman's Blood was mentioned in the 1929 novel *A High Wind in Jamaica*. Hangman's Blood consists of porter ale, rum, gin, whisky, port, and brandy. And in 1960, Anthony Burgess (*A Clockwork Orange*) wrote in the *Guardian* newspaper (England) about this same cocktail, "It tastes very smooth, induces a somehow metaphysical elation, and rarely leaves a hangover...I recommend this for a quick, though expensive, lift."

···

TYPES OF BEER

ALE

Individual households, small inns, and pubs (public houses) made ale from 8000 BCE to the 1400s. From the 1500s to the present, ale had been mostly made commercially. Styles of ales include stout, porter, bitter, brown, wheat, cream, lambic, and pale. Popular ale brands include Guinness, Newcastle Brown, Bass Ale, Redhook, Sam Adams Porter, Sierra Nevada Pale Ale, and Blue Moon.

LAGER

Produced in the Czech Republic in 1842, Pilsner Urquell was the first commercial pilsner lager. It is still made today. Most people think that all lagers have a clear yellow color, but this is untrue. Creating a lager has to do with the bottom fermenting yeast, time, and temperature. Styles of lager include pilsner, bock, dry, ice, dunkel, and amber. Popular lager brands include Budweiser (and all the others like Coors, Michelob, etc.), Stella Artois, Shiner Bock, Warsteiner Dunkel, Keystone Ice, Corona, and Negra Modelo.

···

CORONA COCKTAILS

In 1996, the Corona Limon became popular. It is easy to make—just pour a shot of Bacardi Limon rum in a Corona beer. Another popular Corona cocktail is a Corona Margarita where you insert an opened bottle of Corona into a large Margarita.

···

BEER WORDS TO KNOW

- ABV - Alcohol by volume.

FUN BEER FACTS

› Beer is just liquid bread.

› It has been said that Russia did not consider beer to be an alcoholic beverage until 2013.

› The world's most expensive bottle of beer, "Vieille Bon Secours," ale costs $1,000.

› A Scottish brewery makes the strongest beer in the world, called Snake Venom. Its alcohol content is 67 percent ABV. To compare, Budweiser has a 5 percent ABV.

› According to Wikipedia, the country that drinks the most beer in the world is the Republic of Nauru—formerly known as Pleasant Island—an island country in Micronesia in the Central Pacific.

› In 2012, Amsterdam starting paying alcoholics in beer to pick up trash in the streets.

› On October 17, 1814, in London, England, eight people drowned when the Meux and Company Brewery's beer vats burst, pouring almost 1.5 million liters of beer through the streets.

11

IT'S ALL ABOUT THE GRAPES: WINE

•••
A BRIEF HISTORY OF WINE

In 2007, UCLA archaeologists found what appears to be a winery located in an Armenian cave that dates back to 4100 BCE. It contained grapevine remnants, drinking vessels, a wine press, and pottery jars for storage.

However, no one knows when wine was first invented. Many researchers think that it dates back to 6000 BCE. Art, archaeological digs, and writings show us that many civilizations used wine in ceremonies, religion, special occasions, medicinally, and in the home.

Engraving of Ancient Romans mixing wine and water in a large bowl. © *Oleg Golovnev / Shutterstock*

In the 1500s, wine was brought from Europe to South America. Wine production was attempted in Florida, Virginia, and Canada in the 1600s, but Spanish missions are responsible for bringing grapevines to California in the 1700s, which was the beginning of America's wine industry. By 1805, they established Sonoma's first winery. The Californian wine industry skyrocketed in the 1800s due to the Gold Rush and Europe's phylloxera problem. Phylloxera are microscopic bugs that eat grapevine roots. So for many decades, Europe could not produce wine.

Wine sales spiked again in the 1990s because craft microbrews were taking over the alcohol market and the wine industry wanted to compete. Up until then your wine choices at a restaurant were simply Burgundy, Chablis, or rosé, but in the 1990s restaurants were offering up to one hundred bottles of wine on their menus.

The Top Ten Things to Know About Wine

1. No one knows when wine was first invented.
2. Wine is made from fermented fruit. The most popular fruit used is grapes.
3. Even though there are over 10,000 varieties of grapes in the world, only around 300 are used for commercial wine.
4. Juice from all grapes is clear. It's the skins that give it color.
5. France and America are the top producers of wine, and all fifty U.S. states make wine.
6. "Appellation" means where (geographically) the grapes were grown.
7. "Vintage" means what year the grapes were harvested.

8. It takes about 600 grapes to make a bottle of wine, and there are 50 million bubbles in a bottle of champagne.

9. On Thanksgiving, Americans drink more wine than on any other day of the year.

10. The most popular cocktails made with wine include French 75, Sangria, Champagne Cocktail, Wine Spritzer, Kir, Kir Royale, Mulled Wine, Americano, Martini, and Manhattan.

...

TYPES OF WINE

Basically, all wine falls into two categories: red and white. From there they break down into still, sparkling, and fortified.

RED WINE

Red wine is made from black grapes. Black grapes have a reddish-bluish color. The grape skins are used during production. To make pink-colored wines like rosé and white Zinfandel, the skins are left on for a little bit then discarded. Popular commercial red grapes are Cabernet, Merlot, Pinot Noir, Zinfandel, and Beaujolais.

WHITE WINE

White wine is made from grapes that appear light green. White wine can also be made from black grapes if the skins aren't used. Popular commercial white grapes are Chardonnay, Pinot Grigio, Riesling, and Sauvignon Blanc.

FORTIFIED WINE

"Fortified" means ingredients such as sugar, brandy, herbs, or botanicals have been added to the wine. These include sherry, port, Madeira, and vermouths. The first three are often referred to as dessert wines.

...

ALL ABOUT BUBBLY (CHAMPAGNE, PROSECCO, CAVA, AND OTHER SPARKLING WINES)

Sparkling wine is the number-one alcoholic beverage used to celebrate occasions such as weddings, birthdays, and anniversaries. Just like Post-it notes, Super Glue, and penicillin, sparkling wine is a result of a happy accident.

Northern France (Champagne region) has a short growing season, and during the winter, fermentation would stop inside the wine bottles. As spring approached, the temperature rose, fermentation started again, and the bottles of wine would burst. A French Bénédictine monk named Dom Pérignon spent most of his adult life—until he died in 1715—trying to figure out a way to stop the bubbles.

By the early 1800s, the House of Veuve Clicquot (which was run by a woman) worked out a lot of champagne's issues by using thicker bottles, better corks, and riddling (getting out the sentiment in the bottom of the bottle). Countries such as Italy, Spain, and the United States. thereafter began putting the word "champagne" on their sparkling wine labels, which sparked the Champagne Wars. In 1919, laws were passed mandating that only champagne produced in the Champagne region of France could use the word "champagne" on its label. Today, Italy labels its sparkling wine as "prosecco"; Spain labels it as cava; and the United States just uses the term "sparkling wine."

...
WINE WORDS TO KNOW

- **Blend**: a blend of different wines.
- **Body**: weight and fullness of a wine, which you can discern when you have it in your mouth.
- **Bordeaux**: the area in Southwest France that is considered one of the best wine-producing regions in the world.
- **Brut**: French for "dry."
- **Demi-sec**: French term meaning "half dry."
- **Finish**: the taste in your mouth after swallowing wine.
- **Sulfites**: a natural by-product of the wine fermentation process.
- **Tannin**: Grape skins contain tannins, and the taste is dry or astringent like a strong cup of tea.
- **Varietal**: the main grape the wine is made from.
- **Vintage**: the year the grapes were harvested.

FUN WINE FACTS

› Champagne comes in eight bottle sizes. The largest is called Nebuchadnezzar and is equal to twenty standard 750 ml bottles.

› In 1863, French chemist Angelo Mariani infused Bordeaux wine with three types of coca leaves in the bottle and called it Vin Tonique Mariani. Two ounces contained twelve milligrams of cocaine. It was technically sold as a medicine that worked as an appetite suppressant, stomach stimulant, and helped with depression. It won a Vatican Gold Medal after Pope Saint Pius X and Pope Leo XIII endorsed it. In addition, it is believed that there were over 7,000 endorsements written by physicians. In 1884, John Pemberton from Atlanta, Georgia, replaced the wine with cola extract and soda and Coca-Cola was born.

› During the American Prohibition, grape juice concentrate was sold with instructions for how not to let it ferment—basically, telling consumers how to make wine at home.

› James Bond may be known for Vodka Martinis, but in the novels and films, he drinks champagne more than any alcohol.

› If a wine bottle is corked with real cork, then store the bottle on its side so the cork does not dry out.

› Be careful when opening a bottle of champagne and never point the cork at a person or a brea.k.a.ble object, because the cork can come out at 100 mph.

› Madeira is mentioned in William Shakespeare's play *Henry IV, Part One*, when Falstaff is accused of trading his soul for a chicken leg and a chalice of Madeira.

› In 2004, the hit independent film *Sideways* had bartenders' tongues turning sideways saying Pinot Noir one hundred times a night.

› Every third week in November, you can consume a sense of unity with the world by drinking the same wine—at the same time—with your global brothers and sisters. It is called "It's Beaujolais Nouveau Time!" Beaujolais Nouveau (BOH-zoh-LAY NO-voo) is bottled six to eight weeks after harvest and is distributed around the world within a week. This allows the opportunity to share the experience. Look up at the moon while drinking and you will share two experiences at the same time.

› The world's largest wine bottle is the sign for the Boondocks Lounge in Tucson, Arizona.

12

WHAT TO DRINK BEFORE AND AFTER DINNER: APERITIFS AND DIGESTIFS

...

A BRIEF HISTORY OF APERITIFS

An aperitif (uh-PAIR-uh-TEEF) is a before-dinner drink meant to stimulate the appetite. It's also a perfect way to socialize before dinner. No one knows the exact moment in history this ritual started, but it was all the rage in the late 1700s through the early 1900s.

The two countries that have embraced aperitifs the most are France and Italy. France spells it "aperitif" and Italy spells it "aperitivo." Today, those who like to partake of this before-dinner ritual agree and disagree on what makes a proper aperitif. The general rule is that it should be light, crisp, and refreshing.

...

POPULAR APERITIFS FROM AROUND THE WORLD

Popular spirits drunk in aperitif cocktails, and also on their own, include Aperol, Campari, Cynar, and Pimm's No. 1. Popular aperitif cocktails include the Pimm's Cup, Campari and soda, and Aperol and soda.

...

FORTIFIED WINE-BASED APERITIFS

Lovely wine-based bubbly aperitifs include champagne, prosecco, and cava.

Other light wine-based aperitifs include fino sherry, tawny port, Lillet, Lillet Rose, and light (dry) vermouths such as Cocchi Americano, Cocchi Americano Rosa, Dolin Blanc, and Noilly Prat dry.

Popular wine-based aperitif cocktails include the Champagne Cocktail, Wine Spritzer, and an Americano made with dry vermouth.

...
A BRIEF HISTORY OF DIGESTIFS

Italian limoncello liqueur. © *Gudrun Muenz / Shutterstock*

Digestifs are after-dinner drinks meant to help with digestion. Digestifs tend to be heavier and sometimes sweeter than aperitifs. No one knows when this drinking custom started, but it's fair to assume that experimenting with beverages to help settle one's stomach after a large meal has been a continuous venture.

Drinking digestifs in restaurants is not popular in America, mostly because restaurants look to turn tables for maximum sales. Europeans, on the other hand, embrace digestifs. They tend to relax and linger after a large meal.

POPULAR DIGESTIFS FROM AROUND THE WORLD

Each country tends to have its favorite digestif. In Italy it's limoncello; Germany, schnapps; Greece, ouzo; and Mexico, añejo tequila.

Other popular digestifs include absinthe, Chartreuse, Calvados, Sambuca, aged whiskeys, añejo rum, Fernet, Grand Marnier, and B&B. Popular digestifs cocktails include the Brandy Alexander, Grasshopper, Absinthe Drip, Rusty Nail, and Sazerac.

FORTIFIED WINE-BASED DIGESTIFS

Heavy wine-based digestifs include cream sherry, ruby port, Cognac, armagnac, grappa, pisco, and sweet vermouths such as Antica Formula Carpano, Cocchi Vermouth di Torino, Dolin Rouge, and Cinzano Rosso.

Popular wine-based digestif cocktails include the Manhattan, Rob Roy, Blood and Sand, Vieux Carré, and Negroni.

FUN APERITIF AND DIGESTIF FACTS

> Up until 2006, Campari got its red color from carmine dye that comes from an insect called the Armenian cochineal. Their bodies are dried then turned into a powder and then boiled in ammonia. This ancient coloring is still used today in lipsticks, eye shadows, ice cream, yogurt, and many products that are pink/red in color. In America it is required to list the ingredient on the label as carmine or cochineal extract.

> The Lillet (luh-LAY) used in James Bond's Vesper is no longer available, but the best substitute is Cocchi (ko-KEY) Americano.

> Grappa and pisco are pomace spirits. Pomace (also called "must") are the remains from wine making that includes, stems, seeds, skins, pulp, and anything else left from pressing grapes for wine. Grappa is made in Italy and pisco in Peru and Chile.

> Rémy Martin's King Louis VIII Cognac costs around $2,200 a bottle, and the bottle is made of crystal. Very high-end bars will carry it. It was seen and mentioned in the 1988 film *Cocktail*, Rihanna mentioned it in a 2015 song, it was mentioned on the TV show *The Larry Sanders Show,* and it shows up in many rap songs by artists such as Young Jeezy, Young Buck, Lil Wayne, T-Pain, and Yung Joc.

13

THE GREEN FAIRY: ALL ABOUT ABSINTHE

•••

A BRIEF HISTORY OF ABSINTHE FROM THE 1790S TO THE 1860S

Artemisia absinthium (a.k.a. grand wormwood) is an herb that grows wild in Switzerland and France, and has been used medicinally for thousands of years because of its acclaimed virtues as a digestive aid and nerve tonic.

Henri-Louis Pernod and Henri Dubied opened the first commercial absinthe distillery in Couvet, Switzerland, near the French border in 1797. They relocated to Pontarlier, France, in 1805, whereupon the Pernod Fils distillery became the world's largest producer of absinthe, and would retain that position until it was disbanded following the French absinthe ban in 1915.

During the French conquest of Algeria (1830–1847), soldiers were issued rations of absinthe because it was believed to prevent malaria and other diseases associated with unclean water. French soldiers returning from their service carried their taste for absinthe home with them, and absinthe soon became the fashionable drink of cafés that catered to the bourgeoisie.

•••

A BRIEF HISTORY OF ABSINTHE FROM THE 1860S TO THE PRESENT

Beginning in the 1860s, the insect responsible for phylloxera began ravaging the vineyards of continental Europe. The plague particularly affected France, and was commonly referred to as the Great French Wine Blight. France even offered a cash prize to anyone who could cure the blight. Three botanists were called in to find a solution. In the meantime, however, the grape harvest declined and the price of wine rose accordingly. It was during this time that the popularity of absinthe increased, becoming the preferred tipple of the common people. The increased demand saw yearly increases in production, the price was lowered, and absinthe emerged as a nationally fashionable drink and object of global commerce.

Ted A. Breaux at the Combier Distillery in Saumur, France, cleaning an antique absinthe still, following a distillation of Jade absinthe; 2014. © *Ted A. Breaux*

Nearly thirty years would pass before the wine industry recovered from the widespread blight, but the masses were now hooked on absinthe. Famous artists, poets, and writers praised the virtues of the green spirit, and even nicknamed it La Fée Verte (the Green Fairy). Its popularity had crossed oceans by this point—a bar on Bourbon Street in New Orleans was opened in 1874 that would become the Old Absinthe House. One can still visit this bar and view the original built-in absinthe fountains on the backbar.

So why (starting in the 1900s) was absinthe beginning to be banned worldwide? Because the wine industry promoted the notion that absinthe was a poison, aiming to specifically demonize grand wormwood, in attempts to recover its lost market share. Both the wine industry and the temperance movement capitalized upon the cheap, adulterated versions of the drink imbibed by poor alcoholics in an effort to smear the entire category. This attack was promoted by a well-funded publicity campaign that advertised absinthe as a source of moral corruption and the ruin of modern society.

In America, absinthe was banned from 1912 to 2007, which created an unfilled void when it came to classic cocktails that called for the spirit. After unraveling almost a century's worth of falsehoods and myths, New Orleans native and chemist Ted A. Breaux and Viridian Spirits, LLC, obtained approval to introduce Lucid Absinthe Supérieure as the first genuine absinthe sold in the American market in ninety-five years.

The Top Ten Things to Know About Absinthe

1. "Absinthe" is a French word that means "wormwood." Wormwood is an herb that can have convulsive properties if used to excess.
2. Absinthe is pronounced AB-sent.
3. Pernod (purr-NO) was the very first commercial absinthe.
4. Absinthe does not make you hallucinate.
5. Green Fairy is a nickname for absinthe.
6. La fée verte is French for Green Fairy.
7. Absinthe was banned in America in 1912.
8. New Orleans native, chemist, and absinthe historian Ted A. Breaux and Viridian Spirits, LLC, are responsible for bringing absinthe back to America in March 2007. They spent $500,000 to get the Alcohol and Tobacco Tax and Trade Bureau (TTB) to drop the American ban on absinthe.
9. Historic partaking of absinthe does not include setting anything on fire.
10. The real reason absinthe was banned is because the wine industry wanted their business back.

•••

FIVE POPULAR ABSINTHE COCKTAILS

When using absinthe in a cocktail, two challenges are posed. One is that its prominent flavor is anise, which some casually associate with "black licorice." The other is that it's very high-proof.

ABSINTHE BLOODY MARY

This absinthe drink may sound odd, but the herbs in the absinthe actually go well with the herbs and spices in the Bloody Mary mix.

The Recipe

Pour the following ingredients into a tall 12-ounce glass:
- 1.5 ounces absinthe
- 5 ounces Bloody Mary mix

Add ice, stir, then garnish as you choose.

ABSINTHE SUISSESSE

Believed to be invented at the Old Absinthe House in New Orleans.

The Recipe

Chill a cocktail glass, then pour the following ingredients into a blender:
- 1.5 ounces absinthe
- .5 ounce orgeat syrup
- .5 ounce heavy cream
- 1 egg white
- Half-cup ice

Blend for five to ten seconds, then pour into a chilled cocktail glass.

THE ABSINTHE DRIP

In the first hundred years of absinthe's existence, it was drunk as an Absinthe Drip. An Absinthe Drip requires six things: absinthe, a glass, a slotted absinthe spoon, a sugar cube, an absinthe fountain, and ice-cold water.

The Recipe

- 1 ounce absinthe
- 5 ounces ice water
- 1 sugar cube

Instructions: First, take the glass of your choice and add six ounces of water so you can eyeball how high you'll need to drip the water. Pour out the water and dry the glass. Next, fill an absinthe fountain with ice and water. Now pour the absinthe into the glass, set a slotted absinthe spoon across the rim, then place the sugar cube on top. Position this setup under the spigot of the absinthe fountain and then slowly drip water over the sugar cube until it melts and you have reached the six-ounce level. Stir and enjoy.

As the water mixes with the oil in the absinthe, it will turn cloudy. There are all kinds of absinthe glasses, spoons, fountains, and more that you can purchase. It all depends on how far you want to take your Absinthe Drip experience.

Absinthe drip fountain at the Bourbon O Bar on Bourbon Street. © *Brian Huff*

OBITUARY COCKTAIL

This cocktail was invented at the oldest bar in New Orleans, Lafitte's Blacksmith Shop.

The Recipe

Chill a cocktail glass, and then in a mixing glass add the following:
- .25 ounce absinthe
- 2 ounces gin
- .25 ounce dry vermouth

Add ice, then stir and strain into a chilled cocktail glass.

DEATH IN THE AFTERNOON

It is said that in Spain, Ernest Hemingway invented this cocktail while writing his nonfiction bullfighting book of the same name. One thing is for sure—it is lethal.

The Recipe

In a chilled champagne glass add:
- 1 ounce absinthe
- 5 ounces chilled champagne

14

An Essential Ingredient: Bitters

•••
A BRIEF HISTORY OF BITTERS

No one knows the exact time when bitters started, but it's agreed that it was first used medicinally. In 1712, Richard Stoughton, a British clergyman, received a patent for Magnum Elixir Stomachicum, which was an alcohol-based herbal infusion. It was the second compound medicine in the world to receive a patent. Soon, the public was calling it Stoughton's Bitters. In 1730, he exported it to America.

Bitters is made of selected herbs, spices, seeds, dried fruit peels, flora, barks, botanicals, or roots of one's choice—a witch's brew of sorts—then preserved in a base of high-proof alcohol. However, some bitters are nonalcoholic and made with glycerin. In the 1800s, these elixirs were advertised as cure-alls and sold in 750 ml bottles. Today, due to the cocktail revolution, there is a huge assortment of bitters on the market just like there was back in the 1880s. Bitters can be dashed into fizzy water and drunk to calm a stomachache, and you can use bitters in food and drinks to add flavor. Bitters doesn't taste bitter as the name implies. When used in cocktails, it simply adds a dash of concentrated flavor. Most say it seasons the cocktail in the same way salt seasons food. The best way to taste test bitters is through your nose. No, do not sniff. Dash a couple drops in your palm, rub your palms together, then cover your nose and mouth and smell.

If you'd like to experiment with making your own medicinal bitters, then these herbs and other plants may be worth exploring: amla berry, ashwagandha, astragalus root, bamboo stem, burdock root, Bupleurum, dandelion root, ellagitannin, fo-ti, gotu kola, gubinge, holy basil, Indian gooseberry, Japanese knotweed, jiaogulan, kudzu leaf, licorice root, maca, mallow leaf, moringa leaf, pine bark, pine needles, pine pollen, red clover, rosehip, sea buckthorn, Siberian ginseng, suma, watercress, and yellowdock root.

ANGOSTURA BITTERS

Since 1824, Angostura bitters has stood the test of time. In 1862, Don Carlos Siegert from Trinidad first exhibited it at the Great London Exposition. The cocktail Pink Gin was invented at the same time, and was called Amargo Aromatico. Angostura bitters won a medal at the 1873 World's Fair in Vienna, Austria. Many cocktails call for the bitters, including the Champagne Cocktail, Vieux Carré, Pisco Sour, Old-Fashioned, Pink Gin, Manhattan, Rob Roy, Singapore Sling, Planter's Punch, and Zombie.

PEYCHAUD'S BITTERS AND BOKER'S BITTERS

Johann Boker created Boker's bitters in 1828 and one hundred years later, it went extinct. Adam Elmegirab re-created Dr. Adam Elmegirab's Boker's Bitters in 2009. © *Adam Elmegirab*

The next two most popular bitters in the 1800s were Peychaud's Bitters (1857) from New Orleans and Boker's (1828) from New York. Peychaud's is the red bitters used in a Sazerac or Vieux Carré cocktail. If you ever visit New Orleans, just pop into the local grocery store and take a bottle or two home with you. Boker's bitters was found in many cocktail recipe books before becoming extinct, but thankfully it has been raised from the dead by Dr. Adam Elmegirab's Bitters. Some of the vintage cocktails that called for Boker's include the Japanese Cocktail, Martinez, Manhattan, and Crusta.

ORANGE BITTERS AND FEE'S BITTERS

Orange bitters was called for in the first known Martini recipe seen in print, in 1862. After Prohibition until the early 2000s the only bitters available was Angostura. When Regans' Orange Bitters No. 6 was produced in 2005 by cocktail author, historian, and bartender Gary Regan, it opened the bitters floodgate. Fee's Bitters, who had been in business in Rochester, New York, from 1835, also saw a decline in sales when Prohibition began, so they focused on altar wines and continued with wine until the 2000s when the cocktail culture started to flourish. As of 2016, Fee's now offers seventeen types of bitters, botanical waters, syrups, and more.

BITTERS BOTTLES

You may have noticed many little bottles all around the drink-making station of your local bar. Those are bitters bottles. Some will be purchased bitters and some will be made from scratch by your bartenders.

BITTERS AROUND THE WORLD

Modern bitters bottles on bartop. © *GKondor83 / Shutterstock*

Today, there are too many bitters companies to mention and many bartenders are making their own bitters. Never in the history of the cocktail culture has there been so many flavors to choose from. Check out these flavors: Gumbo, Tex-Mex, Memphis BBQ, Holiday Pie, Figgy Pudding, Mi Casa, Creole, Celery Shrub, Hellfire, Winter Melon, Orange Cream, Hoped Grapefruit, Jamaican Jerk, Cherry Bark, Blackstrap, Roasted Macadamia, Wild Mountain Sage, Palo Santo, Vanilla Chai, Hair of the Dog, Bitter Frost, Smoked Chili, and Wormwood Bitters.

Some of the top companies producing bitters around the world include AZ Bitters Lab, Basement Bitters, Bittercube Bitters, Bitter End Bitters, Bittered Sling Bitters, Dr. Adam Elmegirab's Bitters, Dram Bitters, El Guapo Bitters, Fees's Brothers Bitters, Hella Bitter, Old Men Bitters, Scrappy's Bitters, the Bittered Truth Bitters, the Cocktail Experiment Bitters, and Urban Moonshine Organic Bitters.

DIGESTIVE BITTERS

There are also spirits that have bitter qualities, and many countries have their own. They are measured into cocktails in ounces, not dashes. The most popular include Amer Picon, Aperol, Averna, Becherovka, Campari, Cynar, Fernet, Branca, and Jägermeister.

• • •

HOMEMADE BITTERS PREPARATION

Before you turn your kitchen into a DIY bitters lab, it is best to prepare.

Here are some items to gather:

- A few quart-sized Mason jars.
- Any high-proof liquor (80 proof or higher). A lot of beginners like to start with vodka because it's neutral. But later you can try other spirits such as whiskey and tequila. Just keep in mind they will add to the flavor.
- Filters of some sort like cheesecloth, a fine strainer, or a coffee filter.
- Small dropper or bitters bottles of your choosing.
- Fancy or plain labels of your choosing, or just use masking tape.
- A small funnel to fit into the small bottles.
- Your choice of herbs, spices, seeds, dried fruit peels, whole fresh fruit, flora, botanicals, roots, etc. To help you get started think dried fruit, dried citrus peels, dried flora, coffee beans, peppercorn, star anise, cracked whole nutmeg, juniper berries, cherry bark, etc. Barks may be easier to find online.
- Once you hunt and gather your ingredients, put them in the jar and fill with the spirit. It will need to infuse for several weeks to draw out the flavor. Each day you should agitate the jar to mix up everything. When ready, strain the mixture into another jar using cheesecloth or a very fine strainer. Some people with use both.
- The solids that you catch in the strainer then need to be put into a pot with some water and brought to a boil, then simmered for fifteen minutes. Put all of that mixture into a separate jar and let sit for one week.
- When ready, strain out the solids. The solids can be thrown away. Combine the two jars of liquid you've created, and if the end result has sediment in the bottom or floating in the mixture, you'll need to strain it again.
- Lastly, you can add a little sweetener to make it more palatable. You can use honey, maple syrup, molasses, or rich simple syrup (two parts sugar to one part water dissolved into a syrup). Shake it all up, and now you are ready to bottle.

• • •

HOMEMADE BITTERS RECIPES

Here are some basic recipes to get you started:

BASIC BITTERS

Makes 16 ounces

- Pinch cardamom
- Pinch caraway
- Pinch coriander seeds
- 1 cup dried bitter orange peel
- 2 cups grain alcohol
- 2 tablespoons honey

Combine all the ingredients into a sterilized jar with a lid and allow to sit in a cool dark place for three weeks, agitating it every day. When ready, strain through cheesecloth or a fine strainer into another jar. Bring the solids caught in the strainer to a boil with water and then simmer for fifteen minutes. Put all that mixture into a lidded jar and allow to sit for one week. When ready, strain and combine with the first strained jar. Add the sweetener, shake, and then funnel into dropper or bitters bottles.

BOURBON PECAN BITTERS

Makes 16 ounces

- 1/2 cup roasted pecans
- 2 whole cloves
- 1 cinnamon stick
- 1 vanilla bean, split
- 1 tablespoon wild cherry bark
- 1 tablespoon gentia root
- 2 cups high-proof Bourbon
- 2 tablespoons maple syrup

Combine all the ingredients into a sterilized jar with a lid and allow to sit in a cool dark place for three weeks, agitating it every day. When ready, strain through cheesecloth or a fine strainer into another jar. Bring the solids caught in the strainer to a boil with water and then simmer for fifteen minutes. Put all that mixture into a lidded jar and allow to sit for one week. When ready, strain and combine with the first strained jar. Add the sweetener, shake, and then funnel into dropper or bitters bottles.

LAVENDER BITTERS

Makes 16 ounces

- 1 cup dried lavender
- 1/2 cup orange peels
- 1 vanilla pod, split
- 2 cups grain alcohol
- 2 tablespoons agave nectar

Combine all the ingredients into a sterilized jar with a lid and allow to sit in a cool, dark place for three weeks, agitating it every day. When ready, strain through cheesecloth or a fine strainer into another jar. Bring the solids caught in the strainer to a boil with water and then simmer for fifteen minutes. Put all that mixture into a lidded jar and allow to sit for one week. When ready, strain and combine with the first strained jar. Add the sweetener, shake, and then funnel into dropper or bitters bottles.

ORANGE BITTERS

Makes 16 ounces

- 1 cup orange peels
- 2 cardamom pods
- Pinch coriander seeds
- 1 teaspoon fennel seed
- 10 drops gentian extract
- 2 cups grain alcohol
- 2 tablespoons rich simple syrup

Combine all the ingredients into a sterilized jar with a lid and allow to sit in a cool, dark place for three weeks, agitating it every day. When ready, strain through cheesecloth or a fine strainer into another jar. Bring the solids caught in the strainer to a boil with water and then simmer for fifteen minutes. Put all that mixture into a lidded jar and allow to sit for one week. When ready, strain and combine with the first strained jar. Add the sweetener, shake, and then funnel into dropper or bitters bottles.

15

What Exactly Is a Cocktail Mixer? A Guide to Making Your Own

Mixers are generally nonalcoholic ingredients that provide balance and flavor when mixed with alcohol to create a cocktail. Just remember: to make the best-tasting cocktail, always go fresh.

...

LIST OF COCKTAIL MIXERS

JUICES

The main juices most bars stock include cranberry, grapefruit, lemon, lime, orange, and pineapple. Other juices that bars could offer include apple, carrot, clam, olive, pomegranate, and tomato.

CARBONATED SODA

The main sodas most bars stock include cola, diet cola, ginger ale, lemon-lime, soda water, tonic water, and Perrier. Other sodas that bars could offer include Dr. Pepper, root beer, ginger beer, and anything they would need for a special cocktail on the menu.

SWEETENERS

Unless you are rimming a glass edge or making an Old-Fashioned the old-fashioned way, sugar behind the bar is mostly used in a liquid state called "simple syrup." This is because the liquid mixes better in cocktails than granulated sugar. Many bars make their own simple syrup because it's easy! To make two cups of simple syrup, all you need is one cup of granulated sugar and one cup of warm to hot water. Mix in a blender or a saucepan until the sugar dissolves and you've made simple syrup. This syrup can be kept in the refrigerator for a month.

Other sweeteners a bar can stock include agave nectar, coconut cream, grenadine, gomme syrup, honey, orgeat syrup, pureés, or any flavored syrup the bar needs for certain cocktails on their menu.

DAIRY

The most common dairy mixer behind bars is half-and-half (half milk and half cream). Other dairy mixers that could be found behind bars are cream, eggs, eggnog, ice cream, and unsalted butter. Some bars carry nondairy plant-based options that include soy milk, almond milk, rice milk, and coconut milk.

OTHER MIXERS

Other popular mixers behind a bar include Bloody Mary mix, strawberry mix, Margarita mix, Piña Colada mix, sweet-and-sour mix, apple cider, coffee, tea, hot chocolate, hot water, and apple cider vinegar. The first five mixers mentioned can be purchased, but those products are low-quality fake options. It's best to make them yourself.

Many added ingredients can be added, stirred, or shaken into a cocktail to enhance the flavor and texture. Some of these include, spices, herbs, and sauces such as steak sauce, Worcestershire, and hot sauce.

• • •

HOMEMADE COCKTAIL MIXER RECIPES

SIMPLE SYRUP

Have you ever tried to mix a spoonful of sugar in your iced tea only to find the sugar at the bottom of the glass? This is why it's easier to mix syrups into cocktails. Simple syrup is the base of all syrups and it's very easy to make. If you want to avoid sugar and need a low glycemic option then try Markus Sweet, Monkfruit sweetener, stevia, or xylitol sweet.

Makes 2 cups

- 1 cup water, hot or boiling
- 1 cup granulated sugar of your choice

Now, there are a few ways you can combine the water and the sugar to create simple syrup. Just choose the one that works for you.

1. Pour the sugar and hot or boiling water into a blender, and then blend until sugar is dissolved (about a minute).
2. Pour the sugar and hot or boiling water into a large jar or bottle and secure the lid, and then shake until sugar is dissolved (about a minute).
3. Bring the water to almost boiling in a pot, add the sugar, and then stir until dissolved.

Allow the syrup to cool and then store in bottles or jars in the refrigerator for up to a week. If you need to make more, then increase the portions. The sugar in this base recipe can be replaced with honey, agave, Splenda, maple syrup, brown sugar, or whatever you want.

Now, let us say, for example, that you want to make a ginger syrup. All you need to do is add hot ginger-flavored water with the sugar and you will have ginger syrup. To make ginger-flavored water, you would wash some gingerroot, cut it in slices, put it into a pot with water, and then bring to a boil. Once it starts to boil, turn it down to simmer for about thirty minutes so it extracts the ginger flavor from the gingerroot. When ready, strain out the ginger and then add your sugar to the ginger water. Mix until the sugar melts and voila! You made ginger syrup.

Now, let us say you want to make cucumber syrup. Well, cucumbers are more delicate than gingerroot, so you'll want to infuse sliced cucumbers with water in a jar and then let sit on the counter for a few hours. You can agitate the jar a few times to help the cucumbers release flavor faster. When finished, just strain the cucumber water into a pot and set on medium. For the sugar to melt, you will need to heat the cucumber water warm enough.

You now know how to make any simple syrup or any flavored simple syrup you want with any fruit, vegetable, spice, or herb. In addition, when making citrus syrup from lemons, limes, oranges, etc., you only use the rind of the fruit, not the meat.

Grenadine: Replace the water portion with pomegranate juice.

Tea Syrup: Add tea bags to the water when heating. When you are ready for the next level, get creative and try combinations such as honey-ginger syrup, mint-agave syrup, cinnamon-orange syrup, jalapeño-maple syrup, etc.

MARGARITA MIX

Why use store-bought Margarita mix when you can make the real (and better) stuff at home? If you want to avoid sugar and need a low glycemic option, then try Markus Sweet, Monkfruit sweetener, stevia, or xylitol.

Makes 6 cups

- 2 cups fresh lime juice
- 2 cups simple syrup
- 2 cups water

Blend ingredients in a blender for ten seconds, or shake ingredients together in a large lidded jar, then stop and do a taste test. Some people like sweet mix and some like sour. Some like to add a little orange juice. Just adjust the amount of simple syrup, water, or lime juice according to your personal preference. This will keep in the refrigerator for two days and you can always freeze it.

SWEET-AND-SOUR MIX (OFTEN CALLED SOUR MIX)

The egg whites will put a nice frothy top on top of a Whiskey Sour. If you want to use the mix for a Rum Punch or Long Island Iced Tea, you can leave them out. If you want to avoid sugar and need a low glycemic option, try Markus Sweet, Monkfruit sweetener, stevia, or xylitol.

Makes 6 cups

- 2 cups fresh lemon juice
- 1/2 cup fresh lime juice
- 2 cups simple syrup
- 4 organic egg whites
- 1 cup water

Blend ingredients in a blender for ten seconds, or shake ingredients together in a large lidded jar, and then stop and do a taste test. Some people like sweet mix and some like sour. Just adjust the amount of simple syrup, water, or lemon juice according to your personal preference. With egg whites, it will only keep half a day. Without egg whites, it will keep two days and you can always freeze it.

PIÑA COLADA MIX

It is easy to make real Piña Colada mix, so there's no reason to buy the stuff on the shelf. You can find the Coco López in the mixer section of your local grocer.

Makes 10 cups

- 1 (46-ounce) can of pineapple juice (fresh-squeezed pineapple juice)
- 2 (15-ounce) cans of Coco López coconut cream
- 6 drops vanilla extract

Blend all the ingredients in a blender for five seconds, then refrigerate. It will last for two days and you can always freeze it.

STRAWBERRY DAIQUIRI MIX

You will thank yourself for taking the time to make your own strawberry mix. If you want to avoid sugar and need a low glycemic option, then try Markus Sweet, Monkfruit sweetener, stevia, or xylitol.

Makes 5 cups

- 2 cups unsweetened frozen strawberries, semi-thawed
- 1/2 cup fresh lime juice
- 1 cup simple syrup

Blend all the ingredients in a blender for about ten seconds. Stop, taste test, and then adjust the amount of simple syrup, lime juice, and strawberries according to your personal preference. Refrigerate. It will last for three days and you can always freeze it. If you want it to last two weeks, leave out the fresh lime juice and add to the blender when making a Strawberry Daiquiri or Margarita.

BAR PUNCH

Need something quick to make a Rum Punch without having to pick up five containers? Then just batch these ingredients together. If you need less, cut the recipe in half.

Makes 1 gallon

- 4 cups fresh-squeezed orange juice
- 4 cups pineapple juice
- 2 cup homemade grenadine
- 4 cups sweet-and-sour mix, without egg whites

Pour all ingredients into a gallon container. It will last for three days and you can always freeze it.

BLOODY MARY MIX

This recipe will get you started making your own Bloody Mary mix. You can adjust it to your own taste preferences. You can also add other ingredients such as roasted garlic, rosemary, basil, beef bouillon cubes, wasabi, avocado, apple cider vinegar, chili powder, and bitters.

Makes 1 gallon

- 2 ounces lime juice
- 8 ounces A.1. sauce
- 4 ounce raw horseradish (optional)
- 8 ounces Lea & Perrins Worcestershire sauce
- 1 heaping tablespoon black peppercorns, blended
- 1 heaping tablespoon celery seed, blended
- 2 (46-ounce) cans whole plum tomatoes
- Water as needed
- Dashes of Tabasco sauce, if desired

Add the lime juice, A.1. sauce, horseradish, and Worcestershire sauce into a large open-mouthed container. Pour the celery seed and peppercorns in a blender and blend on high for thirty seconds, and then dump into the large container. Fill the blender halfway with the whole plum tomatoes and then add water to fill. Blend on high for twenty seconds. Fine-strain into the container. Continue this step until all the tomatoes have been blended and strained. Mix all ingredients, pour into sterilized jars or bottles, and refrigerate.

ROSE WATER

This recipe is for rose water, but you can use the petals of any nontoxic flower to make fragrant water.

Makes 1 cup

- 3 cups filtered water
- 2 cups rinsed rose petals
- 1 ounce vodka

Pour petals and the water into a pot, then bring to a boil. Simmer, covered, for thirty minutes. Cool, then strain into a sterilized container or bottle. Add vodka for preservation.

16

THE JEWELRY OF THE DRINK: COCKTAIL GARNISHES

Ask any girl and she will tell you that a cocktail garnish is the jewelry of the drink. Could you imagine a classic Martini served without an olive or a Manhattan without a cherry? It just would not be the same. Garnishes on cocktails were simple from the 1700s to the late 1990s, but when Martini bars popped up all over America between the late 1990s and the mid-2000s, they offered menus with 100+ flavored Martinis. Garnishes consisted of a lot of double-dipped rims of chocolate, caramel, honey, crushed candy, crumbled Oreos, flaked coconut, nuts, sprinkles, and more. This time period overlapped with the beginning of the craft cocktail movement, so the cocktail culture pendulum was swinging to both ends of the spectrum. You could compare it to the mid-1970s to the early 1980s music industry tension, when there were two groups of music lovers: fans of disco and those of rock 'n' roll.

Today, most of the frou-frou Martinis with store-bought mixers and cheap booze are gone, and there is always a new crazy garnish because it's fun. Since 2010 the craft cocktail culture has taken their well-thought-out elegant garnishes to a whole new level.

•••

THE TOP FIVE EDIBLE COCKTAIL GARNISHES EVERY BAR HAS

1. Limes
2. Lemons
3. Olives
4. Cherries
5. Oranges

Cocktail garnishes can be anything edible such as fruit, vegetables, herbs, spices, flora, candy, baked goods, dairy, and even meat products. The only limit when it comes to garnishes is your imagination. Yes, there are common bar garnishes, but most bartenders like to experiment with new garnishes. Generally, the garnish is placed on top of a cocktail, but it can also be placed on the rim. The garnish flavor should always complement the flavor of the cocktail.

•••

FRUIT GARNISHES

Olives are classified as a fruit because they are formed from the ovary of the flower. This particular fruit has the possibility of being stuffed. Most come already stuffed with a red pimento pepper. From the late 1990s to the mid-2000s, Vodka Martinis with blue cheese–stuffed olives were all the rage. Today, you can make your own stuffed olives. Stuffing ideas include cheese of your choice, roasted garlic, Italian sausage, nuts, jalapeño, pickled onion, pepperoni, or anchovies.

COMMON FRUIT GARNISHES

Apples, cherries, bananas, blackberries, blueberries, coconut, cucumbers, grapes, grapefruit, lemons, limes, watermelon, olives, oranges, pineapples, raspberries, and strawberries.

NOT SO COMMON FRUIT GARNISHES

Apricots, avocados, boysenberries, cranberries, dates, dragon fruit, figs, raisins, guava, kiwi, kumquat, lychee, mango, melon, nectarine, blood oranges, tangerine, papaya, passion fruit, peaches, pears, plums, star fruit, and tomatoes.

•••
VEGETABLE GARNISHES

COMMON VEGETABLE GARNISHES

Celery, green onions, pearl onions, pickled beans, and pickled okra.

NOT SO COMMON VEGETABLE GARNISHES

Beets, ginger, and rhubarb.

•••
HERB GARNISHES

COMMON HERB GARNISHES

Basil, chives, cilantro, dill, lavender, lemongrass, mint, rosemary, sage, and thyme.

NOT SO COMMON HERB GARNISHES

Borage, caraway, catnip, fennel, garlic, parsley, oregano, and tarragon.

•••
SPICE GARNISHES

Spice garnishes can be mixed with salt or sugar and then put on the rim of the glass. They can also be sprinkled (or grated) on top of a cocktail that has a frothy head or on top of whipped cream. Some can be used in their whole form such as cinnamon sticks and star anise.

COMMON SPICE GARNISHES

Black pepper, cayenne, celery salt, chili powder, cloves, cinnamon, nutmeg, salt, star anise, and vanilla beans.

NOT SO COMMON SPICE GARNISHES

Ancho chili, anise seed, bay leaf, cumin, caraway seed, crystallized ginger, saffron, and white pepper.

FLORA GARNISHES

A Vanda orchid was first garnished a cocktail in Hawaii, by bar legend Harry Yee, in 1957. Since around 2005, bartenders have been searching for beautiful, nontoxic, edible flora to use in their cocktails. All common fruits, vegetables, and herbs go through a flowering stage, and all of these are nontoxic and safe to use. It's more important to know what flora is toxic and not safe to use as a garnish in your cocktail. For example, during the holiday season you may think that a sprig of mistletoe would be a perfect garnish for your holiday cocktail, but mistletoe is toxic. Always search the internet before using any questionable flora as a garnish.

NONTOXIC FLORA GARNISHES

Aloe Vera, angelica, orchids, daisy, dandelion, chamomile, chrysanthemum, clover, eucalyptus, forget-me-nots, gardenia, hibiscus, impatiens, jasmine, lavender, lilac, magnolia, marigold, orchid, pansy, peony, primrose, rose, snapdragon, sunflower, tulip petals (not the bulb), violet, water lily, and zinnia.

TOXIC FLORA GARNISHES

Angel's trumpet, azalea, belladonna (also called deadly nightshade), bird of paradise, bluebell, buttercup, calla lily, daffodil, English ivy, foxglove, hyacinth, hydrangea, iris, lily of the valley, lucky bamboo, mistletoe, morning glory, rhubarb leaves, star of Bethlehem, sweet pea, tobacco, tomato leaves, and wisteria.

CANDY AND BAKED GOODS GARNISHES

Garnishing with candy and baked goods (such as cookies) started in the late 1990s when the flavored Martini craze began. Before then, the sweetest cocktail garnish was a sugared rim. Because you have so many ingredients to choose from, this category of garnishes is totally up to your imagination. Here are some ideas: rock candy sticks, sugarcane sticks, chocolate-covered strawberries, Tootsie Pops, fortune cookies, a glazed doughnut set horizontally on the glass rim, gummy worms, licorice straws, marshmallows, Peeps, and placing a cookie horizontally on the rim and then poking a hole for a straw.

RIMMER GARNISH IDEAS

When rimming a glass at home, all you need is two plates. One plate will hold your dry garnish (salt, sugar, sprinkles, crushed cookies, etc.) and the other plate will hold the wet garnish that acts as a glue so the dry garnish can stick to the glass. Lemon or lime juice can be used for salts and sugars, but you will need something stickier to attach crushed cookies, sprinkles, etc. Some good choices include melted chocolate and syrups.

There are many flavored and colored sugar and salts that you can purchase, but you can also make your own at home. Sugar and salt are staples in the rimming world. For sugar you can use white, raw, brown, and powdered. If you want to color it, you just need some food coloring and plastic storage bags. When using salted rims on cocktails, you want to use a coarse kosher salt and not table salt. Sugar and salt can be combined with a myriad of spices and herbs to create a new flavor. Combinations might include cinnamon-sugar, cayenne-sugar, edible gold flake and sugar, dried cilantro and salt, cracked black pepper and salt, and dried basil and salt. As for crushing candy and cookies, double-bagging plastic storage bags and then banging the treats with a mallet until crushed is the best way.

Other rimming garnishes to try are sprinkles, Pop Rocks, flaked coconut, Cajun spices, edible pearl dust, chocolate powders, shaved chocolate, and crushed nuts.

...

DAIRY GARNISHES

The most popular dairy cocktail garnish is whipped cream. You can make your own whipped cream by whipping cream and sugar, or in a pinch you can pick up a can at your local grocery store. The most popular alcoholic drinks that use whipped cream are hot coffee, cider, and chocolate drinks.

...

BLOODY MARY GARNISHES

Since the 1970s the Bloody Mary has been the winner for the most edible garnishes of any cocktail in the world. Vintage Bloody Mary ads from the 1930s through the 1960s show very little garnishing for the Bloody Mary: one celery stalk, one lemon, and a lemon and celery stalk. The olive makes an appearance in the 1960s.

Bloody Mary garnishing from the 1970s through the 1990s included salted rims, Cajun spice rims, pickles, pickled beans, green onions, cherry tomatoes, peel-and-eat shrimp, oyster on the half shell, and blue cheese-stuffed olives.

In the 2000s, the Bloody Mary Bloody Bar was born. Vodka companies approached popular restaurants and bars offering free signage, menus, infusion jars, and, of course, a discount on their vodka. The establishment would set up a table filled with containers with a variety of garnishes, hot sauces, and mixes for guests to choose from. With time and for competition's sake, the garnish choices got more insane—well, insane for that time. Choices included beef jerky, hard bacon strips, Slim Jims, pizza-themed garnishes with rims of Parmesan cheese and pepper flakes, spaghetti-themed garnishes with meatballs, olive brine to make it dirty, an assortment of cheese cubes, and so much more.

Steve Schumacher's "Fried Chicken Bloody Mary" at Sobelman's Pub & Grill in Milwaukee, Wisconsin. © *Steve Schumacher*

By 2012, the BM bars began to fade and a new, exaggerated Bloody Mary craze was born. Dave Sobelman from Sobelman's Pub & Grill in Milwaukee is given credit for the ultimate, most excessive, over-the-top Bloody Mary to date. He calls it a Chicken Fried Bloody Mary and it's garnished with a whole fried chicken.

Today, many bars are offering personalized Bloody Mary check-off menus. You are given a printed card and pen and you simply check off the items you want—choices such as vodka, rimming, and garnishes—for your Bloody Mary. Basically they are saving the time and trouble of setting up a table and keeping a small Bloody Mary bar behind the bar.

BLOODY MARY FRUIT GARNISHES

Cucumbers, lemons, limes, olives, and pineapple.

BLOODY MARY VEGETABLE GARNISHES

Asparagus, avocado, brussels sprouts, carrots, celery, baby corn, cocktail onions, fried onion rings, green onions, jalapeño poppers, mushrooms, peppers (all types), pickles (all types), pickled beans, pickled okra, radishes, and tomatoes (all types).

BLOODY MARY ANIMAL-BASED GARNISHES

Bacon, beef jerky, calamari, cheese (all kinds), cheeseburgers, cheesecake, chicken (all kinds; parts and whole), clams, cocktail sausages, crab, crawfish, fish (all kinds), ham, hot dogs, lobster, mac & cheese, meatballs, mussels, oysters, pepperoni, pizza (whole and sliced), ribs, salami, sandwiches (all kinds), shrimp, Slim Jim, and steak.

• • •
COCKTAIL DECORATIONS AND TOOLS

Probably the most iconic nonedible cocktail decoration is the paper parasol (also called the cocktail umbrella).

Cocktail decorations and tools mainly consist of pics (also called picks) and straws. Pics help hold an edible garnish near the top of your drink so it doesn't sink to the bottom, and straws help you sip the cocktail—if you choose not to drink from the rim—and also stir it up more if you desire.

Pics can come in sizes in length from three inches to twelve inches and they can be made of bamboo, wood, plastic, and metal. There are hundreds of pic designs in the world plus companies that specialize in creating logo picks.

Straws can come in sizes in length from five-and-a-half inches to eighteen inches. Most are made of plastic, but they can also be made of paper, bamboo, metal, and glass. Some can bend and some are fat.

Other popular nonedible decorations are little plastic animals and creatures that sit on the rim of your glass. These shapes include monkeys, mermaids, elephants, and giraffes. Lots of bars will have special decorations for signature drinks. For example, Tropical Isle in New Orleans has a drink called the Shark Attack that comes with a blue hollow plastic shark. The bartender pours grenadine (blood) inside the shark and then nose-dives it into your drink. Other decorations you may run across include a bamboo back scratcher, Krazy Straws, rim-hanging shot glasses, hot test tubes filled with booze and pushed into your drink, and indoor drink sparklers.

• • •
CRAZY COCKTAIL GARNISHES

Every day bartenders come up with new techniques for creating garnishes. International bartender competitions tend to have amazing, intricate, food-styled garnishes that replicate those of a five-star chef. Others are clever, experimental, or just plain over-the-top. Here are several examples to give you inspiration:

1. Eau de Vie—a craft bar in Sydney, Australia offers beautiful presentations for all their cocktails. One fun presentation is called "Lady's Leg," which is prepared in a vintage late-1930s cocktail shaker in the shape of a lady's leg complete with a high-heeled silver shoe. The cocktail uses a house-made cranberry sorbet instead of cranberry juice, giving the drink a creamy and soft texture. It is served in sexy vintage champagne coupes. View their stunning gallery of cocktails at eaudevie.com.au/sydney.

2. The Cocktail Professor team from Amsterdam has some of the best drink presentations and garnishes in the world (view their website, Facebook, and Instagram). Examples include an edible paper plane on a twisted classic Aviation cocktail; a twisted Old-Fashioned garnished with an edible wax seal; a cocktail served in a glass pipe that you can suck to drink and blow to blow bubbles; a cocktail with a small bag of pineapple caviar clipped on the rim with a mini clothespin; a cocktail with a swipe of white chocolate then torched coconut on the side of the glass as opposed to the rim; and several smoking cocktails.

Lady's Leg Cosmopolitan from Eau de Vie in Sydney, Australia. © *Eau de Vie Sydney*

3. At the Chicago tiki bar Three Dots and a Dash, the Treasure Chest (for eight) is a rummy drink served in and garnished with orchids, skulls, and other items one might see in a treasure chest.

4. The Black Ant in New York City serves a cocktail that is rimmed with salt and crushed black ants. The Mexican black ants are supposed to be an aphrodisiac. Oh, they also say that it pairs well with an order of Tlayuda con Chapulines, which are crunchy tortillas with sautéed grasshoppers.

5. Victor Tangos in Dallas serves a cocktail made with house-made oyster mushroom syrup and garnished with a candied shiitake mushroom.

6. Cassia in Santa Monica offers a cocktail that is garnished with a spoon of sea urchin roe.

7. In the London bar Nightjar, garnishes include a matcha green-tea cookie, an origami bird sprayed with perfume, and a dried starfish.

8. In New York City, Shigefumi Kabashima created a cocktail that sits in an ice-filled, skull-shaped glass and is garnished with a burning stick of sacred palo santo.

9. Canadian Frankie Solarik is a bar chef who is blowing minds with his garnish techniques. He says: "It's the idea of presenting a drink as a dish. I strive to compose cocktails with the same visual, visceral, and taste appeal, and complexity that is possible within a dish. The general goal for me artistically is to challenge the conventional thought as to what's possible within the medium of a glass." View his gallery on his website, and photos on Facebook, to grasp the beauty and inventiveness of his mind.

10. Lounge Bohemia in London created the Bubble Bath Martini. It's garnished with rose foam and a baby rubber ducky.

17

On the Rocks: A Brief History of Ice for Cocktails

Ice is one of the most important ingredients in cocktail making. It must be respected and kept clean. The cold water dilution that ice provides when stirring or shaking a cocktail is essential to the taste of a cocktail.

In 1883, Mark Twain published *Life on the Mississippi* and on page 117 he says, "In my time, ice was jewelry; none but the rich could wear it. But anybody and everybody can have it now." In the early 1800s, a twenty-three-year-old businessman from Boston named Frederic Tudor looked out on a white frozen pond and saw nothing but green. Tudor became the "Boston Ice King" and he soon learned that harvesting ice from lakes and ponds proved to be an extremely labor-intensive business. Workers dealt with freezing temperatures, sharp tools, heavy blocks of ice, and methods of keeping the blocks from melting. Ice in the first part of the 1800s was only available to the wealthy—like Twain said—but by the 1850s it grew into a commodity. Tudor transported ice to many places around the world—creating the ice trade. And since water freezes on lakes and ponds in many more places than just Northeast America, it didn't take long for other ice harvesting companies to open.

By the 1800s some warm Southern cities built artificial ice factories. Twain gives us a glimpse of the past (in his book) through his observations of visiting a New Orleans ice factory:

Sunk into the floor were numberless tin boxes, a foot square and two feet long, and open at the top end. These were full of clear water; and around each box, salt and other proper stuff was packed; also, the ammonia gases were applied to the water in some way which will always remain a secret to me, because I was not able to understand the process. While the water in the boxes gradually froze, men gave it a stir or two with a stick occasionally—to liberate the air-bubbles, I think. Other men were continually lifting out boxes whose contents had become hard frozen. They gave the box a single dip into a vat of boiling water, to melt the block of ice free from its tin coffin, then they shot the block out upon a platform car, and it was ready for market.

Joseph Ambrose cutting ice blocks for his boutique ice company, Favourite Ice in Washington DC; 2016. © *Mat Cabral*

Twain goes on to describe how some of the clear blocks of ice have items frozen inside such as bouquets of flowers, French dolls with satin dresses, and other pretty items that were placed on platters in the center of dinner tables to cool the room.

In 1889 and 1890, America had record-breaking warm winters and ice harvesting came to a dead stop. By 1900, there were almost 1,000 ice plants in America delivering to bars, grocers, and homes. Ice was delivered in the form of ice blocks; then the buyer could chip, shave, or hand-saw it.

Today, we have commercial ice machines, and since the start of the current cocktail revolution, there has been a demand for blocked ice in craft bars—so small boutique ice shops have popped up. One good example is Favourite Ice (favouriteice.com), the first custom ice company in Washington, DC, which is headed up by Joseph Ambrose and Caleb Marindin. They provide special cut ice to many craft bars in the DC area.

...

TYPES OF ICE

Many craft bars today have "ice programs." This means that they produce and offer a variety type of ice. The ice can come from a machine or molds, or be handmade. Types include crushed ice, pebbled ice, shaved ice, ice spheres (balls), large cubed ice, cylinder ice, ice blocks, and of course, whatever else the imagination will spark.

CRUSHED ICE

Crushed ice is like the ice you would use to make a snow cone. A variety of machines costing anywhere from twenty dollars to two thousand dollars can be used to crush ice. Some bartenders use a "Lewis" canvas bag to make crushed ice. You place ice into the bag and then bang on it with a mallet until the ice is crushed.

PEBBLED ICE

Pebbled ice is also called pellet and nugget ice. It is soft little pieces of ice. The best comes from a machine and the best place to buy it is at your local Sonic Drive-In. They use the ice for their famous slushies and sell ten-pound bags of it for one dollar. When using it for cocktails, it is best to add this ice last or the alcohol and ingredients will melt it down too fast.

SHAVED ICE

Shaved ice is just what it sounds like. A sharp blade shaves the surface of the ice, which results in a soft and very fine snow-white fluffy ice. New Orleans is famous for their Snow Balls that use this type of ice. The liquid ingredients do not sink to the bottom like in a snow cone; rather they become part of the ice.

ICE SPHERES

© GLACE LUXURY ICE

A two-inch luxury ice cube from Gläce Luxury Ice. © *Gläce Luxury Ice*

The ice sphere (ball) was created in Japan. In Japan, ice is highly respected. Most bars do not own ice machines; they rely on ice delivery service, then cut the ice into blocks. Around 2005, the ice sphere became most famous shape that Japanese bartenders would make. They made it by hand with an ice pick and took between five and seven minutes. Videos can be seen on YouTube. By 2010, Americans began to make ice ball molds that anyone could purchase. They can be easily found by googling. Alternatively, in a pinch you can fill up water balloons and freeze them by keeping their form the roundest you can.

In 2008, Roberto Sequeira from San Francisco launched the first luxury high-quality ice company, Gläce Luxury Ice (glaceice.net), offering ice spheres (balls) and large cubes delivered to your door. Today, they supply luxury ice to Disneyland, Hilton Properties, Avia Hotels, Mandarin Oriental Hotel, and the Pebble Beach Resorts.

LARGE CUBED ICE

One-inch cubes are the most popular cubed size. They make expensive commercial machines or you can purchase silicone molds. Again, the same science applies in that this ice dilutes less water into your drink.

CYLINDER ICE

Cylinder ice is long cylinder–shaped to fit down into a tall glass.

ICE BLOCK

This is where it all started. Many craft bars like to have a block of ice visible so you can watch bartenders use an ice pick to chip off ice for your drink—like in the old days. Bartenders will also take the block and cut it down into different-sized square shapes for a variety of glasses and cocktails.

...

HOMEMADE ICE RECIPES

You can make your own ice creations at home by using various molds, ice trays, recycled items, and various other things found around the kitchen.

HOMEMADE CRUSHED ICE

If you don't have a crushed ice machine, you can place ice in the center of a cloth napkin or kitchen towel, wrap it up, and then whack on it with a mallet or something heavy with a handle. Just be careful not to hit your fingers.

SILICONE ICE TRAYS AND MOLDS

This is the easiest way to make fun-shaped ice. Silicone ice trays and molds come in a variety of shapes. Always buy large shapes because the small ones melt very fast in a drink. You can even flavor your ice by freezing juices and other mixers such as coconut water, cucumber water, coffee, ginger beer, or whatever you want. You can also add flowers, candy, pieces of fruit, or anything else that sparks your imagination.

HOMEMADE ICE BLOCKS

A block of ice can be used in a punchbowl to keep the punch cold. Just recycle a half-gallon milk or juice carton by cutting off the top. Clean the container, fill it with water, and then freeze. When you need the block of ice, rip the paper carton off and place it in the punch bowl. You can also freeze juice or a mixer that is in the punch, so the block only melts mixer in the bowl and does not dilute the punch with water.

Another way to use the paper cartons is to set a bottle of liquor or liqueur of your choice into the carton, then fill two-thirds with water and freeze. When frozen, tear away the paper and you have a block of ice around a bottle. Throughout the freezing stages you can add sliced fruit, herbs, flowers, or anything you want.

My Glass Is Half Full ice cylinder; 2013. © *Cheryl Charming*

In 2014, I came up with what I call the "glass is half full" technique. I didn't want to spend any money on molds, so I boiled distilled water and filled up Old-Fashioned glasses half with water. I then covered the glasses in plastic wrap and kept them in the freezer until needed. When ready, I removed a glass from the freezer, discarded the plastic, and strained the cocktail on top of the ice. To take it a step further I purchased lighted coasters to present the cocktail.

CLEAR ICE

On a small scale, you can make almost clear ice by purchasing distilled water then boiling it three times. Just bring it to a boil, shut it off to cool, and then repeat the process. Use this water to fill ice cubes trays, ice ball molds, etc.

On a large scale—without getting a local company involved—you can make your own clear block of ice using the directional freezing technique that was created in 2009 by popular drinks writer and blogger Camper English. Items you will need are: a large hard-sided Igloo cooler, a large reach-in freezer (like the kind your parents kept on the back porch), water, a handsaw, a hammer, a chisel, and a good pair of rubber gloves. Directional freezing is a simple method to make crystal clear ice by controlling the direction that water freezes.

The simplest (and original) way to make a clear ice block by directional freezing is to fill a hard-sided picnic cooler with water, place it into a freezer, and allow it to freeze with the cooler's top off. The water will only freeze into ice from the top-down, and only the last 25 percent or so of the ice block that forms will be cloudy. If the block is removed from the freezer before this point, one will have a perfectly clear slab of ice. Otherwise, the bottom cloudy portion of the ice block can be cut off from the clear part.

18

Bar Hopping: Famous Cocktails from Around the Globe

...
THE UNITED STATES OF AMERICA
(BY STATE AND CITY)

CALIFORNIA

Zombie—Hollywood

The Zombie was invented by Ernest Raymond Beaumont Gantt, a.k.a. Donn Beachcomber/Don the Beachcomber/Donn Beach (1907–1989). Beach is credited for opening the first tiki Polynesian-themed bar, Don's Beachcomber, just half a block off Hollywood Boulevard in 1933 (1722 North McCadden Place). He invented the Zombie here in 1934. Four years later he moved across the street and renamed it Don the Beachcomber (1727 North McCadden Place). It closed in 1985 and condominiums have been built in both locations. Gantt also served the Zombie at the 1939 New York World's Fair.

The challenge of being the best at something is that people want to steal from you, so bartenders from other tiki bars would watch what bottles Gantt's bartenders were picking up, counting the pours, writing down everything they could to steal recipes. Even bartenders from Trader Vic's (375 miles away) would make the trek down to Hollywood. So, Don decided to cover his mixer bottles, then labeled them #1, #2, #3, and so on. The only issue with this was that over time no one knew the true ingredients of the Zombie anymore.

Jeff "Beachbum" Berry dressed up as a zombie, after finding the original Zombie recipe, holding a Zombie cocktail. © *Jonpaul Balak*

Jeff "Beachbum" Berry to the rescue! This "Bum" is responsible for reviving the modern tiki culture starting in 1998 with his book *Grog Log*. He began a Zombie ingredient quest in 1994 and it lasted until 2005. You can check out the story at his website beachbumberry.com. In a nutshell, it took eleven adventurous years to crack the Zombie code. Berry code cracking was written up in many publications.

Hands down, the best place to drink a Zombie is at Beachbum Berry's Latitude 29 located in the quaint Bienville Hotel in the French Quarter, New Orleans.

Mai Tai—Oakland

"Mai Tai" is Tahitian for "out of this world," which translates to "very good." One-legged from childhood, Victor Jules Bergeron was inspired by Don the Beachcomber's tiki restaurant and bar in Hollywood, so in 1934 he borrowed money from his aunt to open his own Polynesian-themed restaurant and bar in Oakland, California, called Hinky Dinks (6500 San Pablo Avenue). In 1939, he renamed it Trader Vic's and opened franchises in Seattle, Hawaii, and San Francisco. He went on to open thirty-one more franchises in America and around the world. Today there are eighteen franchise locations with two of them in America: Atlanta, Georgia, and the flagship Emeryville, California.

Beachbum Berry's tiki bar, Latitude 29 in the Bienville Hotel in New Orleans, Louisiana. © *Jochen-Hirschfeld*

On a summer night in 1944, Bergeron made up a drink for his visiting Tahitian friends, Ham and Carrie Guild, and after taking one sip, Carrie said, "Mai Tai—Roa Ae!" so Vic named it Mai Tai. Most bars don't carry a couple of key ingredients for the Mai Tai (orgeat almond syrup and orange Curaçao) and will substitute amaretto and triple sec. Also, the number-one thing to know about a Mai Tai is that it is not red. It should be yellowish with a dark rum floater and garnished with a mint sprig and lime.

The Mai Tai was all the rage in the late 1950s and early 1960s because it made its way into the 1961 Elvis Presley film *Blue Hawaii*.

The best places to order one: Latitude 29 in New Orleans, Smuggler's Cove in San Francisco, Three Dots and a Dash in Chicago, and Otto's Shrunken Head in New York City.

Tequila Sunrise—The Trident Restaurant & Bar—Sausalito

They should've called it "Being in the Right Place at the Right Time Sunrise." Bartender Bobby "Robert" Lozoff invented the Tequila Sunrise at age twenty-two in 1969 while working for the Trident in Sausalito, California (ten miles from San Francisco)—his first year of bartending. At the time, the Trident was a popular hang for rock 'n' roll celebs. Regulars included Janis Joplin and Carlos Santana, and the late comedian/actor Robin Williams was a busboy. The Trident was known for very attractive waitresses, and some say it was ahead of its time by offering a juice bar and espresso.

On a Monday night in June 1972—the Trident was normally closed on Mondays—Lozoff and two waitresses were called in to work a Rolling Stones American Tour kickoff party of around thirty-five people. Mick Jagger walked up to the bar and ordered a Margarita from Lozoff, who then asked him if he had ever tried a Tequila Sunrise. Jagger said "no." So, Lozoff made one for Jagger, and he loved it! Lozoff says that the thing Jagger liked the best is that it only needed three ingredients—tequila, orange juice, and grenadine—so the band could make them while on tour. In 2010, Keith Richards published a book titled *Life* and in chapter nine, sentence one reads, "The '72 tour was known by other names—the Cocaine and Tequila Sunrise tour."

Lozoff's Sunrise did not start off with three ingredients. He first made it with tequila, orange juice, commercial sweet-and-sour mix, soda water, and a crème de cassis floater served in a chimney glass (tall glass). Lozoff says that eventually grenadine was used in place of the cassis. In fact, due to the Trident being extremely high volume, sometime between 1969 and 1972 the recipe shortened altogether. Lozoff was known as the fastest bartender in San Francisco. It was his bartender "thing" pumping out multiple volumes of drinks to guests. With the help of McKesson Liquor Distributing Corporation in San Francisco and the manager of the Trident, Jose Cuervo was contacted about printing the drink recipe on the back of the bottle. Cuervo learned that the Trident was selling more of their tequila than any bar in America, and Lozoff's recipe was put on the bottle. And as if things couldn't get any better, in April of 1973, the Eagles released their song "Tequila Sunrise," which blew that sunrise out of the water. In 1974, it made it into *Mr. Boston's Bartender's Guide.*

Inventor of the Tequila Sunrise, Bobby "Robert" Lozoff, holding a Tequila Sunrise in Hawaii in 2016 at age sixty-nine. © *Jose Cuervo Tequila*

What happens when a bartender creates a famous drink? Well, in Lozoff's case, nothing. In November of 2016 he said, "Unfortunately I was too young to capitalize on the deal and made no money. As a matter of fact, I received no recognition until writer Jeff Berkhart wrote his *National Geographic* article about me in 2012."

Lozoff moved to Lahaina, Maui, Hawaii, in 1976 and opened up a Trident-like bar and restaurant called Blue Max at 730 Front Street. He decorated it with a big stuffed owl and black-and-white photos of Hawaiian World War II aircraft—and of course served his Tequila Sunrise. Blue Max attracted the same musical giants: Elton John, Stevie Nicks, and too many more to mention. Today, the building is a Chicago pizzeria. Here's a fun fact: Lozoff doesn't drink alcohol and never did. After retiring from the restaurant/bar business in 1989, he became a Mac technician. He says he spent his money on planes, boats, and Rolexes. Today, he still lives in Hawaii and teaches computer classes.

To be fair, bartender Gene Sulit created a cocktail called Tequila Sunrise at the Arizona Biltmore Hotel in the 1930s. The ingredients included tequila, lime juice, crème de cassis, and soda water; no Rolling Stones party was ever hosted there.

HAWAII

BLUE HAWAII—O'AHU

Harry Yee invented the Blue Hawaii in 1957. In the 1950s, Hawaii was on track to be a U.S. state, which it became in 1959, so the islands began a phase of exotic paradise construction to attract tourists. Large tropical getaways were built on every island and the largest of these was the Hawaiian Village on the island of O'ahu.

Hawaii became a state in the same year the *Hawaiian Eye* TV show's exterior shots were filmed at the Hawaiian Village. *Hawaiian Eye* gave Americans a glimpse of what Hawaii was like—too bad the show wasn't in color. The Hawaiian Village is where thirty-seven-year-old bartender Harry Yee invented the drink Blue Hawaii in 1957. Yee was born on September 26, 1918 and started his bartending career at the age of thirty-two. He worked at the Hawaiian Village for thirty years and in 1957 was asked by Bols to help promote their new product, Bols Blue Curaçao—and the Blue Hawaii was born. To be clear, Yee invented the Blue Hawaii, not Blue Hawaiian.

The Blue Hawaiian became an American knockoff once Bols Blue Curaçao made it to nationwide bars and has no real recipe or inventor. At the time there weren't any popular "Hawaii" drinks. Tourists were just ordering Mai Tais, Zombies, Planter's Punches, Piña Coladas, and Grasshoppers. When defining a drink from Hawaii, Yee said, "A Hawaiian drink to me is something they don't get back home."

When asked about the Vanda orchid garnish in the Blue Hawaii, Yee said, "We used to use a sugarcane stick and people would chew on the stick and then put it in the ashtray. When the ashes and cane stuck together it made a real mess, so I put the Vanda orchids in the drink to make the ashtrays easier to clean."

Yee is also credited with using the first paper parasols in cocktails. He invented other tropical cocktails, including the Tropical Itch, Hawaiian Eye, Guava Lada, Hot Buttered Okolehao, Scratch Me Lani, Catamaran, Naughty Hula, Hukilau, Diamond Head, Village Sunset, and Wahine's Delight. His Tropical Itch is garnished with a bamboo Chinese back scratcher, and the Hawaiian Eye became famous in America between 1959 and 1963 because *Hawaiian Eye* featured the drink.

Today, the Hilton Hawaiian Village still sells Yee's Blue Hawaii but sadly, they do not use his exact recipe or garnish anymore. On their menu, they sell another drink called Blue Ocean that is closer to the real recipe, except that it uses Jamaican rum in place of Puerto Rican rum. It's been said that Yee would hold up every Blue Hawaii he made to make sure it was the color of the Pacific Ocean. If that is true, then he must've only worked day shifts.

LOUISIANA (NEW ORLEANS)

Without a doubt, New Orleans wins for the most popular cocktails of any city in the world.

BRANDY CRUSTA—JEWEL OF THE SOUTH

Italian-born Joseph Santini (1817–1874) created the Brandy Crusta, which made it into the first known American cocktail recipe book *How to Mix Drinks or The Bon-Vivant's Companion: The Bartender's Guide* by Jerry Thomas (Thomas or an editor misspells his name as Santina). It is believed that Thomas visited Santini at the City Exchange Restaurant and Bar or at Santini's bar, Jewel of the South, while visiting New Orleans in the 1850s. The Brandy Crusta is famous because it is considered the gateway cocktail— using fresh citrus juice—that led to the creation of the Sidecar and even the Lemon Drop Martini. Maybe it was a way for Santini to add a squeeze of Italian heritage in a cocktail, since Italy is known for their lemons.

Santini was born in Trieste, Italy, and the 1840 Census shows Santini living with another young male in an area of Gentilly called Milneburgh in the New Orleans area. Milneburgh is on the shore of Lake Pontchartrain. While most of America did not experience the railroad until the late 1880s, the Pontchartrain railroad became the second working railroad in 1831. It carried passengers and goods to New Orleans and back on a five-mile track and was used mostly as a weekend getaway destination, depending on which way you were traveling. In 1840, Milneburgh had two hotels, two barrooms, a grocery store, and a bakery. It's possible that Santini worked in one of these barrooms.

In 1841, Santini was given a head barkeeper position by a fellow Italian friend at the Splendid Bar in the St. Charles Hotel. The St. Charles at this time was the most lavish hotel in all of New Orleans. From the outside, it looked exactly like the nation's White House. In the month of April 1842, several ads were run in the *Times-Picayune* announcing Santini opening the bar at the Washington Hotel in Lake Pontchartrain. The ad says,

"Opening of the Washington Hotel, Lake Pontchartrain. Mr. Joseph Santini has the honor to inform the public, that he will open the above Hotel for the reception of visitors, on Sunday, the 3d inst. The Bar will be furnished with the choicest Liquors. The Restaurant will be under the direction of Mr. Mayer."

In February 1855, at age thirty-seven, Santini opened his elegant—and often referred to as "pretentious"— bar, the Jewel of the South, on the corner of St. Charles and Gravier, one block from the French Quarter and across the street from the St. Charles Hotel where Santini used to work (the hotel had just been rebuilt due to an 1851 fire). This bar would later be home to Charles Ramos (Ramos Gin Fizz) and the Sazerac Bar when they moved out of the French Quarter after Prohibition.

Santini owned four businesses on Gravier between St. Charles and Carondolet: a less pretentious bar called the Parlor with the attached Corona Cigar Shop, and another cigar shop called Intimidad ("privacy" in Spanish), which was attached to the Jewel. George B. Ittmann was Santini's head barman. In newspaper articles, Ittmann had been described as a "scientific mixologist who is to the Jewel what Hamlet is to Shakespeare." Other New Orleans businesses open at this time in history included Lafitte's Blacksmith Shop, Old Absinthe House, Sazerac Coffee House, Antoine's, Tujague's, Café du Monde, the Court of Two Sisters, and the first artificial ice factory.

On Dec 29, 1868, Santini announced in the paper that he was retiring from the Jewel and handed it over to head bartender George B. Ittmann. In 1874, while in France with his daughter Marietta, who was pursuing her vocal studies abroad, Santini died at fifty-seven. The day is not exact, but it is agreed that it was either August 9, 11, or 12. Santini's body did not make it to New Orleans for his funeral until October 18. He is buried at St. Louis Cemetery No. 3 at 3421 Esplanade. Mrs. Margaretha Santini (age forty-eight) assumed ownership of the saloons. She eventually retired to Biloxi, Mississippi, and lived to be 103 years old.

Inventor of the Brandy Crusta, Joseph Santini, while visiting France in 1867. © *Diana Lehman (Santini's great-great-granddaughter)*

With direction from Chris McMillian, I found Santini's great-great-granddaughter Diana. Diana shared photos and eleven pages of Santini's liquor inventory that was recorded after his death. Some items of interest include Boker's bitters, Peychaud's Bitters, Newfoundland bitters, Dr. J. Hostetter's bitters, Guaco bitters, Sazerac Cognac, orgeat syrup, orange-flower water, Jamaican rum, Holland gin, arrack, Old Tom gin, Scotch, Irish whiskey, Bourbon, rye whiskey, green and yellow Chartreuse, Bénédictine, kirschwasser, absinthe (spelled absynthe), cassis, Noilly Prat vermouth, many fruit brandies, and almost 1,000 bottles of wine including Madeira, sherry and port.

In 1948, David A. Embury published a Brandy Crusta recipe in his book *Fine Art of Mixing Drinks* with the addition of maraschino liqueur.

Santini was very involved in the arts and aiding in children's education. Articles show that he hosted events to raise money for widows and orphaned children. At the New Orleans Locquet Young Ladies Institute on Camp Street, he provided "Santini Medals" to the female students who excelled in French and elocution (the skill of clear and expressive speech). The Institute gave him a set of gold cufflinks engraved with an open book on one side and the word "education" on the other. Santini was also a Mason of the Maconnique Lodge.

GRASSHOPPER—TUJAGUE'S

Tujague's opened in 1856 and is currently the second oldest restaurant in New Orleans. They have never shown any documentation, but claim to be the inventor of the Grasshopper.

The story: in 1919 the second owner, Philip Guichet, took second place in a New York City cocktail recipe contest and that's it. The drink is green and creamy and tastes like melted chocolate mint ice cream. It rose in popularity in the 1950s and 1960s and then again between 2007 and 2015 due to the popular TV show *Mad Men*. If you visit Tujague's for a Grasshopper today, you'll discover that somewhere through the years, bartenders took it upon themselves to alter the recipe by adding a floater of brandy.

HURRICANE—PAT O'BRIEN'S

If you ask people all over the world to name a bar in New Orleans, they will most likely answer "Pat O'Brien's."

On November 6, 1894, Benson Harrison O'Brien, a.k.a. Pat O'Brien (1894–1983), was born in Chattanooga, Tennessee. O'Brien was a first-generation American whose father left North Tipperary County, Ireland, during the potato famine. O'Brien grew up in Birmingham, Alabama, with three sisters, and after going through a couple of marriages and kids, he made his way to New Orleans alone in 1929 at the age of thirty-five.

O'Brien stood six-foot-four, wore white suits, preferred petite five-foot-tall women, and became one of the best bootleggers in Louisiana and Mississippi. With his outgoing, gregarious personality, it did not take him long to know the bar owners and seek investors to open his own speakeasy.

O'Brien opened a speakeasy and named it Mr. O'Brien's Club Tipperary (nicknamed Tips) on the corner of Royal and St. Peter streets. The password was "Storm's Brewin." By December 3, 1933, O'Brien moved into the French Quarter at 638 St. Peter and opened Pat O'Brien's liquor store two days before the official repeal day—probably because he already knew many cops. Today this location is a small tourist center. Friends wanted O'Brien to open another bar, so three years later he moved to a larger space one block away at 718 St. Peter—the current location.

It is believed that Pat O'Brien, at age forty-eight, invented the Hurricane in 1942, and it's said that it took him two weeks of testing to get it right. He served it in a twenty-two-ounce hurricane lamp–shaped glass (now called a Hurricane glass), and locals were upset that the drink cost sixty cents when other drinks at the time cost only fifteen cents. O'Brien had to announce in the local paper that it cost that much because it contained four ounces of rum. The story goes that the sole reason the Hurricane was invented was that O'Brien wanted whiskey. At the time, whiskey was in short supply, so distributors told him that if he would purchase many cases of rum, they would sell him one case of whiskey. Other stories say if he purchased one case of rum, he could get one bottle of whiskey, but in any case, the Hurricane was born.

My friend Scott Touchton was the GM of Pat O'Brien's from 2000-2014 told me that the original 1942 recipe was 4 oz rum, lime juice, orange juice, and passionfruit syrup served in a 22 oz Hurricane glass. However, another cocktail friend, Philip Greene (a distant relative of Antoine Peychaud) discovered a 1941 Ronrico rum recipe book that lists a "Hurricane Punch" made with 4 oz Ronrico rum, lime juice, lemon juice, and passionfruit syrup served in a 24 oz special blue glass. The instructions say to "Waring mix" half of the drink (Waring is a brand of blender that came out in the 1930s) then pour the blended mixture over a half glass of Ronrico ice. I'm not sure what "Ronrico ice" is, but the real question is "Did Pat O'Brien know about the Hurricane Punch recipe?" No one will ever know.

Sadly, today the popular red drink is not made with fresh-squeezed juices like it was back then, but made with a Kool Aid–type mixture and then bottled at Pat O'Brien's local bottling plant, in which they make huge batches, transport it to the bar, and then store it in a tank that has several lines running to all the bars. Special guns were created for all the bars so that a bartender can fill up three Hurricanes at a time in three seconds.

Indoors, they serve the drink in a twenty-two-ounce Hurricane glass and charge you for the glass. If you don't want the glass, you have to take it to a bartender to get three dollars back. If you choose to keep the souvenir glass, they box up a clean glass and put it into a logo bag with some extra souvenirs. If you want a Hurricane to-go, then it is served in a sixteen-ounce white logo plastic cup.

There have been variations on the recipe, but one thing that is for sure is it was always a red-colored drink, which should come from red passion fruit syrup. Local newspaper articles on public drunkenness talked about the sidewalks being red from Hurricane vomit and spills in the 1940s and 1950s. At that time, Pat O'Brien's was so busy that the city had to employ police officers to monitor the outside of the building. If you want to enjoy a fresh Hurricane the way it tasted in 1942, walk one block to the Bourbon Orleans Hotel Bar.

RAMOS GIN FIZZ

Henry Charles "Carl" Ramos (1856–1928) invented the Ramos Gin Fizz in 1888 and served it until 1919 when he was forced to close for Prohibition. As a farewell gift to New Orleans, he published his recipe in the local paper.

Ramos was a first-born, first-generation American from German parents. He was born in Indiana and made his way to New Orleans around the age of fourteen. He married at age twenty-three and then by age thirty-one, Ramos and his brother took ownership of Pat Moran's Imperial Cabinet in 1888. It was located on the corner of Carondelet and Gravier, which is two blocks outside of the French Quarter from Bourbon Street. Sadly, the building is no longer there today. No one knows what inspired Ramos to create a cocktail, but he did and he named it "Ramos's One and Only One Gin Fizz." A Gin Fizz at the time contained four ingredients: gin, lemon juice, sugar, and soda water (the same ingredients in a Tom Collins). Ramos doubled the ingredients by adding lime juice, cream, egg white, and orange-flower water. Drink historian David Wondrich writes in his book *Imbibe!* that the *Kansas City Star* anointed the Imperial Cabinet "the most famous Gin Fizz in the world" in 1900. Wondrich also discovered that Ramos went through 5,000 eggs a week, owned America's largest hennery, and during 1900's Mardi Gras, employed six bartenders and one black man as a "shaker boy."

In 1907, Ramos sold the Imperial Cabinet and moved one block, taking over the Stag Saloon at 712 Gravier. This location was directly across the street of the entrance to the grandest hotel in the city at the time, the St. Charles Hotel and where Joseph Santini's the Jewel of the South was located previously. St. Charles is the main street for Mardi Gras parades, and during Mardi Gras 1915, it's believed that Ramos hired a chain of thirty-two "shaker boys" who would shake and pass down the shaker tins of fizzes in a long line.

Other New Orleans businesses open at this time in history include Lafitte's Blacksmith Shop, Old Absinthe House, Sazerac Coffee House, Antoine's, Tujague's, Café du Monde, the Court of Two Sisters, Commander's Palace, La Louisiane, Jackson Brewing, Café Sbisa, Galatoire's, Arnaud's, Acme Oyster House, Central Grocery, Broussard's, and America's first nightclub at the Gruenwald (now the Roosevelt Hotel), the Cave. Other New Orleans creations around were: muffaletta sandwich, beignets, Oysters Rockefeller, Barq's soda, Dixie beer, and Tabasco.

Ramos died in 1928, but Governor Huey "Kingfish" P. Long resurrected Ramos's Gin Fizz after Prohibition and made it known that it was his favorite cocktail. Once he took a political trip to New York and stayed at the New Yorker Hotel. After taking one sip of the New Yorker's Fizz, he called the Roosevelt in New Orleans with orders "to send his best gin fizzer to New York by plane so he could teach these New York sophisticates how to make it correctly." The story goes that the next day Sam Guarino, head bartender at the Sazerac Bar, arrived in New York and spent three hours schooling his Northern counterparts on the proper way to make a Ramos Gin Fizz. Drink historian and today's most famous New Orleans bartender, Chris McMillian, shares a YouTube video titled "Huey teaches us," which shows film footage of Long standing behind the Sazerac Bar testing out a Ramos Gin Fizz.

To date, there are five bars that have been famous for executing the Ramos Gin Fizz and two can be visited today.

1. **The Imperial Cabinet** • Ramos's first New Orleans bar, located on the corner of Carondelet and Gravier.

2. **The Stag Saloon** • Ramos's second New Orleans bar, located on the corner of St. Charles and Gravier.

3. **The Cadillac Bar** • After French native New Orleans waiter Achilles Mehault "Mayo" Bessan lost his job due to Prohibition, he decided to take himself and his nineteen-year-old bride across the border where alcohol still flowed. They settled in Nuevo Laredo, Tamaulipas, across the Rio Grande from Laredo and Texas. In 1926, Bessen bought the Caballo Blanco Bar and renamed it the Cadillac Bar. In 1929 he moved the bar and reopened with *muy grande* signs advertising his favorite New Orleans cocktail, "The Famous Ramos Gin Fizz." Bessan served both New Orleans cuisine and Mexican cuisine. Sadly, the Cadillac Bar is no longer around today, but the good thing is that you can order a Ramos Gin Fizz in America.

4. **The Sazerac Bar** | The Roosevelt Hotel • They trademarked the name Ramos Gin Fizz after Prohibition and have been known for making Ramos Gin Fizzes since.

5. **Bourbon O Bar** | The Bourbon Orleans Hotel • In 2013, as bar director I learned three things when researching Henry Charles "Carl" Ramos.
   - Ramos went into the paint business during Prohibition.
   - The local hardware store, three blocks from the bar—Mary's Ace Hardware on Rampart Street—was where Ramos lived.
   - The front room into his house is where the paint section is today.

I entertained the idea of shaking Ramos Gin Fizzes with a paint can shaker, but this proved to be too expensive (and messy), in 2014 I asked William Grant & Sons to buy the bar a $1,000 Asian bubble tea shaker that would shake the Hendrick's Gin Ramos Gin Fizz for six minutes.

SAZERAC

On June 23, 2008, in a 62–33 vote, the Louisiana House of Representatives proclaimed the Sazerac New Orleans's official cocktail. Actually, it is the first city in the world to have an official cocktail!

Most agree that the Sazerac would not be what it is today if it was not for Antoine Amedee Peychaud (1803–1883). Peychaud (pay-SHOWED) was French, but it's not known when he came to New Orleans because he was one of the many who fled a chaotic evacuation during the Haitian Revolution (1791–1804).

What we do know is that in 1832, nineteen-year-old Antoine Amedee Peychaud partnered with druggist A. Duconge at 123 Royal Street—the street numbers changed in 1896, so the address translates to 437 Royal between St. Louis and Conti today. By 1834, Peychaud bought the apothecary and it is believed that he began producing his father's family bitters recipe. According to the *New Orleans Bee*, Peychaud's apothecary became a place to hang after Concorde Blue Mason's Lodge meetings and, using his bitters, Peychaud served brandy toddies. Peychaud was said to measure the toddies using a double-ended eggcup/jigger, then called a coquetier (ko-k-tay), which the word "cocktail" was once thought to have originated from. It's also believed that the Sazerac got its name from a brandy of the same name, however some cocktail historians disagree.

In 1849, Peychaud expanded by opening a second apothecary in the French Quarter. In 1854, at age fifty-one, Peychaud's wife, Celestine, left him a widower with three children, aged sixteen, twelve, and six. In 1857, Peychaud marketed his bitters in the New Orleans Bee newspaper and by 1858, he had two major bitters competitors, Baker's and Hostetter's, so he aggressively marketed Peychaud's Bitters. The 1860 Census shows that Peychaud had ten people living in his household, so it is assumed that he was hard at work selling bitters to support everyone. By 1867, Peychaud opened his third apothecary in the French Quarter.

By 1869 when he was sixty-six, Peychaud's children were grown, and it is assumed he probably wanted to slow down, so he sold his apothecaries and made bitters for Thomas Handy, who owned the popular Sazerac Coffee House (bar). The Sazerac Coffee House (the best coffeehouse in its time) was the number-one place where the Sazerac was served for fifty solid years until 1920 (Prohibition). Today, the spot where the Sazerac Coffee House was located is at 124 Royal. It was a Holiday Inn from 1984 to 2015 and is now a Wyndham Hotel. In addition, in 1869, Peychaud's Bitters received the Diploma of Honor at the Grand Exhibition of Altona, Germany.

In 1872, Thomas Handy became the importer of Sazerac brandy, extended the bar to be 125 feet long, and employed eighteen bartenders. One year later, Peychaud sold the Peychaud's Bitters recipe to Handy. It is said that the recipe for brandy was replaced by rye whiskey and a dash of absinthe was added. This was probably because of the issues with Europe's grapevines being destroyed and absinthe becoming trendy. It is also believed that the Sazerac was always made with rye whiskey from the beginning. It should also be noted that there is another man who many believe created the rye whiskey Sazerac Cocktail by the name of William "Billy" Wilkinson. Wilkinson was a bartender at the Sazerac Coffeehouse.

In 2016, I was given Joseph Santini's 1874 inventory list by his great-great-granddaughter and it shows that Santini owned fifteen bottles of Sazerac Cognac. Was the Sazerac made with this or with rye whiskey? Cocktail historians are still researching.

In 1908, the Sazerac recipe made it into the first known cocktail book in William T. "Cocktail Bill" Boothby's The World's Drinks and How to Mix Them. In the 1930s, The Roosevelt Hotel bought the Sazerac recipe and named their hotel bar the Sazerac Bar.

In 2012, I located Antoine Peychaud's grave. He is buried with his sister Lasthenie Peychaud in St. Louis Cemetery No. 2 between Conti and St. Louis streets in New Orleans.

Vieux Carré–Carousel Bar | Hotel Monteleone

The Vieux Carré has been listed on the Carousel Bar's menu since 1934. Vieux Carré translates to "Old Square" / "French Quarter." This cocktail was invented by head bartender Walter Bergeron (1889–1947). It's is a riff on the Sazerac, which had been popular in New Orleans for over 75 years. The Vieux Carré ingredients are rye whiskey, Cognac, sweet vermouth, Bénédictine, Peychaud's Bitters, Angostura bitters, and a lemon twist. It has become a staple cocktail in New Orleans and the world.

When Bergeron was born in Thibodaux, Louisiana, both his parents were only thirteen years old (Louis Klebert Bergeron and Florence Prioux). As you might have guessed, this young love affair did not survive and both eventually went their separate ways. Walter went with his father who married Amanda Benoit. This union gave Walter two brothers, Phillip and George Bergeron. While researching via Ancestry.com I was able to communicate with a relative named Aunt Punkin' who told me Walter was a very funny man (she used the word comical). She said he loved drinking beer with his brothers and making jokes. She also said his body frame was short and stocky whereas his brothers were tall and lean.

Bergeron moved to New Orleans in 1907 and began his bartending career sometime between 1917 and 1919 (age twenty-eight to thirty) as a hotel bartender, but it's assumed he tended bar at a speakeasy in 1920 (Prohibition) because the 1930 U.S. Census says he was employed in a cigar store, which was a good cover for a speakeasy. In 1934 (after Prohibition), Bergeron went back to a legal bartender position in a hotel. It is assumed the hotel was the Hotel Monteleone at 214 Royal because Bergeron's wife, Jeanne, died in April 1934, leaving him a widower with four children aged eighteen, twelve, nine, and three. It's believed with this much responsibility he would have sought steady employment.

The 1940 U.S. Census says Bergeron worked as a bartender at a hotel forty-eight hours a week with a yearly income of $1,580 (almost $27,000 in 2017). Bergeron died of a heart attack at age fifty-seven in a grocery store on a cool, rainy night—Thursday, February 13, 1947—five days before Mardi Gras and one day before the Mardi Gras weekend celebrations. He lived at 6006 Dauphine Street. He is buried at St. Vincent De Paul Cemetery.

During a 2013 phone conversation with Bergeron's only living child, eighty-three-year-old Klebert (cluh-BARE), he spoke fondly of visiting his father at the Carousel Bar in 1940 at the age of ten. He said he remembered it well because there was a boy his age playing with a shiny red toy fire truck. He said the truck was left unattended at one point, so he walked over to touch it and then told his dad that he wanted one. Bergeron told him to get away from the truck because it belonged to the hotel owner's son. Klebert talked for thirty minutes about how his dad always worked in the daytime so he could be home at night. He said his father woke up at 6 a.m. and returned home at 7 p.m. While visiting his father at the bar, he remembered watching men order drinks, his father mixing drinks, and the smell of smoke. Klebert died in 2014. I have located Klebert Bergeron II and Klebert Bergeron III on Facebook in hopes of gaining a photo of Walter, but sadly the grandson and great grandson of Walter Bergeron have declined to speak with me. I will keep trying.

OTHER NEW ORLEANS COCKTAILS

- **Absinthe Suissesse**—Invented at the Old Absinthe House.
- **Café Brûlot Diabolique (Devilishly Burned Coffee)**—Invented in the 1890s by the founder's son, Jules Alciatore, at Antoine's, the oldest restaurant in New Orleans (1840). It's a show-stopping, flaming concoction of coffee, Cognac, and spices served in special cups.
- **Cajun Martini**—Invented and registered in 1986 by Chef Paul Prudhomme at K-Paul's (416 Chartres) by infusing jalapeños with vodka. He called it "Chef Paul Prudhomme's original K-Paul's Cajun Martini 'Totally Hot.'" One year later, Prudhomme produced a premixed bottled Cajun Martini, and on the bottle, it said "made with Taa.k.a. Vodka, vermouth, and cayenne peppers."
- **Cocktail à la Louisiane**—Invented in the 1880s in the restaurant of the same name. You can visit the bar that took over the space, 21st Amendment, at 725 Iberville Street.
- **Frozen Irish Coffee**—Invented in 1991 by Jim Monaghan Sr. at Molly's on the Market.

- **Hand Grenade®**—Invented and trademarked by Earl Bernhardt and Pam Fortner in 1984 at their original Tropical Isle (600 Bourbon). It was created for the 1984 Louisiana World Exposition and today is the number-one to-go drink seen on Bourbon Street.
- **Obituary Cocktail**—Invented at Jean Lafitte's Blacksmith Shop, which is the oldest bar in New Orleans. The cocktail's subtitle is "The High Brow of All Low Brow Drinks."
- **Roffignac**—Count Louis Philippe Joseph de Roffignac was the ninth mayor of New Orleans and its last French mayor from 1820-1828. He was responsible for the beautification of the French Quarter by adding cobblestone streets and gas lamps. The residents loved him so much that they made a drink in his honor. It was sold up until 1986 and then died off. Recently, it has made an appearance at many fresh craft bars in New Orleans.

ADOPTED NEW ORLEANS COCKTAILS

Many people think these cocktails were invented in New Orleans—but the city only took them under its wings: Absinthe Drip, Bloody Mary, Fleur de Lis, French 75, Milk Punch, Mint Julep, Pimm's Cup, Scarlett O'Hara, and Tom and Jerry.

NEW YORK

LONG ISLAND ICED TEA—OAK BEACH INN

Long Island bartender Robert "Rosebud" Butt claims to have invented this drink. On his website liicetea.com he wrote, "The world-famous Long Island Iced Tea was first invented in 1972 by me, Robert Butt, while I was tending bar at the infamous Oak Beach Inn. Nicknamed 'Rosebud' by OBI owner Bob Matherson, I participated in a Cocktail creating contest. Triple Sec had to be included, and the bottles started flying. My concoction was an immediate hit and quickly became the house drink at the OBI."

By the mid-1970s, every bar on Long Island was serving up this innocent-looking cocktail, and by the 1980s it was known the world over. Though it looks like the iced tea your mom serves on a summer day, it is actually a combination of five different alcohols, with a splash of Coke.

The PBS series *Inventors* documented Butt on February 22, 2013 on film. The clip can be seen on YouTube under the title *Long Island Iced Tea | INVENTORS | PBS Digital Studios*. Butt makes the Long Island Iced Tea in his bright white open-cabinet kitchen with seven ingredients lined up on his counter: Smirnoff vodka, Seagram's gin, Bacardi rum, Jose Cuervo gold tequila, Dekuyper triple sec, commercial sweet and sour, and Coca-Cola. He pours a shot of each spirit (without a jigger). A shot could be 1 ounce, or 1.25 ounces, or even 1.5 ounces, depending on the establishment. So, this drink—according to Butt—could contain between 5 and 7.5 ounces of booze! Today, almost all bartenders pour half shots to make the total alcohol count 2.5 ounces. Many establishments have guidelines of how many ounces of alcohol can be in one drink. However, if you're home in your kitchen like Butt was in the video, make the darn thing any way you want, because you'll only be drinking one.

MANHATTAN—NEW YORK CITY

The earliest-known recipes for the Manhattan appear in three 1884 cocktail books: George Winters' *How To Mix Drinks*, J.W. Gibson, *Scientific Bar-Keeping*, and O.H. Byron's *The Modern Bartender's Guide*.

From what we know, the Manhattan was the signature cocktail at the Manhattan Club in New York in the 1870s. Back then it was made with equal parts rye whiskey and sweet vermouth with a dash (or two) of orange bitters, but who invented it is unclear.

There are two different stories. The broken record story is that it was created at the Manhattan Club for a dinner party being thrown by Lady Randolph Churchill to celebrate Samuel Tilden's election as governor in 1874. However, cocktail researchers discovered that the Lady was in England pregnant with Winston Churchill at this time.

The second story comes from an article written in the 1923 *Valentine's Manual of Old New York* (Volume 7) by a sixty-one-year-old bartender named William F. Mulhall, who had been mixing drinks in New York City for thirty years. He talks about New York bartenders, bars, fights, bouncers, prices, popular cocktails, and not-so-popular cocktails in detail for eleven pages. Mulhall starts the article talking about his first day of work at the Hoffman House at the corner of Twenty-Fifth and Broadway in September 1882. Eight pages in he mentions the Manhattan:

"The Manhattan cocktail was invented by a man named Black, who kept a place ten doors below Houston Street on Broadway in the sixties—probably the most famous mixed drink in the world in its time. The cocktail made America famous and there were many varieties of them—in fact, the variety was infinite—I remember at the Hoffman in the old days, a gentleman would come in and sit down to a table with his party and the waiter would come over and order his particular formula for the party. We had many private formulas for mixed drinks in the Hoffman and the bartenders had to learn them by memory, too, so that the order could be served quickly."

In 1882, the first known mention of a Manhattan cocktail was in the *Sunday Morning Herald* from Olean, New York: "It is but a short time ago that a mixture of whiskey, vermouth, and bitters came into vogue."

VIRGINIA

Mint Julep

David Wondrich is—hands down—America's number-one cocktail historian. He calls the Mint Julep the "first true American drink." His most current Mint Julep findings come from Virginia in 1770. However, Wondrich feels that highly recognized New York City bartender Orsamus Willard, a.k.a. Willard, is responsible for making the iced version popular.

Wondrich also says it started out as a rum-based cocktail, then whiskey, then brandy, then Bourbon. Since 1938, the Kentucky Derby has been promoting the Mint Julep as their official cocktail, much like Wimbledon promotes the Pimm's Cup.

As far as we know, in 1803 the Mint Julep was first seen in print in a London publication, *Travels of Four Years and a Half in the United States*, by John Davis. And in 1837, novelist Captain Frederick Marryat popularized the Mint Julep through his descriptions of American Fourth of July celebrations by writing, "I must descant a little upon the Mint Julep, as it is, with the thermometer at 100? One of the most delightful and insinuating potations that was ever invented, and may be drunk with equal satisfaction when the thermometer is as low as 70? As the ice melts, you drink. I once overheard two ladies in the room next to me, and one of them said, "Well, if I have a weakness for any one thing, it is for a 'Mint Julep!'"—a very amiable weakness, and proving her good sense and taste. They are, in fact, like the American ladies, irresistible."

MULTIPLE LOCATIONS: COSMOPOLITAN—GOLDEN VALLEY, MINNEAPOLIS, PROVINCETOWN, MASSACHUSETTS, CLEVELAND AND CINCINNATI, OHIO, SAN FRANCISCO, CALIFORNIA, NEW YORK, NEW YORK, AND MIAMI, FLORIDA

Gary Regan once said, "The Cosmopolitan is the last true classic cocktail to be born in the twentieth century", and this is true—but—the Cosmopolitan would never have reached international fame and prevailed mainstream as long as it has if it had not been for the HBO show *Sex and the City*, which ran between 1998 and 2004. This time in history coincided with the height of the "flavored Martini craze," so its impact was immense. But how did the Cosmopolitan make its journey to the TV show? Well, as you probably guessed, there are a few stories around its creation.

I have been researching the Cosmopolitan since 2006 when I first surfed the internet to learn when the Cosmopolitan was first seen and mentioned in the HBO show *Sex and the City*. When I discovered that no one knew the answer, I walked to the Orlando Downtown Library and checked out all the *Sex and the City* VHS tapes. Over the years I kept a Cosmopolitan file, but then started to aggressively research the origin of the cocktail in 2015 for this book. Please understand that my Cosmopolitan research is just that—research. You need to realize that none of the bartenders connected to the Cosmopolitan would have ever guessed in a million years that one day this cocktail would become world famous. Try to imagine if someone contacted you with questions from thirty to forty years ago. It took most a little time to remember back that far, which required many emails, texts, and phone calls to gather the information. At times I do give my thoughts, but for the most part, I share what I recorded. Everyone has their truth and their story. You, the reader will need to connect your dots. Respectfully, I do not share personal information about them, others, or celebrity stories that felt to me to be "off the record" conversations. In conclusion, I feel very fortunate to locate as many people as I did before it was too late to record their stories.

The nutshell version of my research is that two bartenders, at two different times (fourteen years apart), in two different cities (1800 miles apart) created a cocktail with almost identical ingredients and named it the same name—Cosmopolitan. These bartenders are Neal Murray and Cheryl Cook. Two New York City bartenders claim to be the first to have upgraded the Cosmopolitan recipe by using quality ingredients, however, only one of them has been credited. Their names are Melissa Huffsmith and Toby Cecchini. And then there is Dale "King Cocktail" DeGroff who independently upgraded the Cosmopolitan. Each person's Cosmopolitan recipe is in Chapter 19 Cocktails 101: A Guide to Classic, Modern Classic, Popular, Famous, Official IBA, and Standard Cocktails.

Author Candace Bushnell wrote a column for *the New York Observer* called *Sex and the City* between 1994-1996, and the column lead to a hit HBO show by creator Darren Star (1998-2004). The rest is history—as well as *her*story.

I believe the Cosmopolitan derived from the Kamikaze, the Kamikaze from the Vodka Gimlet, and the Vodka Gimlet from the Gimlet (made with gin). Before I share my research, there are a couple of cocktails the cocktail community would probably like me to share—The 1933 Cosmopolitan Daisy and Ocean Spray's 1968 Harpoon. In the 1933 book *Pioneers of Mixing Drinks at Elite Bars* published by the American Travelling Mixologists, there is a cocktail named Cosmopolitan Daisy that some believe to be an early version of the Cosmopolitan. I don't agree. The Cosmopolitan Daisy is made with gin, orange liqueur, lemon juice, and raspberry syrup with a raspberry garnish—making the only common ingredient orange liqueur. In 1968, Ocean Spray cranberry juice promoted the "Harpoon" in a 25-cent recipe booklet titled *Mix Around with Cranberry Juice*. I know because

I found this fifty-year-old booklet and purchased it. Here is the exact recipe: Harpoon "A whale of a drink" 1 ounces [sic] Ocean Spray Cranberry Juice Cocktail, 1 ounce vodka, light rum, or gin. Serve over the rocks or tall with soda. Suggested garnish: a splash of lime or lemon optional. Serves 1.

Honestly, there are too many things to pick apart in this recipe, so I'll give you that pleasure. I find it amusing that they describe 1 ounce of spirit and 1 ounce of juice as "A whale of a drink."

Neal Murray • Golden Valley, Minnesota and San Francisco, California

I first tried to contact Neal Murray in December 2016 and heard back from him on April 15, 2017. We have been communicating ever since. Here is the story he has shared with me.

Murray was born in St. Paul, Minnesota in 1951 to politically influential parents of European, Native American, and African descent. When he was ten-years-old, his family moved to Roseville, Minnesota. His parents had a white woman/friend buy their land in Roseville because at the time people of color were not allowed to purchase and build homes in this area. As a young boy, he had been in the room with many political figures including President John F. Kennedy, Robert Kennedy, and Evert Dirksen, to name a few. He got to meet Vice President Hubert Humphrey, Vice President Walter Mondale, and a couple of Minnesota governors all before he was in high school. Murray was a high achiever and grew up being the "only black kid in school" from fifth grade to twelfth grade. Out of 1200 students in junior high, he was the president of the student council. In high school, Murray was the vice president of the junior class, student council, and the canteen council that planned the dances. As a senior, he was to become student council president but he told the school principal he would like to see the first woman in the history of the school become student council president. Murray then convinced the principal to let him create a new conference-wide student council. After meeting with all thirteen principals, he founded and became president of a Suburban Conference Student Council representing 22,000 students in thirteen high schools.

In the second semester of 1975, while studying political science at the University of Minnesota, Murray applied for a bartender position—without experience—at the Cork 'n Cleaver Steakhouse in Golden Valley located at 905 Hampshire Avenue South (it's a Volvo car dealership now). I was not able to obtain the rights to a 1981 Cork 'n Cleaver image that I found, but you can view it at slphistory.org/wayzatabuildingsnorth. Murray applied for the position with the encouragement from two college friends who worked at the Cork 'n Cleaver, Michael Hannah and John Peterson. Murray made it through the interview and hiring process quickly but learned from Hannah and Peterson that he would not be getting the job because he was black. The restaurant accountant called Murray a week later to tell him that the managers would be out of town and if he could learn to be a bartender in four days, then she would hire him. As any good college student would, Murray bought Mr. Boston's Bartender Guide and crammed for three days. By the fall, he was still employed and noticed changes in cocktail trends. Murray watched the Gimlet (gin and Rose's lime juice) change into a Vodka Gimlet and then into the shooter Kamikaze (Vodka Gimlet with triple sec). One cold autumn night, Murray was experimenting with cocktails and made a connection between a Cape Cod (vodka and cranberry with a lime garnish) and the Kamikaze. He poured a little cranberry juice in the Kamikaze then shook and strained it into a stemmed cocktail glass (Murray made it with Gordon's vodka, Leroux triple sec, Rose's Lime Juice, and Ocean Spray cranberry juice). A regular sitting at the bar asked Murray about the pink drink. At first, Murray didn't have an answer, but then smiled and said, "I just thought it needed a little color," making a joke about how he was hired. The regular said, "How cosmopolitan!" and the Cosmopolitan was born.

I have not been able to locate college classmates and coworkers Michael Hannah or John Peterson (yet), but in 2017 I was able to speak with other friends, Greg Harris and Steve Knapp, who had visited Murray at the Cork 'n Cleaver. Fun fact: Murray, Harris, and Knapp were high school classmates with Richard Dean Anderson, better known as MacGyver. I talked to Harris (born in 1950), and he confirmed that he and his wife Patty did indeed visit Murray at the Cork 'n Cleaver, but admitted he's never been a "mixed drink person" and does not remember the Cosmopolitan. He said he would ask his wife if she remembers and get back with me. I never heard back. It took some time to connect with Steve Knapp (born in 1950) as he lives in an off-grid cabin without a car, phone, or internet six months out of the year. Murray told me that when Knapp was in high school, he rode his bicycle from St. Paul to Vancouver, British Columbia and that he still rides hundreds of miles every year. Anyway, I finally was able to speak with Knapp over the phone, and he was full of energy. He remembered Murray's Cosmopolitan, remembers visiting Cork 'n Cleaver with Harris, told me about a farewell John Denver concert he worked before Denver moved to Colorado, and some other bars he tended bar at Butler Square in Minneapolis, Minnesota. Knapp even suggested that I contact bar schools to see what year the Cosmopolitan first entered into their curriculum. I contacted Ricky Richard, the owner of Crescent Bartender School founded in 1983 (crescent.edu), and he researched for me. He discovered that the Cosmopolitan recipe was in his curriculum around 1990.

In 1977, Murray moved to Washington, DC to take a position as a congressional intern. While traveling to visit friends, Murray always ordered a Cosmopolitan explaining to each bartender that it was a Kamikaze with cranberry juice served up in a cocktail glass. He ordered the cocktail everywhere he traveled including Boston, Manhattan, Atlanta, Miami, airport bars, and every bar he visited up and down the East Coast.

In 1979, Murray gave up politics and moved to San Francisco to study psychology at San Francisco State University. While in school he worked as a waiter at Enzo's restaurant in the Embarcadero Center then at Kimball's—not once pushing the Cosmopolitan. But all that changed in 1981 when he handed his 30th resume of the day to co-owner, Tom Clendening, at a New Orleans cuisine restaurant called the Elite Café (2049 Fillmore Street). Murray accepted a waiter position because even in this day and time you still did not see black bartenders. Murray recommended the Cosmopolitan cocktail to his customers, and with time it became famous with the locals. The first bartender Murray taught to make the Cosmo was Michael Brennan. I spoke with Brennan (born in 1952) over the phone in 2017, and he remembered Murray, other coworkers, and remembered making many Cosmopolitans. Today he is a famous San Francisco artist (michaelbrennanart.com). Brennan has designed many spaces, restaurants, and bars in San Francisco and you can check out his latest unconventional design work at the Curio Bar that opened June of 2018 (775 Valencia Street).

I also spoke with co-worker and waiter Hugh Tennent. During my research on Tennent, I found a small September 10, 1982 article in *The Honolulu Advisor Hawaii* newspaper that read "Honolulu adwoman Lynn Cook was dining at the Elite Café in San Francisco, and her waiter was Hugh Tennant, [sic] grandson of artist Madge Tennant [sic]". Hugh's grandmother Madeline "Madge" Grace Cook Tennent (1889–1972) was considered the most important individual contributor to Hawaiian art in the 20th century. I found Tennent via his sister, Madge Walls, who is a writer and lives in Oregon. It took quite a while to connect with Tennent because he does not have an email address, doesn't text, and rarely answers his cell phone. I left several messages then finally, one December day in 2017, he answered. Tennent (born in 1947) lives in Hilo, Hawaii. For fun, he drives a tour van, but his passions are golf and cars. Tennent was very outgoing and remembered Murray, Brennan, and Cosmopolitans at the Elite Café. He also recalled another bartender named Willie Karnofsky and talked about him for quite some time about how back in the day he was a model and golfer. In 2018, I called Karnofsky (born in 1956) via the phone number on his website at golfcoachwill.com. He remembered the Elite Café days, Murray, Brennan, and Tennent, but sadly did not remember serving the Cosmopolitan. But he said his focus at the time was golf.

In 1984, Murray often visited Union Street bars and always ordered the Cosmopolitan. Singer Boz Scaggs owned one bar he often visited called Blue Light Cafe. Also in 1984, he left the Elite Café to be part of the opening crew at the Café Royale (2050 Van Ness). But in 1985, Fog City Diner General Manager, Douglas "BIX" Biederbeck hired Murray as a bartender to help serve a celebrity clientele. Bill Higgins, Bill Upson, and Cindy Pawlcyn owned the Fog City Diner. Within five years it became a national hot spot due to Visa featuring it in a commercial—just search VISA Fog City Diner on YouTube. While at Fog City Diner, Murray created his first Cosmo spin-off by switching out the vodka for Mt. Gay Barbados Rum and called it a Barbados Cosmopolitan. It became an instant hit in the gay community. By 1988 Douglas "BIX" Biederbeck went on to be a true San Francisco restaurateur. He opened his first restaurant, BIX (56 Gold Street), which is a swanky jazz bar that just celebrated its 30th year and still employs two original white-jacketed barmen, Bradley Avey and Bruce Minkiewicz. Biederbeck became part of the Real Restaurant Group and opened many more San Francisco restaurants. In 2008, he released a book called *Bixology*. On page 11, he writes, "We were the first West Coast restaurant to re-spark the current Martini boom. It's a little hard to imagine that, only twenty years ago, the white-wine spritzer, gin and tonic, and occasional sweet drink were the calls of choice. The Cosmopolitan had only recently been invented, and there were about six vodkas known to man." I contacted Biederbeck via the BIX website (bixrestaurant.com), and to my surprise, he called me at 5 PM central time on November 22, 2017. He remembered hiring Murray at Fog City Diner and even put the Barbados Cosmopolitan on his BIX menu. He said, "It was a good drink." We chitchatted about how I lived in New Orleans and how BIX was a jazz bar. He ended our conversation by suggesting that I contact the Fog City Diner owner and chef at the time, Cindy Pawlcyna—a pioneer in the development of wine country cuisine. At Fog City Diner, she was pairing cheeseburgers with champagne. Today she has four cookbooks, and one is a James Beard Award winner. She has also been nominated twice for the James Beard Foundation award for Best Chef in California. I was able to contact Pawlcyn via her website cindypawlcyn.com. Like Murray, she grew up in the Minneapolis area and made her way to San Francisco in 1979. Her email said that, of course, she remembers the Cosmopolitan at Fog City Diner. It was one of her favorite cocktails, and it was very popular among the customers. She said that the waiters referred to it as a "girl drink."

Neal Murray in 2017. © *Neal Murray*

In 1986, Murray was given a VIP card by a Fog City Diner customer to the famous Limelight nightclub in New York City (20th Street and Sixth Avenue). So, he and friend Dana Williams flew to the Big Apple to use the card. Sure enough, the card got them to the front of the line, and they walked in immediately. And of course, Murray ordered a Cosmopolitan explaining to the bartender how to make it. Murray said he also visited Area (157 Hudson Street), and Milk Bar (2 Seventh Avenue South), each time ordering a Cosmopolitan. Would this be the first time the Cosmopolitan was ordered in New York City?

In 1989, Julie Ring from Julie's Supper Club (1123 Folsom Street) hired Murray to become her head bartender and part owner of Miss Pearl's Jam House (601 Eddy Street in the Phoenix Hotel). Murray said that Ring didn't realize Murray had a large following around San Francisco with his Cosmopolitans. He introduced another new Cosmo twist called the Cactus Cosmo made with aloe Vera juice and tequila.

Murray traveled a lot throughout his life, and he always ordered a Cosmopolitan at every bar he visited. He went on to work at many San Francisco restaurants as a consultant and general manager, and in 2016 he retired. Murray now enjoys traveling and writing about restaurants through his website chasingcuisine.com. In April of 2018, he visited me at the Bourbon "O" Bar in New Orleans.

JOHN CAINE • PROVINCETOWN, MASSACHUSETTS, CLEVELAND AND CINCINNATI, OHIO, AND SAN FRANCISCO, CALIFORNIA

When you google the Cosmopolitan cocktail, the name John Caine always comes up in association with Provincetown, Ohio, and San Francisco. I was able to locate Caine in November of 2017 in San Francisco where he has lived with his wife since 1987. All of the Cosmopolitan related internet articles I read on Caine gave me the impression that he was quite boisterous and energetic. So, his first email reply to me on November 27, 2017 did not surprise me when it said, "Hey Cheryl, Good to hear from you and yes I am still quite vain in this ego-based business of cocktail culture and love talking about myself...still!" His second email reply said, "Let's be clear. I did not invent the Cosmo."

Caine (born in 1959) first heard of the Cosmopolitan cocktail around 1984 when he worked at The Rusty Scupper in Cleveland, Ohio (corner of 14th and Euclid Streets). He said, "My gay coworkers went on pilgrimages to gay capitals such as P-town (Provincetown). I'd be working with them when each one recounted 'magic nights' celebrating freedom of expression all along talking about this drink—The Cosmo."

When The Rusty Scupper closed in 1984, Caine moved to Cincinnati, Ohio for his 8th year of undergraduate school. Caine was one of those people who loved college. He said it was easier than real life. Caine took a bartender job at The Diner (1203 Sycamore Street) and worked there for three years. It's where he met his future wife, Sarah as well. Just the way he heard about the Cosmopolitan in Cleveland, so was true in Cincinnati.

In 1987, the couple decided to move to where restaurant service is more of a career—San Francisco. Caine worked a few places in the city, but then finally found himself working for Julie Ring at Julie's Supper Club (1123 Folsom Street). Caine said Julie's was a great supper club where Julie layered in Frank Sinatra and James Brown music. Later into the night, Caine changed the music to hip cocktail lounge mixes. He said bar top dancing was the norm. Caine taught the staff how to make a Cosmopolitan and Julie would introduce Caine as the inventor of the cocktail. Caine did not tell me that he denied it, he just said, "I had to explain that I was merrily along for the ride with a good go-to cocktail. Julie's sold a lot of Martinis, so it was a perfect environment for the Cosmopolitan." I believe there's a connection here with how Anthony Dias Blue came to write the Cosmopolitan recipe from Julie's Supper Club in the first known book to mention the Cosmopolitan in *The Complete Book of Mixed Drinks* in 1993.

Caine has opened many restaurants and bars in San Francisco and currently owns two: ATwater Tavern (295 Terry A Francois Blvd) and HIDive Restaurant (28 Pier). Caine lists a Cosmopolitan on his Atwater Tavern menu. You can view it at atwatertavern.com. It's the very first cocktail on the menu: John Caine's Famous Cosmopolitan by John Caine. It says, "A popular choice from the fern bars of Cleveland; this original recipe was brought to San Francisco by John when he moved to the city in 1987. Made with Absolut, cranberry, and lime." (Yes, the orange liqueur is not listed.)

As for Provincetown, I have contacted fifteen people from the 1980s who lived and partied in P-town, and only three have returned my emails (one owned a bar). All three contacts do not remember a cocktail called Cosmopolitan during that time. So, this leads me to believe that since the Cosmopolitan was first introduced to San Francisco in 1981 and not introduced to New York City or Miami yet, that Caine's Ohio gay coworkers were visiting San Francisco and not Provincetown. I have also tried to contact Julie Ring, but no such luck yet.

Patrick "Paddy" Mitten • San Francisco, California and New York, New York

I believe that Patrick "Paddy" Mitten is the bartender who brought the Cosmopolitan from San Francisco to New York City in October of 1987.

Mitten was born in Coventry, England in 1965. He attended the Royal Ballet School in London then in 1985 went to work for the San Francisco Ballet for a year. When his Visa expired, Mitten took a bartender position that paid "under the table" at the Patio Café (531 Castro Street). It was here that he first learned of the Cosmopolitan cocktail. Mitten distinctly remembers his manager, Alan Mary Kay, walking in one day saying, "I just tried a new cocktail, and it's pink! It's called a Cosmopolitan. It's a Kamikaze with cranberry, but served as a Martini." Mitten said that Kay was very colorful and loved the color pink, which is why he loved the Cosmo. Both Mitten and I have tried to locate Kay, but no such luck yet.

By 1987, all of Mitten's friends, including his partner, had died of AIDS, so he made a fresh start and moved to New York City on the weekend of September 27 for the closing of the famous Paradise Garage nightclub (84 King Street). In October, he took a bartender position in the East Village at the Life Café (343 E 10th St B). I emailed the then owner Kathleen "Kathy" Life in November of 2017 to see if she remembered Mitten working for her in the late 1980s. She said, "Yes, I do remember him. He was charming. A very nice, pleasant young man and a very good employee." By the way, the Life Café became famous in 2005 when it was a film location for the famous table walking scene in the musical drama film adapted from the Pulitzer and Tony Award-winning musical, *Rent*.

I learned of Mitten through communicating with Melissa Huffsmith, a Life Café co-worker. Huffsmith is the girl who Toby Cecchini wrote about in his book who first told him about a San Francisco cocktail called the Cosmopolitan, but more on that later.

Mitten adored Huffsmith. He said she was intelligent, funny, and sexy. Mitten also told me of another co-worker named Peter Pavia. I emailed Kathy Life again and asked if she remembered Pavia, and she said, "Yes, I remember Pete very well. I can hear his distinct voice. He worked for me for quite a long time. He was smart, interesting, had a good sense of humor, a great employee, and confident behind the bar. I enjoyed his good nature when on duty. I believe he was a writer, when not tending bar."

So, Mitten taught Pavia, Huffsmith, and the entire staff how to make the San Francisco pink Martini called a Cosmopolitan. They sold them to customers in Martini glasses, but the staff drank them on the rocks in to-go cups. Mitten said he served a Cosmo to Madonna and he even served one to Sarah Jessica Parker when they were filming the pilot of *Sex and the City*.

Mitten is still tending bar today. He lives in the seaside town of Brighton, England and works at the historic Grand Hotel (grandbrighton.co.uk).

MELISSA HUFFSMITH-ROTH, PETER PAVIA, TOBY CECCHINI, PAUL BACSIK, DALE DEGROFF, AND CANDACE BUSHNELL • NEW YORK, NEW YORK

MELISSA HUFFSMITH-ROTH

Finding Melissa was a vital piece of the New York City Cosmopolitan puzzle because she is the co-worker who Toby Cecchini mentions in his 2003 book *Cosmopolitan: A Bartender's Life* who first told him about the San Francisco Cosmopolitan.

I received a couple of friendly email replies from Huffsmith in November and December in 2017. I also emailed back in June of 2008 to verify a few dates. She began her Cosmopolitan story with "The real Cosmo story:" She said that she first learned of the Cosmopolitan from Life Café co-worker, Patrick "Paddy" Mitten. She said Mitten learned to make the Cosmopolitan in San Francisco and the recipe was a Kamikaze with a little cranberry juice. She said, "We used to make them in big milkshake to-go cups". After speaking with two coworkers (Mitten and Pavia), I now know that she meant the "staff" drank Cosmos on the rocks in go cups.

Huffsmith left the Life Café to take a bartender position at The Odeon in April of 1989. She says that she remembers the exact month because she had a series of "April" jobs; she started The Odeon April of 1989, left The Odeon five years later in April for a bartender position at Lucky Strike (59 Grand Street), and then left Lucky Strike in April.

When Huffsmith started working at The Odeon, her manager was Paul Bacsik. One night Bacsik was making her a shift drink and Huffsmith requested a Cosmopolitan. Bacsik didn't know what it was, so Huffsmith told him how to make it. She explained that it was vodka, triple sec, and Rose's lime with a splash of cranberry juice. When Bacsik asked her what kind of vodka to use, she felt experimental (because at Life Café they did not have upgraded brands), so she decided to try Absolut Citron since it was new, Cointreau, fresh lime juice, and cranberry juice. She said it was yummy. Huffsmith went on to say that the fresh lime juice gave the drink a beautiful, refreshing cloudy light pink lemonade look and all the bartenders started making them for the regulars.

I asked Huffsmith if she remembers serving any celebrities and she said, "I served everyone. Literally everyone." She particularly remembered designer Gordon Henderson being one of the biggest preachers of the word of the Cosmo because he loved the cocktail and made everybody he brought into The Odeon try one. She concluded with, "Pretty soon we started getting calls from other bars about the recipe. It became a thing. Other people have different recollections, but that's the real story. Fun, right? Let me know if you have any more questions."

In the second email, I asked Huffsmith if she remembered working with a co-worker named Toby Cecchini and she said, "Yep! I know he wrote a book and claims ownership of the Cosmo recipe. I haven't read the book, but if there is a Melissa in there, then it's me". She also mentioned in another email that Cecchini was a waiter when she started working at The Odeon in April of 1989. Huffsmith is who told me about Patrick "Paddy" Mitten who then told me about Peter Pavia.

Huffsmith is from Boxford, Massachusetts and currently lives in Astoria, New York. She is a New York City-based editor, photographer, and musician. You can view her website at mhredit.com and Instagram at melissahroth.

PETER PAVIA

Peter Pavia and Melissa Huffsmith started working at Life Café around the same time in January 1988—the same time that Patrick "Paddy" Mitten introduced them to the Cosmopolitan. One of his first sentences to me was, "Yes, Patrick 'Paddy' Mitten was without a doubt the man who brought the Cosmopolitan to New York City." Pavia talked about how he drank a "raspy little concoction" called the Kamikaze in bars from 1975-

1980, and the Cosmopolitan was essentially a pink Kamikaze with the only modification being a dash of cranberry juice. He said, "And Patrick showed me how to make it."

I asked Pavia if he ever made them in go cups. Pavia said, "The bartenders at Life Café certainly made drinks to-go in large paper cups, although this would be illegal in New York City. There were two categories of liquor licenses in the State of New York: on-premises and off-premises. You could not consume drinks at an off-premises establishment such as a liquor store and conversely, aren't supposed to buy liquor to take out from a restaurant or bar".

As for Huffsmith, he said that Life Café was a hangout for East Village locals and when Huffsmith went to The Odeon she brought the drink much higher visibility because that bar attracted a much more urbane and moneyed international crowd and the surge in the drink's popularity was exponential. Now of course, as bartenders will do, modifications were made, and the biggest shift was with the syrupy Rose's lime with fresh lime juice, and as a nascent cocktail culture took hold, the ingredients were of a higher quality. He continues by saying, "It has been well said that success has a thousand fathers while failure is an orphan, and a number of players who were around at the time, claimed authorship of the Cosmopolitan."

After Life Café, from 1991-1992 Pavia worked as a fill-in bartender at a Soho bar called Kin Khao (171 Spring Street) that was managed by Toby Cecchini (Cecchini worked at The Odeon before that). I texted Cecchini, but he said he did not remember Pavia. Anyway, Pavia said the overwhelming number-one popular drink at Kin Khao was the Cosmopolitan.

From 1994-1996, Pavia worked at another Soho bar called Match (160 Mercer Street) and was making many Cosmos with some of them quaffed by none other than Candace Bushnell herself. Bushnell wrote the *Sex and the City* column for the New York Observer between 1994-1996, which soon lead to the hit HBO show. Pavia's last shift was at the Uptown Match at 29 East 65th Street. On that night he met his lovely wife.

Pavia is the author of *Dutch Uncle*, *The Cuba Project*, and co-author of *The Other Hollywood: The Uncensored Oral History of the Porn Film Industry*. His work has appeared in many publications including *the New York Times*, *New York Post*, *GQ*, *Detour*, and *Gear*. He lives in New York with his wife and daughter.

Toby Cecchini

Toby Cecchini (cha-KEE-nee) is a first-generation American who grew up in Madison, Wisconsin. In 1951, his dad emigrated from Florence, Italy to Madison and was an artist and great cook. He allowed his children to drink watered down wine at the dinner table, and had a unique way to make a pitcher of gin and tonics.

Cecchini documented his twenties and thirties in his 2003 memoir *Cosmopolitan: A Bartender's Life*. In the book, he talks about waiting tables to put himself through college in Madison, then in his junior year he signed up for a France college program where he learned a lot about wine. Cecchini made his way to New York City by following a girl he had met in Paris, but in his words, it "blew apart." He said one afternoon in 1987, he recognized The Odeon neon sign from the 1984 Jay McInerney novel's cover *Big Lights, Big City* and decided to take a waiter position long enough to make money to return to France. He writes, "I had no idea I would leave the Odeon, four years later, a wholly changed man."

While reading Cecchini's book, I enjoyed learning new words—with each digital page turn, I clicked words to discover their meaning. I meant to ask him for excerpt permission, but I ran out of time to meet a contracted deadline. You can read an excerpt from the first chapter of his book at nytimes.com/2003/10/19/books/chapters/cosmopolitan.html. Cecchini's Cosmopolitan story is a few pages long and begins with the sentence, "I did not invent the Cosmopolitan." You can read it on Google Books or go the Amazon route. The book has three different covers now; the burgundy one is the original. I feel the book gives the impression that Cecchini learned about the Cosmopolitan in 1987 from a girl named Melissa. However, when I spoke with Cecchini, he said it was 1988. That's fine, everyone messes up a year or two. But Melissa (and others) said she didn't start working at The Odeon until 1989 and Cecchini was still a waiter at that time. Like I said in the beginning, I'm just reporting the research.

The story in Cecchini's book says one night Melissa told him about a drink some girl from San Francisco made for her at Life Café, where Melissa had worked before. The drink was made with vodka, Rose's lime, and grenadine and was called a Cosmopolitan. He says they both decided it could be better by using Absolut Citron, Cointreau, fresh lime juice and enough cranberry juice "to give it a demure pink blush." They decided to shake it extra hard to make it frothy and opaque, then garnished it with a lemon twist. It was just another drink of many they made up. The drink eventually became a private staff drink. Soon customers began ordering them, and they wondered how they learned about their staff drink. They soon were making a couple hundred a night and even tried to push the price up to eight dollars to help slow down the demand, but people kept ordering them.

Ms. Franky Marshall was so lovely to connect me with Cecchini. I emailed him in December of 2016, and we spoke on the phone in early January 2017. Throughout the year I would bug him with questions via text. He was always very kind. If I annoyed him with questions, I would have never known. Cecchini remembers serving Cosmopolitans to Madonna and Sandra Bernhard several times. He recalls Madonna beckoning him to make her one. He said she called him "boyfriend." In 1999, a friend (probably female) excitedly told Cecchini that his cocktail was on the hit HBO show *Sex and the City*. Cecchini was like, "What?" He had never seen the show, and I forgot to ask if he has ever sat down and watched it since. In 2005 or 2007 (he can't remember the exact year) he saw the Cosmopolitan on a bar menu in Warsaw, Poland, that credited him as the inventor—it was then he realized the impact and popularity of the Cosmopolitan. Through the years, bartenders ridiculed him for making "that stupid drink"—a drink that they had to make a hundred times a night for women across America. There were probably plenty of bartenders he never heard from who would have liked to thank him for filling up their tip jars.

Cecchini worked at The Odeon for four heyday years then went on to manage the Soho bar Kin Khao (171 Spring Street) for almost seven years before he became co-owner with Gavin Brown of Passerby in Chelsea (436 West 15th Street) for nearly ten years. In 2013, he opened the Long Island Bar in Brooklyn (110 Atlantic Avenue) with Joel Tompkins. Cecchini writes for *Food and Wine*, *GQ*, *New York Times*, and *Saveur*.

Paul Bacsik

I first learned of Paul Bacsik (born March 3, 1954) from Melissa Huffsmith. I emailed him on November 22, 2017, and heard back from him the same day, then we spoke over the phone after Thanksgiving. I loved listening to his stories. Bacsik was hired at The Odeon as a bartender in 1984. Then, in 1986, he was promoted to bar manager and wine director while also picking up three bartender night shifts a week. Bacsik worked for The Odeon for fourteen years until 1998. He says he and Toby Cecchini are still good friends and even sells wine to his Brooklyn bar. When Cecchini was a waiter, Bacsik asked permission to make him into a bartender. Ownership agreed and Cecchini was all for it. Bacsik asked about Melissa and what was she doing then told me that she was his absolute favorite person to tend bar with.

Bacsik remembered a lot of things: the Cosmopolitan, celebrity stories, and Gary Farmer who was the most charismatic bartender he ever saw—he was so charming people didn't mind waiting to be served by him. In 1984, Farmer left for a position at another celebrity-fueled restaurant, Indochine (430 Lafayette Street) then in 1985 moved to Miami Beach to open a bar called The Strand. In March of 1989 Farmer played a part in the Miami Beach Cosmopolitan—which was totally independent of the Cosmopolitan at The Odeon (more on Farmer in the Miami section of the Cosmo story).

Bacsik is from Rahway, New Jersey, attended college at The University of Connecticut, and today lives in New York, New York. He is the co-owner of Little Wine Company (littlewinecompany.com).

Dale "King Cocktail" DeGroff

I write about Dale "King Cocktail" DeGroff in Chapter 21 Behind the Bar: The Fifteen Most Influential American Bartenders, so I will keep this strictly Cosmopolitan related.

There is a November 2015 YouTube video with DeGroff talking about what he knew of the Cosmopolitan. Just search "Dale DeGroff Cosmopolitan." In the video DeGroff says he first drank a Cosmopolitan at the Fog City Diner in San Francisco, came back home to the Rainbow Room, and made an improved version with quality ingredients. Oh, and of course, he garnished it with his signature flamed orange peel that he learned from Beverly Hills bartender Pepe Ruiz who first did it in 1970 when creating a cocktail called The Flame of Love for Dean Martin. DeGroff goes on to say that he then learned that a bartender named Toby Cecchini was already making an improved version of the Cosmopolitan at The Odeon. Next, the Associated Press at the Rainbow Room Sony Grammy party took a photo of Madonna drinking DeGroff's Cosmopolitan then put it out on the wire with the caption, "Madonna drinking the Cosmopolitan at the world-famous Rainbow Room." This led to DeGroff getting hired by Absolut and Ocean Spray which gave quite a boost to DeGroff's career.

In January of 2017, DeGroff emailed me a blurb for this book. I thanked him, then told him I was doing Cosmopolitan research and requested some dates. 1. what year did you visit Fog City Diner? And 2. what year was the Grammy party? I had calculated guesses, but I like to be thorough and ask the source. He told me that he was on his Whiskey, Gamblers, and Flying Horses Tour, but would ask some friends if they can remember. I bugged him with fifteen more emails until June 6, 2018, but ran out of time. So, the best I can guess is that DeGroff visited Fog City Diner in 1990 or 1991 because in the video he says after he retooled the Cosmopolitan, he learned that someone named Toby Cecchini at The Odeon was making a similar Cosmopolitan. Cecchini wrote in his book that he worked at The Odeon from 1987-1991, and further research has him tending bar in late1989-1991.

If I could only find the Madonna photo drinking DeGroff's Cosmopolitan with the headline he gave to the Associated Press who put it out on the worldwide wire, I would then know the exact year. But I couldn't find it. So, there are three things from DeGroff's video I needed to match up: The year the Grammys left Los Angeles for New York City for the first time in a long time, the years the Grammy's were held in New York City at Radio City Music Hall, and the years Sony hosted a Grammy party was at the Rainbow Room. Well, the longest stretch that the Grammy's were in Los Angeles was from 1982-1987. The awards show then went to New York City's Radio City Music Hall in 1988, , but I have not been able to find any information for 1988. The years that the Grammy's were held in New York City at Radio City Music Hall are 1991, 1992, 1994, and 1998, but, 1998 is probably out because DeGroff said Frank Sinatra was at the party and Sinatra spent time in the hospital the first part of 1998, then died in May. This leaves one more thing to narrow it down; the Sony Grammy Party at the Rainbow Room. In 1991, CBS held their Grammy party at the Rainbow Room (there are ten pictures on Getty Images). In 1992, a *New York Times* article documented a Polygram party at the Rainbow Room. In 1994, Sony held their party at The Metropolitan Museum of Art not the Rainbow Room, however, the book *U2: A Diary* by Matt McGee documents the Grammy Legend Award being presented to Frank Sinatra by Bono at the Grammys, then goes on to mention a "post-show party" at the Rainbow Room. 1994 is also the year DeGroff's Cosmo recipe made it into a newspaper, but not until November. With all of that information, I want to say the year was 1994—but— there's one more year to consider—1997. The Grammy ceremonies were at Madison Square Garden, not Radio City Music Hall. In interviews, DeGroff has said that he added the Cosmopolitan to the Rainbow Room menu in 1996 then after, the Madonna photo happened. I did find a 1997 post Polygram Grammy party at the Rainbow Room in the June-July issue of Vibe magazine, but it just showed and image of singer Seal. DeGroff emailed me and said he is trying to contact his Associated Press friends to find the Madonna photo but it's difficult because 1997-1998 was the time they were transferring everything to digital. So, basically, I'm back to square one of searching for the Madonna photo.

CANDACE BUSHNELL

I was shocked to discover, two days after sending an email on November 7, 2017, that the famous Candace Bushnell has actually responded. Bushnell is an American journalist, author, and television producer. Between 1994-1996 Bushnell wrote the *Sex in the City* column for *the New York Observer*. The column was about her and her friends dating in the city. Instead of using her own name, she created an alter-ego with the same initials as hers—Carrie Bradshaw. While writing the column, she also freelanced at *Vogue* and one assignment was to write about Darren Star who had created *Beverly Hills 90210* and *Melrose Place* with Aaron Spelling. Well, soon after the two became friends they hung out together with the real-life Mr. Big, Ron Galotti (the publisher of *Vogue* at the time) and author and screenwriter Bret Easton Ellis. In 1996, her columns were collected in book form with a title of the same name. This all lead to the HBO show created by Darren Star that ran from 1998-2004, which we all know was the show that rocketed the Cosmopolitan cocktail around the world.

I asked Bushnell if she remembered drinking Cosmopolitans and she wrote, "Hi Cheryl Charming—Thanks for writing to me. Back in the late eighties/early nineties 'designer' spirit brands like Absolut were making a big push for the club crowd. Bret Easton Ellis and I were going out every night and one night we started drinking them. We'd always drank vodkas with cranberry juice and the Cosmo, with the fresh lime juice, seemed like a good alternative. Once we had our first Cosmo, we couldn't stop drinking them. And I pretty much made everyone else drink them too. When Darren and I first met, in 1995, I took him out on the town and introduced him to the Cosmo. I think I may have even posed for photographs with a Cosmo. I suppose it was my signature drink, and because Carrie was my alter-ego, she naturally had to drink them as well! Hope this helps. Best, Candace." I wrote her back of course with a few more questions, but never heard back. I was totally satisfied with the one email.

CHERYL COOK, GARY FARMER, AND BOB DEAN • MIAMI BEACH, FLORIDA

Cheryl Cook

In 1999—my second year of having an email address—I began to receive emails asking if I was "Cheryl from Florida who created the Cosmopolitan." What felt like thousands of emails later, Cheryl Cook and I finally became Facebook friends on July 20, 2015. Over a year later I began to ask her questions about her Cosmopolitan story.

I read Gary Regan's Cosmopolitan article where Cook told him that she created the Cosmo in 1985; this seemed odd to me because I remember tending bar on a Caribbean cruise ship in 1988 when Absolut Citron was introduced. Cook told me that 1985 was a wild guess when talking with Regan because it was so long ago and she really did not remember. I later learned that The Strand opened in 1985, so that may have been a past date that was prominent in Cook's memory. While listening to Cook's story through my iPhone earbuds with pen and paper in hand, she mentioned that she named the drink after a *Cosmopolitan* magazine with a pink cover that the hostess was showing everyone who walked in the door. There was an article on The Strand and the hostess called "The Maître d' is a Ms." Cook continued with her story, but my head lit up like a 1000-watt lightbulb. I interrupted, "Wait! Cheryl, do you have the magazine?" She said no. I told Cook that all we have to do is find that magazine and we will know the exact month and year that you made your Cosmopolitan. I started researching and soon learned that the magazine put out one pink cover each year, so I went to eBay and bought five of them from 1987-1992. The winner was the March issue of 1989. After snapping photos of the article pages, I mailed Cook the copy as a gift.

In 1983, with a theater degree, Cook began working as a production manager for a performing arts high school program which became New World School of the Arts in Miami. In 1987, Cook was hired by a professional theater company called New World Theatre. She received her Equity card. The Strand (671 Washington Avenue) was home to the New World Theatre Company, but there's not a lot of money in the theater, so with three years of bartending experience under her belt, she took a position behind the bar to pay her bills, but her ultimate goal in life was to keep working in the theater in some shape or form.

The Strand opened in December of 1985 and was co-owned and ran by Gary Farmer (formally of Indochine and The Odeon in NYC). The restaurant and bar provided Miami's first hang that welcomed all sexual orientations and attracted a star-studded clientele. In March of 1989, a couple of things coincided: The Strand was mentioned in a *Cosmopolitan* magazine and Cook was given a new product to create a cocktail—Absolut Citron. Cook says her liquor rep asked her to create a cocktail with the new vodka, so she decided to make the cocktail pink to match the cover of the magazine—in Cook's words—"oh so pretty in pink" (a popular phrase at the time from the 1986 film *Pretty in Pink*). The ingredients were a Kamikaze with a splash of cranberry juice. She stirred it in a mixing glass (16-ounce pint glass), then strained it into a conical-shaped cocktail glass (google Libby cocktail glass 8882 to see the glass) because she said flavored Martinis were popular among women and she wanted to use that type of glass She garnished the drink with an old-school lemon twist (the short kind that was often precut vertically around the circumference of a lemon), then offered it as a taste test to friend and co-worker Christine "Crispy" Soloperto. She told Cook it was good, then asked what she was going to name it. They looked over at the magazine, giggled, then said, "Cosmopolitan!" I tried to contact Soloperto, but was not able to get ahold of her. She is a celebrity in South Beach and considered royalty. You can find many Google images and even a YouTube video of her if interested.

Soloperto was the first person to taste the Cosmopolitan and Bob Dean was the second. Dean worked as a bartender one block away at the Lasso Cocktail Bar. More on Dean later. Cook said within hours, everyone in the room was drinking them. When the Absolut Citron ran out, she remembers having to quickly make impromptu lemon vodka by squeezing lemons into Absolut vodka bottles. She made thousands of Cosmopolitans, and soon they became popular in other bars on the strip. Cook says, "Eight mixing glasses had to be lined up and ready for orders of Cosmopolitans at all times."

Cook served many celebrities and had many stories. She vividly remembers serving Madonna and Sandra Bernhard—many times. When the Cosmopolitan went what today we would call "viral" from *Sex and the City*, Cook just assumed that the show's costume designers, Patricia Field and Rebecca Weinburg were responsible for introducing the cocktail to the writers because Field and Weinburg were regulars of hers.

Cook worked at The Strand until it closed, then went down the street to tend bar for Borocco Restaurant, serving even more Cosmopolitans. She became known as "The Martini Queen of South Beach." Sometime during the early 1990s, Italian *Vogue* took photos of her Cosmopolitan, so somewhere out there is a photo of Cook's Cosmopolitan in an Italian *Vogue* magazine.

In 2011, Jake Burger from Absolut vodka was scheduled for a Cosmopolitan video interview with Dale DeGroff, but he had to cancel, so Burger contacted Cook to set up an interview in Miami. Cook had just lost her mother, so the day was dark and gloomy for her and she honestly does not remember much about it. She never heard anything afterwards.

On November 30, 2012, Gary Regan posted an article on his website titled "The Birth of the Cosmopolitan." You can read it for yourself at gazregan.com/the-birth-of-the-cosmopolitan. Regan had been searching for Cook since the mid-1990s and finally received an email from Cook on September 25, 2005, at 11:24 Eastern Standard Time.

Local Miami Beach historian Jeff Donnelly wrote a proposal to the city for its 100th birthday (celebrated in March of 2015) to honor Cheryl Cook for creating the Cosmopolitan. Cook's Cosmo celebration was to be held at City Hall, but then they learned that the crowd was going to be between 250-300 attendees, so they moved it to The Delano Hotel. Cook was presented a proclamation both at the hotel and City Hall. She was amazed to see all the old crowd from back in the day—faces she had not seen in over 25 years!

Cook has produced twenty-seven shows in Atlantic City, worked as an event planner, and was a semifinalist for Event Solutions Magazine's 2006 "Creative Director of the Year." Most currently, Cook taught for Diageo's "Learning for Life" program at Florida International University. Her students assisted the 2016 World Class Cocktail Competition that was held in Miami. Probably my favorite thing throughout my communication with Cook was all the retro photos she shared of her Cosmo and more.

Gary Farmer

Thursday, January 18, 2018, at 1:20 PM was a happy day for me; it ended my fourteen-month search for Gary Farmer. "Hello Miss Charming, Odd we haven't met. I visit New Orleans often and can usually be found drinking somewhere. Susan Brustman forwarded your email. I am happy to answer your questions via email, but please do not share my address. I have a vivid recollection of the day and circumstances that led Cheryl Cook to invent and name the Cosmo at my restaurant The Strand, and would be happy to share with you. Kind regards, Gary. Sent from my iPad."

Susan Brustman was one of many people I contacted on my search to find Farmer, but it only takes one! She first heard about him in 1978. This is documented in the 2015 book by Myrna Katz Frommer and Harvey Frommer *It Happened in Miami, the Magic City: An Oral History*. I also found more information about Farmer and The Strand in Steven Gaines 2009 book *Fool's Paradise: Players, Poseurs, and the Culture of Excess in South Beach*. Cheryl Cook told me there was a 1992 article in *New York Magazine* called "SoHo in the Sun" that mentioned The Strand and showed images of South Beach. This one can be found in Google Books. And you can read a December 18, 1987, article from the *Sun-Sentinel* by googling "Strand: A Place for People Watching in South Beach." I have more, but like I said in the beginning—fourteen months!

Farmer worked at The Odeon in New York City in the early 1980s. He told me that he took bartending very seriously. He said "I was a total cocktail geek, collecting books and recipes from the 1920s and 1930s; I even wrote a monthly cocktail column for *GQ*. In my previous suit-and-tie career, I had frequented the old classic cocktail bars—the original Monkey Bar, the Polo Bar at the Westbury, the Oak Bar, the Carlyle...sophistication and class. A long time ago." I checked on the *GQ* column and indeed found one from 1984, the same year he left The Odeon to manage Indochine.

Through the books that I mentioned, I learned that Farmer was tired of the rat race of New York City and wanted to return to California, but Brustman talked him in coming to South Beach to help spark the turnaround of the area. And that he did. After finding the perfect location, Farmer went through six layers of linoleum and two of carpet to find the original terrazzo floor. Yes, the flower arrangements were exotic, and tables were blanketed in thick white linen, but the lighting was indirect and flattering, so everyone looked good, and mirrors were strategically placed so you could people-watch around corners because Farmer believes the most important product is people. He wanted a diverse clientele such as people in tuxedos sitting next to people in bathing suits. He did not want a cookie-cutter type of staff, so he hired artists, actors, athletes, and a mix of interesting people.

Farmer's and Cook's Cosmopolitan stories were an excellent front of the house/back of the house perspectives. Farmer told me that Absolut was the fashionable vodka of the time and its citron flavor had just been introduced. His salesman dropped off a free case on the very day they were hosting a group of female alumni (from Brown University, he thinks) with complimentary hors-d'oeuvres and a cash bar. Farmer said that Cook had come in early to set up, and he told her to come up with a "feature cocktail" using the Absolut Citron. He said, "Cheryl was a very serious gal and gave it serious thought." He went on to describe Cook's process; The Strand had popularized classic Martini glasses, so it had to be that glass and the color had to be pink because women like pink drinks. Cook fiddled around with the recipe until she was satisfied, and Farmer approved. Cook suggested the name Cosmopolitan because the hostess had been featured in a *Cosmopolitan* magazine story called "When the maître d' is a Ms." (he thinks, but close enough) with a full-page photo of the hostess, Natalie Thomas, opposite the title page. Thomas was very proud of the article and kept a copy of it, open to her picture, on the front desk. Cook thought naming the cocktail after the magazine would be a smart marketing choice. Farmer thought for sure there had to be a Cosmopolitan cocktail already in existence, but there was not one listed in either of the two cocktail books they kept behind the bar, so he gave Cook the green light. The alumni ladies, of course, loved it, and when the restaurant customers (mostly regulars) saw all those pink Martinis, they just had to have one too. Farmer said, "And that's how the Cosmopolitan cocktail was born. I was there. We never made a big deal about it, but they sold like crazy." Farmer ended his Cosmo story by saying, "Cheryl Cook's local celebrity actually came a few years later, when I sold The Strand, and she became Miami's most famous Martini maker at a cool bar called 821 on Lincoln Road. Her Martini nights were PACKED."

Farmer is very private, so I do not have any personal information to share.

Bob Dean

I learned of Bob Dean through Cheryl Cook. Dean's Cosmo connection is being the second person to taste Cook's Cosmopolitan. I was able to speak with him briefly in November of 2017. He was a hoot!

Dean remembered that day in March 1989 like it was yesterday. He said that he worked at the Lasso Lounge across the street from The Strand and Crispy Soloperto walked in at 5 p.m. and said, "Bob! Cheryl just invented a great cocktail called the Cosmopolitan." She told him the ingredients, he made two, (I'm guessing they clicked glasses), and they drank them.

Nashville, Tennessee is Dean's hometown. When he worked in South Beach, he was commuting from Dania Beach in Fort Lauderdale. He said the Lasso Lounge was supposed to be haunted and was also considered the best locals bar in South Beach at the time. Currently, Dean is living in Santa Monica, California and still tends bar! He is also a comic, actor, and has his own podcast show on iTunes called *The Bob Dean Show*. On August 6, 2017, he taped episode 25 "Machine Guns Bad, Cruise Ships and Cosmopolitans," in which he calls up his old friend in Miami, Cheryl Cook. The best place to start listening is 2:20.

FUN COSMO MEDIA FACTS

▸ **1993** On April 23, the first known book to mention the Cosmopolitan is *The Complete Book of Mixed Drinks* by Anthony Dias Blue.

▸ **1994** On November 16, the first known newspaper to publish a Cosmopolitan recipe was *The Central New Jersey Home News* (New Brunswick, New Jersey). Dale "King Cocktail" DeGroff contributed his recipe.

▸ **1998** On April 9, the first known Cosmopolitan cocktail seen and mentioned on a television show was *ER*. It was season 4 episode 17, and the writer was Linda Gase.

▸ **2002** On June 21, the first known film to show and mention a Cosmopolitan is *Juwanna Mann*.

▸ **2003** On June 10, the first known song to mention a Cosmopolitan is "Cosmopolitans" written and performed by Erin McKeown.

Moscow Mule—New York City or Los Angeles

The Moscow Mule was Smirnoff vodka's first cocktail introduced to America. As for the history, well, there are a lot of moving parts in the story and most are without documented proof.

There's a 1947 Polaroid camera bar-hopping picture-taking road trip (but no photos); a 1941 Russian immigrant named Sophie with 2,000 solid copper mugs (but no vintage mugs); a 1930s spirit company salesman named John from Connecticut selling Smirnoff vodka (this is true); a Cock 'n Bull Los Angeles celebrity bar and restaurant owner named Jack, with too much ginger beer in stock, who says he invented it in New York City; and Jack's head bartender, Wes, who said he was cleaning out the Los Angeles basement, found too much vodka and ginger beer in stock, and he invented it—whew!

Magazine ads in the 1950s and 1960s advertised the Moscow Mule to bring the drink to semi-success, but in 1962 when James Bond drank Smirnoff Vodka Martinis in the first James Bond film, *Dr. No*, well, that's when Smirnoff vodka and the shaken-not-stirred Martini spread like wildfire around the world.

The Moscow Mule had a resurrection around 2010, and variations of the drink could be found on almost cocktail menu by 2016.

More American Cocktails

Other cocktails / mixed drinks invented in America with little to no history include the Alabama Slammer, Appletini, Bushwhacker, Cape Cod, Chocolate Martini, Colorado Bulldog, Flaming Dr. Pepper, Fuzzy Navel, Harvey

Wallbanger, Jack Rose, Lynchburg Lemonade, Martini, Melon Ball, Mudslide, Pink Lady, Sex on the Beach, Tom and Jerry, and Washington Apple.

···
AROUND THE WORLD

BRAZIL

CAIPIRINHA

The Caipirinha (kye-purr-REEN-yuh) is Brazil's national drink. It's made with cachaça (kuh-SHA-suh), which is Brazilian rum. There are hundreds of brands of cachaça in Brazil.

There are several stories about its history, but a recently found 1856 Paraty document (near Rio de Janeiro) says, "Because [of the concern with cholera and water], by necessity we began mixing medium aguardiente with water, sugar and limes, because it was prohibited to drink straight water." Aguardiente is rum.

BELGIUM/BRUSSELS

BLACK RUSSIAN—HOTEL METROPOLE

It is believed that Hotel Metropole bartender Gustave Tops created the Black Russian in 1949 for American socialite Perle Mesta (U.S. Ambassador to Luxembourg). The Hotel Metropole, still in business today, is one of Brussels's most important historical landmarks.

BERMUDA

DARK 'N STORMY

The Dark 'n Stormy is the official cocktail of Bermuda, and the first thing you should know is that it's registered, which means you cannot legally make a Dark 'n Stormy with any rum other than Gosling's Black Seal rum. The company owns the trademark on the name, clothing, kits containing rum and ginger beer, bar services, and a premixed version of the drink.

There are other trademarked cocktails in the world, including New Orleans's Hand Grenade and Chef Paul Prudhomme's Cajun Martini. In 1936, the New York Supreme Court ruled that an authentic "Bacardi Cocktail" had to be made with Bacardi Rum.

The Dark 'n Stormy was created in the early 1900s and obtained an American trademark in 1991. Its origins come from the highly successful ginger beer factory that was run as a subsidiary to the Royal Naval Officers' Club in Bermuda. They soon discovered that a splash of the local black rum (Gosling's) was just what the ginger beer was missing. The name is said to have originated when an old salt (a teller of sea stories) observed that the drink was the "color of a cloud only a fool or dead man would sail under," which was probably followed by "Barman, I'll have another Dark 'n Stormy."

Englishman William Gosling and his son James set sail in 1806 aboard the *Mercury* carrying £10,000 of wine and spirits (that's almost $1 million in 2018 currency). They stopped over in Bermuda—not meaning to make Bermuda their destination—and decided to stay and set up shop. Soon they sent for more family members.

In 1824, Gosling brothers James and Ambrose opened a wine and spirits shop in Bermuda, and in 1857, they renamed it Gosling Brothers. It's assumed that one day they looked around at their stock and thought, "Hey! We spend all this time selling other people's alcohol, why don't we make our own to sell?" However, there was one problem—there was not enough land on Bermuda to grow crops. Therefore, they imported oak barrels of rum distillate from the Caribbean. James and Ambrose did a lot of experimenting with blending for a long time, and soon the distinctive black rum was ready to be sold.

Malcom Gosling, the current face of Gosling's Black Seal rum and great-great-great grandson of Ambrose Gosling in 2014. © *Gosling's Black Seal Rum*

They decided to sell it directly from the barrel, so customers could come into the shop and fill up their bottles with the "Old Rum." After World War I, James and Ambrose recycled champagne bottles from the British Officers' Mess, and used black sealing wax to seal the corks. Bars began to stock the rum and patrons would ask for the "black seal" rum. Later, a play on words and images gave birth to the little, barrel-juggling "Black Seal" bottle label.

Today, the company's face is Malcolm Gosling, who is the gregarious great-great-great-grandson of Ambrose Gosling. Malcolm is out spreading the Gosling's Rum gospel around the world. Maybe in his travels he will run into the other world-popular Gosling, who goes by the name of Ryan, and could put Gosling's Rum sales through the roof.

CUBA

CUBA LIBRE, DAIQUIRI, AND MOJITO

Cuba is famous for these three cocktails, and thanks to esteemed cocktail historians Anistatia Miller and Jared Brown, we have the most updated information on these cocktails from their 2012 book *Cuban Cocktails*.

"Cuba Libre" translates to "Free Cuba," and the cocktail is simply made with rum, cola, and a squeeze of lime. It is often said that Teddy Roosevelt and his Rough Riders invented it in 1898 during the Spanish-American War, but Coca-Cola did not make it to Cuba until 1902. What we do know is that a drink from 1872 named Cuba Libre was mentioned in the *New York Herald*; however, its ingredients consisted of honey and hot water. The next known publication of the Cuba Libre is in the 1928 book *When It's Cocktail Time in Cuba*, by Basil Woon, who wrote that it was available at the American Club in Havana. In 1935, the *New Yorker* published the exact recipe but with the name Carioca Cooler (Carioca was a brand of rum). The drink makes an appearance in many other publications up to 1979 that vary in glass types and sizes.

DAIQUIRI

Today's Daiquiri consists of three ingredients: rum, lime juice, and sugar. The most common story of its invention comes from a man named Cox, and it is said to have been named after the Cuban beach town Daiquiri.

It is pretty much agreed upon that the Daiquiri was an invention of sailors as an elixir to prevent and cure scurvy (a disease resulting from a lack of Vitamin C). For many years, it was confused with the Bacardi Cocktail, but a 1699 memoir by Captain William Dampier titled *A New Voyage Round the World* said: "Ships coming from some of the Caribbean Islands are always well stored with Rum, Sugar, and Lime-Juice to make Punch, to hearten their Men when they are at work getting and bringing aboard the Salt; and they commonly provide the more, in hopes to meet with Privateers, who resort hither in the aforesaid Months, purposely to keep a Christmas, as they call it, being sure to meet with liquor enough to be merry with, and are very liberal to those that treat them."

There are many versions of rum and sugar being mixed with lemon juice starting in 1734, but the first time a recipe mentions lime juice is in the 1914 book *Drinks by Jacques Straub*, which called it a Daiquiri Cocktail. Author Hugo R. Ensslin called it a Cuban Cocktail in 1916, and a 1934 Havana Club compliment card called it a Havana Club Special.

Restaurant critic G. Selmer Fougner (1885–1941) published the recipe under the name "Daiquiri" in 1935 and, one year later, *Sloppy Joe's Cocktails Manual* did the same. From then on it pretty much stayed the same with the exception of flavored spin-offs. The Frozen Daiquiri was first published in the 1976 and 1979 *Bacardi Party Book*.

Mojito

Much like the Cosmopolitan being a marriage between a Cape Cod and a Kamikaze made with lemon vodka, the Mojito is a marriage of a Daiquiri and a Rum Mint Julep. Today, the Mojito is made with five ingredients: rum, lime, sugar, mint, and fizzy water.

In a 1981 book by Fernando G. Campoamor, the author talks about a drink called the "Draque" (Spanish for dragon). This 1586 mixture of aguardiente de caña (rum), sugar, and Cuban hierbabuena (mint) appears to be named after Sir Francis Drake and given to him—and his sailors—as medicinal rations. These ingredient combinations appear in print again in 1753 and 1838.

The year 1910 was the first time that the word "mojito" made it into a cocktail recipe. It was at the La Concha Bar at the Hotel-Balneario in Havana, Cuba, when a bar attendant named Rogelio created a cocktail with rum, lemon juice, sugar, Angostura bitters, and soda water. As you probably noticed, if you leave out the bitters, then all that is missing is the mint and lime.

The drink went though many variations, but finally in 1935 Bar la Florida in Havana served a drink called Mojito Criollio that contained four ingredients of the Mojito we know today. The only difference is that it called for lemon instead of lime.

Finally, in Havana's Sloppy Joe's 1936 *Cocktails Manual*, we see a cocktail named Mojito made with rum, lime, sugar, mint, and soda water. Due to the Cuban Revolution in 1959, no one could visit Cuba. Sloppy Joe's closed in 1965 and reopened in 2013.

ENGLAND/LONDON

Pimm's Cup—Pimm's Oyster Bar

James Pimm (1798–1866) invented the Pimm's Cup in 1823. Not only did Pimm create the cocktail, he invented the gin-based spirit used in the cocktail as well.

Pimm was a farmer's son from Newnham, Kent, but was educated in Scotland. During his early twenties, he moved to London and sold fish. At age twenty-five he opened his first oyster bar across from Buckingham Palace. His Pimm's No. 1 tonic contains a secret mixture of herbs and liqueurs that was created to aid digestion.

Pimm began large-scale production in 1851 to keep up with sales to other bars, and then in 1859 it was sold commercially.

Pimm opened many more oyster bars, and then at age sixty-seven—one year before he died—he sold his businesses and the rights to his name.

Many New Orleans visitors think the Pimm's Cup was invented at the French Quarter restaurant and bar Napoleon House. The Napoleon House first became a restaurant in the 1940s, and it's not known how they became famous for the Pimm's Cup. One might guess that an Englishman had something to do with it. Today, the Pimm's Cup is the official drink of Wimbledon.

FRANCE

MIMOSA—PARIS

Part-Austrian and part-Jewish bartender Frank Meier is credited with inventing the Mimosa in 1923 at the Hotel Ritz Paris. His first name for the drink was Champagne Orange. Meier started working at the hotel in 1921 as the first head bartender in Café Parisian. Today, the bar is named Bar Hemingway. Meier published an art deco cocktail book in 1936 titled *The Artistry of Mixing Drinks*. The book contains only his favorite cocktail recipes.

You should know that England also invented a cocktail of the same ingredients (different portions) and named it the Buck's Fizz.

MEXICO

MARGARITA

The Margarita has three ingredients: tequila, triple sec (orange liqueur), and lime juice. We'll probably never know the true story of who invented Mexico's national drink—the Margarita. Truthfully, it's like playing a round of the TV game show of *To Tell the Truth*.

- Carlos "Danny" Herrera claimed he invented it in 1938 at his restaurant Rancho La Gloria (five miles south of Tijuana, Mexico) for Ziegfeld dancer Marjorie King.
- A bartender named Willie created it for Marguerite Hemery at the Dos Republicos in Matamoros, Tamaulipas, Mexico.
- Enrique Gutierrez said he created it in Tijuana, Mexico, for movie actor Rita Hayworth, whose birth name was Margarita Cansino.
- Bartender Don Carlos Orozco said he invented it at Hussong's Cantina in Ensenada, Mexico, in 1941 for a woman named Margarita.
- Francisco "Pancho" Morales said he invented it on July 4, 1942, at Tommy's Place Bar near the El Paso border when a woman asked for a Magnolia.
- An Acapulco bar owner named Margaret Sames said she invented it.

ITALY/VENICE

BELLINI—HARRY'S BAR

Bartender and owner of Harry's Bar, Giuseppe Cipriani (1900–1980), invented the Bellini in 1931 in Venice, Italy. Cipriani was born in Verona, Italy. Before becoming a bartender, Cipriani wanted to travel around and learn as much as he could. He worked in a watch factory, a pastry kitchen, and as a waiter in some very elegant upper-class hotels in France, Belgium, and Italy. The owner of the Hotel Europa told him that he should be a barman because he had the right tone with clients and knew many languages. This planted a seed within Cipriani and thus started his dream of opening an elegant bar where the customers did not have to walk through an intimidating grand entrance and lobby to get to the bar.

Enter Harry Pickering. Pickering was a young, wealthy American student who was traveling with his aunt so she could help Pickering stop drinking so much. They ended up getting in a fight, and the aunt left him with very little funds. Cipriani decided to loan Pickering 10,000 lira. Time passed and one day Pickering reappeared and gave Cipriani back his money with an interest payment of 30,000 lira (totaling around $200,000 in 2017 dollars). So, Cipriani opened Harry's Bar on May 13, 1931.

Kings, presidents, and celebrities throughout the years have visited Harry's Bar, and the Bellini is still served today.

PERU

Pisco Sour

From 1916 to 2014 the Pisco Sour was believed to be invented by Victor Vaughen "Gringo" Morris (1873–1929), a native of Salt Lake City, Utah, at Morris Bar, his American Bar in Lima, Peru.

However, in 2014, Peruvian writer Raúl Rivera Escobar scanned a 1903 Lima pamphlet published by S. E. Ledesma and then uploaded it online. It showed a cocktail by the name "Cocktail" containing all the ingredients of a Pisco Sour. Morris was not in Peru in 1903, so there is no way he could've known about the pamphlet, but it's common for different bartenders to create a cocktail with the same ingredients.

PUERTO RICO

Piña Colada

The Piña Colada (translated to "strained pineapple") is Puerto Rico's national drink, but no one knows the true story of its invention. The first time the words "Piña Colada" were seen in print was in a 1922 travel magazine that said, "But best of all is a Piña Colada, the juice of a perfectly ripe pineapple—a delicious drink in itself—rapidly shaken up with ice, sugar, lime and Bacardi rum in delicate proportions. What could be more luscious, more mellow and more fragrant?" As you can see, there is lime juice in place of the coconut, so this drink could have easily just been called a Pineapple Daiquiri.

As for the Bacardi reference, Bacardi was Cuban rum at the time, but expanded to Puerto Rico in 1936. Then during the Cuban Revolution (1959), Bacardi left Cuba. There was a similar Cuban drink created in the 1920s with coconut water, but the modern Piña Colada uses Coco López coconut cream.

Coco López was invented in Puerto Rico by agriculture professor and scientist Ramón López Irizarry (1897–1982) who used government grant funds to create an easier way to extract the cream from the coconut pulp. Irizarry perfected the process in 1949 at age fifty-two. He sold the company in 1966 and died a millionaire sixteen years later.

There are three stories claiming the creation of the Piña Colada, and most lean toward number one.

1. San Juan's Caribe Hilton bartender Ramón "Monchito" Marrero Perez claimed to have created the drink on August 16, 1954, by using the new product Coco López cream of coconut at the Beachcomber Bar.

2. San Juan's Caribe Hilton bartender Ricardo García claimed to have created the drink during a coconut cutters union strike in 1954.

3. Barrachina Restaurant bartender Ramón Portas Mingot claimed he created the drink in 1963.

SINGAPORE

SINGAPORE SLING—THE LONG BAR | RAFFLES HOTEL

The Long Bar in the Raffles Hotel has claimed the Singapore Sling, however, many cocktail historians do not agree. The hotel says Hainanese-Chinese head bartender Ngiam Tong Boon created it, and they even have an original handwritten recipe in the Raffles Hotel Museum. On their menu it says, "The Singapore Sling was created at Raffles Hotel at the turn-of-the-century by Hainanese-Chinese bartender, Mr. Ngiam Tong Boon."

In the hotel's museum, visitors may view the safe in which Mr. Ngiam locked away his recipe books, as well as the Sling recipe jotted on a bar chit in 1936 by a visitor to the hotel who asked the waiter for it. Over the years there have been variations on the recipe, which started with four ingredients and includes seven ingredients today.

19

Cocktails 101: A Guide to Classic, Modern Classic, Popular, Famous, Official IBA, and Standard Cocktails

...

WHAT EXACTLY ARE THE DIFFERENCES BETWEEN A CLASSIC, MODERN CLASSIC, POPULAR, FAMOUS, OFFICIAL IBA, AND STANDARD COCKTAIL?

CLASSIC COCKTAIL

A "classic" cocktail has stood the test of time and is well known in cocktail culture around the world. They are generally classy and documented. Many come from cocktail recipe books from the 1880s through the 1940s, which were written by bartenders. Examples include the Martini, Manhattan, Mint Julep, and Old-Fashioned. Other vintage classics that may sound new to unseasoned bartenders include the Aviation, Blood and Sand, Clover Club, and Corpse Reviver.

MODERN CLASSIC COCKTAIL

A "modern classic" cocktail is a recent category—due to the cocktail revolution. It is a cocktail that has become a classic in modern time. As time passes, new categories will probably be added (that will more than likely be categorized by periods of time), but for now, it is safe to say that a modern classic could span between present time and back thirty years.

Modern classic cocktails can go viral as a result of media; however, that has not happened since the Cosmopolitan in 1999. Some can be discovered on cocktail menus that then attract the attention of the media. Good examples of this include the Benton's Old-Fashioned invented by New York City bartender Don Lee when he created a new spirit infusion technique he calls fat washing. He then made a bacon-flavored whiskey to use in his cocktail. Or when Portland bartender Jeffrey Morgenthaler barrel-aged a barrel of Negronis. These two are examples of doing something that has never been done before, but not all modern classic cocktails need be this way. They can be as simple as Paul Harrington's Jasmine or Dick Bradsell's Bramble. Modern classic cocktails can also come from winning competitions or from a menu that has won awards.

POPULAR COCKTAIL

A "popular" cocktail can be popular for a short period like a Toasted Almond from the 1980s, Purple Hooter from the 1990s, or Incredible Hulk from the 2000s, but if it remains popular for many years, it then becomes famous. It can be famous locally or globally. Locally famous cocktails include Detroit's Hummer, Alabama's Yellowhammer, and Maryland's Black-Eyed Susan. World-popular cocktails include the Piña Colada, Margarita, and Long Island Iced Tea.

OFFICIAL IBA COCKTAIL

An official IBA cocktail comes from the International Bartenders Association. The association was founded on February 24, 1951, in the Saloon of the Grand Hotel in Torquay, England. It is an international organization representing the best bartenders in the world and sanctions a list of official cocktails. The IBA has three categories of cocktails: The Unforgettables, Contemporary Classics, and New Era Drinks. The IBA categories will have some classics, modern classics, popular, famous, and standard cocktails.

STANDARD COCKTAIL

A "standard" cocktail is likened to a standard piece of music. All good musicians should be able to play many standards in many genres. Similarly, a good bartender anywhere should be able to make a standard cocktail or mixed drink. Mixed drinks are simple and often fall into the two-ingredient highball category such as a Screwdriver, Rum & Coke, Gin & Tonic, etc. There are standards in classic cocktails, popular cocktails, famous cocktails, and even official IBA cocktails categories.

TYPES OF COCKTAILS

In vintage cocktail books, types organized many cocktails. Bartenders who study these books still use these types as guidelines. Some bartenders will say that eleven types are too many and they can be condensed to four or five types:

- **Cobbler**—contains a spirit, sugar, and a garnish of fruits.
- **Collins**—contains a spirit, lemon juice, simple syrup, and carbonation.
- **Daisy**—contains a spirit, lemon juice, and a sweetener such as gum syrup, raspberry syrup, or grenadine.
- **Fix**—contains a spirit, lemon juice, and sugar, and is served with crushed ice.
- **Fizz**—like the Collins, it contains a spirit, lemon juice, sugar, and carbonation. Almost like a Sling.
- **Flip**—contains a spirit, egg, sugar, and spice (no cream).
- **Egg Nog**—contains a spirit, egg, sugar, spice, and cream.
- **Julep**—contains a spirit, sugar, and mint.
- **Punch**—started with containing five ingredients served in a large bowl for communal drinking: spirit, citrus juice, water, sugar, and spice.
- **Rickey**—contains a spirit, lime juice, and club soda.
- **Sling**—contains a spirit, lemon juice, sugar, and sometimes carbonation, and is served in a tall glass, almost like a Fizz.

••• COCKTAIL MAKING TIPS

PRE-CHILLING AND HEATING GLASSWARE

A cocktail glass needs to be chilled so it does not warm a shaken and strained cocktail. You can keep glasses in the freezer, or before you make the cocktail, place ice (or ice and water) into the cocktail glass so it will be chilled when you are ready to fill it. Simply discard the ice when necessary. Hot cocktails should be served in warmed (preheated) mugs for a similar yet opposite reason.

TOOLS

Tools needed: cocktail shaker (two-piece Boston or three-piece cobbler), mixing glass (or use the sixteen-ounce pint glass of the Boston shaker), jigger or jiggers (with measures for .25 ounce, .5 ounce, .75 ounce, 1 ounce, and 1.5 ounce), wide peeler for large citrus zests and peels, channel knife for thin zests and spirals, a sharp knife for cutting garnishes, Hawthorne strainer, a manual citrus squeezer, and assorted glassware.

TIN VS. GLASS

These recipes will instruct you to pour the ingredients into a shaker tin. This refers to a three-piece cobbler shaker tin because it is assumed that these cocktails will be made at home.

If making them behind a commercial bar, then you would add the ingredients to the sixteen-ounce pint mixing glass or second half of a Boston shaker.

INGREDIENTS

JUICES

When a juice is called for in a recipe, it means fresh-squeezed juice. This particularly applies to lemon, lime, grapefruit, orange, and pineapple.

CHERRIES

Cherries for garnishing should be real (not clown-nose-red fake cherries). A good brand is Luxardo or use fresh cherries.

•••
ALPHABETICAL RECIPE LIST OF CLASSIC, MODERN CLASSIC, POPULAR, FAMOUS, OFFICIAL IBA, AND STANDARD COCKTAILS

AMERICANO

Classic, popular, famous, IBA Unforgettable, and standard.

Add ice to a rocks glass or Old-Fashioned glass, then pour in:
- 1 ounce Campari
- 1 ounce sweet vermouth
- 1 ounce soda water
- Gently stir, then garnish with an orange slice.

Gaspare Campari invented the Americano in the 1860s in his bar, Caffè Campari, in Milan, Italy. The name of the cocktail changed from Milano-Torino to Americano in the early 1900s when it became popular with American tourists.

Variation

Negroni: replace the soda water with gin.

AVIATION

Classic.

Chill a cocktail glass, then pour the following into a shaker tin:
- 2 ounces gin
- .5 maraschino liqueur (like Luxardo)
- .5 ounce lemon juice
- .25 ounce crème de violette (like Rothman & Winter)
- Add ice to the shaker tin and shake, then strain into the chilled cocktail glass. Garnish with a cherry.

BACARDI COCKTAIL

Classic and IBA Unforgettable.

Chill a cocktail glass, then pour the following into a shaker tin:
- 1.5 ounces Bacardi light rum
- 1 ounce lime juice
- 1 ounce grenadine
- Add ice to the shaker tin and shake, then strain into the chilled cocktail glass. Garnish with a cherry.

In the early 1930s, Bacardi learned that New York bartenders were making the Bacardi Cocktail with other branded rums, so they took a case to New York's Supreme Court. In 1936, Justice John Walsh ruled that the Bacardi Cocktail must be made with Bacardi rum.

Variation

Daiquiri: replace the grenadine for simple syrup.

BELLINI

Famous and IBA Contemporary Classic.

Chill a champagne flute, then add the following:
- 4 ounces prosecco, cold
- 1.5 ounces fresh peach puree, cold
- Stir gently.

Bartender and bar owner Giuseppe Cipriani (1900–1980) invented the Bellini in 1931 at his bar, Harry's Bar, which is located in Venice, Italy.

Variation

Puccini: replace the fresh peach puree with fresh mandarin juice.

Rossini: replace the fresh peach puree with fresh strawberry puree.

Tintoretto: replace the fresh peach puree with fresh pomegranate juice.

BETWEEN THE SHEETS

Classic and IBA Unforgettable.

Chill a cocktail glass, then pour the following into a shaker tin:
- 1 ounce Cognac
- 1 ounce white rum
- 1 ounce triple sec
- .75 ounce fresh lemon juice
- .25 ounce simple syrup
- Add ice to the shaker tin and shake, then strain into the chilled cocktail glass.

The Between the Sheets is believed to have been invented by Harry MacElhone at Harry's New York Bar in Paris, France, in the 1930s.

Variation

Side Car: omit the rum, replace the triple sec with Cointreau, and add a sugared rim.

BLACK RUSSIAN

Classic, popular, famous, IBA Contemporary Classic, classic, and standard.

Add ice to a rocks glass then pour in:
- 1 ounce vodka
- 1 ounce coffee liqueur
- Stir gently.

It is believed that bartender Gustave Tops created the Black Russian in 1949 at the Hotel Metropole in the Belgian city of Brussels, for American socialite Perle Mesta (US Ambassador to Luxembourg).

Variation

White Russian: add 2 ounce cream.

Mississippi Mudslide: add 1 ounce cream and 1 ounce Irish cream.

Sombrero: omit the vodka and layer 1 ounce cream on top of the coffee liqueur.

Smith & Kerns/Kearns: replace the vodka with soda water and add 1 ounce cream.

Smith & Wesson: add 1 ounce cream and 1 ounce soda water.

Colorado Bulldog: add 1 ounce cream and 1 ounce cola. Often this drink is served in a tall glass and ingredient portions are raised.

Dirty Mother: replace the vodka for brandy.

Dirty White Mother: replace the vodka with brandy and add 1 ounce cream.

Toasted Almond: replace the vodka with amaretto and add 1 ounce cream.

Roasted Toasted Almond: add 1 ounce amaretto and 1 ounce cream.

Girl Scout Cookie: replace the vodka for white crème de menthe and add 1 ounce cream.

BLOODY MARY

Popular, IBA Contemporary Classic, and standard.

Add the following to a tall 12-ounce glass:
- 1.5 ounces vodka
- 5 ounces tomato juice
- .5 ounce lemon juice
- .5 ounce Worcestershire sauce
- Dash of Tabasco
- Celery salt and pepper to taste
- Add ice gently, then stir. Garnish as you wish.

This recipe is from the IBA. If you make or purchase a Bloody Mary mix, then you would just combine the spirit and the mix. Who invented the Bloody Mary is not quite clear, but most believe it was either Fernand Petiot at Harry's New York Bar in Paris, France, or George Jessel in New York City. Both claimed they created the drink in the 1920s.

Variation

Bloody Maria: replace the vodka with tequila.

Bloody Caesar: add 3 ounces clam juice.

Red Snapper: replace the vodka with gin.

Bloody Joseph: replace the vodka with Scotch.

BLUE HAWAII

Famous.

Fill a 12-ounce Hurricane glass with ice, then add the following:
- .75 ounce vodka
- .75 ounce Puerto Rican rum
- .5 ounce blue Curaçao (preferably Bols)
- 1 ounce pineapple juice
- .5 fresh lemon juice
- .5 ounce simple syrup
- Stir to mix and add water dilution. Garnish with pineapple slice and orchid and serve with aloha.

This is the exact recipe from the inventor, Harry K. Yee. Yee who invented the Blue Hawaii in 1957 at the Hawaiian Village on the island of O'ahu. Not to be confused with the Blue Hawaiian, which no one really knows the recipe for because it was made up by many trying to copy the Blue Hawaii.

Harry Yee at age ninety-eight in 2016 holding a Blue Hawaii from the Hilton Hawaiian Village where he created it in 1957. © *Dennis Oda*

BRAMBLE

Modern Classic and IBA New Era Drink.

- 2 ounces gin
- 1 ounce fresh lemon juice
- 1 ounce blackberry liqueur
- Prepare an Old-Fashioned glass with crushed ice, then pour the first two ingredients into a shaker tin. Add ice to the shaker tin, shake then strain over the crushed ice, then gently stir. Pour the blackberry liqueur over the top of the drink in a circular fashion and garnish with a lemon slice and two blackberries.

Invented in the 1980s by bartender Dick Bradsell at Fred's Club in London, England.

BRANDY ALEXANDER

Classic, IBA Unforgettable, and standard.

Chill a cocktail glass, then pour the following into a shaker tin:

- 1 ounce Cognac
- 1 ounce dark crème de cacao (white cacao can be used if you do not have dark)
- 1 ounce fresh cream
- Add ice to the shaker tin and shake, then strain into the chilled cocktail glass. Garnish with fresh grated nutmeg.

Variation

Alexander: replace the Cognac with gin.
Grasshopper: replace the Cognac with green crème de menthe and the dark cacao with white cacao.
Pink Squirrel: replace the Cognac with crème de noyaux and the dark cacao with white cacao.
Golden Cadillac: replace the Cognac with Galliano and the dark cacao with white cacao.
Banshee: replace the Cognac with banana liqueur and the dark cacao with white cacao.

BRANDY CRUSTA

Classic and famous.

Prep a small fancy 5-ounce wine glass (with a narrow diameter rim) by moistening the outside of the glass—near the rim—one inch in height with a lemon slice, then roll in granulated sugar. The result will be a one-inch band of sugar around the rim. Take a whole lemon and a wide peeler (or paring knife if you're skilled) and peel the entire rind off in one long piece. Coil the lemon rind the size of the diameter of your glass and place inside at the top. Some of the rind should be sticking up a little higher above the rim and be able to stay secured on its own. Pour the following into a shaker tin:

- 2 ounces Cognac or brandy
- .5 ounce lemon juice
- .5 ounce orange Curaçao

- 1 dash Angostura bitters
- Add ice to the shaker tin and shake, then strain into the prepped glass.

The Brandy Crusta is known as the first "fancy cocktail" and the first cocktail to use citrus juice. Joseph Santini in New Orleans invented it sometime in the early 1850s. The cocktail made it into the first known American cocktail recipe book, *How to Mix Drinks or The Bon-Vivant's Companion: The Bartender's Guide* by Jerry Thomas and precedes the Side Car and Lemon Drop Martini.

CABLE CAR

Modern classic.

Prep the rim garnish by adding a half-cup granulated sugar and one teaspoon of ground cinnamon into a plastic bag, shake to mix, then pour out on a saucer or plate. Run a lemon slice around the rim of a chilled cocktail glass. then dip into the cinnamon-sugar mixture. Pour the following into a shaker tin:
- 1.5 ounces Captain Morgan Spiced Rum
- .75 ounce Marie Brizard Orange Curaçao
- .5 ounce simple syrup
- 1 ounce lemon juice
- Add ice to the shaker tin and shake, then strain into the chilled rimmed cocktail glass. Garnish with an orange spiral.

Invented in 1996 by craft cocktail pioneer Tony Abou-Ganim at the Starlight Room in San Francisco's Sir Drake Hotel.

CAIPIRINHA

Classic, popular, famous, and IBA Contemporary Classic.

Muddle half of a lime that is cut into two pieces and two teaspoons of granulated sugar in the bottom of a rocks glass or old-fashioned glass. Fill the glass with ice, then pour in the following:
- 2 ounces cachaça

- Stir to mix and to melt in a little water dilution in the drink.

This is Brazil's national drink.

CAPE CODDER

Popular and standard.

Add the following to a 10–12 ounce highball glass:
- 1.5 ounces vodka
- 4 ounces cranberry juice
- Add ice, then garnish with a lime wedge.

Variation

Vodka Cranberry: omit the lime wedge.

Scarlett O'Hara: replace the vodka with Southern Comfort.

Sea Breeze: use equal parts cranberry and grapefruit juices.

Bay Breeze: use equal parts cranberry and pineapple juices and omit the lime wedge.

Woo Woo: add 1 ounce peach schnapps and adjust the vodka portion to 1 ounce.

CHAMPAGNE COCKTAIL

Classic, IBA Contemporary Classic, and standard.

- Chill a champagne flute or coupe. Place a sugar cube on a palm-held napkin or into the bowl of a bar spoon, then dash 2–3 dashes of bitters onto the sugar cube. Drop the bitters-soaked cube into the chilled champagne glass, then add the following:
- 4 ounces chilled champagne.

The first mention of the Champagne Cocktail was in 1855 in the book *Panama in 1855* by Robert Tomes. Tomes's version included ice and brandy. The next time it was seen in print was in the first American cocktail recipe book, *How to Mix Drinks* by Jerry Thomas, which included a lemon peel garnish and a small lump of ice. There have been slight variations of the cocktail over the years, but the one given is the most common.

CLOVER CLUB

Classic and IBA Unforgettable.

Chill a cocktail glass, then fill a shaker tin half full with ice and add:

- 2 ounces gin
- .75 ounce French dry vermouth
- .75 ounce raspberry syrup
- .75 ounce lemon juice
- 1 egg white
- Shake well, then strain into the chilled glass.

Variation

Clover Leaf: add a spring of fresh mint when shaking, and then garnish with a mint sprig.

COSMOPOLITAN

Modern Classic, popular, famous, IBA Contemporary Classic, and standard.

The stories for each of the five Cosmopolitans can be found in Chapter 18 Bar Hopping: Famous Cocktails from Around the Globe.

NEAL MURRAY'S COSMOPOLITAN

Pour the following into a shaker tin with ice:

- 1.5 ounces Gordon's vodka
- .75 ounce Leroux triple sec
- .75 ounce Rose's lime
- .5 ounce cranberry juice
- Shake, then strain into a conical-shaped cocktail glass. Garnish with a lime wedge.

MELISSA HUFFSMITH-ROTH'S COSMOPOLITAN

Chill a conical-shaped cocktail glass, then pour the following into a shaker tin:
2 ounces Absolut Citron vodka

- 1 ounce Cointreau
- 1 ounce lime juice
- .5 ounce cranberry juice
- Add ice to the shaker tin and vigorously shake, then strain into the chilled cocktail glass. Garnish with a lemon twist. Melissa says, " The color should be a pale ballet pink and cloudy from the fresh lime juice and ice—clean and refreshing like a pink lemonade for grownups.

TOBY CECCHINI'S COSMOPOLITAN

Chill a conical-shaped cocktail glass, then pour the following into a shaker tin:

- 1.5 ounces Absolut Citron vodka
- .75 ounce Cointreau
- .75 ounce lime juice
- .75 ounce cranberry juice
- Add ice to the shaker tin and shake, then strain into the chilled cocktail glass. Garnish with a lemon twist. To be authentic, make an old-school lemon twist by cutting the ends off a lemon and then cutting halfway into the lemon lengthwise (not the circumference). Hull out the lemon meat with a spoon, so you are left with the whole rind. Roll up the rind, insert a toothpick (or bar pick) through the roll to secure, then cut slices to make curled lemon twists.

Toby Cecchini old school lemon twists.
© *Cheryl Charming*

DALE "KING COCKTAIL" DEGROFF'S COSMOPOLITAN

This recipe is from DeGroff's 2002 book, *The Craft of the Cocktail*. Originally, the vodka he used was Absolut Citron and the triple sec was Cointreau.

Chill a conical-shaped cocktail glass, then pour the following into a shaker tin:

- 1.5 ounces Ketel One Citron vodka
- .5 ounce triple sec
- .25 ounce lime juice
- 1 ounce cranberry juice
- Add ice to the shaker tin and shake, then strain into the chilled cocktail glass. Garnish with a flamed orange zest.

CHERYL COOK'S COSMOPOLITAN

Pour the following into a mixing glass filled with ice:

- 2 ounces Absolut Citron vodka
- .5 ounce triple sec
- .5 ounce Rose's lime
- .5 ounce cranberry juice
- Stir, then strain into a conical-shaped cocktail glass. Garnish with a lemon twist. To be authentic, make this old-school lemon twist by cutting one end of a lemon then cutting about eight vertical incisions around the lemon. When needed, pull off a twist.

CUBA LIBRE

Popular, IBA Contemporary Classic, and standard.

Add the following to a 10-ounce highball glass:

- 1.5 ounces light rum (preferably Cuban)
- 4 ounces Cola
- Add ice, then garnish with a lime wedge.

Variation

Rum & Coke: omit the lime wedge.

DAIQUIRI

Classic, popular, famous, IBA Unforgettable, and standard.

Chill a cocktail glass, then pour the following into a shaker tin:

- 1.5 ounces light rum
- 1.5 ounces simple syrup
- 1 ounce lime juice

Add ice to the shaker tin and shake, then strain into the chilled cocktail glass.

Cheryl Cook old school lemon twists. © *Cheryl Charming*

DARK 'N STORMY

Popular, Famous, IBA New Era Drink, and standard.

Add the following to a tall 12-ounce glass:
- 1.5 ounces Gosling's Black Seal rum
- 5 ounces ginger beer
- Add ice, then garnish with a lime wedge.

DEATH IN THE AFTERNOON

Popular, Famous, IBA New Era Drink, and standard.

Chill a champagne flute, then add the following:
4 ounces dry champagne, cold
- 1 ounce absinthe (like Lucid)
- Gently stir. Some will not find this sweet enough; so if you desire, you can add simple syrup or a sugar cube to taste.

ESPRESSO MARTINI

IBA New Era Drink

Chill a cocktail glass, then pour the following into a shaker tin:
- 1.5 ounces premium vodka
- 1 ounce Kahlúa coffee liqueur
- .5 ounce simple syrup
- 1 shot strong espresso
- Add ice to the shaker tin and shake, then strain into the chilled cocktail glass. Garnish with three coffee or espresso beans in the center to resemble flower petals.

Invented by Dick Bradsell at London's Fred's Club in the late 1980s. Bradsell made it at the request of an up-and-coming model, Kate Moss, who wanted a cocktail that could both wake her up and mess her up.

FRENCH 75

Classic, popular, famous, IBA Contemporary Classic, and standard.

Chill a champagne flute, then add the first ingredient. Pour the last three ingredients into a shaker tin:
- 4 ounce dry champagne, cold
- 1 ounce Cognac
- .5 ounce simple syrup
- .5 ounce lemon juice
- Add ice to the shaker tin and shake, then strain on top of the champagne and then garnish with a lemon twist.

Variation

French 75 (British style): replace the Cognac with gin.
French 76: replace the Cognac with vodka.

GODFATHER

Classic, IBA Contemporary Classic, and standard

Add ice to a rocks glass or an Old-Fashioned glass, then pour in:
- 1.5 ounces Scotch
- 1.5 ounces amaretto
- Stir gently.

Variation

Godmother: replace the Scotch with vodka
French Connection: replace the Scotch with Cognac

GRASSHOPPER

Classic, popular, famous, IBA Contemporary Classic, standard.

Chill a cocktail glass, then pour the following into a shaker tin:
- 1 ounce white crème de cacao
- 1 ounce green crème de menthe
- 1 ounce cream or half-and-half
- Add ice to the shaker tin and shake for 10 seconds, then strain into the chilled cocktail glass.

HEMINGWAY DAIQUIRI

Classic and IBA Contemporary Classic.

Chill a cocktail glass, then pour the following into a shaker tin:

- 2 ounces light rum (preferably Cuban)
- .25 ounce maraschino liqueur
- .25 ounce simple syrup
- .75 ounce grapefruit juice
- .5 ounce lime juice
- Add ice to the shaker tin and shake, then strain into the chilled cocktail glass. Garnish with a floating lime wheel if desired.

HURRICANE

Popular and famous.

Add the following to a large 22-ounce Hurricane glass:

- 2 ounces light rum
- 2 ounces gold or dark rum
- 1.5 ounces red passion fruit syrup (like Monin)
- 1 ounce lime juice
- 4 ounces orange juice
- Add ice, stir, and add more ice if needed, then garnish with an orange slice and cherry.

It is believed that Pat O'Brien invented the Hurricane in 1942 in New Orleans. Sadly, today if you order one at Pat O' Brien's in New Orleans you will get a mass-produced red Kool-Aid-type drink. If you only have a 16-ounce Hurricane glass, then cut the portion of the rum to 1.5 ounces each.

IRISH COFFEE

Popular, famous, IBA Contemporary Classic, and standard.

- 1.5 ounces Irish whiskey
- 1 ounce simple syrup
- 5 ounces hot coffee
- 2 ounce cream float
- Warm an 8–10 ounce coffee glass, then add the first three ingredients. Float the cream on top.

The Buena Vista Café in San Francisco makes 2,000 Irish Coffees a day. In 2008, they were entered into the Guinness Book of Records for making the largest Irish Coffee.

JACK ROSE

Classic.

Chill a cocktail glass, then pour the following into a shaker tin:

- 2 ounces Laird's applejack
- .5 ounce lemon juice
- .5 ounce lime juice
- .5 ounce handmade grenadine
- Add ice to the shaker tin and shake, then strain into the chilled cocktail glass.

Some claim this cocktail is made with lemon juice while others say lime, so this recipe covers both. Laird & Company (lairdandcompany.com) has been making applejack (apple brandy) since the 1600s and is the oldest distillery in America. President George Washington wrote the family a letter asking for the recipe and President Abraham Lincoln sold it in his saloon. Today, ninth generation Lisa Laird is the face of Laird & Company—the first woman to hold this position.

Lisa Laird, the ninth-generation owner of the oldest distillery in America, Laird & Company. © *Lisa Laird*

JASMINE

Modern Classic.

Chill a cocktail glass, then pour the following into a shaker tin:

- 1.5 ounces gin
- .75 ounce lemon juice
- .25 ounce Campari
- .25 ounce Cointreau
- Add ice to the shaker tin and shake, then strain into the chilled cocktail glass. Garnish with a lemon twist.

Cocktail godfather Paul Harrington invented the Jasmine in the early 1990s. It was named after his roommate's last name. Years later he learned that the roommate spelled his last name without the "e" on the end.

KIR

Classic and IBA Contemporary Classic.

Chill a champagne flute, then add the following:

- 4 ounces dry white wine, cold
- 1 ounce crème de cassis (black currant liqueur)

Variation

Kir Royale: replace the wine with dry champagne.
Cardinal: replace the white wine with red wine.
Kir Impérial: replace the cassis with raspberry liqueur.
The Kir (rhymes with ear) is named after the French Mayor Felix Kir (1876–1968) of Dijon in Burgundy.

LEMON DROP MARTINI

Modern Classic, popular, and standard.

Rim a chilled cocktail glass with sugar, then pour the following into a shaker tin:

- 1.5 ounces lemon vodka
- 1 ounce triple sec
- 1 ounce lemon juice
- .5 ounce simple syrup

- Add ice to the shaker tin and shake, then strain into the chilled rimmed cocktail glass, and then garnish with a lemon twist.

Variation

Flavored Lemon Drop Martini: replace the lemon vodka with other flavored vodkas.

LAST WORD

Modern classic and popular.

Chill a cocktail glass, then pour the following into a shaker tin:

- 1 ounce gin
- 1 ounce green Chartreuse
- 1 ounce maraschino liqueur (like Luxardo)
- 1 ounce lime juice
- Add ice to the shaker tin and shake, then strain into the chilled cocktail glass.

The Last Word is believed to have been invented by a bartender from Detroit, Michigan, named Frank Foggerty.

LONG ISLAND ICED TEA

Popular, famous, IBA Contemporary Classic, and standard.

- .5 ounce vodka
- .5 ounce gin
- .5 ounce light rum
- .5 ounce blanco tequila
- .5 ounce triple sec
- 1 ounce simple syrup
- 1 ounce lemon juice
- 1 ounce cola
- Fill a 12–14 ounce tall glass with ice, then add the first seven ingredients. Top with more ice, add the cola, and then garnish with a lemon wedge.

Variation

Long Beach Tea: replace the cola with cranberry juice.

Miami Tea: replace the cola with Sprite and the triple sec with blue Curaçao.

MAI TAI

Popular, famous, IBA Contemporary Classic, and standard.

Add ice to an old-fashioned glass, then pour the following into a shaker tin:
- 1 ounce Rhum Clément VSOP Martinique rum
- 1 ounce Appleton Estate Extra dark Jamaican rum
- .5 ounce orange Curaçao
- .5 ounce orgeat syrup
- 1 ounce lime juice
- .25 ounce simple syrup
- Add ice to the shaker tin and shake, then strain over the glass of ice. Garnish with a half-spent lime shell and mint sprig.

The Mai Tai is Tahitian for "out of this world," which translates to "very good." Vic Bergeron a.k.a. Trader Vic invented it in 1944. This recipe is from Jeff "Beachbum" Berry. In 1944, the recipe called for seventeen-year-old J. Wray & Nephew rum, but it is extinct. Beachbum says these rums will make it taste like the original Mai Tai.

MARGARITA

Classic, popular, famous, IBA Contemporary Classic, and standard.

Chill a cocktail glass, then pour the following into a shaker tin:
- 1.5 ounces tequila
- .5 ounce Cointreau (or triple sec)
- .75 ounce lime juice
- .75 ounce simple syrup
- Add ice to the shaker tin and shake, then strain into the chilled cocktail glass. Garnish with a lime. If you desire salt, then you can prep the glass with a rim of coarse kosher salt. In addition, if you would like it on the rocks, then strain over an old-fashioned glass filled with ice.

No one knows who invented the Margarita, but there are several who claim to. It is, however, Mexico's national cocktail.

Variation

Golden Grand Margarita: use gold-colored/aged tequila and Grand Marnier in place of the Cointreau.
Blue Margarita: substitute blue Curaçao for the Cointreau.

MARTINI

Classic, popular, famous, IBA New Era Drink, and standard.

Chill a cocktail glass, then pour the following into a mixing glass:
- 2 ounces London dry gin
- 1 ounce French dry vermouth
- Add ice to the mixing glass and stir, then strain into the chilled cocktail glass. Garnish with a green olive, lemon twist, or both.

Variation

Vodka Martini: replace the gin with vodka and shake instead of stir.
Dirty Martini: add 1 ounce olive brine.
Dry Martini: use half the amount of vermouth.
Very Dry Martini: omit the vermouth.
Perfect Martini: use equal parts dry and sweet vermouth.
Gibson: garnish with a pickled cocktail onion.
Bronx: a Perfect Martini with 1 ounce orange juice added.
Burnt Martini: a splash of Scotch is added.
Dry Martini Cocktail from William Boothby in 1907: equal parts gin and vermouth and a dash of orange bitters.
No one knows who invented the Martini. There are several stories and varied recipes, but that is all we have.

MANHATTAN

Classic, popular, famous, IBA Unforgettable, and standard.

Chill a cocktail glass, then pour the following into a mixing glass:

- 2 ounces rye whiskey
- 1 ounce sweet vermouth
- 1 dash Angostura bitters
- Add ice to the mixing glass, then stir and strain into the chilled cocktail glass. Garnish with a cherry.

Variation

Rob Roy: replace the rye whiskey with Scotch whisky.

MIMOSA

Classic, popular, IBA Contemporary Classic, and standard.

Chill a champagne flute, then add the following:

- 4 ounces champagne
- 2 ounces orange juice
- Garnish with an orange slice or orange twist or strawberry.

A Buck's Fizz and a Mimosa are the same drink.

MINT JULEP

Classic, popular, IBA Contemporary Classic, and standard.

- Drop four mint sprigs into the bottom of an 8-ounce stainless-steel julep cup or highball glass and gently tap with a muddler to release the oils. Fill the glass with cracked ice, then add the following:
- 2 ounces Bourbon whiskey
- 1 ounce simple syrup

The Mint Julep is one of America's oldest cocktails, dating back to the late 1700s when it was made without ice.

MOJITO

Classic, popular, famous, IBA Contemporary Classic, and standard.

Drop two mint sprigs (about 10 leaves) into the bottom of a tall 12-ounce glass and gently tap with a muddler to release the oils. Then add the following:

- 2 ounce light rum (Cuban preferably)
- 1 ounce lime juice
- 1 ounce simple syrup
- 3 ounces soda water
- Add ice, stir gently, then garnish with a mint sprig.

A medicinal version of this drink for sailors was first mentioned in 1586. The first known time it was seen in print with these exact five ingredients was in Havana's Sloppy Joe's 1936 *Cocktails Manual.*

MONKEY GLAND

Classic and IBA Unforgettable.

Chill a cocktail glass, then pour the following into a shaker tin:

- 2 ounces gin
- 1.5 ounces orange juice
- .25 ounce absinthe
- .25 ounce grenadine
- Add ice to the shaker tin and shake, then strain into the chilled cocktail glass. Garnish with an orange zest. For more absinthe aroma, keep absinthe in a small spray bottle, omit the absinthe in the recipe, then spray over the top of the finished cocktail.

Invented in Paris by either bartender Frank Meier or Harry MacElhone in 1923. The name comes from a famous doctor of the time who believed that grafting monkey gland (testicle) tissue onto human males would provide longevity and rejuvenation.

1. Vesper. © *Wollertz / Shutterstock*
2. Modern Sidecar. © *Brent Hofacker / Shutterstock*
3. Mint Julep. © *Brent Hofacker / Shutterstock*

3

6

4. Clover Club Cocktail. © Elena Demyanko / Shutterstock

5. Sazerac. © Brent Hofacker / Shutterstock

6. Classic Margarita. © Brent Hofacker / Shutterstock

MOSCOW MULE

Classic, popular, IBA Contemporary Classic, and standard.

Add the following to a 12-ounce copper cup or old-fashioned glass:

- 1.5 ounces Smirnoff vodka
- 5 ounces ginger beer
- Add ice, then garnish with a lime wedge.

Variation

Dark 'n Stormy: replace the vodka with Gosling's Black Seal Rum.

Kentucky Mule: replace the vodka with Kentucky Bourbon.

Tennessee Mule: replace the vodka with Tennessee whiskey.

Mexican Mule: replace the vodka with tequila.

Irish Mule: replace the vodka with Irish whiskey.

Scottish Mule: replace the vodka with Scotch whisky.

Kentucky Mule: replace the vodka with Bourbon.

Ginger Mule: replace the vodka with gin.

Chilcano: replace the vodka with pisco.

The Moscow Mule is America's first vodka drink that introduced Smirnoff vodka.

NEGRONI

Classic, popular, famous, IBA Unforgettable, and standard.

Add ice to a rocks glass or old-fashioned glass, then pour in:

- 1 ounce gin
- 1 ounce Campari
- 1 ounce sweet vermouth
- Gently stir, then garnish with an orange slice or twist.

Variation

Americano: replace the gin with soda water.

OLD-FASHIONED

Classic, popular, IBA Unforgettable, and standard.

- Drop a sugar cube into the bottom of an Old-Fashioned glass, dash with four dashes of Angostura bitters, then add .25 ounce of water. With a muddler, crush the sugar cube, and stir with the muddler until dissolved. Add the following:
- 2 ounces Bourbon or rye whiskey
- Drop in a chunk of ice (preferably one you've picked from a block of ice), then add an orange zest. In the "old" days, they would icepick off chunks from blocks of delivered pond ice. You can make your own ice chunks by filling a metal baking pan with water, or by cutting off the tops of dairy (and nondairy) paper containers, cleaning them, then filling them with water and freezing.

Variation

The original Old-Fashioned (late 1700s–early 1800s): omit the ice chunk, replace the orange twist with a lemon twist, and serve with a small spoon in the glass. The spoon always stays in the glass.

Old-Fashioned in the mid to late 1800s: replace the orange twist with a lemon twist.

Wisconsin Old-Fashioned: replace the whiskey with brandy, muddle an orange wedge and cherry, replace the sugar cube with 1 ounce simple syrup, fill the glass with ice, stir and garnish with an orange wedge and cherry.

PIÑA COLADA

Classic, popular, famous, IBA Contemporary Classic, and standard.

Pour the following into a blender:

- 1.5 ounces light rum (preferably Puerto Rican)
- 3 ounces pineapple juice
- 1 ounce Coco López coconut cream
- Add a half-cup of ice, then blend for 10 seconds. Pour into a poco grande glass (or glass of your choice) and garnish with a pineapple wedge and cherry.

The Piña Colada is Puerto Rico's national cocktail.

Variation

Bushwhacker: replace the light rum with dark rum and add 1 ounce coffee liqueur.

Bahama Mama: add 1 ounce orange juice, .5 ounce lime juice, and .5 ounce grenadine (basically a marriage between a Rum Punch and a Piña Colada).

Miami Vice: layered half Piña Colada and half Strawberry Daiquiri.

Painkiller: add 1 ounce orange juice and grate fresh nutmeg on top.

PISCO SOUR

Classic, famous, IBA New Era Drink, and standard.

Chill a cocktail glass then pour the following into a shaker tin:

- 1.5 ounces pisco
- .75 ounce simple syrup
- 1 ounce lime juice
- 1 egg white, raw
- Add ice to the shaker tin and shake, then strain into the chilled cocktail glass. Garnish with three dashes of Angostura bitters on top.

The Pisco Sour is Peru's national cocktail.

RAMOS GIN FIZZ

Classic, famous, and IBA Unforgettable.

Chill an 8-ounce juice glass, then pour the following into a shaker tin:

- 1.5 ounces Old Tom gin
- .5 ounce lemon juice
- .5 ounce lime juice
- 1 ounce simple syrup
- 1 ounce heavy cream
- 1 small egg white
- 1 dash orange-flower water
- Add a half-cup of ice to the shaker tin and shake for five minutes. Add 1 ounce soda water to the

chilled glass, then strain cocktail into the chilled glass to the top.

Charles Ramos created the Ramos Gin Fizz in 1888 at his New Orleans bar, the Imperial Cabinet. It is believed that he employed a line of "shaker boys" to shake and pass down the cocktail in an assembly line.

RUSTY NAIL

Classic, popular, IBA Unforgettable, and standard.

Add ice to a rocks glass or Old-Fashioned glass then pour in:

- 2 ounces Scotch whisky
- 1 ounce Drambuie
- Gently stir, then garnish with a lemon twist.

SAZERAC

Classic, popular, famous, IBA Unforgettable, and standard.

- Set out two Old-Fashioned glasses and chill one by adding ice and water into it. In the second glass add a sugar cube, .5 ounce of water, and 4 dashes of Peychaud's (PAY-showds) bitters—it must be Peychaud's. With a muddler, crush the sugar cube, and stir with the muddler until dissolved. Add the following:
- 2 ounces rye whiskey
- Add ice, then stir with a bar spoon. Empty the first glass chilling with iced water, then add .25 ounce of absinthe and swirl inside the glass to coat. Strain the mixture from the second glass into the first glass, then garnish with a lemon twist. You can keep absinthe in a small spray bottle and spray the inside of the glass if so desired. You can also use .5 ounce simple syrup in place of the sugar cube and water.

It is said that this preparation method was the original way the Sazerac was made. Today, you can skip the second old-fashioned glass and just use a mixing glass. The Sazerac has been New Orleans's official cocktail since 2008.

SCREWDRIVER

Popular, IBA Unforgettable, and standard.

Add ice to an Old-Fashioned or highball glass, then pour in:

- 1.5 ounces vodka
- 5 ounces orange juice
- Garnish with an orange wedge.

In 1959, the *Washington Post* published, "It was in Ankara during World War II that a group of American fliers invented a drink called the 'Screwdriver'—orange juice and vodka—because they couldn't stand Turkish vodka. This was a slur on Ankara's estimable cuisine which at its worst is never so dreadful as the Screwdriver."

Variation

Madras: use equal parts orange and cranberry juices.
Fuzzy Navel: replace the vodka with peach schnapps.
Hairy Navel: add 1 ounce peach schnapps.
Sex on the Beach: add 1 ounce peach schnapps to the Madras.
Harvey Wallbanger: float 1 ounce Galliano on top.
Melon Ball: add 1 ounce melon liqueur.
Alabama Slammer: add .5 ounce sloe gin, .5 ounce Southern Comfort, and .5 ounce amaretto.

SEA BREEZE

Popular, IBA Contemporary Classic, and standard.

Add ice to an Old-Fashioned or highball glass, then pour in:

- 1.5 ounces vodka
- 2.5 ounces grapefruit juice
- 2.5 ounces cranberry juice
- Add ice then garnish with a lime wedge.

SEX ON THE BEACH

Popular, IBA Contemporary Classic, and standard.

Add ice to an Old-Fashioned or highball glass, then pour in:

- 1 ounce vodka
- 1 ounce peach schnapps
- 2.5 ounces cranberry juice
- 2.5 ounces orange juice
- Garnish with an orange wedge.

SIDECAR

Classic, Famous, IBA Unforgettable, and standard

Chill a cocktail glass, then pour the following into a shaker tin:

- 2 ounces Cognac
- 1 ounce Cointreau
- 1 ounce lemon juice
- Add ice to the shaker tin and shake, then strain into the chilled cocktail glass.

Variation

Modern Sidecar: add a sugared rim.

SINGAPORE SLING

Classic, famous, and IBA Contemporary Classic.

Add ice to a tall 16-ounce glass (or Hurricane glass) then pour the following into a shaker tin:

- 2 ounces gin
- 1 ounce cherry brandy or Cherry Heering
- .5 ounce Cointreau
- .5 ounce Bénédictine
- 3 ounces pineapple juice
- 1 ounce lime juice
- 1 dash Angostura bitters
- Add ice to the shaker tin and shake for two seconds, then strain over the ice. Garnish with a pineapple slice and cherry.

It is claimed that the Singapore Sling was invented at the Raffles Hotel in Singapore. It is believed that the original recipe was lost, but these are the ingredients known today.

STINGER

Classic, IBA Unforgettable, and standard.

Chill a cocktail glass, then pour the following into a shaker tin:

- 2 ounces brandy
- 1 ounce white crème de menthe
- Add ice to the shaker tin and shake, then strain into the chilled cocktail glass.

Variation

Vodka Stinger: replace the brandy with vodka.

TEQUILA SUNRISE

Popular, Famous, IBA Contemporary Classic, and standard.

Add the following to a tall 12-ounce glass:

- 1.5 ounces tequila
- 5 ounces orange juice
- Add ice, then pour in 1 ounce grenadine. It will sink to the bottom creating a gradient (sunrise) effect. Garnish with orange slice and cherry.

Variation

Tequila Sunset: replace the grenadine with blackberry brandy.
Caribbean Sunrise: replace the tequila with rum.
Vodka Sunrise: replace the tequila with vodka.
The Tequila Sunrise was invented by Bobby Lozoff in 1969 at the Trident in Sausalito, California.

TOMMY'S MARGARITA

Modern classic and IBA New Era Drink.

Chill a cocktail glass, then pour the following into a shaker tin:

- 2 ounces reposado tequila
- 1.5 ounces lime juice
- .75 ounce agave nectar
- Add ice to the shaker tin and shake, then strain into the chilled cocktail glass.

Created by Julio Bermejo at Tommy's Mexican Restaurant in San Francisco in the early 1990s.

VESPER

Famous, and IBA New Era Drink.

Chill a cocktail glass, then pour the following into a shaker tin:

- 3 ounces Gordon's gin
- 1 ounce Smirnoff vodka
- .5 ounce Cocchi Americano
- Add ice to the shaker tin and shake, then strain into the chilled cocktail glass. Garnish with a large thin slice of lemon peel.

The Vesper is a fictional cocktail first seen in Ian Fleming's 1953 novel *Casino Royale*. It is named after Bond's love interest. In the casino, Bond asks for "three measures of Gordon's, one of vodka, half a measure of Kina Lillet. Shake it very well until it's ice-cold, then add a large thin slice of lemon peel. Got it?" Kina Lillet is extinct, so the closest substitute is Cocchi Americano.

VIEUX CARRÉ

Classic and famous.

Add ice to an Old-Fashioned glass, then pour in:

- 1 ounce rye whiskey
- 1 ounce Cognac
- 1 ounce sweet vermouth
- .25 ounce Bénédictine
- 2 dashes Peychaud's Bitters
- 2 dashes Angostura bitters
- Gently stir, add more ice if needed, then garnish with a lemon twist.

The Vieux Carré (VOO- ka-RAY) translates into "old square," which means the French Quarter where it was invented by head bartender Walter Bergeron at the Carousel Bar in the Hotel Monteleone in 1934.

WHISKEY SOUR

Classic, popular, IBA Unforgettable, and standard.

Add ice to an Old-Fashioned glass then pour the following into a shaker tin:

- 1.5 ounces Bourbon whiskey
- 1 ounce simple syrup
- 1 ounce lemon juice
- 1 egg white
- Add ice to the shaker tin and hard shake for 30 seconds, then strain over the ice. Garnish with half orange slice and cherry. This cocktail can be served up in a cocktail glass as well.

Variation

Amaretto Sour: replace the Bourbon with amaretto.
Vodka Sour: replace the Bourbon with vodka.
Scotch Sour: replace the Bourbon with Scotch.
Apricot Sour: replace the Bourbon with apricot brandy.
Midori Sour: replace the Bourbon with Midori melon liqueur.

WHITE LADY

Classic and IBA Unforgettable.

Chill a cocktail glass, then pour the following into a shaker tin:

- 2 ounces gin
- .5 ounce Cointreau
- .5 ounce lemon juice
- 1 egg white
- Add ice to the shaker tin and shake, then strain into the chilled cocktail glass.

Invented by bartender Harry MacElhone at Ciro's Club in London, then revamped to this recipe ten years later at Harry's Bar in Paris.

ZOMBIE

Famous.

Pour the following into a blender:

- 1.5 ounces gold Puerto Rican rum
- 1.5 ounces dark Jamaican rum
- 1 ounce 151-proof Lemon Hart Demerara rum
- .75 ounce fresh lime juice
- .5 ounce Falernum
- 1 teaspoon grenadine
- 6 drops Pernod
- 1 dash of Angostura bitters
- .5 ounce Don's mix (2 parts grapefruit juice to 1 part cinnamon-infused sugar syrup)
- Add 3/4 cup of small ice and blend for 5 seconds, then pour into a tiki mug or tall glass.
- Add ice to fill, then garnish with a mint sprig.

Don the Beachcomber created the Zombie at his bar in Hollywood in 1934.

20

LOOK IT UP: THE BEST ONLINE COCKTAIL SOURCES

•••
COCKTAIL RECIPE SITES

We have all been there. We google a cocktail recipe—or any subject for that matter—from one of our internet-enabled devices and a plethora of choices appear. We do not know where to start. We think, "If it's at the top, does that make it the best?" Well, as far as cocktail recipe sites go, there is no need to worry anymore—just bookmark these.

COCKTAILDB • cocktaildb.com

This database is by cocktail historian and author Ted Haigh. It has been around since 2000 and has all your classic cocktails. You will also learn a thing or two while browsing.

DIFFORD'S GUIDE • diffordsguide.com/cocktails

London-based Simon Difford has probably been to more bars than anyone in the world. He is a renowned and respected drinks expert and has been a huge source for cocktail culture information for years. *Difford's Guide* used to be just cocktail recipes, but it has expanded to *everything cocktail*—the recipes with color photos are still there.

KINDRED COCKTAILS • kindredcocktails.com

This is a modern craft cocktail recipe database for enthusiasts and professionals. It is for a community of like-minded "kindred spirits" sharing and collaborating. You can collect recipes shared by others to build your own cocktail book, find a cocktail you want, concoct your own recipes, and categorize recipes for easy searching, grouping, and printing.

INTERNATIONAL BARTENDERS ASSOCIATION (IBA) • iba-world.com

The IBA Cocktail recipes are in three categories: The Unforgettables, Contemporary Classics, and New Era Drinks.

WIKI WEBTENDER • wiki.webtender.com

Look for the "All Recipes" link. There is a lot of information here. Pål Løberg created the first cocktail recipe database on the internet, Webtender, in 1995. The recipe section of that site, however, is not managed anymore, but this wiki version will satisfy you if you need some quick information on a cocktail plus more.

COCKTAIL + DAVID WONDRICH

David Wondrich had an amazing cocktail section for Esquire.com for thirteen years. As of July 2016, Wondrich left *Esquire*, but if you google "The name of a cocktail + David Wondrich," links will pop up. Wondrich is America's number-one drink historian and award-winning cocktail writer.

• • •
COCKTAIL BLOGS

Blogging has been around since 1994, but with most new things, it takes time to trickle down to the masses. The majority of America did not have an email address until the early 2000s, and that address would have been through AOL (America Online). But when WordPress launched a free online content management system in 2003, it made it easier for average people to create a space for themselves on the internet without having to pay money to have a website developed. Between 2006 and 2014 the web was inundated with cocktail-related blogs that are now defunct. There are a few popular cocktail blogs that have recently stopped updating, but you can peruse their archives. These include cocktailchronicles.com and spiritsandcocktails.wordpress.com.

ALCADEMICS • alcademics.com

Alcademics drinks blogger, Camper English in San Francisco. © *Camper English*

Popular drinks writer Camper English lives in San Francisco and started this drink blog in 2006 as a spin-off of his personal website. English has traveled the world learning and sharing about drinks and has contributed to publications including *Popular Science*, *Saveur*, *Details*, *Whisky Advocate*, *Drinks*, *Liquor*, and many more. English pioneered directional freezing to obtain crystal-clear ice, has an incredible Flickr photo page from his worldly cocktail travels at flickr.com/photos/cramper, a great Instagram page at instagram.com/alcademics, and published a book titled *Tonic Water: A.k.a., G&T, WTF.*

BOOZE MOVIES: THE 100 PROOF FILM GUIDE • boozemovies.com

William T. Garver first started writing an article for *Modern Drunkard* magazine titled "Soused Cinema." Then in December 2006, Garver started his *Booze Movies* blog that not only shows clips of drink seen in film, but also comes with reviews of the film.

TALES OF THE COCKTAIL • talesofthecocktail.com/news

Tales of the Cocktail was the world's first cocktail festival. Their blog/news page will keep you updated on many things going on in the cocktail world.

The Liquid Muse drinks blogger, Natalie Bovis, in Sante Fe, New Mexico; 2014.
© Doug Merriam

Other current and popular cocktail blogs include 12bottlebar.com, artofdrink.com, chuckcowdery.blogspot.com, cocktailwonk.com, drinkhacker.com, gastronomista.com, goodspiritsnews.com, jeffreymorgenthaler.com, professorcocktail.com, stirandstrain.com, and theliquidmuse.com.

...

ONLINE COCKTAIL MAGAZINES

CLASS MAGAZINE • diffordsguide.com

Simon Difford is responsible for uniting the international cocktail community. He started Difford's Guide *Class* magazine in August 1997 and with Difford's passion for the cocktail culture, it grew from 16 pages to 150 monthly glossy pages, but then the internet took over and he was forced to sell. Difford was able to take it back over in 2009 and in 2010 won a Tales of the Cocktail Spirited Award. In 2014, the printed magazine was laid to rest, and now everything is online. It's highly recommended to join his newsletter to receive updates. The information on this site is rich and immense.

IMBIBE

Imbibe launched in 2005 and immediately started winning awards. This drink magazine (and now you can get it digital online) quenched a thirst for the growing craft cocktail movement at the time. Some of its many awards include a 2012 James Beard Journalism Award for Best Wine, Spirits or Other Beverage Writing, four Maggie Awards, and two Tales of the Cocktail Spirited Awards.

LIQUOR • liquor.com

Liquor is a James Beard Award-winning and Tales of the Cocktail Spirited Award-winning digital publication dedicated to good drinking and great living. They employ a huge network of award-winning writers, master mixologists, and spirits experts who travel the globe. Their top-shelf board of advisors are the best in the business: Jacques Bezuidenhout, Dale "King Cocktail" DeGroff, H. Joseph Ehrmann, Simon Ford, Allen Katz, Jim Meehan, Gary Regan, Julie Reiner, Aisha Sharpe, Willy Shine, and David Wondrich.

Other current and cocktail online magazines include bartender.com and chilled.com.

MODERN DRUNKARD MAGAZINE • drunkard.com

Modern Drunkard Magazine is a little on the crusty side, but can be entertaining—a junk food drinking mag, if you will. Boston saloon owner Hiram Flannery Rich started it in 1905 when a critic from the *Boston Globe* gave his saloon a bad review. Rich handwrote ten rebuttal newsletter issues, then handed them out to his regulars to read. It was a hit, so Rich started a regular newsletter that was first called *Genteel Drunkards Drink at Hiram Rich's Real Irish Saloon*, but after the Great Fire of 1909, he launched a Boston-wide edition, renaming it the *Genteel Drunkard*. The first editions were crude, obscene, and controversial to the point where the Women's Christian Temperance Union, with their hatchets, raided the magazine office four times. This made the publication even more popular. During Prohibition, the magazine was renamed *Modern Drunkard Magazine* and would give a list of passwords to speakeasies. Today, it's an online magazine, and you can browse online issues in their archive.

PUNCH • punchdrink.com

Punch is a James Beard Award-winning online magazine in collaboration with Ten Speed Press that writes about cocktails, spirits, wine, and beer.

•••
COCKTAIL WEBSITES OF INTEREST

EUVS (EXPOSITION UNIVERSELLE DES VINS ET SPIRITUEUX) • euvs.org

In 1958, Paul Ricard started the EUVS museum and today has amassed a collection of over 8,000 bottles of wine and spirits from around the world, as well as drink menus and more dating back to the 1860s. In 2007, esteemed drink historians and writers Anistatia Miller and Jared Brown came on board to increase the collection. The site also has a complimentary cocktail menu creator and so many other interesting things to browse through. The most fun part of the website is the digital library of vintage cocktail recipe books that you can flip through. You can find the library easier by going to euvslibrary.com

BEACHBUM BERRY • beachbumberry.com

The Bum is the number-one tiki god in the world.

MINISTRY OF RUM • ministryofrum.com

Ed Hamilton is a rum fanatic and actually lives on a boat and sails from one Caribbean island to the next exploring rum. He even came out with his own brand in 2015.

COCKTAIL VIDEOS OF INTEREST

When you search how to make a cocktail on YouTube, there will be one correct video for every ten. Here are some video sources to help get you started off on the right foot.

SMALL SCREEN NETWORK • smallscreennetwork.com

You will find some of the best videos for inspiration and for learning at this website. The best ones to watch include *Inspired Sips with the Liquid Muse*, *Kathy Casey's Liquid Kitchen*, *Raising the Bar with Jamie Boudreau*, *The Morgenthaler Method*, and *The Proper Pour with Charlotte Voisey*. You can also search titles on YouTube and watch them there.

LIQUOR • liquor.com

Liquor.com has a video section with over one hundred videos to view.

BAR TIMES • bar-times.com

The website is in Japanese, so subscribe to their YouTube channel to watch the fascinating and beautiful style of Japanese bartending.

21

BEHIND THE BAR: THE FIFTEEN MOST INFLUENTIAL AMERICAN BARTENDERS

We will never know about the thousands of popular beverage servers throughout history in villages, towns, and cities who served liquid libations with passion, but it is agreed that they probably had a lot in common with the passionate bartenders of the past three centuries. It can be challenging to list fifteen influential bartenders in America, because, of course, there are more than this. But this is a good start.

Many things can make a bartender memorable: personality, being the best at something, writing books, being recorded in media, starting a new trend, being respected and recognized by peers, pioneering a new method, or all of the above.

CATO ALEXANDER

New York socialite William Dunlap wrote, "Who has not heard of Cato Alexander's? Not to know Cato's is not to know the world." Cato Alexander (1780–1858) was born in New York City as a slave and deemed free by the "Act for the Gradual Abolition of Slavery." As a young boy, he worked at an inn and even helped President George Washington on and off his horse. Around 1812, he opened a tavern in an area of New York City that today is considered Midtown East (around Second Avenue and Fifty-Fourth Street). He was famous for his brandy punch, gin cocktails, juleps, and eggnogs. His bar stayed open until the 1840s, and he was very well known among the elite and wild young men of the city. The five-mile carriage ride (or gallop on a horse) from Lower Manhattan was often turned into a race to Cato's. The book *Cyclopaedia of American Literature, Vol. 1* refers to Cato's as a celebrated road tavern with a view of a dusty road, cabbage garden, and horse shed. The interior was decorated with elegant furniture, offered rooms to let, and Mrs. Cato was a notable cook. Cato lent money to many of his patrons and sadly, most never paid him back. This caused him to lose his tavern.

ORSAMUS WILLARD

Orsamus "Willard" (1792–1876) was born in Massachusetts and is famous for being the first bartender in New York City to make fancy cocktails. He was also known for making the best iced Mint Juleps—ice was the new hot commodity—at the City Hotel lobby bar. The hotel at the time was the grandest of the city and used to be the governor's mansion. He was also known for his Apple Toddy made with baked apples (this one was written up in newspapers), Gin Cocktail, and Extra-Extra Peach Brandy Punch. Willard was known to have a photographic memory, was ambidextrous, and was one of those who could get by on two hours of sleep a day. For a good twenty-five years, anyone who was anyone locally or abroad knew "Willard of the City Hotel." Before becoming a bartender, he worked as a schoolteacher, and after his bar career, he moved back home to the country in Massachusetts, where he farmed and raised children. Even though he gained much fame as a bartender, he never wrote a cocktail recipe book to leave behind—or at least not one that we know of.

JEREMIAH P. THOMAS

"Professor" Jerry Thomas (1830–1885) is known as *the* American cocktail godfather because he published the first known American cocktail recipe book: *Bar-Tender's Guide, How to Mix Drinks or The Bon-Vivant's Companion*. He is also known for traveling the world with a set of silver bar tools. Thomas was born in Sackets Harbor, New York, on October 13, and it is assumed that he was a first-born son because his father's name was Jeremiah as well.

Drawing of "Professor" Jerry Thomas making a Blue Blazer.
© *Anthony Joseph Filippone*

The family moved to New Haven, Connecticut, when Thomas was in his early teens, and by sixteen he was working in a bar. After a couple of years, he set out to travel the world, and he moved around a lot: San Francisco, New York City, St. Louis, Chicago, South Carolina, New Orleans, and London. Thomas opened four saloons in New York City, and the first one can still be seen at Broadway and Ann Street below the Barnum's Museum. Thomas invented many cocktails, but the one he is most known for is the Blue Blazer; to make it, he poured a stream of hot whiskey back and forth between metal cups, creating an arc of fire. He was a performer behind the bar and showmaster who liked to dress bejeweled in diamonds while making cocktails with silver bar tools. The James Beard Award-winning book *Imbibe!*, by David Wondrich, tells the story of his life.

HARRY JOHNSON

Harry "The Dean" Johnson (1845–1930) was born aboard a German ship (of which his father was the captain) somewhere between Poland and Lithuania. While not technically American, he did tend bar all over the country. He is famous for his published books, *Harry Johnson's Bartenders' Manual,* which were published in 1882, 1888, and 1900. He is also known for publishing a cocktail specifically named "Martini." Johnson did not just fill his books with recipes; he gave lists of instructions on "how to attend a bar," what to wear, how to conduct yourself, how to train someone, how to treat patrons, opening bar duties, collecting money when you are in a rush, rules of using a gigger (yes, with a "g"), etc. When he was sixty-five years old, Johnson said in an interview that he actually published his first cocktail recipe book at fifteen, and the publisher sold 10,000 copies with six weeks. This may have been true, but not one single copy has been found. Johnson first tended bar in San Francisco, then moved to Chicago in 1868 to open a bar. He said that a New Orleans barkeeper with the last name of Le Boeuf wrote to him about entering a national competition to be held in New Orleans. Johnson said the competition consisted of a bartender standing behind the bar and twelve people walking up and ordering cocktails. On his turn, the group called "bartender's choice" for twelve whiskey cocktails. Johnson lined up twelve glasses in two rows, then stacked a pyramid of cocktail glasses on top. He served the whiskey cocktails in waterfall form. The prize was said to be $1,000 ($18,500 in 2018 currency). Johnson went back to Chicago, and a few years later the great Chicago Fire of 1871 put him in debt. Johnson married, tended bar in

Philadelphia, then moved to New York City, where he owned several bars and published a few books (in English and German). It is also believed that he started a bar school. Johnson died in Berlin, Germany, in 1930.

WILLIAM T. BOOTHBY

William T. Boothby (1862–1930) was born in San Francisco and known as "Cocktail Bill." Boothby tended bar in New York, Chicago, Philadelphia, New Orleans, and Kansas City, but he is most known for working at San Francisco's Palace Hotel bar in the late 1800s to early 1900s. In 1891, he published *Cocktail Boothby's American Bartender* and then revised it in 1890. During the Great Earthquake and Fire of San Francisco (1906), the printing plates were destroyed, so his third and best edition was published in 1908 and titled *The World's Drinks and How to Mix Them.* As a child, Boothby performed on stage in minstrel shows, so this experience served him well behind the bar.

HUGO ENSSLIN

Hugo Ensslin (1876–1963) was born in Germany but tended bar in New York City. He is known for publishing the last cocktail recipe book before the American Prohibition, titled *Recipes for Mixed Drinks.* It contains 400 recipes, but the most famous cocktail in the book is the Aviation. The book also mentions new ingredients not seen before, which includes triple sec, grenadine, and applejack. Post-Prohibition bartenders published many of his recipes in their books. Ensslin was not a flashy bartender and did not tend bar at esteemed New York City hotel bars. He worked lower-class hotel bars and was fine just doing what he was doing. It has been said that he influenced Harry Craddock.

VICTOR JULES BERGERON

Victor Jules Bergeron, a.k.a. Trader Vic (1902–1984), is famous for creating Trader Vic's, the drink (and food) empire, which makes him the most successful bartender of all time. He was born to French-Canadian parents in San Francisco on December 10. His mother was known for being an excellent French cook and his father, a waiter at the famed Fairmont Hotel, later became a grocery store owner. On April 18, when Bergeron was four, his parents rushed him to the hospital for a foot amputation due to a bone disease, and at 5:12 a.m., the San Francisco Earthquake of 1906 struck the northern coast of California. It has been said that he remembered his father carrying him out of the hospital while he watched bricks fall. By the next available amputation appointment, the disease had spread and more than his foot needed amputating. After recovery, his parents bought him a canoe and encouraged rowing to build upper body strength, and as an adult, Bergeron would tie in the boat scenario to explain the loss of his leg, saying, "The sharks got it." The disease kept creeping up his leg, which also kept his parents in debt.

By the time he was thirty-two, the disease subsided and Bergeron borrowed money from his aunt to open a beer parlor in Oakland, California, called Hinky Dinks. In 1939, inspired by a trip to Cuba and Don the Beachcomber's tiki bar and restaurant in Hollywood, Bergeron changed the name of his bar and restaurant to Trader Vic's. In 1941, Trader Vic's was put on the map when San Francisco journalist Herb Caen wrote, "The best restaurant in San Francisco is in Oakland." Four years later, Bergeron invented the world-famous Mai Tai. Bergeron went on to open a chain of twenty-five Trader Vic's around the globe. Today there are eighteen Trader Vic's with twelve located in the Middle East. There is only one remaining store in America, which is located in Atlanta, Georgia, on the lower level of the Hilton Atlanta. Bergeron wrote two bartenders' guides, six cookbooks, and one biography in 1973 titled *Frankly Speaking: Trader Vic's Own Story*. In his lifetime, Bergeron spent time fighting with California veterans' hospitals for better rehabilitation programs for veterans who had lost limbs. Bergeron was ambidextrous, an artist, married twice, and had four children, who took over the franchise in 1972.

ERNEST RAYMOND BEAUMONT-GANTT

Ernest Gantt (1907–1989), a.k.a. Don the Beachcomber, is considered the father of the tiki movement. He opened the first Polynesian bar and restaurant, Don's Beachcomber, in Hollywood. Gantt was born in Mexia, Texas, on February 22 and at seven years old was sent on a bus to Mandeville, Louisiana (across the lake from New Orleans), to live with his wealthy grandfather. Within one month, he was traveling the Caribbean on his grandfather's yacht and walking French Quarter cobblestone streets. Later, he left to travel the world, worked on steamships, and bootlegged. In 1934, he opened America's first Polynesian-themed restaurant and bar in Hollywood, California, with the tagline "If you can't get to paradise, I'll bring it to you." A few years later, he moved across the street and renamed it Don the Beachcomber.

Gantt's bar was visited by all the famous faces of the time, and they loved his foul-mouthed myna birds. He is known for inventing over eighty cocktails, but the Zombie is the most popular and was served at the 1919 World's Fair in New York.

During World War II, Gantt joined the U.S. Army and returned with a Purple Heart and a Bronze Star. He also learned that his wife, Cora Irene "Sunny," opened sixteen Don the Beachcombers around America. They soon divorced, and Gantt left to live in Hawaii where he opened another bar, made some Hawaiian singers famous, remarried, and died a poor man. Today there is one store in Huntington Beach, California, and in 2015, Ernest Coffee Shop and Bootlegger Tiki Bar opened in Palm Springs, California, in the same building that housed one of the Don the Beachcomber restaurants.

DALE "KING COCKTAIL" DEGROFF • kingcocktail.com

Dale "King Cocktail" DeGroff was born in Quonset Point, Rhode Island on September 21, 1948, to Armand and Carmella DeGroff. He is credited for kick-starting the craft cocktail revolution.

At the University of Rhode Island, he studied to be an actor. Around 1973, DeGroff entered the F&B business as a dishwasher, waited tables at Charley O's in Rockefeller Center, and landed his first private bartender gig in 1976 at the Gracie Mansion. He scratched his acting itch by moving to Los Angeles where he tended bar at the famous Hotel Bel-Air, had two sons with his wife Jill and began to take bartending seriously.

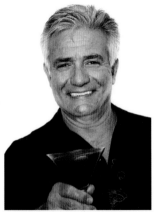

A 2006 photo of Dale DeGroff for his second book, *The Essential Bartender: The Art of Mixing Perfect Drinks*. © David Kressler

In 1985, famed New York restaurateur Joe Baum lured Degroff back to New York City to create a nineteenth-century bar program at Aurora Restaurant. In 1987, he headed up the bar program for Baum's Rockefeller Center's Rainbow Room and rose to fame by introducing a fresh classic cocktail menu unlike any others in the city. A photo was taken of Madonna drinking DeGroff's retooled Cosmopolitan and his career shot through the roof.

DeGroff has won a James Beard award, Julia Child, and many more. His books include *The Craft of the Cocktail* and *The Essential Cocktail*. He travels the world judging, consulting, and sometimes even giving shows with his guitar through monologue and song. He lives in West Hempstead, NY with his wife and business partner Jill, who is also a saloon artist.

GARY REGAN • gazregan.com

Gary "Gaz" Regan (REE-gan) was born in Lancashire, England, in 1951 and lived over his parents' British pub for the first two years of his life. He is most famous for helping pioneer the craft cocktail movement and being a prolific cocktail writer. His mom named him Gary because she didn't want his name turned into a short nickname, but for some unknown reason at the time, a new nickname for anyone named Gary was Gaz.

The first cocktail Regan consumed was a room-temperature Gimlet. This was after his parents opened another pub when he was twelve. By age eighteen, Regan was working weekend bartender shifts learning the pub business from his dad and the bartenders who worked for his dad. One year later, he quit school to work in his parents' pub full-time. He also got married, but then divorced at age nineteen.

Regan always had a fascination with New York City, which came from reading Superman comic books as a kid, so he made the trek to Superman's Metropolis and landed a job at a British pub called Drake's Drum. Regan credits his learning from bar owner David Ridings, who stressed the importance of hospitality. Regan went on to work numerous bars around the city. He soon combined his experience with his love of writing and was picked up by many food- and beverage-related magazines. His first published book was 1991's *The Bartender's Bible*, and soon after he wrote a regular column for the *San Francisco Chronicle*, "The Cocktailian," for thirteen years. In 2003, Regan published his most popular book, *The Joy of Mixology*. To date he has published sixteen books, launched an orange bitters, conducts two-day workshops, judges cocktail competitions, and has won many awards. Regan also chose to be public about his mouth cancer. Today, he lives in the Hudson Valley, New York, and six times a year tends bar at the award-winning Dead Rabbit in New York City. He also puts out a weekly newsletter.

CHARLES ANTHONY ABOU-GANIM • themodernmixologist.com

Charles Anthony "Tony" Abou-Ganim was born in Port Huron, Michigan, to Lebanese and Irish parents George and Dorothy Abou-Ganim on April 14, 1960. He is most famous for helping pioneer the craft cocktail movement.

Pioneer of the craft cocktail movement Tony Abou-Ganim. © *Tim Turner Studios*

Named after two bartenders in the family—Uncle Charles and Cousin Tony—Abou-Ganim was destined to be a bartender. On his eighteenth birthday, the family sat him on a barstool in the Brass Rail (his cousin Helen David's bar), and his cousin Tony began lining up a row of cocktails in front of him. Abou-Ganim remembers being fascinated watching the care and skill it took to make each cocktail and he didn't even know—then—that they were all classic cocktails (Manhattan, Tom Collins, Whiskey Sour, etc.). Two years later, in 1980, he began training as a bartender with his cousin Helen. The first two cocktails he remembers making was a made-from-scratch B&B and Manhattan, but his goal career was to be an actor.

In 1993, at the Rainbow Room in New York City, Abou-Ganim visited another bartender, Dale DeGroff, whose goal was also to be an actor. DeGroff made Abou-Ganim a Negroni served up (it was challenging to find a bartender who knew what a Negroni was at the time), and all the memories from the classic cocktails served to him at his eighteenth birthday came flooding back. It was then that Abou-Ganim decided to be the best bartender he could be.

In San Francisco, Abou-Ganim began making fresh cocktails at Jack Slick's Balboa Café, Harry Denton's, Po (Mario Batali's first restaurant), then Harry Denton's Starlight Room on top of the Sir Francis Drake Hotel, where he launched his first specialty cocktail menu. In 1998, Abou-Ganim was selected by Steve Wynn to develop the cocktail program for all twenty-three bars at Bellagio Las Vegas. Today, Abou-Ganim's home base is Las Vegas, but he travels the world as a consultant, trainer, and educator in all things cocktail. In 2010, he published *The Modern Mixologist* and in 2017, Abou-Ganim opened his own bar in the Libertine Social at Mandalay Bay in Las Vegas. It is the bar that has the large blue neon light that says, "Stay Wild."

CHRIS MCMILLIAN • revelcafeandbar.com

Chris McMillian was born in Shreveport, LA on March 6, 1961 and is known for being the most famous bartender in New Orleans. McMillian reeks of old-school style and is a walking, talking encyclopedia of all things cocktail.

McMillian moved to New Orleans in 1984 and took his first bartender job in 1994 at the Chateau Sonesta Hotel on Iberville in the French Quarter, and by 1999, he moved across the street to the Richelieu Bar inside Arnaud's. It was here where he became famous for his Ramos Gin Fizzes and is credited for creating the technique where the meringue would rise over the rim of the glass. In 2000, the Ritz-Carlton Hotel opened and McMillian took over the helm of the Library Bar, where bar enthusiasts from around the world would come see the master work his craft. McMillian and his wife, Laura, were founding members of the Museum of the American Cocktail in 2002 and have organized many cocktail seminars.

McMillian has been written up in several magazines and newspapers, has been a guest speaker at the Smithsonian, and possesses the largest collection of New Orleans cocktail information of anyone in the world. In 2015, he McMillian and his wife, Laura opened their first bar, Revel Café & Bar at 133 North Carrollton Avenue. The coveted place to sit at this fourth-generation bartender's bar is near the well of his Tobin Ellis Signature Cocktail Station, so you'll be in earshot of enlightening spiritual stories of the cocktail he is making, or a story he feels like sharing. The first cocktail McMillian made was a Whiskey Sour.

He and his wife have six children and nine grandchildren, and in 2016, McMillian published *Lift Your Spirits: A Celebratory History of Cocktail Culture in New Orleans*.

TOBIN ELLIS • barmagic.com

Tobin Ellis was born in Los Gatos, California, in 1970 and raised in Rochester, New York. He first rose to international fame in 2007 when he was selected as America's number-one bartender to compete against Iron Chef Bobby Flay in his TV show *Throwdown! with Bobby Flay*.

Ellis began his hospitality career nearly twenty years earlier as a dishwasher and slinging at college dives. Shortly after college, he became an NSO bar trainer for TGI Friday's opening restaurants around the country. In 1997, he cofounded and served as first president for the FBA (Flair Bartenders' Association) and launched the first flair bartending website. In 1999, Ellis opened a second-floor speakeasy behind an unmarked door in Syracuse, New York, serving obscure tequilas, fresh Margaritas, and classic cocktails. Ellis was recruited as head bartender at Caesars Palace, Las Vegas, in 2000 and finished his bartending career at PURE Nightclub in Las Vegas after winning a handful of major cocktail competitions including a USBG (United States Bartenders' Guild) national title.

Ellis then launched "Social Mixology," the world's first pop-up speakeasy series, which spanned the globe with unique themed pop-up parties where a password was required. His unique hospitality design company has designed and opened bars worldwide, and most recently, Ellis collaborated with the Perlick Corporation to launch the Tobin Ellis Signature Cocktail Station, which won the 2016 Good Design Award given out to companies including Apple, BMW, Porsche, and Bang & Olufsen. These days Ellis splits his time between Las Vegas and his home in Rochester, New York, providing hospitality consulting and design services for companies including Ritz-Carlton, Waldorf-Astoria, Starbucks, Ace Hotels, and a select handful of others. Being a prolific writer, Ellis has worked as a published columnist and advertising creative (copywriter), is left-handed, and was making Gin & Tonics for his father at age ten—he drank and ordered virgin Gin & Tonics.

SASHA NATHAN PETRASKE

Sasha Petraske (1973–2015) was born in Manhattan on March 6 and is famous for opening Milk & Honey, a small, unadvertised cocktail den, without a sign, with limited seating, strict rules, and an unconventional reservation system serving pre-Prohibition crafted cocktails—in a time when the Cosmopolitan and Martini bars were the rage. He was a pioneer in the craft cocktail movement and spawned Prohibition-style speakeasies worldwide.

High school bored Petraske, so he dropped out, worked at a café, rode a bicycle across America, lived in San Francisco, then joined the Army for three years. He returned home and worked at a bar called Von and then became inspired to open his own bar when seeing a small hidden bar called Angel's Share (hidden inside a Japanese restaurant). He answered an ad in the *Village Voice* for a small commercial space at 134 Eldridge Street for $800 a month and learned that the owner was a friend from the fifth grade. Petraske promised that his bar would be quiet and would not disturb neighbors, so his secret bar theme fit perfectly for the space. The bar opened on New Year's Eve 1999.

Petraske went on to open London Milk & Honey, Little Branch, White Star Absinthe Bar, Mercury Dime, the Varnish, Dutch Kills, Middle Branch, Milk & Honey 2.0, and a consulting company with Christy Pope and Chad Solomon called Cuffs & Buttons. In 2015, he signed a contract to write his first book for Phaidon Press and planned to open a bar in Brooklyn called Falconer, but died on August 21. In 2016, his widow, Georgette, honored the publisher's contract and handed over his book, *Regarding Cocktails*. Petraske was also known for starting the "bartender's choice" on cocktail menus and bringing back the use of jiggers. He will always be remembered wearing light-colored suits and black slicked-back hair as if he had stepped out of the pages of the novel *The Great Gatsby*.

Christian Delpech, the number-one flair bartender in the world. © *Christian Delpech*

Delpech was born in Buenos Aires, Argentina, on February 25, 1977, and is known as the best flair bartender in the world. Ever.

At age seventeen while he was tending bar in Buenos Aires, the film *Cocktail*, starring Tom Cruise, inspired Delpech to think about bartending in a whole new way. He entered a local flair competition at Hard Rock Café in 1998 and won first place in flair. In 1999, Delpech expanded his horizons and moved to Spain where he tended bar and performed tableside magic in Tenerife, Madrid, and on the island of Ibiza. By 2002, he was hired at the number-one flair bar in the world, Carnival Court in Las Vegas, Nevada.

Delpech has won over seventy first-place awards around the world and since the craft cocktail revolution, his favorite flair competition is "Blue Blazer," where the quality of the cocktail counts for 60 percent of the score.

Delpech's matrix-style of flair is fluid, beautiful, and elegant—all the while flashing smiles to the audience with a twinkle in his eye as he moves his body around objects as opposed to objects moving around him.

In 2016, Delpech was the first non-Cuban to win "King of Daiquiri" at the famous Floridita bar in Cuba. In celebration of the Floridita's 200th anniversary in 2017, all past winners competed for the title.

Delpech lives in Miami, where he tends bar at the historic Fontainebleau and owns the American Bar Academy by Christian Delpech. If Delpech were alive in the 1800s, he would have been one of the barkeepers described in the 1856 article found in the *Brooklyn Daily Eagle*, which read, "The barkeeper and his assistants possess the agility of acrobats and the prestidigitative skill of magicians. They are all bottle conjurors.—They toss the drinks about; they throw brimful glasses over their heads; they shake the saccharine, glacial and alcoholic ingredients in their long tin tubes."

INFLUENTIAL BARTENDERS OUTSIDE AMERICA

Again, there are many to mention, but this is a good start.

Harry Craddock (1876–1963), Constante Ribalaigua Vert (1888–1952), Harry MacElhone (1890–1958), Joe Gilmore (1922–2015), Peter Dorelli (1941–present), Salvatore Calabrese (1955-), Richard Arthur "Dick" Bradsell (1959–2016), Colin Peter Field (1961–present), and Tony Conigliaro (1971–present).

GLOBAL BARTENDER ORGANIZATIONS

Almost every industry has professional organizations to facilitate networking and growth. Here are some bartender organizations:

USBG (United States Bartenders' Guild)

usbg.org • facebook.com/TheUSBG • Started in 1948 and currently has chapters in fifty cities. Their mission is to unite the hospitality community to advance professional bartending. The best way to get involved is to see if your city has a USBG Facebook page.

IBA (International Bartenders Association)

iba-world.com • Established in 1951 and currently has members from sixty-two countries around the world.

FBA (Flair Bartenders' Association)

barflair.org • Founded by Tobin Ellis and Alan Mays in 1997 and currently has 10,000 members worldwide. The FBA is a community for flair bartenders, and they offer workshops, seminars, and flair bartending competitions.

Facebook

Almost every large city has a "bartender" Facebook page.

Reddit

reddit.com/r/bartenders • Reddit has been active since 2006. They currently have 36 million users. There are 10,000 bartenders in the Reddit community.

22

CHANGING THE WAY WE DRINK: CRAFT BARS

...
WHAT IS A CRAFT BAR?

The term "craft bar" came from Dale "King Cocktail" DeGroff. His first published book, *The Craft of the Cocktail: Everything You Need to Know to Be a Master Bartender*, officially kickstarted the modern craft culture movement.

Between the 1950s and 1990s (and into the beginning of the millennium), most bars in America used inferior fabricated ingredients, yet recipe books from the 1800s through the 1940s called for fresh ingredients. If you made a Whiskey Sour, you used fresh lemon juice. Margarita? Fresh lime juice. Quality and freshness is the foundation of what the modern-day craft cocktail movement is about. It is nothing new—your grandmother did it this way. We just forgot, or wanted to cut costs, and allowed companies to capitalize on the ignorance of the masses.

Many craft bars hand-make their own syrups and mixers, seek out forgotten spirits, have different ice choices, and incorporate little used spices and herbs. They peruse vintage recipe books and put fresh artisanal spins on new creations. It can be compared to a passionate chef studying classic cookbooks and then making his or her own sauces, soups, pasta, breads, etc., from scratch. For many years in restaurants, there has been a huge disconnect between the kitchen and the bar. But today—finally—quality in both food and drink is offered by most restaurant/bar venues.

DeGroff is credited with watering the cocktail renaissance seeds in the late 1980s. The *New York Times* declared he was "single-handedly responsible for what's been called the cocktail renaissance." With lots of liquid sunshine, the seed grew to around thirty craft bars in America by 2005 and by 2018, the number reached over 1000.

...
AMERICAN CRAFT COCKTAIL BEGINNINGS TIMELINE

1960s–1990s – Many bars in San Francisco did not experience a cocktail revolution because they never stopped making classic cocktails with fresh ingredients. Some of these bars include Henry Africa's, the Zuni Café, Balboa Café, BIX Jazz Bar, Dartmouth Social Club, Golden Gate Grill, Enrico's, and Stars.

1985 – Dale "King Cocktail" DeGroff heads up restaurateur Joe Baum's restaurant Aurora making classic cocktails he learned in Jerry Thomas's 1862 book.

1987 – Dale "King Cocktail" DeGroff begins a gourmet approach to recreating classic cocktails at restaurateur Joe Baum's current project, the Rainbow Room in New York City (65th floor of 30 Rockefeller Plaza).

1987 – Del Pedro makes fresh classic cocktails at celebrity-owned Sam's Café in New York City (100 Crescent Court, Suite 140). He then went on to work at Les Halles, the Hotel Knickerbocker, Grange Hall, and Pegu Club, and in 2012 opened his own bar called Tooker Alley in Brooklyn (793 Washington Avenue).

– Brother Cleve takes a bartender position at his friend's bar, Hoodoo BBQ in Boston (97 Massachusetts Avenue) and introduces a classic cocktail menu.

– Barnaby Conrad III publishes *Absinthe: History in a Bottle*.

1989 – Kathy Casey pioneers the kitchen-to-bar-chef movement. She develops liquidkitchen.com and rolls out the first craft cocktail program on a cruise ship.

1990 – Julio Bermejo at Tommy's Mexican Restaurant makes a decision to be rid of all the inferior tequilas and brings in 100 percent blue agave tequilas. Bermejo starts a tequila club and by 1999, Tommy's was the epicenter number-one tequila bar in America.

– Bartender Murray Stenson serves classic cocktails at Il Bistro in Seattle, Washington (93 Pike Street).

– Chris Israel and Bruce Carey open Zefiro, the first fresh classic bar in Portland, Oregon (500 Northwest Twenty-First Avenue). They bring on Peggy Boston as bar manager and she puts out a classic cocktail menu.

1991 – Gary Regan publishes *The Bartender's Bible*.

menu driven

GARY WOLF

The lost art of mixology
An Enrico's bartender rediscovers Cuban cocktails

Bottoms Up *Enrico's barman Paul Harrington is a throwback to the days when business lunches entailed powering down three martinis.*

The August 1992 *San Francisco Bay Guardian* newspaper clipping of Paul Harrington. © *Paul Harrington*

1992 – Paul Harrington is recognized in San Francisco's *Bay Guardian*. The title of the article reads, "The Lost Art of Mixology; An Enrico's bartender rediscovers Cuban Cocktails." Paul talks about making Mojitos, Aviations, and Hemmingway Daiquiris.

– Bartender Danny Rosenberg offers a menu of recipes he found in old cocktail recipe books at Grange Hall in New York City (50 Commerce Street). Coworkers include Toby Maloney and Del Pedro.

– Steve Olson a.k.a. Wine Geek starts a beverage consulting company.

1993 – NOLA scientist Ted A. Breaux becomes intrigued by the Old Absinthe House and actively researches the mysterious spirit.

– While working on the John Hughes film *Baby's Day Out* in Chicago, Ted Haigh spots a sign that reads "Chicago's Oldest Wine & Spirits Merchant." Every weekend, he buys buy up vintage (and extinct) bottles that include Abbott's bitters, 1930s gin, and vintage crème de menthe, then ships them home to California. His new hobby of collecting and researching vintage cocktail culture is born.

– Inspired by Dale "King Cocktail" DeGroff, Francis Schott starts a fresh bar program at his restaurant, Stage Left, in New Brunswick, New Jersey (5 Livingston Avenue).

1994 – Jeff "Beachbum" Berry begins his search for the original Zombie ingredients (it takes eleven years).
– Beverage director Steve Olson, along with Tom Colicchio and Danny Meyers, opens Gramercy Tavern and introduces fresh crafted and classic cocktails in New York City (42 East Twentieth Street).

1995 – The first cocktail websites are launched on a new media platform called the World Wide Web. Websites that focus on fresh classic cocktails are:

- Paul Harrington a.k.a. "The Alchemist" of www.cocktailtime.com (defunct) puts out a beautiful color cocktail section of classic cocktails complete with history and notes on the first commercial web magazine: www.hotwired.com (defunct).
- Jared Brown and Anistatia Miller launch www.martiniplace.com (defunct) on Halloween. They now own mixellany.com.
- Author and beverage consultant Robert Plotkin launches www.barmedia.com.
- Just for fun, the other first cocktail-related websites to launch on the New World Wide Web included www.ardentspirits.com, www.barasterie.com, www.barmagic.com, www.barnonedrinks.com, www.barproducts.com, www.bartender.com, www.cocktail.com (defunct), www.drinkboy.com, www.kingcocktail.com, www.martiniclub.com, www.misscharming.com, www.thebartend.com (defunct), www.webtender.com, www.worldwidedrinks.com, and www.zigysmartinilounge.com (defunct).

– Tony Abou-Ganim becomes inspired in 1993 after meeting Dale "King Cocktail" DeGroff at the Rainbow Room. By 1995, Tony introduces fresh classic cocktails at Harry Denton's Starlight Room at the Sir Francis Drake Hotel in San Francisco (450 Powell Street).
– Steve Olson begins teaching "Gin Cocktail Clinics" helping consumers make fresh and classic cocktails in their homes. The clinics lasts for five years and employs over 100 bartenders as consultants teaching the program in six major cities in America, reaching up to 300 consumers per show, with as many as 25 bartenders working the show with Olson. The list of people who worked with the clinics includes Don Lee, Jim Meehan, Phil Ward, Eric Alperin, Jon Santer, Carlos Yturria, Jacques Bezuidenhout, Misty Kalkofen, Sean Kenyon, John Lermayer, Tad Carducci, Charles Joly, right hand Leo DeGroff, and the ringleader, Andy Seymour.
– Julie Reiner learns classic cocktails from Linda Fusco at the Red Room in San Francisco (827 Sutter).
– Peggy Boston opens the fresh bar program at Saucebox in Portland, Oregon. Bartenders included Lucy Brennan and Marcovaldo Dionysos.
– Nick Mautone makes his own cocktail onions, brandied cherries, and more for fresh cocktails at Gramercy Tavern in New York City (42 East Twentieth Street).

1996 – Dale DeGroff sets up the Pravda bar program and trains the bar staff in New York City (281 Lafayette Street) Among the bartenders are Jason Kosmas and Dushan Zaric.
– Todd Thrasher heads up the bar at Café Atlantico in Washington, DC (405 Eighth Street) and adds five Latin cocktails to the menu that include Caipirihna, Caipiroska, Mojito, Pisco Sour, and a traditional Bolivian drink called the Shoofly. In 1991, Thrasher trekked to see Dale "King Cocktail" DeGroff at the Rainbow Room.
– Dave Nepove makes fresh cocktails at Enrico's in San Francisco for ten years. He earns the nickname Mr. Mojito.
– Steve Olson and Doug Frost travel the world for five years teaching the Sterling School of Service and Hospitality Spirits Program—a one-day bartender spirits certification class. In 1997, I attend their class at Walt Disney World.
– Paulius Nasvytis squeezes fresh juice and makes classic cocktails at the Velvet Tango Room in Cleveland, Ohio (2095 Columbus Road). By 2005, VTR is a full craft cocktail bar.

– Marcovaldo Dionysos makes classic cocktails as daytime bartender at Enrico's Sidewalk Café in San Francisco (504 Broadway). Later he works at the Absinthe Brasserie & Bar, Bourbon & Branch, Harry Denton's Starlight Room, and Smuggler's Cove.

– Yokocho Japanese Restaurant opened in Greenwich Village in 1994 (8 Stuyvesant Street), but by 1996, Japanese trained bartender Shinichi Ikeda begins training bartenders in Angel's Share—a secret bar behind a door inside the restaurant—how to make classic craft cocktails with hand-chipped ice. Rules posted on the door say: "No more than four people in a group, no standing, no screaming, and no shouting."

– Ted A. Breaux obtains his first unopened bottles of pre-ban absinthe.

– Steve Olson sets up the bar program at Mirezi in New York City (59 Fifth Avenue) with Asian-inspired handcrafted cocktails.

1997 – F. Paul Pacult publishes the groundbreaking book *Kindred Spirits: The Spirit Journal Guide to the World's Distilled Spirits and Fortified Wines.*

– Dale "King Cocktail" DeGroff sets up the bar program at the Greatest Bar on Earth on top of the World Trade Center in New York City (107th floor in Tower One).

– George Delgado tends bar in the Windows Bar on top of the World Trade Center in New York City, making classic and fresh cocktails. The night before 9/11/2001, he teaches a cocktail and spirits class.

– Julie Reiner is featured on the front page of the food section in the *New York Times* using seasonal fresh fruits, spices, and tea while tending bar at C3 in the Washington Square Hotel in New York City (103 Waverly Place).

– Quench, on the Food Network, brings cocktails to TV with hosts Andrea Immer Robinson and Steve Olson.

– *The Happy Hour*, a nationally syndicated radio show with Paul Pacult and Gary Regan, introduces cocktails to the consumers.

– Dale DeGroff invites Audrey Saunders to help work special events with him at the Rainbow Room.

– Jared Brown and Anistatia Miller publish *Shaken Not Stirred: A Celebration of the Martini.*

– Josh Childs opens Silvertone Bar & Grill in Boston with a fresh and classic bar program.

– Gary Regan publishes *New Classic Cocktails.*

1998 – Paul Harrington and Laura Moorhead publish the game-changing *Cocktail: The Drinks Bible for the 21st Century.* It was based on the section of classic cocktails at www.hotwired.com.

– Bill Russell-Shapiro and Eric Vreede open the craft bar Absinthe Brassiere & Bar in San Francisco (398 Hayes Street). Bartenders included Scott Beattie and Marcovaldo Dionysos.

– Patrick Sullivan opens B-Side Lounge—considered Boston's first fresh classic cocktail bar (92 Hampshire Street). Brother Cleve helps with the cocktail menu and tends bar for three years. Other bartenders include Misty Kalkofen, John Gertsen, Jackson Cannon, Dylan Black, Dave Cagle, Joe McGuirk, and Andy McNees.

– Tony Abou-Ganim is hired to bring classic fresh cocktails to all twenty-three bars at Bellagio in Las Vegas (3600 South Las Vegas Boulevard). Included in the opening is Bridget Albert, who becomes Abou-Ganim's protégé.

– Jeff "Beachbum" Berry publishes *Beachbum Berry's Grog Log.*

1999 – Dale "King Cocktail" DeGroff and Audrey Saunders head up the craft bar Blackbird in New York City (60 East Forty-Ninth Street).

– Tobin Ellis opens a craft and classic cocktail bar with a tequila focus hidden behind an unmarked door and up a flight of stairs above a pizza shop in Syracuse, New York, called the Stoop (309 West Fayette Street).

– Toby Cecchini opens Passerby in New York City (436 West Fifteenth Street).

– Steve Olson sets up the craft bar program at Russian Tea Room in New York City (150 West 57th Street).

– Marion's Continental on the Bowery serves fresh craft cocktails in New York City (354 Bowery).

– Eleven Madison Park restaurant serves classic cocktails in New York City (11 Madison Avenue).

2011 The award-winning cocktail writer and drink historian David Wondrich.
© *Danny Valdez*

– David Wondrich begins to update the online version of *Esquire*'s 1949 *Handbook for Hosts*.

– Gary Regan launches www.ardentspirits.com.

– The Campbell Apartment in New York City serves classic cocktails (Grand Central Terminal, 15 Vanderbilt Avenue).

– Ted A. Breaux becomes the first to analyze vintage absinthe using modern science, the results sparking a paradigm shift in our understanding of the infamous spirit.

– Inspired by Angel's Share, Sasha Petraske opens Milk & Honey on New Year's Eve in New York City (134 Eldridge Street).

– Chris Hannah makes fresh cocktails at the Duck News Café in Kitty Hawk, North Carolina (1564 Duck Road). Later, in 2004, Hannah heads up the French 75 Bar in New Orleans (813 Bienville Street).

2000 – Sasha Petraske hires his first bartender, Toby Maloney, at Milk & Honey in New York City. Other employees to follow include Christy Pope, Joseph Schwartz, Wilder Schwartz, Kelvin Perez, Elizabeth Sun, and Chad Solomon.

– Ryan Magarian joins Kathy Casey Food Studios and develops global fresh craft bar programs.

2001 – Lucy Brennan opens the craft bar Mint in Portland, Oregon (816 North Russell Street).

– Ted Haigh launches DrCocktail.com.

– Drew Levinson begins to travel with Steve Olson designing innovative beverage programs for nationally acclaimed restaurants.

– Gary Regan begins conducting a series of two-day bartender workshops called Cocktails in the Country. And Jonathan Pogash is one of the first students.

– Jonathan Pogash starts tending bar at the Russian Tea Room following Steve Olson's fresh juice program.

– Jamie Boudreau launches his *Spirits and Cocktails* blog (spiritsandcocktails.wordpress.com).

– Carlos Yturria tends bar at Ba.k.a.r making classic cocktails in San Francisco (448 Brannan Street).

2002 – Dale "King Cocktail" DeGroff publishes the book that officially kicks off the craft cocktail movement, *The Craft of the Cocktail: Everything You Need to Know to Be a Master Bartender*.

– Principal bartender John Gertsen works with bar manager Ryan McGrale to create a fresh classic cocktail program at No. 9 Park in Boston (9 Park Street).

– Murray Stenson serves classic cocktails at Zig Zag Café in Seattle, Washington (1501 Western Avenue #202).

– Sasha Petraske opens Milk & Honey in London in 2002 (61 Poland Street).

– Duggan McDonnell serves fresh classic cocktails at Wild Ginger in Seattle, Washington (1401 3rd Avenue).

– Tales of the Cocktail—the first cocktail festival—is launched in New Orleans by Ann Rogers.

– Jeff "Beachbum" Berry publishes *Intoxica*.

– William Grimes publishes *Straight Up or On the Rocks: The Story of the American Cocktail*.

2003 – Eastern Standard opens in Boston, which radicalizes the way those in Boston look at the art of cocktail making (528 Commonwealth Avenue).

– LeNell's Boutique Liquor Shop opened in Brooklyn (416 Van Brunt Street).

– Julie Reiner opens Flatiron Lounge, the first high-volume craft cocktail bar in New York City (37 West 19th Street). Bar staff includes Katie Stipe, Lynnette Marrero, John Blue, Phil Ward, Brian Miller, Toby Maloney, Dushan Zaric, and Jason Kosmas.

– Eben Freeman becomes known as a molecular mixologist at WD-50, a molecular gastronomy restaurant and bar in New York City (50 Clinton Street).

– Murray Stenson becomes head bartender at the Zig Zag Café.

– Gary Regan publishes *The Joy of Mixology*.

2004 – The Museum of the American Cocktail is founded in New Orleans by Dale and Jill DeGroff, Chris and Laura McMillian, Ted Haigh, Robert Hess, Phil Greene, and Jared Brown and Anistatia Miller.

– Ted Haigh publishes *Vintage Spirits and Forgotten Cocktails*.

The award-winning bar Employees Only in New York City. © *Emilie Baltz*

– Dushan Zaric and Jason Kosmas open the award-winning bar Employees Only in New York City (510 Hudson Street).

– Stefan Trummer takes craft cocktails to another level at Upstairs at Bouley in New York City (130 West Broadway).

– Jeff "Beachbum" Berry publishes *Taboo Table*.

– Brian Van Flandern serves classic crafted cocktails as head barman at Michelin three-star restaurant Per Se in New York City. One year later, he is credited for starting the global "tonic water" revolution by creating his own tonic water from scratch.

– Bartender and drink blogger Jeffrey Morgenthaler launches his drink blog jeffreymorhenthaler.com. Later, Morgenthaler heads up the award-winning Clyde Common in Portland, Oregon. Morgenthaler is also credited with making barrel-aged cocktails popular.

2005 – Sasha Petraske opens Little Branch in New York City (22 7th Avenue South).

– Chemist turned bartender Darcy O'Neil launches his blog *Art of Drink*. O'Neil goes on to write the award-winning book *Fix the Pumps* and also resurrects extinct drink products such as acid phosphate, lactart, and Abbott's bitters.

– Audrey Saunders opens Pegu Club in New York City (77 West Houston Street). Bar staff included Toby Maloney, Chad Solomon, Phil Ward, Jim Meehan, Sam Ross, and Brian Miller.

– Ryan Magarian partners with Christian Krogstad in making Aviation Gin. In 2018, actor Ryan Reynolds purchases the company.

– Dave Arnold starts working at the French Culinary Institute.

– Paul Clarke launches the first blog dedicated to the cocktail, *Cocktail Chronicles*.

– David Wondrich publishes *Killer Cocktails*.

– Derek Brown starts a cocktail blog, *DC Drinks*.

Midnight Rambler in the basement of the Joule Hotel. © *Mei Chen*

2006 – Sasha Petraske, Christy Pope, and Chad Solomon start Cuffs & Buttons—a beverage consultant and catering company. In 2014, Christy Pope and Chad Solomon open their own bar, Midnight Rambler in Dallas, Texas (1530 Main Street).

– Jamie Boudreau opens the craft bar Vessel in Seattle, Washington (624 Olive Way). Then in 2011 Boudreau opens the award-winning Canon in Seattle (928 Twelfth Avenue).

– Charlotte Voisey—sounds like "noisy"—is one of the first brand ambassadors and princesses of the cocktail world, handpicked by William Grant & Sons to represent Hendrick's gin.

– Wayne Curtis publishes *And a Bottle of Rum: A History of the New World in Ten Cocktails.*

– Popular drinks writer Camper English launches the *Alcademics* drink blog.

– Karen Foley publishes the award-winning drinks magazine *Imbibe*.

– San Francisco Cocktail Week starts its first year.

– Jared Brown and Anistatia Miller publish *Mixologist: The Journal of the American Cocktail Vol. 1.*

– Dale "King Cocktail" DeGroff, Steven Olson, Doug Frost, Paul Pacult, David Wondrich, and Andy Seymour open Beverage Alcohol Resource (BAR) in New York City.

– Todd Smith and Jon Santer open Bourbon & Branch in San Francisco (501 Jones Street).

– The bartenders of Absinthe Brassiere & Bar publish *Art of the Bar.*

– Francis Schott opens the restaurant Catherine Lombardi with a fresh craft cocktail bar in New Brunswick, New Jersey (3 Livingston Avenue).

– Dave Kaplan and Alex Day open Death + Co. on New Year's Eve in New York City (433 East 6th Street).

– Todd Thrasher opens his first bar, PX, in Alexandria, Virginia (728 Kings Street).

2007 – Don Lee starts training behind the bar at Death & Co., then in the same year helps Jim Meehan at PDT. He invents fat washing by infusing bacon with Bourbon and creates the Benton's Old-Fashioned.

– Eric Seed brings Rothman and Winter crème de violette back into America after being unavailable for almost ninety years.

– Eben Freeman he opens his own bar Tailor (505 8th Avenue).

– Greg Boehm begins to reproduce and publish old cocktail books.

– Jeff "Beachbum" Berry publishes *Sippin' Safari.*

– Lucid absinthe becomes the first wormwood absinthe allowed back into the United States after being banned for ninety-five years—thanks to Ted A. Breaux and Veridian Spirits LLC.

– Duggan McDonnell opens his craft bar Cantina in San Francisco.

– Head mixologist Toby Maloney opens the Violet Hour in Chicago (1520 North Damen Avenue).

– St. Germain elderflower liqueur is introduced.

– Paul Tanguay and Tad Carducci launch Tippling Bros.—a beverage consulting company.

– Jim Meehan opens PDT in New York City (9113 East Marks Place). The telephone booth entrance creates headlines and the TV talk show host Jimmy Fallon talks about it on his show.

– Michael Martensen begins a fresh craft bar program at the Rosewood Mansion on Turtle Creek in Dallas, Texas.

– David Wondrich publishes the James Beard Award-winning *Imbibe!*

– Jared Brown and Anistatia Miller publish *Mixologist: The Journal of the American Cocktail Vol. 2.*

– Tobin Ellis is selected as the number-one bartender in America to compete against Bobby Flay in his TV show *Throwdown! with Bobby Flay*, making Ellis the first successful award-winning flair bartender to cross over to the craft cocktail world.

– Tony Abou-Ganim publishes *Modern Mixology.*

– Colin Kimball launches the Small Screen Network and brings professional online bartending videos to the cocktail community.

2008 – Julie Reiner opens Clover Club in Brooklyn, New York (210 Smith Street). The opening bar staff includes Ms. Franky Marshall, Nate Dumas, Brad Farran, Giuseppe Gonzalez, and Tom Chadwick. Ms. Franky Marshall went on to work at Monkey Bar, the Tippler, Dead Rabbit, and Holiday Cocktail Lounge.

– Sasha Petraske opens White Star absinthe bar in New York City (22 7th Avenue South).

– Robert Hess publishes *The Essential Bartender's Guide.*

– Pernod Ricard USA partners with some of the most highly respected American spirits professionals to launch BarSmarts—an advanced bartender training program. The trainers include Dale "King Cocktail" DeGroff, Steve "Wine Geek" Olson, Doug Frost, F. Paul Pacult, Andy Seymour, and David Wondrich.

– Scott Beattie publishes *Artisanal Cocktails.*

– Roberto Sequeira launches Gläce Luxury Ice, which offers high-quality ice spheres (balls) and large cubes delivered to your door.

– Bridget Albert publishes *Market Fresh Mixology.*

– Dale "King Cocktail" DeGroff publishes his second book, *The Essential Cocktail.*

– John Lermayer is handpicked by rock star Lenny Kravitz and Morgans Hotel Group Vice President of Nightlife Ben Pundole to create a cutting-edge beverage program for the Delano in Miami Beach.

– New Orleans becomes the first city in the world to vote in an official city cocktail—the Sazerac.

– Natalie Bovis publishes the first nonalcoholic craft mocktail book *Preggatinis: Mixology for the Mom-to-Be.*

– Cocktail Kingdom is launched, selling high-quality master mixology bar tools.

2009 – Sasha Petraske opens Los Angeles's first craft bar, the Varnish, with Eric Alperin and Cedd Moses (118 East 6th Street).

The award-winning flair bartender, mixologist, hospitality consultant, and bar equipment designer Tobin Ellis. © *Tobin Ellis*

- Brian Van Flandern publishes *Vintage Cocktails*.
- Sasha Petraske opens Dutch Kills in Long Island City, New York (27–24 Jackson Avenue).
- Phil Ward opens his bar, Mayahuel (304 East 6th Street).
- Kate Gerwin opens Casa Vieja restaurant in Corrales, New Mexico with a fresh craft bar program.
- I help BarProducts.com add a Master Mixology section of bar tools.
- Kathy Casey's book *Sips & Apps* is published and in the book, Dale "King Cocktail" DeGroff mentions her as the first bar chef.
- Philip Ward and Ravi DeRossi head up Mayahuel in New York City (304 East Sixth Street).
- Tobin Ellis launches Social Mixology, the world's first pop-up speakeasy series, which makes underground appearances in New York, Honolulu, Los Angeles, New Orleans, Aspen, Las Vegas, San Francisco, and Miami.

2010 – The millennial generation takes the wheel. Yeah, they tend to be narcissistic, don't understand why they need to pay their dues—run before they can walk—but look where they drove the cocktail culture: they steered away from the speakeasy-styled bars and created casual hangs such Prizefighter, Honeycut, and Mother's Ruin, they opened dive craft bars, tiki bars, and soda fountain bars, grew their own herbs, created barrel-aged cocktails, advanced molecular mixology, cocktails on tap, cold maceration, flair bartenders crossed over to mixology and vice versa, Red Rover Bartenders (celebrity bartenders swapped/traveled to bartend at other bars), organized pop-up bars, produced commercial artisanal syrups, waters, bitters, and more, experimented with plant-based milk, focused on mezcal, tequila, moonshine, and genever forward cocktails, made tattooed bartenders cool, started ice programs, popularized Japanese bar tools, produced their own bar tools, presented food and cocktail pairings, started their own cocktail events, and most importantly, won James Beard Awards. They are not done. In 2018, they have started a serious push to-go straw-less for environmental reasons. Previous generations are very proud, but their only regret is not having the internet / social media bartender community back in their day.

23

SERVING COCKTAILS: A GUIDE TO COCKTAIL VESSELS

•••
A BRIEF HISTORY OF DRINKING VESSELS

The first drinking vessels were made of pottery, wood, metals—or in a pinch—objects such as a cracked coconut shells, animal horns, etc.

The first "glass" was made naturally from black volcanic glass. It is believed that starting around 2000 BCE, the people of Mesopotamia (now Northern Syria and Iraq) would melt volcanic glass, and then pour it into molds to make objects such as bowls and beads. The Romans improved on this idea around 50 BCE by sticking a molten glob on the end of a hollow tube and then blowing it into a shape. By the 1400s, glassmaking techniques greatly advanced. In the 1600s, and especially the 1700s, elegant glassware was found in most homes.

In the early 1800s, barkeeps only had about five types of bar glasses. By the end of the century, the first-rate bars had a glass for everything, sometimes totaling twenty-five types of bar glasses.

•••
BASIC COCKTAIL GLASSWARE

A glass is the first thing you or a bartender will grab before making a cocktail. Now, of course, you can drink a Mai Tai from a recycled pickle jar, but if you live in the civilized world, you will want to drink cocktails in their proper glassware. At home, you can get away with delicate cocktail glassware, but in most bars you will find more durable glassware for obvious reasons.

From left to right: highball, rocks, Old-Fashioned, Double Old-Fashioned, Collins, shot, brandy snifter, champagne flute, champagne saucer/coupe, champagne trumpet, champagne tulip, cocktail coupe, cocktail conical, cordial, Hurricane, Irish coffee, Margarita, poco grande, punch cup, sherry, and tiki mug.

STURDY GLASSWARE

HIGHBALL

Seven to nine ounces. Most bars do not stock real highball glasses and just use short Old-Fashioned glasses, calling them highballs. Vintage films from the 1930s through the 1950s often show what is considered a highball glass.

ROCKS

Around five to eight ounces and used for shooters and, of course, drinks on the rocks such as one-spirit (normally whiskey) or two-spirit drinks like a Rusty Nail or Black Russian.

OLD-FASHIONED

A nine-to-twelve-ounce, short, stocky glass, making it perfect for a highball such as a Scotch & Water, Gin & Tonic or—of course—an Old-Fashioned. Sometimes it is called a lowball glass.

DOUBLE OLD FASHIONED

A twelve-to-fourteen-ounce, short, sturdy glass that is a little bigger than an Old-Fashioned glass. People who do not like the awkwardness of a tall glass will like these. It is also called a bucket glass.

COLLINS

A ten-to-twelve-ounce glass (also called a chimney glass) that is tall and thin with straight sides.

SHOT

One-and-a-half-to-two-ounce short glass designed for shots of liquor.

STEMMED GLASSWARE

BRANDY SNIFTER

Snifters can be found in sizes five to twenty-four ounces. They are used for brandy or Cognac; however, many spirits can be served in a snifter, including Sambuca (don't forget the three coffee beans), Grand Marnier, a fine tequila, a single malt Scotch, etc. Some bars like to use snifters for Brandy Alexanders and Milk Punches.

CHAMPAGNE FLUTE

This will be a six-ounce glass (for a five-ounce pour) for champagne and champagne drinks.

CHAMPAGNE SAUCER/COUPE

A six-ounce glass for champagne and champagne drinks.

CHAMPAGNE TRUMPET

A six-ounce glass for champagne and champagne drinks that is a type of flute. It is tall and V-shaped like a trumpet.

CHAMPAGNE TULIP

A six-ounce glass for champagne and champagne drinks that is a type of a flute. It has a curvy shape.

Cocktail Glass/Coupe

Cocktail coupes can range from five to ten ounces in size. Vintage coupes are on the small side, while modern coupes will be a little larger.

Cocktail Glass / Conical

These conical-shaped cocktail glasses are often referred to as a Martini glass. They range in sizes six to twelve ounces. Large Martini glasses are meant for cocktails that have mixers added to them.

Cordial

A cordial glass will be a small glass holding up to two ounces.

Hurricane

A twelve-to-twenty-two-ounce hurricane lamp–shaped glass that is used for tropical drinks.

Irish Coffee

A seven-to-ten-ounce glass mug used for hot drinks, or the traditional version, which is a stemmed glass without a handle (the latter is used at the Buena Vista Cafe where they make 2,000 Irish Coffees a day). If you use a larger mug at home, you will need to double up the booze to compensate for the extra size.

Margarita

A Margarita glass has a sombrero-shaped coupe and is between fourteen and sixteen ounces. There are other Margarita glasses with green cactus stems and glasses made of thick, bubbled Mexican glass.

Poco Grande

A Poco Grande glass is a short version of a Hurricane glass. It will be around fourteen ounces, and some bars will use this glass for all their tropical drinks, including Margaritas.

Punch Cup

A punch cup will be around six to eight ounces because punch is meant to be strong and served without ice in the cup.

Sherry

A four-to-five-ounce glass used for sherry and ports. A proper serving is three ounces.

Wine

Wineglasses can be seven to twenty-four ounces. Most bars carry one all-purpose wineglass used for both red and white wines, but "wine bars" will generally use large bowl glasses for reds and slender glasses for white. A proper pour of wine is six ounces; however, some bars will pour five ounces because they want to get five glasses out of a bottle.

NOVELTY

Coconut

The best way to make coconut cups for glassware is to use a band saw to saw off the top quarter part of the coconut and leave in the coconut meat.

PINEAPPLE

Cut the top part of a pineapple off, then hull out the meat. To make hulling easier, invest in a pineapple corer.

TIKI

Tiki mugs come in a variety of shapes and sizes up to twenty-four ounces.

FUN COCKTAIL GLASSWARE FACTS

› In 1884, the G. Winter Brewing Company in New York published a bartender guide listing over twenty-five types of glassware that first-rate saloons should have.

› It has been said that the stemmed coupe glass was modeled after Marie Antoinette's bosom; however, this cannot be true because the glass was invented almost one hundred years before she was born.

› The twelve-ounce conical Martini glass was not created until the late 1990s when the flavored Martini craze happened. Glass producers had to make them larger so the added mixers could fit in the glass.

› The sixteen-ounce pint glass is the most popular all-purpose glass because it can be used for beer, a mixing glass, water, the second half of a Boston shaker, and tall (and double tall) drinks such as Long Island Iced Teas, lemonades, tropical drinks, Bloody Marys, and many more.

› On January 25, 2008, the world's largest champagne fountain was created with 43,680 glasses at the Shopping Center Wijnegem in Belgium.

24

Tools of the Trade: The Essential Cocktail Bar Tools

* * *

···

A BRIEF HISTORY OF COCKTAIL TOOLS

All professions have tools, and in the cocktail world, one bartender stands out on the subject of bar tools: Jerry "Professor" Thomas. Thomas published the very first American cocktail recipe book in 1862, and it is well known that he traveled the world with a set of solid silver bar tools. In the late 1700s to early 1800s, bar tools included punch bowls, silver ladles, citrus reamers and strainers, knives, nutmeg graters, spoons, small wineglasses for measuring, large containers to be used as measuring cups, pestles and mortars, sugar loaf nibs, and a muddler. In the late 1800s, bar tools began to be improved and patented.

···

BASIC BAR TOOLS

From left to right: barspoon, bottle opener, citrus squeezer, corkscrew, grater (microplane), jigger, muddler, Boston shaker, cobbler shaker, Hawthorne strainer, julep strainer, mesh strainer, wide peeler, zester/channel knife.

Only a few tools are needed to make great cocktails and, in a pinch, you can even find substitutes in your kitchen drawers. Sure, you can shake up a cocktail in a lidded Mason jar and strain it through your fingers, but if you want to get serious about cocktail making, then invest in a few tools.

BARSPOON

A barspoon has a long handle and you use it to stir cocktails, layer shots, spoon dry goods like sugar, and guide a thick frozen/blended drink out from the blender pitcher into a glass. Popular cocktails that require stirring include Gin Martinis, Manhattans, and Sazeracs.

To stir a cocktail, add your ingredients into a mixing glass and then add ice. Place the handle of the spoon between your middle and ring fingers, then insert the spoon to the inside of the mixing glass (bowl of the spoon touching the inside of the glass). Keep the bowl on the inside of the glass as you stir around. Twenty revolutions is a good stir.

All alcohols have different weights (densities), and when you layer a shot, you start with the heaviest alcohol on the bottom and the lightest on top. Let us say you want to layer Irish cream on top of coffee liqueur. Simply fill half of the shot glass with coffee liqueur, set the edge of the spoon bowl on top of the coffee liqueur level, and gently pour the Irish cream on the bowl (breaking the fall) so that it gently layers on top of the coffee liqueur. Some bartenders like to use the curved side of the bowl and others like the concave side of the bowl.

BOTTLE OPENER

A bottle opener opens bottles. There are many to choose from. They come in all colors and styles, with retractable reels, belt hooks, and so much more.

CITRUS SQUEEZER

A citrus squeezer squeezes citrus juice, and there are electric, manual, and handheld squeezers to choose from.

CORKSCREW

A corkscrew is also called a wine tool and used to open bottles of wine, stubborn corks on whiskey bottles, and as bottle openers. Many types are available, but real bartenders and wine stewards use a waiter's corkscrew. The best to buy is a "double lever" waiter's corkscrew, which comes with a small built-in knife to cut the foil off a wine bottle, but you will find the knife can serve many other purposes.

GRATER

A grater (microplane) is used mostly to grate fresh spices. Just hold the small, stainless-steel grater over the drink and grate. The most popular drinks that require nutmeg grating include Milk Punch and a Brandy Alexander.

JIGGER

A two-sided measurement tool to measure alcohol for cocktails. They come in about five different sizes. But if you can only buy two, get 1–2 ounce and 1.5–.5 ounce jiggers.

MUDDLER

A muddler is used to crush and mash fruits, sugar cubes, herbs, and more. Never use a varnished or lacquered muddler because those poisons will get into the drink. There are several muddlers to choose from today.

SHAKER TIN

A shaker is used to shake a drink. You can find novelty shakers in many shapes, but they all break down into two types: cobbler and Boston.

Cobbler shakers consist of three pieces and are mostly used by home enthusiasts. A Boston-type shaker consists of two components pieced together to shake a drink—normally a sixteen-ounce mixing pint glass and a twenty-eight-ounce shaker tin.

STRAINER

A strainer keeps ice and other ingredients that have been shaken from falling into the glass. Bartenders today use three types of strainers: Hawthorne, julep, and mesh.

Hawthorne strainers have a metal coil and can be used on top of a shaker tin or a mixing glass. Julep strainers fit at an angle into a mixing glass. A mesh strainer is used as a "double strainer"—meaning that it's held over the glass and used as a second strainer while pouring into the glass from a Boston or julep strainer. It makes sure seeds or small bits are caught before going into the drink.

WIDE PEELER

This is a peeler much like you have at home to peel vegetables but wider to cut citrus rinds.

ZESTER/CHANNEL KNIFE

These cut curly, fancy citrus twists.

THE BEST BAR TOOLS

Every profession has different grades and levels of tools—and bar tools are no exception. A one-stop shop for the leading high-quality bar tools is cocktailkingdom.com. There is also thebostonshaker.com, babsupplies. com, and the master mixology section of barproducts.com.

FUN BAR TOOL FACTS

› In the early cocktail-making days, sherry glasses were used as jiggers. It is also known that eggcups were often used as a jigger. Eggcups were mainly used for breakfast; a soft-boiled egg was placed into the cup, then cracked with a butter knife and eaten out of the shell with a spoon.

› The julep strainer was originally called an ice spoon.

› The barspoon is believed to come from apothecary medicine and pestle spoons.

› In 1932, popular jewelry company Napier produced a silver cocktail shaker with engraved recipes called "Tells-You-How Mixer." The engraved recipes included Alexander, Bacardi, Between the Sheets, Bronx, Clover Club, Dry Martini, Dubonnet, Gin Rickey, Manhattan, Old-Fashioned, Orange Blossom, Pam Beach, Sidecar, and Tom Collins. Initially, it was only sold at Saks Fifth Avenue. Today, you can buy one for around $1,200. Napier went on to produce many more cocktail shakers.

› The muddler was first called a toddy stick and was made of silver or hardwood.

› Double straining (straining with a Hawthorne and mesh strainer held over the cocktail glass) was first done by using a Hawthorne strainer and julep strainer held over the glass.

› To heat cocktails, vintage bartenders would plunge hot iron pokers from the fireplace into drinks. They were either called flip dogs or loggerheads.

› In 1850, the first known published illustration of a two-piece cocktail shaker was seen in the *London News*.

› To authentically strain a cocktail that is stirred in a mixing glass, you should leave the spoon in as you strain.

> In 1868, articles on American cocktails and cocktail shakers were published in two British publications: the British periodical *Notes and Queries* and *Meliora: A Quarterly Review of Social Science*.

> > "This endeavor to get up a system of stimulation has given rise in America to the manufacture of 'cocktail' (a compound of whiskey, brandy, or champagne, bitters, and ice), dexterously mixed in tall silver mugs made for the purpose, called 'cocktail shakers.'"—*Notes and Queries*

> > "They toss the drinks about; they throw brimful glasses over their heads; they shake the saccharine, glacial and alcoholic ingredients in their long tin tubes."—***Meliora: A Quarterly Review of Social Science***

> E. J. Hauck from Brooklyn, New York, patented a three-piece cocktail shaker in 1884.

> In 1889, a man from Connecticut created a metal spring to go around a strainer, and a few years later, the Connecticut company Manning & Bowman improved it and punched holes in it to read "Hawthorne," which was named after the Hawthorne Café in Boston.

> In 1892, Chicago bartender Cornelius Dungan patented the double cone jigger.

Neat or Straight Up: Getting Familiar with Drink-Making Terms

...

DRINK-MAKING TERMINOLOGY

- **Blend:** to mix up ingredients in an electric blender with ice. In America, generally the South says "frozen" and the North says "blended."

- **Build:** fill a glass with large ice and pour in the ingredients. If you have small, thin ice, pour your ingredients in first and then add the ice to avoid a lot of dilution.

- **Chill:** to chill a glass, add ice and then water to the glass and allow it to chill while you are making the drink. Alternatively, keep glasses chilled in the freezer.

- **Float:** gently pour a spirit on top of a drink.

- **Muddle:** to mash up ingredients with a muddler. Crush hard for ingredients like pineapple, citrus, ginger, etc. Softly tap herbs just to release the oils.

- **Neat:** room-temperature-pour straight from the bottle. No ice.

- **On the Rocks:** over ice.

- **Rim:** to add something to the rim of the glass.

- **Roll:** to roll a drink back and forth.

- **Shake:** to shake a cocktail with ice with a cocktail shaker.

- **Strain:** after shaking, strain the cocktail with a strainer.

- **Stir:** pour ingredients into a mixing glass; add ice, and then stir.

- **Straight Up:** a drink that is chilled by shaking or stirring then served cold straight up.

Rules to Drink By: Bar Etiquette

Every profession in the world could list ten things they want you to know. Dentists wish women wouldn't wear lipstick to appointments; off-duty doctors wish you wouldn't ask questions about your aches and pains; and supermarket cashiers wish you would take items out of the basket instead of sitting it on the belt.

The Top Ten Things Bartenders Want You to Know

1. Cash tips are king. It is common in America to be paid bimonthly, so bartenders have to wait two weeks to get their taxed credit card tips. Cash tips are king because it gives the bartender a little spending cash.

2. If a bartender asks you for a valid ID, take it as a compliment. There is a small window in life where you get to be young and beautiful, so enjoy it! Bartenders don't enjoy taking time to check your ID because it slows them down, but they have to follow state laws and work policies in order to keep their jobs.

3. Bartenders lose money if not tipped. Let us say that you do not tip on your $10 drink. The sale of that drink is still reported to the government and then taxed eight percent. The tax is taken out of their hourly pay. So, a $6 an hour bartender job can very quickly turn into a $1 an hour job. It is common for a bartender to not get a check at all.

4. Asking for a drink in a tall glass or with less ice does not mean you get more alcohol. It only means that you get your drink served in a tall glass with extra mixer. A drink with less ice means normal portions of alcohol and mixer with less ice. If you want more alcohol, then you will need to order a double.

5. Be respectful and leave the bar when it closes. Last call is normally given one half-hour before closing, and lights come up when it's closing time. Bartenders have another two hours cashing out, doing paperwork, stocking, cleaning, and hauling out trash before they can go home, so don't add extra time for them.

6. When you say, "Hook me up! Make my drink strong! Make it a good one!" what bartenders hear is, "Hey, I know we don't know each other and you could get fired, but will you please steal some booze for me?" Bars are a store and bartenders are the salespeople. They sell products owned by other people, and therefore cannot give away things that are not theirs. A person who takes things that are not theirs is called a thief. Yes, some bar owners allow a small comp tab, but bartenders use it with discretion and for valid comps—not to steal something for you.

7. Most jobs are either physical or mental. Bartending is both. Bartenders spend their first two hours setting up the bar for the day and their last two hours closing down. Sandwiched in between they are remembering ten things in their head at all times (names, prices, drink orders, tabs, cocktail recipes, etc.), making many five-second decisions (whether you are of age, too intoxicated, safe, etc.), dealing with many personality types, and having to bend, reach, squat, and lift. It's physically and mentally draining.

8. Please do not announce, "I'm a bartender" or "I used to be a bartender" because real bartenders would never say that. Bartenders know you are in the biz by your actions.

9. Please stop handing over multiple cards to split your tabs when the bar is busy. If you insist on paying separately, then begin separate tabs at the beginning or do the best thing by taking turns buying rounds.

10. It is not the bartender's responsibility to charge and take care of your media devices. Bring your charge cord and we will be happy to let you know where the outlets are located. On the media note: please do not push your cell phone in bar staff faces with a cocktail recipe that has more than four ingredients.

• • •

HONORABLE MENTION

Stop being ripped off by lazy bartenders who do not give you the alcohol that you paid for.

Example #1: You order four chilled Patrón Silver shots. When the bartender shakes the tequila with ice (to chill it), water melts into the tequila. All four shots will not fit into four shot glasses now, so make sure you tell the bartender you want all the extra. You paid for it, so you deserve it.

Example #2: You order a frozen drink and the bartender makes it by hand in a blender. Everything in that blender is yours, so do not let them pour the finished drink into a glass, then have some leftover in the blender. You need to ask for the leftover because you've paid for that alcohol.

• • •

HOW TO ORDER A COCKTAIL AT A BAR

1. When a bar is busy, always have your order/orders ready when the bartender approaches you. If you have questions or want to have a conversation about cocktails and choices, then let the bartender know so they can fit in the time needed to do that into their flow. The bartender may set you up with a few ideas and menu to give you a little time, then get back with you. Bartenders want to give you good service, but they also want to give everyone good service. If the bar is slow, then the bartender will be able to spend more time with you.

2. When you know what you want, name the liquor first and your mixer second. Also, "call" your liquor (meaning to call out the brand you want). Examples include: Grey Goose & Cranberry, Jack & Coke, Bombay & Tonic, Ketel One Screwdriver, Knob Creek Rye Old-Fashioned, and Malibu & Pineapple.

3. Well drinks. These are also called rail or house drinks. They are the least expensive mixed drinks. When you ask for a Gin & Tonic, then the bartender is using the cheapest gin to make your drink. However, a lot of corporate bars require the bartender to up sell, so the bartender will ask you if there is a gin you prefer or if you want your favorite gin used, etc. If you truly want the cheapest Gin & Tonic, then help the bartender by asking for a well Gin & Tonic. This eliminates a lot a time and monotony for the bartender.

4. When ordering drinks that require details, always give the details. Examples include: Herradura Reposado Margarita on the rocks with salt; Bombay Sapphire Martini straight up, stirred with an olive and a twist; Belvedere Vodka Martini straight up, shaken with a twist; Double Glenlivet 12, neat with a water back; Hendrick's Negroni with Aperol up; and Jim Beam Rye Manhattan on the rocks. ("Up" is short for straight up. Straight up means that it has been chilled—shaken with ice—then strained into the glass. "Neat" means that it is poured out of the bottle at room temperature.)

5. While the bartender is making your cocktail/cocktails, start getting your money ready. If you want to start a tab, then get your credit card ready. After delivering your cocktail, the next step for a bartender

is to secure a transaction. Many have cameras on them and they are required to follow through with the transaction process.

Here are some common things people say to bartenders and ways to do and say them better.

You: What's good? Surprise me!

It is great that you want to try something new, but please narrow it down. First, we do not know what flavors, spirits, and types of cocktails you like or dislike. Second, we do not know if you are lactose intolerant, allergic to nuts, or have any dietary concerns. We also do not know what you are in the mood for. Are you celebrating something? Do you want something hot, boozy, refreshing, fruity, creamy, classic, etc.? Better ways to ask the bartender include:

- "I like vodka-based drinks with fruity flavors. I also love the taste of ginger, chocolate, or mint. Can you make me something tall and refreshing?"
- "Can you make me something off the top of your head? I'm game for anything. The only spirit I do not like is tequila and the only other flavor I do not like is licorice. I'd like something boozy on the rocks."
- "I'm celebrating! Can you make me something historic made with champagne?"
- "I had a craft cocktail in New York City that had a spicy liqueur in it that I really liked. Could you make me something spicy with Bourbon?"

You: Can I get a beer?

I know they do this in the movies, but it doesn't work in bars. Ask for a beer menu or ask the bartender where you can find the beer menu. Most bars offer many beers.

You: Can we get three shots of tequila?

Yes, you can, but what kind of tequila do you want? Do you want salt? Do you want limes? Ways to order shots of tequila include:

- "Can we get three shots of Patrón Silver with salt and limes?"
- "We need three chilled shots of Don Julio Reposado with limes."
- "We'd like to get three shots of well tequila with no salt or limes."

27

TRENDING: WHAT INFLUENCES OUR IMBIBING

•••
MEDIA INFLUENCE ON COCKTAILS

Media. Is. Communication. It can be spoken, written, or broadcasted on radio, in newspapers, magazines, film, advertising, music, TV, internet, etc. Media can influence voters, the products you buy, your attitude, and a sense of what is or is not important to you. It always reflects and creates culture. It is powerful. So, if you think you don't know the name of a hit TV show featuring a New York City pink Martini being drunk by four attractive female friends—you're wrong. You know the name of the show—don't you? Media is even more powerful in today's world because of the speed of technology. Humans started with the spoken word, which led to cave paintings, smoke signals, handwriting, carrier pigeon, printing press, Morse code, typewriter, radio, vinyl albums, telephone, TV, word processor, cassette tapes, VHS tapes, compact discs, computers, internet, and social networking. Cell phones have become such an integral part of our everyday life that when watching a film or TV show from the 1990s, we often catch ourselves wondering for a few seconds, "Why don't they just call!...oh, it was the nineties."

•••
INFLUENTIAL COCKTAIL MEDIA IN FILM

1934–1947 *THE THIN MAN*

The Thin Man (1934), *After the Thin Man* (1936), *Another Thin Man* (1939), *Shadow of the Thin Man* (1941), 1944 *The Thin Man Goes Home* (1944), and *Song of the Thin Man* (1947).

The *Thin Man* movies are without a doubt the most prolific series of films that highlight cocktails. Actually, it is the only film series. The series are comedic mystery films starring William Powell and Myrna Loy as Nick and Nora Charles. Nick is a retired private detective and Nora is a wealth heiress. Their imbibing cocktails of choice include a Martini, Knickerbocker, Bronx, gin, rye whiskey, and more.

1962 *DR. NO*

The first James Bond film is responsible for jumpstarting the sale of vodka in America—Smirnoff in particular. Before then, most Americans drank whiskey, brandy, rum, and gin. But when Sean Connery made his own Smirnoff Martinis in his hotel room and later ordered Vodka Martinis—shaken-not-stirred—it created a worldwide Vodka Martini frenzy. To date, vodka (still) is the number-one spirit sold in America.

1988 *COCKTAIL*

Many films have bar scenes, but when Tom Cruise introduced the entertainment-starved world to "Flair Bartending," it sparked a sensation. To this day, bar guests will still mention Tom Cruise anytime a bartender makes any kind of fancy movement. Many will ask, "Can you bartend like Tom Cruise?" TGI Fridays began to train their bartenders to perform fancy moves called "flair" in the late 1970s and 1980s. The word probably came from the pieces of flair—an assortment of extra fun pins stuck on server and bartenders suspenders—that the staff was required to wear. "Magic" Mike Werner, a Texas TGI Friday's bartender and trainer, is credited with planting the flair seed when he was flipping bottles around for fun. Werner was the first stacked domino, pushed to create a flair bartending chain reaction. TGI Friday's was the first to host a flair bartending competition, 1986's TGI Friday's Bar Olympics in Woodland Hills, California. The winner of the competition was John "JB" Bandy (Werner won second place). In 1987, Bandy was approached by Touchstone Pictures to be the flair bartending choreographer and bartender trainer for Tom Cruise and Bryan Brown for the 1988 film *Cocktail*. Many drinks were made, seen, and mentioned in the film, but most importantly, it kickstarted the flair bartending phenomenon.

2002 *DIE ANOTHER DAY*

Forty years after skyrocketing the Vodka Martini in 1962, James Bond (played by Pierce Brosnan) did it again—this time with a Mojito. The Mojito is a 1920s classic Cuban cocktail, but brand-new to audiences watching an orange bikini–clad Halle Berry rise from the water, walk to the bar, and have James Bond hand her a Mojito. Ever heard the term "overnight sensation"? Bar guests walked into bars ordering Mojitos and bartenders had zero fresh mint, or zero knowledge of this cocktail. The Mojito is still going strong.

2011 *CRAZY, STUPID, LOVE*

The 1800s Old-Fashioned was made popular again by the hit TV series *Mad Men* (2007–2015), so when charming movie star Ryan Gosling made Old-Fashioneds for himself and Emma Stone in 2011, it threw gas on the fire. Gosling learned his Old-Fashioned–making skills from superstar bartender Eric Alperin, co-owner of the esteemed Los Angeles craft bar Varnish. Today, it is one of the top cocktails men will order.

• • •

INFLUENTIAL COCKTAIL MEDIA IN MUSIC

1945 "RUM AND COCA-COLA," THE ANDREWS SISTERS

The Andrews Sisters in 1945. © *Photofest*

In 1943, this song was a hit in Trinidad. The song was stolen (don't worry, the owner got his day in court), its lyrics revamped, and then introduced to the Andrews Sisters.

It became the number-one song in America. Network radio stations banned it because it mentioned an alcoholic beverage and a brand (Coca-Cola). There were still a lot of dry states in America at the time, but history has proven one thing: when something is banned, it makes it more popular. The demand for the record was phenomenal. Decca Records sold seven million copies. Now, if we only knew the rum and the Coca-Cola sales, because the guess is that it was nothing short of mind-blowing.

1973 "TEQUILA SUNRISE," THE EAGLES

The recipe for a successful Tequila Sunrise:

- 1 cup Bartender Bobby Lozoff inventing it, then making one for Mick Jagger.
- 1 cup Mick Jagger asking for it at bars all over America while on tour.
- 1 cup Jose Cuervo putting the recipe on the back of their bottle in early 1973.
- Stir in a hit song by the Eagles and release it to the masses.

Bartenders from 1973 say that as soon as the song hit the airwaves customers were asking for the drink.

1977 "MARGARITAVILLE," JIMMY BUFFETT

Margaritas had been popular since the 1950s, but when Jimmy Buffett rose to the number-on spot on the charts with the song "Margaritaville," the drink was in high demand in bars everywhere. To meet the demand, bars stocked bottles of fake Margarita mixers. Today, many bars have gone back to using fresh-squeezed lime juice—thank you!

1979 "ESCAPE," RUPERT HOLMES

If you like Piña Coladas and getting caught in the rain, then you will like this song, but ask any bartender from 1979 their least favorite drink to make and they will say—yep!—Piña Colada. And it's all because of Rupert Holmes. Again, to keep up with the demand, the shelves were filled with fake Piña Colada mixers.

1993 "GIN & JUICE," SNOOP DOGG

Unbelievably, gin was not on the drinking radar at this time, so when Snoop Dog's second hit reached the Top Ten, bar guests began asking for it. Most did not understand what they were ordering—they just heard it on a hit song and wanted it. Bartenders were constantly asking, "What kind of juice would you like?" Seagram's reported that their sales shot to over three million cases that year and up to four million through the late 1990s. Soon, Seagram's began making flavored gin.

2001 "PASS THE COURVOISIER," BUSTA RHYMES AND P. DIDDY

Cognac had been mentioned in 1990s rap songs previously, but "Pass the Courvoisier" changed the genre of Cognac overnight. Thoughts of Cognac used to conjure images of men sitting in overstuffed leather chairs smoking cigars and drinking Cognac. This was a game-changer. On NPR in 2009, Courvoisier's marketing manager, Jennifer Szersnovicz, said, "It was huge for the brand and our volumes skyrocketed."

Some previous rap songs with Cognac or a brand of Cognac in their songs:

- 1990 "Humpty Dance," Digital Underground
- 1993 "Gz Up, Hoes Down," Snoop Dogg
- 1994 "The Genesis," Nas
- 1994 "Down for Whatever," Ice Cube
- 1994 "So Much Pain," TuPac
- 1996 "Nas Is Coming," Nas
- 1999 "Next Episode," DRE and Snoop Dog

In 2007, Snoop Dogg was approached by Landy Cognac to put their brand in a rap song. Now, that is the way to do it! One year later, Dogg released the Christmas rap song "Landy in My Eggnog."

...

INFLUENTIAL COCKTAIL MEDIA ON TV

1998–2004 *SEX AND THE CITY*

The very first episode showed Carrie and Samantha drinking Cosmopolitans at Miranda's birthday dinner; however the average viewer would not have known the cocktails were called Cosmopolitans. But on Sunday night, July 19, 1998, in season one episode seven, the cocktail was finally written into the transcript by Darren Star. The voice-over of character Carrie Bradshaw read: "That afternoon I dragged my poor, tortured soul out to lunch with Stanford Blach and attempted to stun it senseless with Cosmopolitans." And the rest is history.

Out of six seasons and 94 episodes, the Cosmopolitan was seen 27 times and mentioned by name four times. In 1999, season two most definitely set the Cosmopolitan tone for the rest of the seasons because the cocktail was seen in ten episodes and mentioned by name in three.

2006 *THE OPRAH WINFREY SHOW*

The *Oprah* show could make someone famous overnight. Any product mentioned skyrocketed in sales, and the same is true for cocktails. In 2006, Oprah Winfrey and Rachael Ray made Lemon Drop Martinis and Pomegranate Martinis. Lemon Drop shot and shooters had been around in the late 1980s and 1990s, but when the "Martini Bar" craze started (late 1990s–mid-2000s), it was common to see Lemon Drop Martinis, so bartenders could easily make it. The Pomegranate Martini was a different story. Bars did not carry pomegranate-flavored anything (juice, flavored liquor, syrup, or liqueur). Of course, as you might imagine, everyone started asking bartenders for Pomegranate Martinis the very same day the show aired. This is when POM brand pomegranate juice began to appear in the grocery stores.

2007–2015 *MAD MEN*

Jon Hamm as Don Draper in *Mad Men*; 2009. © *AMC / Photofest*

Mad Men made many vintage cocktails from the late 1950s and the 1960s cool again. The Old-Fashioned is probably the most popular, but it was nice for bartenders to have twenty-somethings (millions turn twenty-one every day) order cocktails that their grandmothers or grandfathers might have ordered in their youth.

INFLUENTIAL COCKTAIL MEDIA IN PRINT

1905 ABSINTHE DRIP

Absinthe Drip had been enjoyed from the late 1700s, but in 1905, a global absinthe ban made it even more popular. International newspaper headlines in 1905 told the story about a Swiss farmer named Jean Lanfray who drank absinthe and then murdered his wife and daughters. To be fair, the media failed to mention the other alcohol he consumed that day, which included crème de menthe, Cognac, coffee with brandy, six glasses of wine with lunch, a glass of wine before leaving work, and then more wine after. America banned absinthe in 1912 and lifted the ban in 2007. Soon it began popping up in films such as *Moulin Rouge*, *Alfie*, and *Eurotrip*. Absinthe became a mystery, and once bar guests learned that it had been banned for ninety-seven years, they grew more intrigued.

1953 *CASINO ROYALE BY IAN FLEMING*

In the seventh chapter of Ian Fleming's first James Bond novel he created a fictional cocktail that lives on today—Vesper. As far as we know, it is the first time that gin and vodka had been mixed together in a cocktail. Bond requests his order be served in a deep champagne goblet and use three measures of Gordon's, one of vodka, and half a measure of Kina Lillet. Shake it very well until it's ice-cold, then add a large, thin slice of lemon peel.

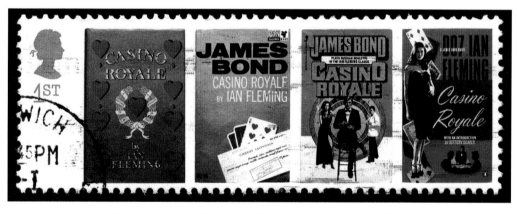

A used 1995 postage stamp from the UK depicting Casino Royale. © *AMC / Photofest*

28

COCKTAILS IN FILM: THE 1930S TO THE 2010S

• • •

A HISTORY OF THE COCKTAIL IN FILM

American Prohibition ended in 1933, which was around the same time Hollywood was releasing "talkies" (films where you could hear the actors speak). Greta Garbo was a huge silent film star in the 1920s and made her talkie film switch in 1930. Her fans were very excited to hear her voice for the first time, and the marketing team stoked the fire by advertising the event with the catchphrase, "Garbo Talks!" Moreover, what were her first words, you ask? "Gimme a whiskey, ginger ale on the side."

It's informative to know that the first time women were allowed into the main room of bars (and not just the small "Ladies' Bar" for prominent women) was the 1920s during Prohibition. Before then, a woman was only allowed in the main bar if she was a prostitute or madam. Therefore, most American women's first bar experience was in illegal, secretive bars between the years 1920 and 1933. The combination of American women being allowed to drink socially and Hollywood's advancing technology created a glamorization of the cocktail.

During the silent film era, there were plenty of imbibing scenes, particularly in Charlie Chaplin films. During American Prohibition, drinking scenes were simply set in countries that were not in Prohibition. A Horse's Neck is ordered in the 1914 film *Caught in a Cabaret*, a Whiskey and Soda is made in the 1917 film *The Idle Class*, and Manhattans are drunk in the 1928 film *Manhattan*.

One thirty-second film should be mentioned. It was an advertisement film titled *DeWar's—It's Scotch*, and was projected on a wall in New York City's Herald Square in 1898. It is the first spirit commercial to appear on film.

• • •

COCKTAILS IN FILM FROM THE 1930S TO THE 2010S

This collection is exclusively cocktail or spirit scenes. There are a plethora of films filled to the brim with champagne, beer, wine, and drinking scenes, and you can see more of those films at William T. Garver's blog, *Booze Movies* (boozemovies.com) and a Facebook page called *Cocktail Cinema*.

Greta Garbo in the 1930 film *Anna Christie*. © MGM / Photofest

1930 – *Anna Christie* • Greta Garbo orders a whiskey with ginger ale on the side.

1932 – *Cock of the Air* • Matt Moore is seen drinking a tableful of Martinis.

1932 – *Grand Hotel* • Joan Crawford, Greta Garbo, and John Barrymore order and drink absinthe at a Berlin bar. In the Grand Hotel, a man tries to get Joan Crawford to order a Louisiana Flip, but she orders absinthe. The man says "Louisiana Flip" eight times. Whiskey is also mentioned.

1932 – *The Old Dark House* • Ernest Thesiger offers a drink to a guest and says, "It's only gin, you know gin...I like gin!"

1934 – *It Happened One Night* • Claudette Colbert and others drink White Ladies.

1934 – *Murder at the Vanities* • Manhattans are used as props during a stage performance.

1934 – *The Thin Man* • William Powell and Myrna Loy drink Knickerbockers, and there is a scene where Powell is giving the bartenders advice on drink making. He says, "The important thing is the rhythm. Always have rhythm in your shaking. Now, a Manhattan you shake to foxtrot time; a Bronx, to two-step time; a dry Martini you always shake to waltz time."

– He also tells Nora, "This will make six Martinis." Nora says to the waiter, "All right. Will you bring me five more Martinis, Leo, and line them up right here." Rye whiskey is also mentioned.

1935 – *After Office Hours* • Clark Gable and Constance Bennett drink Dry Martinis with one olive.

1935 – *Top Hat* • Ginger Rogers and Fred Astaire drink Buck Fizzes.

1936 – *Dodsworth* • Martinis are drunk.

1936 – *My Man Godfrey* • David Niven, the butler, helps himself to Vodka Martinis.

1937 – *Every Day's a Holiday* • Mae West and others drink Bellinis. This movie also introduced the famous one-liner, "You should get out of those wet clothes and into a Dry Martini."

1937 – *Make Way For Tomorrow* • Victor Moore orders drinks for himself and Beulah Bondi: "Two Old-Fashioneds for two old-fashioned people."

1937 – *The Awful Truth* • Cary Grant serves eggnog from a punchbowl.

1938 – *Jezebel* • Mint Juleps are served and whiskey is drunk.

1939 – *Dark Victory* • Bette Davis drinks Pink Gin.

1939 – *Ninotchka* • Greta Garbo drinks a Black Russian.

1939 – *Remember?* • Greer Garson, Lew Ayres, and Robert Taylor drink Imperials.

1940 – *Angels over Broadway* • Rita Hayworth and Douglas Fairbanks Jr. drink Rob Roys.

1940 – *Bank Dick* • W. C. Fields sits at a bar and orders several drinks, but one you can hear and see clearly is absinthe.

1940 – *Foreign Correspondent* • Joel McCrea orders a Scotch & Soda.

1940 – *The Philadelphia Story* • Katharine Hepburn, Cary Grant, and James Stewart drink Kir Royales. Also, James Stewart says, "Champagne's a funny stuff. I'm used to whiskey. Whiskey is a slap on the back and champagne's heavy mist before my eyes."

1941 – *Phantom Submarine* • Anita Louise and others drink Sea Breezes.

1941 – *The Man Who Came to Dinner* • Ann Sheridan drinks a Mint Julep poolside.

1942 – *Across the Pacific* • Humphrey Bogart orders two Planter's Punches.

1942 – *Casablanca* • *Casablanca* has a few famous lines, but the one that mentions alcohol is: "Of all the gin joints in all the towns in all the world, she walks into mine."
– Paul Henreid orders a Champagne Cocktail and two Cointreau, Claude Rains orders two Champagne Cocktails, and Madeleine LeBeau drinks brandy (the boss's private stock). A German officer orders French 75s from Sascha the Russian bartender, and then Madeleine LeBeau says to the bartender, "Put up a whole row of them, Sascha... starting here and ending here." The German officer says, "We'll begin with two."

1942 – *Now, Voyager* • Bette Davis and Claude Rains drink Old-Fashioneds.

1942 – *Woman of the Year* • Katharine Hepburn has a Scotch & Soda.

1943 – *The Heat's On* • Mae West and others drink Martinis.

1944 – *Double Indemnity* • Barbara Stanwyck drinks a Pimm's Cocktail.

1944 – *Laura* • Vincent Price makes a Gin & It.

1944 – *To Have and Have Not* • Lauren Bacall drinks a Daiquiri.

1945 – *The Lost Weekend* • Ray Milland drinks a Rusty Nail.

1946 – *It's a Wonderful Life* • Clarence the Angel orders a Flaming Rum Punch and a Mulled Wine.

1946 – *Humoresque* • Joan Crawford drinks a Tom Collins. She also says. "Do you like Martinis? They are an acquired taste, like Ravel."

1946 – *The Big Sleep* • Lauren Bacall orders a Scotch Mist.

1947 – *Dead Reckoning* • Lizabeth Scott drinks a Ramos Gin Fizz.

1947 – *The Bishop's Wife* • Cary Grant as Dudley the Angel orders a round of Stingers while lunching with ladies from the church.

1948 – *The Big Clock* • Ray Milland orders a Stinger with green crème de menthe, and several raise glasses of Stingers for a honeymoon toast.

1948 – *The Great Gatsby* • Martinis are drunk.

1949 – *DOA* • Edmond O'Brien orders a Bourbon Highball.

1949 – *State of the Union* • Katharine Hepburn orders a Sazerac.

1949 – *Whisky Galore* • A comedy based on a shipwreck and its cargo of whisky.

1950 – *All About Eve* • Bette Davis drinks a Gibson. She also says, "I admit I may have seen better days, but I am still not to be had for the price of a cocktail."

1950 – *Father of the Bride* • Spencer Tracy makes a tray of Martinis for a party, but his guests start asking for other cocktails. Tracy ends up playing bartender in his kitchen and misses the whole party. Cocktails mentioned are Old-Fashioneds, Tom Collins, Mint Juleps, Frozen Daiquiris, Scotch, Bourbon & Waters, and Rum & Cokes.

1950 – *Harvey* • Jimmy Stewart drinks Martinis.

1950 – *In a Lonely Place* • Morris Ankrum orders a Stinger.

1952 – *Moulin Rouge* • The Moulin Rouge is a Paris nightclub, so lots of drinking can be seen. Jose Ferrer plays famous French painter Henri de Toulouse-Lautrec, who is given free Cognac and drinks in exchange for painting posters.

1952 – *The Snows of Kilimanjaro* • Gregory Peck, Ava Gardner, and others drink Gimlets.

1953 – *A Blueprint for Murder* • Joseph Cotton and Jean Peters call for and drink Bacardi cocktails.

1953 – *Bad for Each Other* • Charlton Heston and Lizabeth Scott drink Martinis.

1953 – *From Here to Eternity* • Burt Lancaster and Deborah Kerr drink Screwdrivers. There is also a lot of drinking in this film, and whiskey is seen and mentioned.

1954 – *Rhapsody* • Elizabeth Taylor makes a Mimosa.

1954 – *Sabrina* • Walter Hampden makes a Martini but has trouble getting the last olive out of the jar. He finally pours his Martini into the jar and drinks from it.

1955 – *I'll Cry Tomorrow* • Susan Hayward drinks Martinis.

1955 – *Guys and Dolls* • Marlon Brando gets Jean Simmons to drink several Dulce de Leches in Cuba.

> Simmons: What did you order?
> Brando: Dulce de Leche. *Dulce* is the Spanish word for "sweet." *De* means "of" and *leche* means "milk." Sweet of milk.
> Simmons: Don't they serve it plain?

Brando: Well, only in the mornings. It has to do with the heat. At night, they put a kind of preservative in it.

Simmons: That's interesting. What do they use?

Brando: Bacardi.

Simmons: Doesn't that have alcohol in it?

Brando: Well, just enough to keep the milk from turning sour.

– When Simmons is on her second drink, she says, "It's so delicious. That Bacardi flavoring certainly makes a difference. You know, this would be a wonderful way to get children to drink milk."

Marilyn Monroe and Tom Ewell in *The Seven Year Itch*; 1955. Monroe is holding the "Big Tall Martini" that Ewell made for her. © *mptvimages.com*

1955 – *The Seven Year Itch* • Tom Ewell invites Marilyn Monroe for a drink in his apartment because she does not have air-conditioning and he does. After she arrives, he offers to make her a drink.

Monroe: Do you have gin?

Ewell: Of course. You mean straight gin?

Monroe: No, gin and soda, I guess.

Ewell: Gin and soda?

Monroe: That's wrong. How do you drink gin?

Ewell: There's gin and tonic and gin and vermouth, that's a Martini.

Monroe: That sounds cool. I'll have a glass of that. A big, tall one.

Ewell: Big, tall Martini. (He gets her one.) Well, here you are. Big, tall Martini.

Monroe: Thanks.

Ewell: You're welcome.

Monroe: Very good. Maybe it needs a bit more sugar.

Ewell: I'd strongly advise against putting sugar in a Martini.

Monroe: You would? Why?

Ewell: Well...Take my word for it. No sugar in a Martini.

Monroe: Back home they put sugar in Martinis.

Ewell: Back home? Where?

Monroe: Denver, Colorado.

– Other lines in the film include:

"The human body is a very delicate machine, you can't run it on Martinis and goulash."

"I'm capable of fixing my own breakfast. I had a peanut butter sandwich and two Whiskey Sours."

1956 – *High Society* • Gordon Richards makes Stingers for Bing Crosby, Frank Sinatra, and anyone who needs some "hair of the dog."

1957 – *Kiss Them for Me* • Cary Grant and Jayne Mansfield drink Stingers. He says, "Stingers, and keep them coming."

1957 – *Sweet Smell of Success* • Burt Lancaster and Tony Curtis drink Martinis.

1958 – *Auntie Mame* • The second scene of the film is a cocktail party, and Auntie Mame (Rosalind Russell) descends the stairs talking about how someone is on their way with a gallon of gin. This is because the film begins in the Prohibition year of 1928 (it spans about twenty years), and many cocktails are seen.
– The morning after the party, Mame asks her nephew, Patrick, to tell the butler to bring her a light breakfast of black coffee and a Sidecar. Patrick (Jan Handzlik) is only twelve years old and makes a Martini for a visiting guest. He asks the guest if he would like it dry or extra dry. There is a complete scene of Patrick pouring the gin in a glass pitcher and educating the man: "Stir, never shake—it bruises the gin." Patrick then swirls vermouth around inside a Martini glass, pours it out, and then pours the stirred gin into the glass. He serves it without an olive but asks: "Would you like an olive? Auntie Mame says it takes up too much room in the drink."
– Other drinks seen and mentioned in the film include Mint Juleps, Drambuie, and Cognac. There is also a scene where Mame serves a specialty cocktail called "the Flaming Mame," which is served in a large, stemmed, conical-shaped metal glass with the drink lit on fire. It is a joke she plays on her guests to pay them back for serving her bad cocktails at their house.

1958 – *Cat on a Hot Tin Roof* • Paul Newman has a Hot Toddy.

1959 – *Beloved Infidel* • Deborah Kerr and Phillip Ober drink Sazeracs.

1959 – *North by Northwest* • Cary Grant drinks a Gibson on a train.

1959 – *Our Man in Havana* • Alec Guinness and friends drinks Daiquiris.

1959 – *Some Like It Hot* • Marilyn Monroe makes Manhattans in bed in a water bottle while on a train.

1960 – *The Apartment* • Shirley MacLaine asks for a Daiquiri, Hope Holiday asks for a Rum Collins, and Stingers are mentioned several times.

1960 – *When Strangers Meet* • Kim Novak and Kirk Douglas drink Martinis.

1961 – *Blue Hawaii* • Angela Lansbury throws a cocktail party for Elvis Presley and serves Mai Tais.

1961 – *Breakfast at Tiffany's* • Audrey Hepburn drinks a Planter's Punch.

1961 – *Days of Wine and Roses* • Jack Lemmon orders Lee Remick a Brandy Alexander.

Sean Connery as James Bond in the 1962 film *Dr. No.* © MGM / UA / Photofest

1962 – *Dr. No* • James Bond orders a Vodka Martini shaken, not stirred, and jump-starts the sale of vodka in America. The Vodka Martini goes viral.

1962 – *The Roman Spring of Mrs. Stone* • Vivian Leigh drinks an Americano.

1963 – *Come Blow Your Horn* • Frank Sinatra orders a Rum & Coke.

1963 – *From Russia with Love* • Sean Connery has a Martini.

1963 – *It's A Mad Mad Mad Mad World* • Jim Backus is flying a plane and leaves the controls to mix an Old-Fashioned.

1963 – *The Nutty Professor* • Jerry Lewis plays Buddy Love and orders an Alaskan Polar Bear Heater at the bar. He has to give the bartender the ingredients: "Two shots of vodka, a little rum, some bitters, a smidgen of vinegar, a shot of vermouth, a shot of gin, a little brandy, a lemon peel, an orange peel, a cherry, and some more Scotch. Now, mix it nice, then pour it into a tall glass."

1964 – *Goldfinger* • Sean Connery has a Martini and a Sour Mash Mint Julep.

1965 – *Thunderball* • Sean Connery makes a Vodka Martini with Smirnoff blue and Cinzano dry vermouth. He also orders a Rum Collins.

1967 – *Casino Royale* • David Niven and Peter Sellers drink Martinis.

1967 – *You Only Live Twice* • Sean Connery drinks a Stolichnaya Vodka Martini made with Martini & Rossi dry vermouth.

1968 – *Funny Girl* • Barbra Streisand drinks a Green Crème de Menthe Frappé.

1968 – *The Producers* • Mel Brooks drinks a Manhattan.

1968 – *The Thomas Crown Affair* • Steve McQueen drinks a Martini.

1969 – *Hello, Dolly!* • Barbra Streisand mentions a Rum-Toddy.

1969 – *On Her Majesty's Secret Service* • George Lazenby drinks a Martini.

1970 – *M*A*S*H* • Many Martinis are drunk. Elliott Gould says, "Yes, but a man can't really savor a Martini without an olive, otherwise it just doesn't quite make it."

1971 – *A Clockwork Orange* • Malcolm McDowell and friends drink Moloko Plus.

1971 – *Diamonds Are Forever* • Sean Connery has a Vodka Martini.

1972 – *Avanti* • The bartender makes Jack Lemon a Whiskey Sour.

1973 – *Live and Let Die* • Roger Moore orders a Bourbon & Water, but David Hedison changes the order to two Sazeracs.

1974 – *The Godfather: Part II* • John Cazale orders a Banana Daiquiri.

1977 – *Annie Hall* • Woody Allen imagines a conversation between Diane Keaton's parents. Annie's father says to her mother, "Make me a Martini." The mother replies, "Of course, sweetheart, how would you like it, dear?" Her dad replies, "On white bread with mayonnaise."

1977 – *The Spy Who Loved Me* • Roger Moore drinks a Vodka Martini.

1977 – *Saturday Night Fever* • John Travolta orders a 7&7 twice and a Vodka & Tonic is ordered.

1979 – *Moonraker* • Roger Moore drinks a Vodka Martini.

1980 – *The Blue Brothers* • John Candy asks, "Who wants an Orange Whip? Orange Whip? Orange Whip?, Three Orange Whips!"

1980 – *The Shining* • A ghost bartender drinks a Martini. • 1982 *Evil Under the Sun* – Maggie Smith gives Peter Ustinov a choice of cocktails: White Lady, Sidecar, Mainbrace, or Between the Sheets. He then asks for crème de cassis or banana syrup.

1982 – *Tootsie* • Dressed as a woman, Dustin Hoffman orders Dubonnet with a twist.

1983 – *Gorky Park* • William Hurt says the Stinger is a whore's drink. Later, he orders a Stinger and says, "I am a whore."

1983 – *Never Say Never Again* • Sean Connery drinks two Vodka Martinis. Kim Basinger orders a Double Bloody Mary.

1983 – *Octopussy* • Roger Moore drinks a Vodka Martini.

1983 – *Romancing the Stone* • Kathleen Turner drinks Grasshoppers.

1985 – *Fletch* • Chevy Chase orders a Bloody Mary at a tennis club.

1987 – *The Living Daylights* • Timothy Dalton drinks two Vodka Martinis.

1988 – *Beaches* • Bette Midler orders a Stinger twice.

1988 – *Cocktail* • This film holds the record for the most cocktails mentioned. Three are made and mentioned: Red Eye (beer, tomato juice, spices, and a raw egg), Turquoise Blue (the drink Cruise makes while flairing—it appears to be made with Bacardi light rum, blue Curaçao, and either pineapple juice or sour mix, then split tin strained into a Martini glass), and a Frozen Daiquiri poured into a Hurricane glass. Other cocktails mentioned include Velvet Hammer, Vodka & Rose's, Gilbey's & Tonic, Absolut Rocks, Orgasm, Cuba Libre, Orgasm, Angel Tit, Dirty Mother, Bloody Mary, Martini, Briar Tuck, Screwdriver, Pink Squirrel, Kamikaze, Sex on the Beach, Velvet Hammer, Iced Tea, Alabama Slammer, Death Spasm, Singapore Sling, and Ding-a-Ling.

Tom Cruise as Brian Flanagan in the 1988 film *Cocktail.* © *Buena Vista Pictures / Photofest*

– King Louis XIII is part of a bet and drunk between Cruise and Brown; Brown pours two Rémy Martin Cognacs for him and Cruise; and a Jim Beam bottle is held by Cruise when he hops up on the bar top and cites the "Barman's Poem."

1988 – *Tequila Sunrise* • Mel Gibson drinks Tequila Sunrises.

1989 – *Batman* • The Joker drinks a Martini.

1989 – *License to Kill* • Timothy Dalton orders a medium-dry Vodka Martini.

1989 – *She's Out of Control* • Tony Danza orders a Double Kahlúa Punch, which is served in a pineapple with a parasol.

1989 – *Skin Deep* • John Ritter drinks a Bonzai Sunset.

1990 – *Bonfire of the Vanities* • Alan King orders a Sidecar, then tells Bruce Willis, "I'm not supposed to drink, but I love a Sidecar." He then drinks it, is served another, tells Willis a crazy story, then dies at the restaurant table.

1990 – *The Adventures of Ford Fairlane* • Andrew Dice Clay makes a Sambuca Milkshake.

1991 – *The Doors* • Val Kilmer drinks a Ramos Gin Fizz.

1992 – *Batman Returns* • The Penguin's parents drink Martinis.

1992 – *Bram Stoker's Dracula* • Absinthe is seen and the film's opening line is, "Absinthe is the aphrodisiac of the soul. The green fairy who lives in the absinthe wants your soul, but you are safe with me."

1993 – *Groundhog's Day* • Bill Murray orders a Jim Beam & Water and Andie MacDowell orders a Dubonnet on the rocks with a twist.

1993 – *Mrs. Doubtfire* • Robert Prosky orders a Double Scotch on the rocks and tells the waiter to bring Robin Williams two of them so that he can catch up.

1994 – *Ed Wood* • Johnny Depp orders a Beefeater Martini.

1994 – *Interview with a Vampire* • Brad Pitt is seen drinking absinthe, and then absinthe is mentioned another time.

1995 – *Father of the Bride* • Steve Martin has a daydream in which his son-in-law is a Martini-drinking playboy.

1995 – *French Kiss* • Meg Ryan orders a Sea Breeze.

1995 – *GoldenEye* • Pierce Brosnan orders a Vodka Martini.

1995 – *The Net* • Sandra Bullock orders a Gibson at the Beach Bar.

1995 – *Total Eclipse* • The film's opening scene shows a waiter serving a glass of absinthe, and then Leonardo DiCaprio disrupts a speech about absinthe. Later it shows DiCaprio drinking absinthe.

1996 – *Exit in Red* • Annabel Schofield drinks a Margarita.

1996 – *Happy Gilmore* • Christopher McDonald drinks Martinis.

1996 – *In Love and War* • Sandra Bullock gives Chris O'Donnell a Martini made from gin and castor oil.

1996 – *Mother* • Albert Brooks and Debbie Reynolds have Martinis.

1996 – *Swingers* • Lots of drinks are seen, ordered, and mentioned such as single malt Scotch, Dewar's Scotch, Martinis, and a cocktail called James Bond. Bottles seen at a party are Jack Daniel's, Stoli vodka, and Glenfiddich Scotch. A swing band sings the song "You and Me and the Bottle Makes Three," which mentions a Gin & Tonic in the lyrics.

1996 – *The Evening Star* • Miranda Richardson orders a Bloody Mary.

1996 – *To Gillian on Her 37th Birthday* • Claire Danes drinks two large Zombies.

1996 – *Up Close and Personal* • Michelle Pfeiffer has a Banana Daiquiri.

1997 – *Boogie Nights* • Mark Wahlberg and John C. Reilly have Margaritas. There is also a bartender doing bar tricks.

1997 – *Deconstructing Harry* • Billy Crystal drinks a Martini.

1997 – *Eight Heads in a Duffel Bag* • Andy Comeau, Kristy Swanson, and George Hamilton drink Margaritas.

1997 – *Fathers' Day* • Billy Crystal chugs a Martini in one gulp.

1997 – *George of the Jungle* • Thomas Haden Church makes a comment about a Gin Martini then orders two Black Russians and a White Ape.

1997 – *Jackie Brown* • Pam Grier and Samuel L. Jackson order Screwdrivers at the Cockatoo Inn.

1997 – *Meet Wally Sparks* • Debi Mazar asks for Sex on the Beach.

1997 – *Money Talks* • Heather Locklear's mother drinks a Bloody Mary.

1997 – *My Best Friend's Wedding* • Julia Roberts and Dermot Mulroney order Margaritas.

1997 – *Open Your Eyes* • Fele Martinez and Penelope Cruz drink Rum & Cokes. Eduardo Noriega orders a Whiskey & Coke.

1997 – *Picture Perfect* • Kevin Bacon and Jennifer Aniston drink Martinis.

1997 – *The Ice Storm* • Sigourney Weaver drinks Martinis.

1997 – *The Man Who Knew Too Little* • Bill Murray drinks a Martini.

1997 – *Tomorrow Never Dies* • Pierce Brosnan drinks a Vodka Martini.

1998 – *Bringing Down the House* • Joan Plowright orders a Double 7&7.

1998 – *Deceiver* • Tim Roth drinks a Martini.

1998 – *Fear and Loathing in Las Vegas* • Johnny Depp and Benicio del Toro drink Singapore Slings.

1998 – *Gods and Monsters* • Ian McKellen has two Martinis.

1998 – *Hope Floats* • Sandra Bullock orders a Vodka Tonic.

1998 – *Living Out Loud* • Holly Hunter has a Martini.

1998 – *Practical Magic* • Sandra Bullock makes a Midnight Margarita.

1998 – *The Big Lebowski* • Jeff Bridges drinks many White Russians.

1998 – *The Imposters* • Stanley Tucci has a Martini in a huge Martini glass while others have normal Martini glasses. A Grasshopper is also ordered.

1998 – *The Odd Couple II* • Jack Lemmon drinks a Martini.

1998 – *There's Something About Mary* • Matt Dillon orders a Whiskey Sour.

1998 – *Twice Upon Yesterday* • Penelope Cruz plays a bartender and makes a Gin & Tonic.

1998 – *Wild Things* • Matt Dillon orders Rum & Coke.

1999 – *A Perfect Murder* • Michael Douglas holds a Martini and fixes one for Gwyneth Paltrow.

1999 – *Blast from the Past* • Christopher Walken and Sissy Spacek drink Martinis. Alicia Silverstone brings a Champagne Cocktail to Brendan Fraser.

1999 – *Crazy in Alabama* • Melanie Griffith orders a Hurricane in New Orleans.

1999 – *Cruel Intentions* • Selma Blair finishes her beverage and says it doesn't taste like tea. Ryan Phillippe tells her that it's from Long Island (Long Island Iced Tea).

1999 – *Double Jeopardy* • Bruce Greenwood has a Martini.

1999 – *Eyes Wide Shut* • Todd Field has a Vodka Tonic.

1999 – *Goodbye Lover* • There are Martinis all through this film.

1999 – *House on Haunted Hill* • Famke Janssen has a Martini.

1999 – *Me, Myself, & Irene* • Renée Zellweger and Jim Carrey have Rum & Cokes.

1999 – *The Guilty* • A Double Whiskey Sour is ordered.

1999 – *The World Is Not Enough* • Pierce Brosnan drinks a Vodka Martini.

2000 – *Meet the Parents* • Robert De Niro's favorite drink is a Tom Collins.

2001 – *Best Laid Plans* • Alessandro Nivola and Josh Brolin drink 7&7's.

2001 – *From Hell* • While taking a bath in a claw-foot tub, Johnny Depp makes himself a poisoned absinthe.

2000 – *Cecil B. Demented* • Melanie Griffith has several Martinis.

2000 – *Cheaper by the Dozen* • Bonnie Hunt has a Martini.

2000 – *Chuck & Buck* • Chris Weitz orders a Martini and Mike White orders a Rum & Coke.

2000 – *Down to You* • Selma Blair has an Old-Fashioned.

2000 – *Duets* • Huey Lewis has a 7&7.

2000 – *Joe Gould's Secret* • Stanley Tucci and Ian Holm have several Martinis.

2000 – *Nutty Professor II* • Eddie Murphy orders a 7&7.

2000 – *Reindeer Games* • Ben Affleck orders Rum & Cokes.

2000 – *The Banger Sisters* • Goldie Hawn makes herself a Rum & Coke.

2000 – *The Whole Nine Yards* • Bruce Willis drinks Martinis and Matthew Perry drinks Scotch & Soda.

2001 – *Black Knight* • Martin Lawrence tells Marsha Thomason he wants to have Mai Tais.

2001 – *Blow Dry* • Bill Nighy orders two Gin & Tonics.

2001 – *Crocodile Dundee in Los Angeles* • George Hamilton has a Martini.

2001 – *Down to Earth* • Wanda Sykes mixes a Martini in the car. Chazz Palminteri carries a Martini. Greg Germann and Jennifer Coolidge have Martinis.

2001 – *Heartbreakers* • Jennifer Love Hewitt orders a very dry Martini.

2001 – *Johnny English* • Rowan Atkinson orders a Bloody Mary.

2001 – *Legally Blonde* • Reese Witherspoon's dad drinks Martinis.

2001 – *Monkeybone* • A bartender offers Brendan Fraser a Coma-tini.

2001 – *Moulin Rouge* • Moulin Rouge is an 1890s Paris nightclub, so lots of drinking is seen. Absinthe is drunk and an absinthe fairy flies around at different times in the film.

2001 – *Never Again* • Jill Clayburgh has several Martinis.

2001 – *Rat Race* • Whoopi Goldberg and Lanai Chapman order Mimosas.

2001 – *Tomcats* • Jerry O'Connell is given a Hot Toddy.

2001 – *Vanilla Sky* • Cameron Diaz has a Martini.

2002 – *40 days and 40 nights* • Josh Hartnett buys his date a Martini.

2002 – *About Schmidt* • Jack Nicholson orders a Vodka Gimlet. Jack Nicholson and Kathy Bates drink Manhattans.

Pierce Brosnan as James Bond in the 2002 film *Die Another Day.* He orders Martinis, but the Mojito shot to stardom around the world because of this film. © *MGM / UA / Photofest*

2002 – *Die Another Day* • Pierce Brosnan drinks Martinis, but the viral cocktail in this film is a Mojito. Forty years prior, James Bond exploded the Vodka Martini and now revives the 1920s classic Cuban cocktail, the Mojito.

2002 – *Divine Secrets of the Ya-Ya Sisterhood* • Maggie Smith has a Bloody Mary.

2002 – *Igby Goes Down* • Ryan Phillippe has a Bloody Mary.

2002 – *Hysterical Blindness* • Juliette Lewis orders a Sex on the Beach.

2002 – *Juwanna Mann* • Miguel A. Nunez Jr. asks for a Cosmopolitan, heavy on the vodka.

2002 – *Kissing Jessica Stein* • Jennifer Westfeldt orders a Strawberry Margarita.

2003 – *A Guy Thing* • James Brolin brings Diana Scarwid a Martini.

2003 – *Bad Boys II* • Gabrielle Union and Jordi Molla drink Bacardi Mojitos.

2003 – *From Justin to Kelly* • Katherine Bailess has a Martini and Greg Siff has a Piña Colada.

2003 – *Lost in Translation* • Scarlett Johansson orders a Vodka Tonic. And Bill Murray is in Japan for a whiskey commercial.

2003 – *Matchstick Men* • Sam Rockwell has a Martini.

2003 – *Mona Lisa Smile* • Marcia Gay Harden mentions a Manhattan. Dominic West orders a Jack & Ginger.

2003 – *Recruit* • Colin Farrell works as a bartender and serves Al Pacino a Martini.

2003 – *Stuck on You* • Cher and Greg Kinnear have Margaritas.

2003 – *The Haunted Mansion* • A client of Eddie Murphy's orders three Volcanoes (a house specialty drink).

2004 – *Alfie* • Susan Sarandon pulls out a bottle of illegal absinthe she smuggled and makes two Absinthe Drips for herself and Jude Law.

2004 – *Breakin' All the Rules* • Jamie Foxx buys Gabrielle Union a Double Bloody Mary. Morris Chestnut chugs a Martini and, because of all the olives in front of him, we suspect he's had many.

2004 – *Catwoman* • Halle Berry orders a White Russian and tells the bartender to hold the vodka and Kahlúa.

2004 – *Closer* • Jude Law orders a Vodka Tonic for Julia Roberts.

2004 – *Euro Trip* • Absinthe is drunk in a club by the main characters.

2004 – *Flight of the Phoenix* • Kirk Jones wishes he could have a Bacardi & Coke.

2004 – *I Heart Huckabees* • Jude Law has a Martini and mentions that in the future he will drink Piña Coladas.

2004 – *Ladder 49* • John Travolta and his firefighters order many drinks, including an Irish Car Bomb, 7&7, Sea Breeze, and Margarita.

2004 – *Man on Fire* • Denzel Washington asks for a Jack & Water.

2004 – *Meet the Fockers* • Dustin Hoffman serves a tray of Tom Collinses.

2004 – *Wicker Park* • Matthew Lillard orders a 7&7.

2004 – *Sleepover* • Alexa Vega gets a text message telling her to order a Sex on the Beach.

2004 – *Suspect Zero* • A woman orders a 7&7.

2005 – *Bewitched* • Will Ferrell drinks a Bloody Mary and Nicole Kidman drinks two Martinis.

2005 – *Fun with Dick & Jane* • Jim Carrey, Alec Baldwin, and Tea Leoni have Mimosas.

2005 – *Guess Who* • Ashton Kutcher orders a Vodka Tonic. Zoë Saldana orders Cosmopolitans.

2005 – *In Her Shoes* • Shirley MacLaine makes Cosmopolitans to impress her granddaughter, Cameron Diaz.

2005 – *Kiss Kiss Bang Bang* • Robert Downey Jr. orders a Jack & Soda.

2005 – *Lord of War* • Nicolas Cage drinks a Martini.

2005 – *Monster-in-Law* • Jane Fonda drinks Martinis.

2005 – *Mr. and Mrs. Smith* • Brad Pitt orders and fixes himself a Martini.

2005 – *Red Eye* • Rachel McAdams orders a Bay Breeze at an airport.

2005 – *Rumor Has It* • Jennifer Aniston carries two Bloody Marys.

2005 – *Stealth* • Jamie Fox, Jessica Biel, and Josh Lucas drink Martinis.

2005 – *Thank You for Smoking* • Robert Duvall and Aaron Eckhart have Mint Juleps.

2005 – *The Ice Harvest* • John Cusack orders a Rum & Pineapple Juice.

2005 – *The Hitchhiker's Guide to the Galaxy* • Sam Rockwell drinks a Pan Galactic Gargle Blaster.

2005 – *The Matador* • Pierce Brosnan orders Margaritas.

2005 – *The Upside of Anger* • Joan Allen and Alicia Witt order Bloody Marys.

2005 – *The Wedding Date* • Dermot Mulroney brings Debra Messing a Bloody Mary.

2006 – *Casino Royale* • James Bond orders a Vesper. "Three measures of Gordon's, one of vodka, half a measure of Kina Lillet, shake it very well until it's ice-cold, then add a large, thin slice of lemon peel. Got it?"

2006 – *Phat Girlz* • Joyful Drake orders a Cosmopolitan.

2006 – *The Break-Up* • Keir O'Donnell orders himself and Jennifer Aniston two Apple Martinis.

2006 – *The Pink Panther* • Steve Martin has a flaming drink and, during the cartoon credits, the Pink Panther holds a Martini.

2007 – *Grindhouse* • Many Margaritas are drunk.

2007 – *Perfect Stranger* • Hemmingway Daiquiris are ordered

2007 – *Code Name: The Cleaner* • Cedric the Entertainer talks about having Mai Tais.

2007 – *Enchanted* • A poisoned red Appletini is given to Amy Adams.

2007 – *Shrek the Third* • Prince Charming orders a round of Fuzzy Navels for the bar, and Puss in Boots daydreams of fishing with a pitcher of Mojitos beside him.

2007 – *Zodiac* • Brian Cox orders a Hot Toddy and Jake Gyllenhaal orders an Aqua Velva.

2008 – *27 Dresses* • Katherine Heigl drinks a Vodka Soda and says she has Grey Goose & Red Bull in the fridge.

2008 – *And Then She Found Me* • Bette Midler, Colin Firth, and Helen Hunt have Sake Bombs.

2008 – *Brideshead Revisited* • A dry Martini and a Whiskey & Water are ordered.

2008 – *Forgetting Sarah Marshall* • Jason Segel has a Malibu & Pineapple for breakfast.

2008 – *Ironman* • Robert Downy Jr. orders two dry Martinis.

2008 – *Miss Pettigrew Lives for a Day* • Amy Adams mentions Margaritas and Bellinis.

2008 – *Never Back Down* • A Margarita is seen.

2008 – *Nim's Island* • The captain talks about selling Piña Coladas to tourists.

2008 – *Sex and the City* • No drinks are mentioned but the Cosmopolitan and Flirtini are seen.

2008 – *The Curious Case of Benjamin Button* • Brad Pitt drinks a Sazerac.

2008 – *The House Bunny* • Anna Faris has a Kamikaze. College students talk about Marvin's tasty Margaritas.

2008 – *The Love Guru* • Martinis are ordered.

2008 – *Two Lovers* • Joaquin Phoenix orders a Brandy Alexander.

2009 – *Dorian Gray* • Ben Barnes sits for a portrait painting with a glass of absinthe next to him.

2010 – *Cyrus* • A Vodka Red Bull is seen.

2010 – *Ghost Writer* • Pierce Brosnan is given a Bloody Mary.

2010 – *Iron Man 2* • Scarlett Johansson hands Robert Downey Jr. a Dirty Martini and suggestively asks, "Is that dirty enough for you?"

2010 – *Knight and Day* • A guy orders a Harvey Wallbanger.

2010 – *Leap Year* • Amy Adams drinks a Martini.

2010 – *Marmaduke* • Catherine O'Hara drinks from a pitcher of Bloody Marys.

2010 – *Our Family Wedding* • Forester Whitaker orders a Pink Nipple.

2010 – *Scott Pilgrim vs. the World* • Gin & Tonics are ordered.

2010 – *Shrek Forever* • Shrek drinks Eyeball Martinis.

2010 – *Skyline* • Margaritas are seen and Mimosas are drunk.

2010 – *The Bounty Hunter* • Christine Baranski drinks a Martini.

2010 – *The Switch* • Many cocktails are seen including a Bloody Mary.

2010 – *Valentine's Day* • Anne Hathaway says she's going to need a Mint Julep.

Ryan Gosling in the 2011 film *Crazy, Stupid, Love.* © *Warner Bros.* / *Photofest*

2011 – *Crazy, Stupid, Love* • Many drinks are seen, but Ryan Gosling's drink of choice is an Old-Fashioned. In one scene, Gosling skillfully makes two of them.

2013 – *The Great Gatsby* • Leonardo DiCaprio orders highballs.

2013 – *The Immigrant* • Joaquin Phoenix and Marion Cotillard drink absinthe.

2015 – *100 Years* • John Malkovich and Robert Rodriguez put a bottle of King Louis XIII Cognac into a time capsule, and the planned release date is November 18, 2115.

2016 – *The Nice Guys* • Russell Crowe is handed an orange cocktail with a cherry garnish at a party, but does not drink it because he is a recovering alcoholic. Ryan Gosling drinks Martinis, whiskey, and orders Scotch.

2016 – *Whisky Galore* • A remake of the 1949 comedy about the raiding of a shipwreck and its cargo of whiskey.

2016 – *Whiskey Tango Foxtrot* • The film has a lot of drinking scenes.

2017 – *Passengers* • Michael Sheen plays an android bartender named Arthur on the *Starship Avalon.* Arthur serves Jennifer Lawrence and Chris Pratt Champagne Cocktails.

2018 – A Simple Favor • Blake Lively and Anna Kendrick drink Aviation American Gin Martinis.

29

COCKTAILS IN LITERATURE: FROM SHAKESPEARE TO TODAY

1599 *Julius Caesar*, Shakespeare

– Brutus: Speak no more of her. Give me a bowl of wine.

> In this I bury all unkindness, Cassius.

– Cassius: My heart is thirsty for that noble pledge.

> Fill, Lucius, till the wine o'erswell the cup;
>
> I cannot drink too much of Brutus's love.

1809 *A History of New York from the Beginning of the World to the End of the Dutch Dynasty*, Washington Irving

– "This class of beverages originated in Maryland, whose inhabitants were prone to make merry and get fuddled with mint-julep and apple toddy. They were, moreover, great horse-racers and cock-fighters; mighty wrestlers and jumpers, and enormous consumers of hoecake and bacon. They lay claim to be the first inventors of those recondite beverages, cock-tail, stone-fence, and sherry cobbler."

1821 *The Spy*, James Fenimore Cooper

– The author writes about a fictional character named Betty Flanagan who is based on a real-life character, Catherine Hustler. "Betty had the merit of being the inventor of that beverage which is so well known, at the present hour, to all the patriots who make a winter's march between the commercial and political capitals of this great state, and which is distinguished by the name of 'cocktail.'"

1823 *Saint Ronan's Well*, Sir Walter Scott

– A Gin-Twist is mentioned: "Sir Binco, I will beg the favour of your company to the smoking-room, where we may have a cigar and a glass of Gin-Twist." A Gin-Twist is gin, hot water, lemon juice, and sugar.

1824 *An Essay on the Inventions and Customs of Both Ancients and Moderns in the Use of Inebriating Liquors*, Samuel Morewood

– "Time adds much to the mildness and value of rum, which the planters, it is said, often improve by the addition of pineapple juice."

1838 *The Posthumous Papers of the Pickwick Club*, Charles Dickens

– "Mr. Stiggins was easily prevailed on to take another glass of the hot pineapple rum and water, and a second, and a third, and then to refresh himself with a slight supper previous to beginning again."

1843 *Martin Chuzzlewit*, Charles Dickens

– "He could...smoke more tobacco, drink more rum-toddy, mint-julep, gin-sling, and cocktail, than any private gentleman of his acquaintance." Dickens talks about a large Sherry Cobbler.

1857 *Tom Brown's Schooldays*, Thomas Hughes
– "Here, Bill, drink some cocktail."

1869 *Innocents Abroad*, Mark Twain
– Many cocktails are mentioned, including Champagne Cocktail, Sherry Cobbler, Brandy Smash, Santa Cruz Punch, Eye-Opener, Stone-Fence, and an Earthquake.

>Our general said, "We will take a whiskey straight."
>[A stare from the Frenchman.]
>"Well, if you don't know what that is, give us a champagne cock-tail."
>[A stare and a shrug.]
>"Well, then, give us a sherry cobbler." The Frenchman was checkmated. This was all Greek to him.

– "Give us a brandy smash!" The Frenchman, suspicious of the ominous vigor of the last order, began to back away, shrugging his shoulders and spreading his hands apologetically. The General followed him up and gained a complete victory. The uneducated foreigner could not even furnish a Santa Cruz Punch, an Eye-Opener, a Stone-Fence, or an Earthquake. It was plain that he was a wicked impostor.

1869 *Miscellanies: The Book of Snobs, Sketches, and Travels in London*, William Makepeace Thackeray
– "... the young rakes and viveurs come swaggering in, and call loudly for Gin-Twist."

1872 *Narrative of a Voyage Round the World*, Sir Edward Belcher
– "And then Captain Bening made us a Champagne Cocktail. Half a tumbler of champagne, a little brandy, a little bitters, a little sugar."

1874 *Cross Patch*, Mother Goose
– "Cross patch, draw the latch, sit by the fire and spin; Take a cup and drink it up, and call your neighbors in."
Drinking a cup refers to a bowl of alcoholic punch.

1920 *This Side of Paradise*, F. Scott Fitzgerald.
– This book has the first known literary mention of the Daiquiri.

1925 *The Great Gatsby*, F. Scott Fitzgerald
– "The notion originated with Daisy's suggestion that we hire five bathrooms and take cold baths, and then assumed more tangible form as 'a place to have a mint julep.'"
– "Open the whiskey, Tom, and I'll make you a Mint Julep. Then you won't seem so stupid to yourself. ...Look at the mint!"
– Tom came back, preceding four Gin Rickeys that clicked full of ice. Gatsby took up his drink.
– "They certainly look cool," he said, with visible tension.
– We drank in long, greedy swallows."

1926 *The Sun Also Rises*, Ernest Hemingway
– George the barman serves Jake Barnes a Jack Rose at the Hotel Crillon in Paris.

1927 "Hills Like Elephants," Ernest Hemingway
– A line in the story reads, "Yes," said the girl. "Everything tastes like licorice. Especially all the things you've waited so long for, like absinthe."

1929 *A High Wind in Jamaica*, Richard Hughes

– On page 77, the author mentions a drink called Hangman's Blood that consists of porter ale, rum, gin, whisky, port, and brandy.

1930 *The Glass Key*, Dashiell Hammett

– Ned Beaumont drinks a Manhattan.

1931 *The Maltese Falcon*, Dashiell Hammett

– Sam Spade drinks a Manhattan from a paper cup.

1931 *The Thin Man*, Dashiell Hammett

– Nick and Nora Charles drink several types of Martinis, including the Knickerbocker and Bronx.

1933 *Winner Take Nothing*, Ernest Hemingway

– Brandy, grappa, wine, and champagne are mentioned.

1934 *Love's Lovely Counterfeit*, James M. Cain

– Ben Grace makes Manhattans.

1934 *The Postman Always Rings Twice*, James M. Cain

– Cora makes Bourbon & Cokes and Bourbon & Sodas.

1935 *Trinity Town*, Norman Collins

– "'What would you like—a Bronx or a Sidecar?' 'A Sidecar,' Vicky told him. She had never had a cocktail before."

1939 *Uncle Fred in the Springtime*, P.G. Wodehouse

– "Do we by any chance know of a beverage called May Queen? Its full name is 'Tomorrow'll be all the year the maddest, merriest day for I'm to be Queen of the May, mother, I'm to be Queen of the May'. A clumsy title, generally shortened for purposes of ordinary conversation. Its foundation is any good, dry champagne, to which is added liqueur, brandy, Armagnac, kummel, yellow chartreuse, and old stout, to taste."

1945 *Brideshead Revisited*, Evelyn Waugh

– Anthony Blanche orders four Alexandra Cocktails (Alexander Cocktail) all for himself.

1950 *Across the River and into the Trees*, Ernest Hemingway

– Colonel Cantwell orders two very dry Martinis.

1950 *The Second Seal*, Dennis Wheatley

– "There he went up to his room, sat on his bed for a while, then rang for the waiter and ordered a double Absinthe. When it arrived, he added sugar and water and slowly drank the opal fluid."

1951 *Catcher in the Rye*, J. D. Salinger

– Carl Luce orders a very dry Martini with no olive at the Wicker Bar in the swanky Seton Hotel. Holden Caulfield drinks Scotch & Sodas.

1953   *Casino Royale*, Ian Fleming

"A Dry Martini," he said.

"One. In a deep champagne goblet."

"Oui, monsieur."

"Just a moment. Three measures of Gordons, one of vodka, half a measure of Kina Lillet. Shake it very well until it's ice-cold, then add a large thin slice of lemon peel. Got it?"

"Certainly, monsieur." The barman seemed pleased with the idea.

1953   *The Long Goodbye*, Raymond Chandler

– Philip Marlowe and Terry Lennox drink Gimlets. Lennox says, "A real Gimlet is half gin and half Rose's lime juice and nothing else. It beats Martinis hollow."

1954   *Cat on a Hot Tin Roof*, Tennessee Williams

– At Big Daddy's birthday, Brick drinks a Hot Toddy.

1958   *Breakfast at Tiffany's*, Truman Capote

– A White Angel is made: "Let me build you a drink. Something new. They call it a White Angel," he said, mixing one-half vodka, one-half gin, no vermouth.

1958   *Our Man in Havana*, Graham Greene

– The first sentence in the book reads, "Wormold enjoyed his rum cocktails frozen, with lime."

1958   *Playback*, Raymond Chandler

– Philip Marlowe orders a double Gibson.

1959   *The Galton Case*, Ross MacDonald

– Lew Archer drinks Gibsons and Gin & Tonics.

1960   *Rabbit, Run*, John Updike

– Harry "Rabbit" Angstrom resents the job he works just to earn a living to buy sugar for his wife to put into her rotten old Old-Fashioneds.

1962   *A Clockwork Orange*, Anthony Burgess

– A cocktail invented by the author is called Moloko Plus.

1966   *The Crying of Lot 49*, Thomas Pynchon

– Mrs. Oedipa Maas mixes Whiskey Sours for her and her husband.

1971   *Fear and Loathing in Las Vegas*, Hunter S. Thompson

– "We had actually been sitting there in the Polo Lounge—for many hours—drinking Singapore Slings with mescal on the side and beer chasers."

1971 *Love in the Ruins*, Walker Percy

– Dr. Thomas More describes the Gin Fizz as an egg-based cocktail that is silky and benign shortly before going into anaphylactic shock.

1973 *Breakfast of Champions*, Kurt Vonnegut

– Bonnie, a down-on-her-luck cocktail waitress, says "Breakfast of Champions" every time she serves a Martini.

– Character Dwayne Hoover's Martini of choice is the "House of Lords Martini" made with House of Lords and a twist of lemon peel.

1991 *Harlot's Ghost*, Norman Mailer

– A Martini called the Berlin Station Chief made with Scotch and gin is mentioned.

1993–2012 *Honor Bound* series, W. E. B. Griffin (William Edmund Butterworth III)

– The Sazerac is well liked by Office of Strategic Services (OSS) agent Cletus Frade in this World War II thriller series of eight books.

1995 *Practical Magic*, Alice Hoffman

– "She goes to the kitchen and fixes a pitcher of Margaritas. She takes the pitcher, along with two glasses dipped in coarse salt, out to the backyard and leaves it all beside the two lawn chairs set up near the little garden where the cucumbers are doing their best to grow."

1997 *Mason & Dixon*, Thomas Pynchon

– Cock Ale Punch is a popular drink at the Moon. It is actually made with a rooster.

2001 *Right As Rain*, George Pelecanos

– Ray Boone makes a Whiskey & Coke, then stirs it with a dirty finger.

2003 *The Second Glass of Absinthe*, Michelle Black

– The author talks about an absinthe hallucination.

2005–2013 *Presidential Agent* series, W. E. B. Griffin

– There are references to the Sazerac in this series of books.

2007 *Rebel Angels*, Libba Bray

– The character Gemma Doyle drinks absinthe with her friends at a Christmas Ball.

2011 *The Pale King*, David Foster Wallace

– "Meredith Rand has two gin and tonics and is on her third, slightly more to drink than normal."

2012 *The Cocktail Waitress*, James M. Cain

– Cocktails mentioned include an Old-Fashioned, Martini, Manhattan, Gibson, Whiskey Sour, and Margarita.

2013 *The Firebird*, Susanna Kearsley

– Vodka Martinis are mentioned.

2014 *Girl's Night Out*, Kate Flora

– A Cosmopolitan is on the cover of the book and a Cosmopolitan is mentioned in the book.

2014 *Gone Girl*, Gillian Flynn

– Cocktails mentioned are Mojitos and Gin Martinis.

2014 *The Fault in Our Stars*, John Green

– A Martini is mentioned.

2015 *Beat Slay Love*, Thalia Filbert

– Chef Hannah Wendt makes a Berry Drop made with Grey Goose vodka, huckleberry syrup, lemon liqueur, and candied ginger.

30

COCKTAILS IN TELEVISION: THE 1950S TO THE 2010S

1951–1957 *I LOVE LUCY*

In the hilarious season one, episode thirty, titled "Lucy Does a TV Commercial," Lucy finagles her way onto her husband's show as a pitch girl selling a new medicine product, Vitameatavegamin (contains vitamins, meat, vegetables, and minerals). With each take of the commercial, she takes a sip. The only issue is that she does many takes and the medicine is 23 percent alcohol (46 proof). Needless to say, she becomes intoxicated.

1951–1959 *DRAGNET*

Dragnet is a Los Angeles police detective show. The episode "The Big Bar" (season four, episode eight) opens with an outside bar sign that reads, "Cocktails." The next scene features Sergeant Joe Friday inside the Green Light Tavern investigating a murder. A holdup man who drinks Scotch & Water is sticking up bars, taking the money, then killing the victims.

1958–1964 *THE GARRY MOORE SHOW*

The Garry Moore Show is a variety show that features singers, comedy skits, and more. In 1962, twenty-year-old Barbra Streisand drinks many prop Martinis, as she performs the 1929 song "Happy Days Are Here Again."

1961 *WHITE HORSE SCOTCH WHISKEY* (Commercial)

White Horse Scotch Whiskey puts out a stop-motion TV commercial showing their white horse galloping around the globe. The horse travels to France, Hong Kong, Australia, Mexico, and New York City. People are drinking cocktails with the White Horse Scotch on their balconies, patios, and bars.

1960–1968 *THE ANDY GRIFFITH SHOW*

Andy Griffith plays Andy Taylor, a widowed sheriff in Mayberry, North Carolina (a fictional town). Many episodes deal with moonshiners, a town drinker named Otis turns himself in each week, and Deputy Barney Fife accidently gets drunk a couple times.

In the episode "Andy's Rich Girlfriend" (season three, episode two), Andy takes his date to the nearby town of Mt. Pilot. She talks about New Orleans and orders a Sazerac.

In the episode "Only a Rose" (season seven, episode twelve), Andy is seen carrying a tray of Tom Collinses in his home.

1964–1972 *BEWITCHED*

Bewitched is a fantasy show about a witch who marries a mortal man. Out of the 254 episodes, 169 of them have drinking scenes. In addition, many names of bars are seen or mentioned. Some of these include

Happy Times Bar, Joe's Bar and Grill, the Diamond Slipper, Purple Popsicle Night Club, Elbow Room Cocktail Lounge, and Dundee's Bar.

1972–1983 M*A*S*H

MASH is an acronym for "Mobile Army Surgical Hospital" and the show is about a team of doctors in South Korea during the Korean War (1950–1953). M*A*S*H was first a novel, then a film, and later turned into a TV series. The lead doctor characters, Hawkeye and Trapper John, drink Martinis in almost every episode. They make a gin-making still contraption in their quarters. The complete DVD collection is actually titled *Martinis and Medicine*. In the 1973 episode "Ceasefire," Hawkeye says, "I'll stick with gin. Champagne is just ginger ale that knows somebody."

1972–1978 MAUDE

Maude is an *All in the Family* spin-off. It is set in Tuckahoe, New York, and is about a politically outspoken liberal woman who stands up for the issues of the time. This, however, often gets her into trouble. *Maude* was the first TV show in history to show a gay bar. The episode is called "The Gay Bar" (season six, episode nine). Maude drinks what looks like vodka on the rocks and several cocktails are seen. The episode "Walter's Problem," a.k.a. "Life of the Party" (season two, episode one), deals with Walter (Maude's husband) drinking too much. The home bar is set up and he asks who wants a Bloody Mary. There are five bartenders in ten episodes of this series and many cocktails are seen.

1977–1987 THE LOVE BOAT

The Love Boat is set on a Princess Cruise Line cruise ship. Each week, celebrities young and old guest star, setting sail on humorous and often romantic adventures. Over 1,300 celebrities appear on *The Love Boat*, including Janet Jackson, Zsa Zsa Gabor, Tom Hanks, and Hulk Hogan. Serving all kinds of cocktails, Teddy Wilson plays Isaac the bartender in 250 episodes. There are also other bartenders seen serving drinks, because if you've ever been on a cruise ship, then you know there are several types of bars. The show was a spin-off of a made-for-TV movie, which was based on a novel.

1977–1984 THREE'S COMPANY

This sitcom is set near the beach in Santa Monica, California. It is about three friends named Jack, Chrissy, and Janet becoming roommates. The girls, however, know the landlord would not appreciate the arrangement, so they tell him Jack is gay. (Roommates of different sexes and adding a gay factor were racy concepts in 1977.) The neighborhood bar is the Regal Beagle and throughout the show's seven-year run the bar goes through three bartenders and many cocktails. Jack is watching the bar for the bartender in "Stanley Casanova" (season two, episode ten). He makes two classic Daiquiris, but with tequila. In "Handcuffed" (season four, episode eighteen), Chrissy and Jack play around with handcuffs and accidently cuff themselves together. The problem is that Jack has a date, so Chrissy has to come along to the Regal Beagle while handcuffed to Jack. Three white wines are ordered and cost $5.25. Jack drinks a red cocktail called the Rocket and becomes the life of the party in "Up in the Air" (season six, episode twenty-five). There are also ten episodes that have party scenes and many cocktails are seen.

1979–1983 *ARCHIE BUNKER'S PLACE*

This is an *All in the Family* spin-off. Archie runs his own local bar in Queens, New York. Lots of beer is served and the décor consists of a brass four-spout tap tower on the bartop; framed photographs of sport figures on the wall; trophies, bottles, and glasses on the backbar; and cloth-covered bistro tables with candles and black plastic ashtrays.

In "Relief Bartender" (season four, episode sixteen), Archie is approached by a female bartender, but he thinks only men should be bartenders. She tries to convince him by saying: "Mr. Bunker, I've been a bartender for ten years. I can make over two hundred drinks. I know what goes in them, what to pour them in, and how to serve them. I tell jokes, I'm a good listener, an avid sports fan, and I've thrown out my share of drunks." In the same scene, she makes a Sidecar and a Grasshopper.

Cheers TV show. Shown from left (top row): John Ratzenberger, Roger Rees, Woody Harrelson; (middle row) Rhea Perlman, Ted Danson, Kirstie Alley, George Wendt; (bottom row) Kelsey Grammer, Bebe Neuwirth. © *NBC / Photofest*

1982–1993 *CHEERS*

Cheers wins for having the most scenes in a bar. This is because the show is named after a Boston bar, Cheers. Many drinks are seen through its eleven-year run and its theme song is one of the most beloved.

Cheers theme song ("Where Everybody Knows Your Name")

"Sometimes you want to go, where everybody knows your name. And they're always glad you came."

1987–1994 *STAR TREK: THE NEXT GENERATION*

The bar on this spacecraft is called Ten Forward, located at the forward end of the saucer section, which offers a spectacular view of space. In season two, a bartender named Guinan is added to the cast and played by Whoopi Goldberg. The writers make her a good advisor and counselor for guests, and everyone on board is her guest. There are several bar scenes, she keeps a bottle of high-proof green Aldebaran whiskey behind the bar that was a gift from Jean-Luc Picard, techno terminals on the backbar produce food and drinks, Klingon drinks are served in large smoking metal cups, and guests can entertain themselves with three-dimensional chess.

1988–1998 *MURPHY BROWN*

Murphy Brown is set in Washington, DC, and Murphy and her news coworkers frequent Phil's Bar & Grill for lunch and after work. (These were the years of President George H. W. Bush. and President Bill Clinton's first term.)

In the first few seasons, whenever a new person enters the bar, everyone yells out in unison, "Close the door!" Lots of wine and beer are seen and Murphy always seems to drink a tall, clear drink with a lime wedge. There are many scenes related to drinking and bars that include Murphy singing, along with the bar pianist, "Don't Get Around Much Anymore" (the joke is that she can't sing); Murphy helping Phil financially with his bar; Murphy dealing with a suspected alcoholic worker; Murphy learning that a date is a big partier; and there are many parties thrown for many occasions.

1989–THE PRESENT *THE SIMPSONS*

The Simpsons is a humorous animated TV show set in a fictional American city called Springfield. It is about a family and their town. The show got its start as short animated sketches on *The Tracy Ullman Show*. Over 1,000 celebrities have guest-starred on the show; some multiple times (up to fifty-two).

The bar on *The Simpsons* is Moe's. Moe's has become so popular that in 2015, Orlando Florida's Universal Studio built a replica of Moe's. You can order a Duff Beer, a Flaming Moe, and a Krusty Burger. There are too many drinking scenes to mention, so here are some of the best:

- Duff Beer. Duff Beer is seen in every episode.
- Fudd Beer. It is Duff Beer's rival (Duff spelled backward). It makes its appearance in season three, episode twenty.
- Simpson & Son Revitalizing Tonic. Homer and his father create a tonic and then start bottling it. All goes well until they burn down their childhood home (season six, episode ten).
- Illegal Bathtub Hooch. When Prohibition hits Springfield, Homer sets out to brew his own (season eight, episode eighteen).
- Flaming Moe's. In season three, episode ten, bartender and owner Moe, runs out of Duff Beer, so Homer tells him about the "Flaming Homer" drink he invented. Moe steals the recipe and renames it "Flaming Moe." Moe's bar becomes a hot spot. Even the rock band Aerosmith is suddenly hanging out at Moe's bar and sings a song, "Flaming Moe's," to the tune of the *Cheers* theme song.

1990–1991 *TWIN PEAKS*

Twin Peaks is an FBI investigation show set in the fictional town of Twin Peaks, Washington. Many scenes take place in the roadhouse type of bar called the Big Bang Bar. Lots of beer, whiskey, and free unshelled peanuts are seen along with an industrial lounge singer played by Julee Cruise.

1990–1995 *NORTHERN EXPOSURE*

This show is about a young physician who was able to attend medical school because the state of Alaska paid for his education. The catch is, after graduating, he must pay back Alaska by practicing in a small Alaskan town. The small town has one bar, called the Brick, and it is in almost every episode. It's nothing fancy; just a whiskey and beer bar with an attached restaurant, but it has a feeling of coziness with many conversations at the bar.

1993–1999 *STAR TREK: DEEP SPACE NINE*

This is a spin-off of *Star Trek: The Next Generation*. The bartender and bar owner on *Deep Space Nine* is named Quark. Many drinks are seen throughout the series, but the most popular are Raktajino and a Slug-O-Cola.

1999–THE PRESENT *FAMILY GUY*

Family Guy is an adult animation show set in the fictional city of Quahog, Rhode Island. It revolves around the politically incorrect Peter Griffin and his family. Celebrities are often guests. In fact, over 800 celebrities have appeared as guest stars.

Peter works at a brewery called Pawtucket Ale and patronizes the Drunken Clam. Throughout the series, the Clam attempts several themes, including a British pub, karaoke bar, and a Coyote Ugly theme. In one episode, we learn that Peter has been going to the Clam since 1977, and that in the 1980s it was called St. Elmo's Clam. The Clam also burns down and is rebuilt. Peter is always drinking and has considered working a twelve-step program. On the other hand, he has gotten so drunk that he tries to unicycle down a flight of stairs. In one episode, he orders a Vodka Stinger with a whiskey back.

1998–2004 *SEX AND THE CITY*

Sarah Jessica Parker in *Sex and the City*, Season 5, 2002. © *NBC / Photofest*

Sex and the City is a romantic comedy set in New York City. It follows the lives of four friends. The show was based on a New York column and a book of the same name.

As far as cocktails, in 1999 (the second season) the show made the Cosmopolitan go—in today's terms—viral. Season one mentions the Cosmopolitan once in episode seven, but the Cosmo is seen in ten episodes and mentioned three times in season two. The Flirtini (a champagne cocktail made with vodka and pineapple juice) is another cocktail seen and mentioned. It was ordered in bars for a little while, but the Cosmopolitan reigned queen.

One of the friends dates a bartender, many bars are hopped, and several cocktails are seen and drunk in almost every episode.

1999–2003 *FUTURAMA*

The *Futurama* crowd visits and mentions several bars such as the Hip Joint, O'Grady's Pub, and O'Zorgnax's Pub. A drink called Slurm is popular and the Hip Joint serves Martini Clouds that rain into your glass. There is also a heavy-drinking robot named Bender Bending Rodriguez.

1999–2007 *THE SOPRANOS*

Bada Bing! What else would an Italian-American New Jersey mobster's strip bar be named? Meetings with drinks are held in the club and in the lead character's office in the back. There's drinking in almost every episode. Drinks mentioned include Sambuca, Armagnac, vodka, wine, and homemade wine.

2000–2007 | 2016–THE PRESENT *GILMORE GIRLS*

The *Gilmore Girls* show follows a single mother and her daughter in the fictional town of Stars Hollow, Connecticut. The show is about relationships between its quirky residents.

Miss Patty, played by Liz Torres, is known for making a deceptively strong punch at all the town events and almost every character on the show has a regretful story from drinking it the next day.

In "Red Light on the Wedding Night" (season 2 episode 3), Lorelai Gilmore, played by Lauren Graham, says to her daughter, "Honey, someday, when you're a little older, you will be introduced to something that is extremely seductive but fickle. A fair-weather friend who seems benign but packs a wallop like a donkey kick, and that is the Long Island Iced Tea. The Long Island Iced Tea makes you do things that you normally wouldn't do, like lifting your skirt in public or calling someone you normally wouldn't call at really weird times."

In season five, episode twenty, Lorelai Gilmore's drink of choice is a Gin Martini. Her mother, Emily Gilmore, played by Kelly Bishop, pretends that Lorelai's drink of choice is a Sidecar, then Lorelai says, "No, my drink is a Martini. It's always been a Martini."

In "Twenty-One Is the Loneliest Number" (season 6 episode 7), Emily Gilmore asks the bartender to create a drink called the "Rory" for Alexis Biedel's twenty-first birthday. After tasting it, Scott Patterson comments that it tastes pink.

2001–2010 *SCRUBS*

Scrubs is a medical comedy drama whose main character is Dr. John Michael "J. D." Dorian, played by Zach Braff. There are too many episodes to mention, but you learn quickly that his favorite cocktail is an Appletini.

2002–2006 *THE THIRSTY TRAVELER*

Kevin Brauch hosts this weekly Travel Channel show, and each week he explores a new destination's alcohol, people, customs, and traditions.

2002–2008 *THE WIRE*

The characters in this cop show always gather at Kavanagh's Irish Pub when an officer dies or retires, and on other occasions. Wakes are held with the body on the pool table. Lots of beer, whiskey, and indoor smoking are seen.

2003–2006 / 2013–THE PRESENT *ARRESTED DEVELOPMENT*

Drinking is seen throughout the episodes; especially Martinis Jessica Walter (the mother) drinks. There are also several scenes at a local nightclub called "and Jeremy Piven."

2003–2015 *TWO AND A HALF MEN*

This show is a situation comedy about brothers Charlie and Alan (the two) and Alan's son (the half). After a divorce, Alan (Jon Cryer) and his son move in with brother Charlie (Charlie Sheen) who lives well in a beach house—and the move-in cramps his style, but leads to many laughs. Many drinks are seen throughout the series, and the local bar is called Pavlov's, where every time the bell is rung everyone barks and takes a shot. Alan's favorites drinks are Appletinis and Rum & Cokes.

2004–2006 *DEADWOOD*

This show is set in the 1870s in nonfictional Deadwood, South Dakota. Like every small 1800s town, you would expect to find a saloon, and every episode has a scene in the Gem Saloon. Al Swearengen owns Deadwood's saloon and brothel. He is a known pimp. The handwritten imbibing menu on the backbar includes whiskey, brandy, Old Tom Gin, Blue Blazer, and a drink called the Judge. A large sign advertising ice is also hanging outside. At the time when the show is set, ice was harvested from frozen ponds.

2005–2014 *HOW I MET YOUR MOTHER*

This show is set in New York City starting in 2005 and follows the main character, Ted, and his friends. It is narrated by a voice who retells the story to his children in the year 2030. Every episode of this TV show has one or more scenes that take place at MacLaren's Pub, because this is where the friends sit in a booth, drink, and catch up each day.

There are too many scenes to mention, but some include Marshall inventing a cocktail called the Minnesota Tidal Wave; Lily's funny pregnant drinking scene; Barney creating "Barney Stinson's Hangover Fixer Elixir"; Robin drinking Scotch; Ted dropping a $600 bottle of Scotch; Ted offering to buy the newest Scotch at MacLaren's (Jumbo Jim's Grape Scotch); and the time when Barney and Ted dream of owning a bar, which cuts to them reenacting the famous Tom Cruise/*Cocktail* film scene where both are flair bartending behind the bar.

2005–THE PRESENT *IT'S ALWAYS SUNNY IN PHILADELPHIA*

It's Always Sunny in Philadelphia is about a gang of underachieving friends who own a bar called Paddy's Pub in South Philadelphia. There is drinking and talking of drinking in every episode. Once, they even hold drinking contest.

2006–2008 *THE ULTIMATE COYOTE UGLY SEARCH*

CMT (Country Music TV) aired this reality TV show for three seasons. Fueled by the 2000 film *Coyote Ugly*, this show auditions / exploits female bartenders in competitions with the prize being a position at a Coyote Ugly Saloon and $50,000.

2007–2015 *MAD MEN*

Mad Men is an AMC period drama primarily set in the 1960s. The show is about an advertising agency in New York City and the star character is Don Draper. There is too much to mention because every episode has drinking scenes and most are heavy, hard, three-Martini-lunch, stocked-liquor-cabinet drinking scenes.

One thing *Mad Men* did was to make cocktails from that era popular again. The AMC *Mad Men* website even provides *Mad Men* cocktail recipes. Some of these include the Old-Fashioned, Tom Collins, Blood and Sand, Champagne Cocktail, Blue Hawaiian, Manhattan, Pink Squirrel, Negroni, and Sidecar. One scene to share is the opening scene of season six, where Don Draper and his second wife lounge on a Hawaiian beach. She partakes of a Blue Hawaii that is served in a Hurricane glass.

2007–THE PRESENT *THE GRAHAM NORTON SHOW*

This humorous BBC celebrity talk show hosted by Graham Norton provides liquid refreshment for its celebrity guests. Guests' preferred drink of choice is preset on the coffee table in front of the sofa. There are too many to mention, but one notable cocktail gets a brand mentioned in series fourteen, episode three, when Norton draws attention to Robert De Niro's Hendrick's Cucumber Martini.

2008–2014 *TRUE BLOOD*

True Blood is an HBO horror vampire TV show that is set in Bon Temps, Louisiana (a small fictional town located in the northwest part of the state). The main character is a telepathic human-faerie hybrid named

Sookie Stackhouse. Sookie waitresses at the favorite hang in town, called Merlotte's Bar and Grill, and her best friend, Tara, is the bartender.

The bar sells a new alternative blood source (synthetic blood) for vampires called Tru Blood. It is designed to make humans feel safe around vampires. One year after the show premiered, HBO began selling Tru:Blood as a fictionalized brand to the public. It was a carbonated blood orange drink. Later in the series, Merlotte's Bar & Grill is sold, revamped, and renamed Bellefleur's Bar and Grill and often just called BB&G. As you might guess, every episode has a bar scene; in "Somebody I Used to Know" (season one, episode eight), Tara makes a straight-up Strawberry Daiquiri with the fastest shake in the world.

2008–2010 ON THE ROCKS: THE SEARCH FOR AMERICA'S TOP BARTENDER

Absolut vodka and LXTV (NBC Local Media's award-winning producer of local lifestyle and entertainment programming) search for a bartender with the personality, looks, and skills to become America's Top Bartender. Each week, ten finalists compete for $100,000.

2009–2015 PARKS AND RECREATION

Parks and Recreation is often referred to as *Parks and Rec* and is a political comedy set in the fictional town of Pawnee, Indiana. Leslie Knope, the main character, works at the Parks Department as deputy director and serves on many committees. Her goal is to become the city manager and eventually—her secret goal—president of the United States.

Leslie is cheerful and perky, but inclined to put positive spins on failures. There is drinking throughout the series and a bar called the Snakehole Lounge. This fictional lounge even has its own website (snakeholelounge. com). Their specialty spirit is called snakejuice. Other drinks on the menu include Sweetums Fizz, Viper Milk, and Hiss Juice. In "Two Parties" (season five, episode ten), the guys from work visit a new trendy bar called Essence, which is a molecular mixology bar. They are not impressed with the Whiskey Lotion, Cotton Candy Beer, and vodka served in the form of a light flash. Other drinking scenes include Leslie getting drunk at the zoo; Leslie drinking wine from an illegal gift basket to be part of the boys' club; and an employee building a wooden harp to prove to Leslie that he is capable doing amazing things while drinking alcohol.

2010–THE PRESENT THREE SHEETS

Three Sheets is an international travelogue/bar-hopping series. The title is short for a term for "drunk," "three sheets to the wind." It is hosted by Zane Lamprey, and as you might imagine, there are several educational bar and alcohol scenes in every episode.

2007–2017 THE BIG BANG THEORY

The Big Bang Theory is a sitcom set in Pasadena, California. The show began its first season based around five characters: four geeky science guys and one girl, who is a waitress/bartender trying to be an actress, living across the hall. The show has had many famous scientists appear as guest stars, even Stephen Hawking! The friends visit many restaurants and bars, and there are many scenes involving drinks.

Three of the best that mention drink names include "The Grasshopper Experiment" (season one, episode eight). Here, Penny needs to practice making cocktails, so she sets up a bar in her kitchen and invites the guys over. Leonard orders a Tequila Sunrise; Raj orders a Grasshopper; Sheldon orders a Virgin Cuba Libre; and Howard orders a Slippery Nipple. There is funny interaction between orders. This is also the episode where the friends learn that Raj, who is afraid to talk to women, can talk to women if he drinks. In "The Gothowitz Deviation" (season three, episode three), Howard takes Raj to a Goth bar. Howard drinks a Vodka Cranberry because he says it looks like blood and then makes fun of Raj's light beer. When they offer to buy two girls a drink, the girls ask for light beers. In "The Apology Insufficiency" (season four, episode seven), Penny is tending bar and Sheldon wants to order a cocktail. He opens a drink app on his phone to choose a cocktail and says: "Harvey Wallbanger...ehhh, Sex on the Beach...I hardly think so. Rob Roy, Silk Slipper, Mad Hatter, ohhhhh! I'll have a Rosewater Rickey." Penny serves him a shot of whiskey.

Other drinking-related things to mention include Sheldon getting drunk on beer; Sheldon getting drunk on wine; Sheldon getting drunk on Long Island Iced Teas; the friends patronize a wine bar; and they all go out to a tiki karaoke bar and drink tiki drinks complete with mugs and paper parasols.

2010–2015 BOARDWALK EMPIRE

This is a crime drama series set in Atlantic City during Prohibition. As you might guess, many scenes are set in speakeasy bars (except when they drink in Cuba). Well-known film director Martin Scorsese and actor Mark Wahlberg produce the series. The show's intro has bottles of whiskey washing up on shore.

2010–THE PRESENT NADIA G'S BITCHIN' KITCHEN

Nadia is a YouTuber turned Cooking Channel star. Not only does she cook, but also every once in a while she explores cocktails. In "Girls Night In" (season two, episode six), Nadia makes Cardamom Blood Orange Mojitos. In "Depression Desserts" (season two, episode thirteen), Nadia makes a Bourbon Vanilla Milkshake. In "Bitchin'/Party Guide" (season two, episode sixteen), Nadia shows you how to set up a DIY vodka bar with spicy pomegranate and lemongrass mixers. In *Mad Men* (season three, episode eight), Nadia makes an Old-Fashioned Cocktail–inspired Cherry Pie. In "Hair of the Dog Breakfast" (season three, episode thirteen), Nadia makes a Pineapple-Cilantro Martini rimmed with Chile salt and a Smoky Chipotle Bloody Mary. In "Hipster Brunch" (season three, episode sixteen) Nadia makes a Maple Pink Grapefruit Mimosa, Spiced Orange Mimosa, and Vanilla Pineapple Mimosa.

2014–THE PRESENT BOOZE TRAVELER

The Travel Channel's host Jack Maxwell travels the world drinking his way through alcohol and its customs.

2014–THE PRESENT NCIS: NEW ORLEANS

NCIS: New Orleans is a police series set and filmed in New Orleans, Louisiana. New Orleans is known for having many bars, so there are many bar scenes, bars in the background, and lots of parades and celebrations with people drinking. One notable episode is the opening scene of "The Third Man" (season two, episode twenty-three), which shows and mentions two Sazeracs.

2014–THE PRESENT THE TONIGHT SHOW WITH JIMMY FALLON

Jimmy Fallon succeeded Jay Leno, becoming the sixth *Tonight Show* host. He also succeeded in talking the executives into letting him host in New York City instead of California. Many cocktails have been seen and made on the show. He has also mentioned (a few times) the New York City bar PDT. Justin Timberlake makes an Old-Fashioned with his Tequila 9:01; Gordon Ramsey drinks a cocktail he created called Wake Up, You Donkey;

Fallon presents light saber cocktails in Collins glasses set on lighted coasters with Stinger shots; Anthony Bourdain makes a Negroni; and Rachel Maddow makes a few cocktails.

Fallon also hosts a regular Drinko game with celebrities. Alcoholic drinks normally consist of tequila, sambuca, beer, wine spritzer, peppermint schnapps, champagne, cinnamon whiskey, limoncello, Jägermeister, and absinthe.

2014–THE PRESENT *THE UNITED STATES OF DRINKING*

A Smithsonian TV show hosted by award-winning food writer Josh Ozersky. Josh explores the science and history of all drinking and drinks, and the shows often delve into cocktails and mixology.

2015–THE PRESENT *ASH VS. EVIL DEAD*

This is a comedy horror show set approximately thirty years after the first three *Evil Dead* films. Ash Williams works as a stock boy in the day and drinks in bars at night. In the very first episode of the first season, "El Jefe," Ash walks into a bar, spots a girl sitting alone, and says to the bartender, "Send me down a Moscow Mule and two of whatever the lady is having."

2015–THE PRESENT *BETTER CALL SAUL*

Better Call Saul is a spin-off prequel of *Breaking Bad*. The show starts in 2002 and is set Albuquerque, New Mexico. It follows the story of small-time lawyer Jimmy McGill six years before his appearance on *Breaking Bad* as Saul Goodman. There are many bar scenes.

In "Bali Ha'i" (season 2 episode 6), Rhea Seehorn turns down a Moscow Mule, calling it vintage. Later that evening, she orders herself a Moscow Mule at a bar.

2015–THE PRESENT *COCKTAILS & CLASSICS*

Michael Urie hosts *Cocktails & Classics* with celebrity friends who watch and analyze classic films while sipping cocktails. The show begins with Michael introducing the cocktail.

2016–THE PRESENT *MATCH GAME*

Match Game is a panel game show where celebrities try to match fill-in-the-blank questions with contestants. The show was first aired from 1962 to 1969, then 1973 to 1982, then 1990 to 1991, but in the new 2016 show, the celebrities have an alcoholic drink of their choice. The host is Alec Baldwin.

31

NAME YOUR POISON: COCKTAILS AND ALCOHOL CELEBRITIES DRINK

Celebrities probably attend more parties than the average person and there is a bartender somewhere to serve them. Special thanks for contributions from Kyle Branche and Jennifer Long from Los Angeles who have been tending bar for celebrities in Hollywood for a long time.

- **Alan Jackson:** Bushwhackers on his private yacht.

- **Alfred Hitchcock:** Mimosa.

- **Amy Schumer:** She drinks wine, but used to be a bartender and is known for tipping

- bartenders $1,000.

- **Andy Dick:** Vodka with anything.

- **Andy Garcia:** Negroni and Grey Goose Martini.

- **Andy McDowell:** Midori Sour.

- **Alan Cumming:** Martini.

- **Ava Gardner:** Beefeater gin, Bloody Mary, Whiskey & Coke, Martini, and Mai Tai.

- **Barbra Streisand:** Champagne Cocktail at the Playboy Mansion.

- **Bill Maher:** Vodka & Tonic, with the lime on the side on a napkin preferably placed with tongs because he is a germaphobe.

- **Bing Crosby:** Bourbon and Herradura Tequila.

- **Britt Leach:** Scotch on the rocks.

- **Bob Saget:** Margarita in Los Angeles and he is a great tipper.

- **Buddy Hackett:** Gin Ricky.

- **Cal Ripkin:** Rum Runners served by me at the Grand Floridian Beach Resort in Walt Disney World.

- **CeeLo Green:** Long Island Iced Tea.

- **Charlize Theron:** Pomegranate Blossom at Social in Hollywood.

- **Chevy Chase:** Piña Colada served by me at the Grand Floridian Beach Resort in Walt Disney World.

- **Conan O'Brien:** He loves Appletinis. On August 9, 2011, he said, "After yesterday's six-hundred-point drop, the stock market fell and then got back up again six times today. So basically, the stock market is acting like me after three Appletinis."

- **David Bowie:** Bombay Sapphire Martini.

- **David Krumholtz** (TV show *Numbers*): Patrón Margarita.

- **David Lee Roth:** Jack Daniel's straight from the bottle at every concert.

- **Dean Martin:** Pinch Scotch & Soda, Dewar's Scotch & Soda, and ginger ale on the rocks with a little Scotch on the rim so that it looked and smelled like a drink at the Playboy Mansion.

- **Eddie Money:** Tequila Sunrise.

- **Elizabeth Hurley:** Stinger.

- **Elizabeth Montgomery:** Sidecar, Sazerac, White Wine, Smirnoff Bloody Mary, and Smirnoff Screwdriver at the Playboy Mansion.

- **Elizabeth Taylor:** Scotch, Vodka, Bloody Marys, and Chocolate Martinis. In the 2007 book *Rock Hudson: His Story*, Elizabeth and Rock were filming *Giant* and on a Saturday night in 1955, he and Elizabeth invented the Chocolate Martini. They put vodka, chocolate syrup, and chocolate liqueur in a Vodka Martini and thought it tasted terrific. Rock said, "We were really just kids, we could eat and drink anything and we never needed sleep." He also said one Sunday it hailed and they ran out with a bucket to gather hailstones for Bloody Marys.

- **Ellen DeGeneres:** Tequila and Gin & Tonic and is a good tipper because she used to be a bartender.

- **Elvira** (Cassandra Peterson)**:** Vodka & Soda and Vodka Cranberry.

- **Ernest Hemingway:** Papa Noble, Dry Martini, Bloody Mary, Hemingway Daiquiris, Absinthe Drip, Mojito, Death in the Afternoon, and Planter's Punches.

- **Eva Mendes:** Pink Elephant at the Pink Elephant in New York City.

- **Frank Sinatra:** Bourbon & Water, Scotch & Water, and Jack Daniel's.

- **George Chakiris** (1961 Best Supporting Actor Oscar winner, *West Side Story*)**:** Keoke Coffee.

- **George Clooney:** Raspberry Cheesecake at the Cherry Nightclub in Las Vegas.

- **George Lucas:** Old-Fashioned.

- **Gisele Bündchen:** Peach Passion in Miami.

- **Hal Nederham:** Absolut Citron on the rocks with a twist of lemon.

- **Hulk Hogan:** Piña Coladas served by me at the Grand Floridian Beach Resort in Walt Disney World.

- **Hunter S. Thompson:** Chartreuse on the rocks.

- **Jack Benny:** Gin Martini.

- **Jane Birkin:** Appletini at the Fubar in Paris.

- **Janis Joplin:** A mix of Southern Comfort, Rose's Lime, and soda water.

- **Jayma Mays:** Gin & Tonic with honey.

- **Jeff Gordon:** White Wine Spritzer.

- **Jennifer Aniston:** Margarita. Jennifer is a well-known Margarita lover. In 2015, she told Yahoo's beauty editor-in-chief, "I love Patrón. I also love Don Julio 1942 as nice sipping tequila. It's so yummy, it has a little sweetness to it, which I usually don't like. Justin (her then-husband) actually makes the perfect Margarita with Don Julio 1942 because there's no agave, no sugar, no mix. It's pure tequila, lime juice, and a squinch of Cointreau. It's delicious."

- **Jennifer Lawrence:** Piña Colada.

- **Jerry O'Connell:** Cosmopolitan in Australia.

- **Jessica Biel:** Angry Dragon Martini at the Grand Hotel in New York City.

- **Jessica Simpson:** Grey Goose & Soda and champagne.

- **Jim Belushi:** Rémy Martin XO.

- **JK Rowling:** Gin & Tonic.

- **Joan Crawford:** Whisky Sour made with Scotch at American Bar at the Savoy in London.

- **Jock Mahoney:** Bourbon & Water

- **Joe Namath** (football quarterback): Absolut on the rocks.

- **Joe Pesci:** Gin Martini.

- **John Ashton:** Dewar's & Water.

- **Johnny Depp:** Blueberry & Ginger Bourbon Sour at the Buddha Bar in Paris.

- **Johnny Halliday:** Woodford Reserve Old-Fashioned.

- **John Travolta:** Bombay Sapphire Martini.

- **Jon Bon Jovi:** Chartreuse on the rocks.

- **Julia Roberts:** Scorpino.

- **Karen Carpenter:** Scotch on the rocks.

- **Kate Hudson:** Passionate Saketini at Doku 15 in Toronto.

- **Kate Moss:** Kate told *Playboy* that she orders "French 76" at the Hemingway Bar at the Ritz in Paris.

- **Kelly Ripa:** Jell-O shots

- **Kiefer Sutherland:** Jade Mistress at the Red Pearl Kitchen in Hollywood.

- **Kim Kardashian:** White Russian. On February 9, 2011, Kim told *Bazaar*, "I don't drink. I just started at thirty. A White Russian. I hate the taste of alcohol. White Russians or Midori Sours—that's it."

- **Kylie Minogue:** Lychee Martinis at the Opium in Belfast.

- **Lance Bass:** Appletini in Los Angeles and Mississippi Mule (moonshine ginger beer) at his wedding. Moscow Mule served by me at the Bourbon O Bar in New Orleans.

- **Laura Prepon:** Hurricane at Two Urban Licks in Atlanta, Georgia.

- **Linda Hamilton** (*Terminator*): Long Island Iced Tea served by me at the Bourbon "O" Bar in New Orleans.

- **Liv Tyler:** Strawberry Daiquiri served by me at the Grand Floridian Beach Resort in Walt Disney World.

- **Lou Ferrigno:** Strawberry Daiquiri and Kir.

- **Madonna:** Cosmopolitan made by Patrick "Paddy" Mitten at the Life Cafe in New York City, Cosmopolitan made by Melissa Huffsmith at The Odeon in New York City, Cosmopolitan made by Toby Cecchini at The Odeon in New York City, Cosmopolitan made by Cheryl Cook at The Strand in Miami Beach, Cosmopolitan made by Dale "King Cocktail" DeGroff at the Rainbow Room in New York City, and Pomegranate Martini at the Prime Grill in Los Angeles.

- **Mark Consuelos:** Heineken.

- **Marc McGrath:** Vodka Cranberry.

- **Mario Lopez:** Margarita.

- **Martha Stewart:** Mimosa made with blood orange juice.

- **Martin Landau:** Vodka Martini.

- **Melanie Griffith:** Frozen Margarita served by me at the Grand Floridian Beach Resort in Walt Disney World.

- **Mick Jones** (Foreigner)**:** Stoli on the rocks.

- **Mike Ditka:** Cape Cod.

- **Mike Scioscia** (baseball)**:** Sangria.

- **Mindy Kaling:** Dark 'n Stormy.

- **Naomi Campbell:** Champagne Cocktails at the Absolut Bar in Vienna.

- **Natalie Shaffer** (Mrs. Thurston Howell III on the TV show *Gilligan's Island*)**:** Scotch & Milk.

- **Nicole Richie:** Vodka & Soda.

- **Oliver Reed:** Gin & Tonic and Bloody Mary at Harry's Bar in Paris.

- **Oprah Winfrey:** Tequila, Lemon Drop Martini, Pomegranate Martini, and Moscow Mule.

- **Pamela Anderson:** Mai Tai.

- **Paul Reubens** (Pee-wee Herman)**:** Vodka Cranberry and Vodka & Soda.

- **Peter Lawford:** Rob Roy, Grants & Water, and Pink Lady at the Playboy Mansion.

- **Peter O'Toole:** Sidecar.

- **Pink:** Dirty Martini.

- **President Andrew Jackson:** Whiskey.

- **President Franklin D. Roosevelt:** Martinis, Manhattans, and Bermuda Rum Swizzles.

- **President George H. W. Bush:** Vodka Martinis.

- **President George Washington:** Applejack and Madeira.

- **President Gerald Ford:** Gin & Tonic and Martinis.

- **President Harry Truman:** Old-Fashioneds.

- **President Herbert Hoover:** Dry Gin Martini.

- **President John F. Kennedy:** Daiquiris and Bloody Mary.

- **President Lyndon B. Johnson:** Scotch.

- **President Martin Van Buren:** Whiskey.

- **President Richard Nixon:** Rum & Coke.

- **President Theodore Roosevelt:** Mint Juleps.

- **President Warren G. Harding:** Whiskey.

- **President Woodrow Wilson:** Scotch.

- **Princess Stephanie of Monaco:** Vodka and Pink Lemonade served by me at the Grand Floridian Beach Resort in Walt Disney World.

- **Queen Elizabeth II:** Gordon's Gin & Tonic with three slices of lemon while visiting Australia. And yellow Chartreuse after a fish and chip lunch at Claridges.

- **Raquel Welch:** Champagne Cocktail.

- **Reba McEntire:** anything made with American whiskey.

- **Rebecca Romijn:** Red Pearl at the Red Pearl Kitchen in Hollywood.

- **Renée Zellweger:** a cocktail named Cosmic Messenger.

- **Richard Burton:** Whiskey & Soda, Vodka Martinis, Vodka & Tonic, and Jack & Soda.

- **Richard Chamberlain:** Ketel One Martini with a side shot of cold olive brine.

- **Richard Mulligan** (TV show *Soap*): Opal Nera Black Sambuca.

- **Robert De Niro:** Hendrick's Cucumber Martini on the *Graham Norton Show*.

- **Robert Stack:** Early Times & Water.

- **Ryan Gosling:** Scotch.

- **Ryan Reynolds:** Anything with Aviation American Gin.

- **Sally Field:** Grasshoppers made with vanilla ice cream.

- **Sammy Hagar:** Cabo Wabo Margarita.

- **Shane West:** Jack & Coke.

- **Shirley Jones:** Bombay Sapphire Martini.

- **Simon Le Bon** (Duran Duran): Caipiroska.

- **Skeet Ulrich:** Anything with tequila and he's a great tipper.

- **Slash:** Jack Daniel's on the rocks.

- **Steven Tyler:** Piña Colada served by me at the Grand Floridian Beach Resort in Walt Disney World.

- **Tallulah Bankhead:** Mint Julep, Gin Martini, French 75, frozen Daiquiri, and Manhattan.

- **Taylor Swift:** Whiskey Sour.

- **Teri Garr:** Mai Tai served by me at the Grand Floridian Beach Resort in Walt Disney World.

- **Tony Curtis:** 100-proof Smirnoff on the rocks with a twist.

- **Tyne Daly:** Greyhound.

- **Umberto of Italy** (ex-king): Manhattan with two cherries at the American Bar at the Savoy in London.

- **Valerie Bertinelli:** Cosmopolitan on the rocks, Vodka Cranberry, and Dirty Martini.

- **Vanessa Paradis:** Strawberry Mojito at the Buddha Bar in Paris.

- **Vince Vaughn:** Red Bull and Vodka at the Reserve in Chicago.

- **Whitney Houston:** Belvedere Martini.

32

Neighborhood Watering Holes: Historic Bars Around the World

UNITED STATES OF AMERICA (BY STATE AND CITY)

ALABAMA

Flora-Bama (Est. 1964) | Perdido

Nicknamed "the Bama," this extremely popular dive beach bar, oyster bar, honky-tonk roadhouse, and package store is located at the Florida and Alabama border. At one time, they had over twenty bars with several bands playing. The Bama has made the Bushwacker their signature drink and they are known to hold sold-out annual events such as Super Bowl Chili Cook Off, Mullet Toss, Bulls on the Beach, and Polar Bear Dip. Over seven country singers have mentioned the Bama in song. Some of those artists include Jimmy Buffett, Kenny Chesney, and Blake Shelton.

ALASKA

B&B Bar (Est. 1908) | Kodiak

This oldest bar in Alaska displays their liquor license as proof.

ARIZONA

The Crystal Palace Saloon (Est. 1879) | Tombstone

This oldest bar in Arizona was originally built in 1879, then burned down in 1881. It was immediately rebuilt, then burned down again in 1882, and then was immediately rebuilt a second time. The most famous patron was Doc Holiday. The second story was not a brothel like most saloons; it housed the offices for such notables as US Deputy Marshal Virgil Earp, attorney George W. Berry, and Dr. George E. Goodfellow. Today, the Crystal Palace slogan is "Still Serving Good Whiskey and Tolerable Water."

Drift Inn Saloon (Est. 1902) | Globe

The Drift Inn Saloon is said to be haunted with the ghosts of ladies of the night due to the second level being used as a brothel back then. Today, it is one of the top biker bars.

THE OHIO CLUB (EST. 1905) | HOT SPRINGS

The Ohio Club is the oldest bar in Arkansas. During Prohibition the bar turned into a secret speakeasy and was renamed the Ohio Cigar Store. Out front was the cigar store, but in the back was the bar. It has been said that the club was visited by almost every well-known gangster of the time including Al Capone. Today, there is even a statue of Al Capone sitting smoking a cigar outside on the sidewalk.

Baseball legend Babe Ruth was known to visit because Hot Springs hosted spring training, and as for jazz entertainment, Al Jolson, Mae West, Louis Armstrong, Sammy Davis Jr., and Tony Bennett helped with that. The Ohio Club still has entertainment seven nights a week.

CALIFORNIA

IRON DOOR SALOON (EST. 1852) | GROVELAND

The Iron Door is believed to be the oldest bar in California and gets its name from its swinging cast-iron front doors, which were shipped from England. The bar sits just miles from Yosemite. Today, the saloon's ceiling is covered in wadded-up dollar bills, elk heads hang on the wall, and you can even see a few gunshot holes.

BALBOA CAFÉ (EST. 1913) | SAN FRANCISCO

The elegant Balboa Café has been making classic cocktails since they opened. It's also a classic place to eat American fare and people-watch. The interior has remained mostly untouched since 1913.

BUENA VISTA CAFÉ (EST. 1912) | SAN FRANCISCO

The Buena Vista Café is most known for introducing the Irish Coffee to America in 1952. Today, they serve over 2,000 a day.

ELIXIR (EST. 1858) | SAN FRANCISCO

2015 Elixir Saloon in San Francisco. © *Darren Edwards*

As the second oldest continually operating saloon in San Francisco, Elixir is a testament to the storied saloon history of the wildest of Wild West towns. H. Joseph Ehrmann is the eleventh proprietor since 1858, having lovingly restored its Victorian bones in 2003 and bringing the bar to international renown while playing a significant role in the revival of cocktail culture in the early 2000s. Today, it boasts one of the best whiskey collections in the country and 365 days of service, never closing to the public for private events. As Ehrmann continues to invest in historic research and physical restoration, the saloon is poised to continue serving San Francisco, and the world, for generations to come.

OLD SHIP SALOON (EST. 1851) | SAN FRANCISCO

This oldest saloon in San Francisco sits atop a gold rush ship graveyard. In 1849, *Ship Arkansas* left New York and six months later arrived in San Francisco. It ran aground on Alcatraz, then was brought to shore and converted into a store. In 1851 it became a saloon with a plank entrance. By 1857, the ship was dismantled and built upon. After the Great Earthquake of 1906, a brick building was erected.

MAGIC CASTLE (EST. 1963) | HOLLYWOOD

2013 Award-winning bar magician Doc Eason. © *Doc Eason*

I'm sure you've heard of the world-famous Magic Castle, but just in case you haven't—google it. It's the most unusual club in the world. You can't just walk in, however, there are ways to gain access (again, google it). In 2012, beverage manager Chris Taggart introduced classic and craft cocktails in all five of the Magic Castle bars: W.C. Fields Bar, Grand Salon Bar, Owl Bar, Palace Bar, and Hat and Hare Pub. In 2005, the Academy of Magical Arts Awards held at the Magic Castle, added a new category—Bar Magician. My friend William H. "Doc" Eason is the first to win this award. To date, he has won six awards at the Magic Castle.

THE SALOON (EST. 1861) | SAN FRANCISCO

This bar is believed to be the second oldest bar in California. It has survived earthquakes and fires. Back in the day, the upstairs was a brothel, but today, it is one of the best blues dive bars around. There are too many famous patrons to mention, but the owner's favorite celeb story is the night Johnny Depp took over door duty so the doorman could have a restroom break.

THE TONGA HUT (EST. 1958) | NORTH HOLLYWOOD

Don the Beachcomber opened the first American tiki bar in Los Angeles in 1934, but it closed in 1985. The Tonga Hut is the oldest tiki bar in California. Tiki was hip from the 1930s through the 1960s, but out of style from the 1970s through 2000, but the Tonga held on tight and stood the test of time.

COLORADO

THE MINT (EST. 1862) | SILVERTHORNE

The Mint is the oldest Colorado bar still in operation. It still uses its original name and building and was built fourteen years before Colorado was a state.

CONNECTICUT

GRISWOLD INN TAP ROOM (EST. 1776) | ESSEX

Griswold's sits on the Connecticut River and has operated as a working bar and hotel since the signing of the Declaration of Independence. Fifty years after being in business, the steamboat "golden era" grew in popularity and the Griswold flourished. Many celebrities have visited Griswold's, including George Washington, Mark Twain, Katharine Hepburn, and Albert Einstein. From the 1960s through today, the Griswold has been the backdrop for several TV shows and films.

Palace Saloon (Est. 1903) | Fernandina Beach

Fernandina Beach, Florida, was a major rail and seaport back in 1903, so the Palace Saloon was established. Adolphus Bush, founder of Anheuser-Busch, was the design consultant, and today, many of the designs are still in place, like the embossed tin ceiling, inlaid mosaic floors, mahogany hand-carvings, a forty-foot bar lit with gas lamps, and walls painted with six commissioned murals.

Captain Tony's Saloon (Est. 1958) | Key West

This building has been around since 1852, and it has been a city morgue, icehouse, telegraph station, brothel, cigar factory, and speakeasy. After Prohibition in 1933, it was Sloppy Joe's until 1957, when they moved down the street. This is where Jimmy Buffett got his start, Ernest Hemingway was a regular, and presidents have visited. Oh, there is a tree inside the building that has hung seventy-five people, and the tombstone at its trunk does not mark a real grave, but one of the coroners from the 1800s buried his daughter under the building where the poolroom is located.

HAWAII

Murphy's Bar & Grill (Est. 1891) | Honolulu

The Murphy's Bar & Grill building has had a "retail spirit" license since the 1860s and was first known as the Royal Hotel. In 1891, a bar was built in the hotel, and the waterfront hotel became a gathering place for ship captains, merchants, and gentlemen to meet and drink. Over the years, the bar changed owners and names many times. Since 1987, it has been known as the Royal Hawaiian Hotel, and the bar is called Murphy's Bar & Grill (it's an Irish bar).

Tropics Bar and Grill at the Hilton Hawaiian Village (Est. 1957) | Waikiki

Home of the Blue Hawaii cocktail, Hilton Hawaiian Village, Honolulu, Hawaii, Waikiki Beach. © *Jeff Whyte / Shutterstock*

In the 1950s, Hawaii went through grand construction because they wanted to bring tourism to their islands (they were not a US state until 1959). Hilton's Hawaiian Village started as a small hotel named the Niumalu Hotel in 1928. Then, in 1954, Henry J. Kaiser purchased the Niumalu and eight oceanfront acres, and new construction began. It was renamed Kaiser Hawaiian Village. This is where the legendary bartender Harry Yee invented the Blue Hawaii. Harry also is the first to start putting paper parasols and fresh orchids in drinks, and invented many more cocktails like the Tropical Itch, which was garnished with a bamboo back scratcher. Conrad Hilton bought the Kaiser Hawaiian Village in 1961, the same year Elvis Presley filmed *Blue Hawaii*. Elvis stayed at the new Hilton Hawaiian Village on the fourteenth floor of the Ocean Tower (Ali'i Tower) in the Mahele Suite. The Hawaiian Village was also the birthplace for exotica music.

White Horse Saloon (Est. 1907) | Spirit Lake

Not only is this saloon the oldest in Idaho, it was also the tallest building in 1907. They say that the bar is known to be haunted by a woman named "Big Girl," and many employees over the years have several stories to share. The bar still has its original hardwood floors, and there are eight flophouse rooms upstairs where patrons can crash.

ILLINOIS

The Village Tavern (Est. 1849) | Long Grove

The Village Tavern has been in continuous operation since 1849. The antique thirty-five-foot mahogany bar has been preserved. It even survived Chicago's Great McCormick Place Fire of 1967.

INDIANA

Knickerbocker Saloon (Est. 1835) | Lafayette

The Knickerbocker was the first bar in the state to receive a liquor license. It was named the Gault House, then the Cherry Wood Bar in the 1850s. In 1974 it was renamed Knickerbocker Saloon after a large player piano.

Slippery Noodle Inn (Est. 1850) | Indianapolis

This historic bar began with the name Tremont House and was renamed Slippery Noodle Inn by the new owner's six-year-old son in 1963. Between 1850 and 1863 it was the Concordia House, Germania House, Beck's Saloon, Moore's Beer Tavern, Moore's Restaurant (during Prohibition), then back to Moore's Beer Tavern until 1963. Today, it's an award-winning blues bar with live entertainment seven nights a week.

KANSAS

Hays House (Est. 1857) | Council Grove

In 1857, Daniel Boone's son Seth Hays built this bar and restaurant, and today it is the oldest continuously open bar and restaurant west of the Mississippi and a National Register Historic Landmark.

KENTUCKY

Talbott Tavern (Est. 1779) | Bardstown

The Old Talbott Tavern has been called the oldest western stagecoach stop in America. This dry stone building was built in 1779 and has held up pretty well through the years. Daniel Boone gave a deposition here in 1792, and it has a history of being owned and visited by Bourbon distiller greats such as William Heavenhill, William Samuels (Maker's Mark), and the Beams. Today, the bar is a Bourbon bar.

LOUISIANA

LAFITTE'S BLACKSMITH SHOP (EST. 1722) | NEW ORLEANS

The oldest bar in New Orleans is Lafitte's Blacksmith Shop. It is located on the corner of Bourbon and St. Philip streets. It was built between 1722 and 1732, is named after the privateer (pirate) and entrepreneur (gangster) of the Battle of New Orleans, Jean Lafitte. At night it's lit mostly by candlelight.

CAROUSEL BAR AT HOTEL MONTELEONE (EST. 1886) | NEW ORLEANS

This is the most famous bar to stop by while visiting New Orleans due to its rotating carousel bar. The hotel is known for being the temporary home to writers including Tennessee Williams, William Faulkner, Ernest Hemingway, Eudora Welty, and Truman Capote. As a matter of fact, so many writers in its history hung out in the Carousel Bar that the Friends of the Library Association designated it an official literary landmark in 1999.

MAINE

JAMESON'S TAVERN (EST. 1779) | FREEPORT

This building was built as a residence in 1779 for the town doctor. In 1801, Captain Samuel Jameson bought it and turned it into a tavern with rooms to let. It's known that presidents and writers have lodged here. There is a plaque out front proclaiming it as the "Birthplace of Maine," because records indicate that commissioners met in the northeast corner of the second floor to sign the final papers giving Maine her independence from Massachusetts. Later, it was sold to Richard Codman and became known as Codman's Tavern. Through time, the building became a residence, but it has been a running tavern since 1981. In 2003, celebrity chef Bobby Flay stopped to cook a proper Maine lobster dinner.

MARYLAND

MIDDLETON TAVERN (EST. 1750) | ANNAPOLIS

This tavern has hosted some of the nation's most revered leaders, including George Washington, Thomas Jefferson, and Benjamin Franklin. The Maryland Jockey Club, Freemasons, and the Tuesday Club met here to catch up on events while drinking, smoking, and gambling. The tavern went though many name changes, but the 1968 owners restored its original name.

MASSACHUSETTS

THE GREEN DRAGON TAVERN (EST. 1654) | BOSTON

The Green Tavern was coined "Headquarters of the Revolution" by Daniel Webster. The original Green Dragon Tavern served as the general meeting place and think tank for events that would eventually shape America. Samuel Adams, Dr. Joseph Warren, Paul Revere, and other Founding Fathers met in secret here to discuss events. These secret meetings led to the Boston Tea Party on December 16, 1773, and the departure of Paul Revere on April 18, 1775, on his famous midnight ride to Lexington and Concorde to warn patriots that the "British are coming."

MICHIGAN

OLD TAVERN INN (EST. 1835) | NILES

Michigan's oldest bar is also its oldest business. It started as a stagecoach stop between Chicago and Detroit.

MINNESOTA

NEUMANN'S BAR (EST. 1887) | NORTH ST. PAUL

Their claim to fame is being the oldest continuously running bar. During Prohibition, the bar sold near beer, and the second floor turned into a speakeasy. It is said that the ladies' restroom used to have a life-size picture on the wall of famous bodybuilder Charles Atlas wearing nothing but a fig leaf. When the leaf was lifted, a buzzer would go off in the bar.

MISSISSIPPI

KINGS TAVERN (EST. 1769) | NATCHEZ

As you might expect, Kings Tavern has a lot of history from being a stagecoach and later riverboat stop. The first known proprietor, Richard King, opened a tavern. The building is thought to be haunted by the ghost of Mr. King's mistress, Madeline. Her remains were found in the brick fireplace with a Spanish dagger in her chest. Today, the new owner, Chef Regina Charboneau, turned it into a fresh bar and restaurant practicing the farm-to-table philosophy. They also offer mixology classes.

MISSOURI

O'MALLEY'S PUB (EST. 1842) | WESTON

This bar is hidden almost sixty feet underground in the three-story cavernous cellars of what was the Weston Brewing Company. It was turned into a speakeasy during Prohibition.

MONTANA

BALE OF HAY SALOON (EST. 1863) | VIRGINIA CITY

Known as the oldest watering hole in the state of Montana. Today, two sisters, Gay and Kay (owners), offer ghost tours and Brothel Days with bed races, costume parties, and lectures. Oh, and the city population is 196.

NEBRASKA

GLUR'S TAVERN (EST. 1876) | COLUMBUS

This whitewashed tavern is the oldest bar west of the Missouri River operating continuously in the same building. Legend says that Buffalo Bill Cody visited here while traveling through to attend the funeral of Major Frank North. The tavern is listed in the National Register of Historic Places.

NEVADA

GENOA BAR (EST. 1853) | GENOA

A number of movies have been filmed here including *The Shootist* with John Wayne; *Charley Varrick* with Walter Matthau; *Honkytonk Man* with Clint Eastwood; *Misery* with James Caan, Kathy Bates, Rob Reiner, and Richard Farnsworth; and most recently, *A Place Called Home* starring Ann-Margret. When Raquel Welch visited, she was asked to leave her bra and agreed but insisted that all the other bras be taken down. The black leopard-print bra hanging on the deer antlers behind the bar is hers.

The Diamond Dust Mirror on the back of the bar came from Glasgow, Scotland, in the late 1840s. It was shipped around South America to San Francisco, and then brought by covered wagon (over two hundred miles!). Some musicians who have visited include Willie Nelson, Charlie Daniels, Merle Haggard, Waylon Jennings, Johnny Cash, Slim Pickens, and John Denver.

NEW HAMPSHIRE

The Fox Tavern in the Hancock Inn (Est. 1789) | Hancock

There is no true record of the Inn's original name, but it became known as the Fox Tavern when it passed into the hands of proprietor Noah Wheeler's son-in-law Jedediah Fox. It was known for its balls and dances, which were frequented by the aristocracy of the region. In winter, sleighing parties from neighboring towns would end their journey at the tavern with dinner and dancing. The tavern was on a stagecoach route, and later the railroad came through town. Officials on the first "official" train stop came to the Hancock House for dinner.

Wall murals in one of the bedrooms that had been painted by the famous itinerant artist, inventor, and journalist Rufus Porter were found in the 1900s. Stenciling by Hancock's well-known stencil artist, Moses Eaton Jr., was discovered under layers of wallpaper in the chambermaid's closet. As the two men were known to have worked together, it's likely that these were painted during the same time period, in 1825.

Since we're talking rural New England here, it should come as no surprise that the oldest tavern in the state is in what now operates as primarily a bed and breakfast. This colonial landmark is the oldest inn in New Hampshire, and was a regular hangout for the only guy from the state to ever be president, Franklin Pierce. It's still got a tavern and restaurant, so you can stop in without having to spend a romantic weekend watching the leaves change or some other equivalent unpleasantness.

NEW JERSEY

Barnsboro Inn (Est. 1720) | Sewell

The inn provided lodging, food, and drink from its beginning and has also been known as the Spread Eagle, Crooked Billet Inn, and Barnsboro Hotel. As times changed it turned into just a restaurant and bar. It was built with twelve-by-sixteen-inch square cedar logs and listed in the National Register of Historic Places in Gloucester County in 1973. Today, it features happy hours, comfort food, and an outdoor patio.

NEW YORK

White Horse Tavern (Est. 1800) | New York City

The White Horse Tavern is the second oldest continuously run tavern in New York City. Originally, the bar served men working the piers lining the Hudson River. In the 1950s it became popular with writers and artists, with the most renowned being Dylan Thomas, who found the tavern reminiscent of his favorite haunts in his home country of Wales. Some of the most influential people in jazz and the newly burgeoning folk and rock music scene flocked to the White Horse.

THE OLD '76 HOUSE (EST. 1755) | TAPPAN

Supposed to be New York's oldest tavern. The house was the site used to sign the Orangetown resolutions on July 4, 1774. It was also used as a prison for Major Andre and hosted General Washington and his first officers.

MCSORLEY'S OLD ALE HOUSE (EST. 1854) | NEW YORK CITY

This is the city's oldest continuously operated saloon. Everyone from Abe Lincoln to John Lennon has passed through its swinging doors. Woody Guthrie inspired the union movement from a table in the front with guitar in hand, while civil rights attorneys Faith Seidenberg and Karen DeCrow had to take their case to the Supreme Court to gain access. Women were finally allowed access to McSorley's in 1970, but the first women's restroom was not installed until 1986. As far as female barkeeps, the first one was hired in 1994. If you order beer, then there are two kinds, light or dark, and they give you two of them.

THE KING COLE BAR AT THE ST. REGIS (EST. 1904) | NEW YORK CITY

There are a couple of stories of where the Bloody Mary was invented, and this bar is the focus of one of them. Besides that, the five-star St. Regis Hotel has hosted too many celebrities to mention. Stars who lived at the hotel include Marilyn Monroe, Joe DiMaggio, John Lennon, and Yoko Ono.

NORTH CAROLINA

TAVERN IN OLD SALEM (EST. 1771) | SALEM

The Tavern burned down in 1784, then was quickly rebuilt with brick. In 1832, a wooden connecting building was constructed. Their claim to fame is that President George Washington visited for two nights. Today, they serve locally farmed food, craft cocktails, and beers in an upscale casual environment.

NORTH DAKOTA

PEACOCK ALLEY LOBBY BAR IN THE PATTERSON HOTEL (EST. 1911) | BISMARCK

Peacock Alley has hosted famous patrons such as President John F. Kennedy, Joe Louis, President Teddy Roosevelt, and President Lyndon Johnson. During Prohibition, the bar set up an elaborate alarm system to keep out unwanted guests. The hotel hosted illegal gambling and prostitution, and it's rumored that an underground tunnel once connected the hotel with the nearby train depot. The Patterson ceased hotel operations in the late 1970s, and the rooms were converted into senior housing.

OHIO

YE OLDE TRAIL TAVERN (EST. 1848) | YELLOW SPRINGS

This is the oldest bar in Ohio and is connected to the second restaurant in Ohio. The restaurant has hundreds of signed dollar bills displayed with many signed by celebrities. Other original items hanging on the walls include flasks, steins, and jugs.

OKLAHOMA

EISCHEN'S BAR (EST. 1896) | OKARCHE

This is the oldest bar in Oklahoma. The bar closed during Prohibition and was turned into a restaurant, but the alcohol came back after. Today, the massive backbar was hand-carved in Spain in the 1700s. It was brought from California in the 1950s. Eischen's burned down in 1993, then was rebuilt the same year, and the bar stills stands.

OREGON

HUBER'S (EST. 1879) | PORTLAND

Huber's is known for their flaming signature drink, Spanish Coffee, and turkey sandwiches. During Prohibition, it turned into just a restaurant with a speakeasy in the back.

PENNSYLVANIA

BROAD AXE TAVERN (EST. 1681) | AMBLER

It was first located on an old Indian path that was frequented by farmers and Indians. As the population increased, drinks were added, and it became a place for locals to gather and exchange news. In 1763, Derrick Van Pelt took over the Broad Axe and began horse races along Skippack Road, which became very popular. American Revolutionary soldiers were known to march by led by General Washington. Many soldiers were buried around this area, and it's said later—after the cemeteries had been abandoned—that the fireplace hearth was made from the tombstones of those graves. Today, the tavern is a family-friendly restaurant and bar.

RHODE ISLAND

WHITE HORSE TAVERN (EST. 1673) | NEWPORT

This is the oldest bar in America. It got its name from a white horse symbol mounted on the building. Not everyone could read in those days, so public establishments identified themselves with symbols. The White Horse was a regular haunt for colonists, British soldiers, Hessian mercenaries, pirates, sailors, Founding Fathers, and all manner of early American folk. In 1957, through the generosity of the Van Beuren family, the property was acquired by the Preservation Society of Newport County and meticulously restored.

SOUTH CAROLINA

McCRADY'S (EST. 1778) | CHARLESTON

Edward McCrady built this four-story Georgian house on East Bay Street and opened McCrady's Tavern. It served as a retreat for lowcountry luminaries who congregated at the tavern to imbibe, socialize, and discuss the country's ever-evolving political climate during the American Revolution. It is said that George Washington once was served a thirty-course dinner here. Today, it offers craft cocktails and fine dining.

SOUTH DAKOTA

Buffalo Bodega Bar (Est. 1877) | Deadwood

This is now known as the Buffalo Bodega Gaming Complex, but back then it was the city's eighteenth saloon named after Buffalo Bill Cody, a close friend of original owner Mike Russell.

TENNESSEE

Springwater Supper Club (Est. 1879) | Nashville

Today, this bar is a high-volume rock music venue. It claims to be the oldest bar in Tennessee that has served alcohol continuously (even during Prohibition). It has had a few name changes such as Norma's, and Pirate's Den, before changing it to Springwater Supper Club in 1978. It was opened during the Tennessee Centennial and International Exposition in 1897.

TEXAS

Scholz Garten (Est. 1866) | Austin

August Scholz (1825–1891), a German immigrant and Confederate veteran, built his public bar and café over an old boarding house the year following the end of the Civil War (1866). In 1908, a bowling alley was built inside that is still in operation. During Prohibition, they sold a nonalcoholic brew and served food. In 1995, the building was restored.

UTAH

Shooting Star Saloon (Est. 1879) | Huntsville

This saloon is the oldest in Utah. It had a couple of names before this: Holin's Bar and Clarence's Bar. It is said that its current name came from a patron named Whiskey Joe who was cut off and kicked out of the bar. Whiskey Joe started shooting at the star on the outside of the building, and the name was born. Today, it is decorated with a stuffed St. Bernard dog head, photos of the original owner, business cards, boots, kitchen utensils, magazine articles, funny signs, and more.

VERMONT

Ye Olde Tavern (Est. 1790) | Manchester

This was built by master builder Aaron Sheldon and was distinguished by the sprung floor on its third-floor ballroom and the high square columns of its porch. It was first named the Stagecoach Inn and later renamed to Lockwood's Hotel, then Thayer's Hotel, and Fairview Hotel. In 2002, it was renamed to Ye Olde Tavern. Today, their bar serves vintage classic cocktails and American fare, and provides banquet space.

VIRGINIA

The Tavern (Est. 1779) | Abingdon

The Tavern has hosted such guests as King of France Louis Philippe, President Andrew Jackson, and Pierre Charles L'Enfant. The building has been used for other purposes including a bank, bakery, general store, cabinet shop, barbershop, private residence, post office, antique shop, restaurant, and hospital for wounded Confederate and Union soldiers during the Civil War. In 1984, local attorney Emmitt F. Yeary restored it to a tavern again.

WASHINGTON

THE BRICK SALOON (EST. 1889) | ROSLYN

This is the oldest continuously operated bar in Washington and was the backdrop for the TV show *Northern Exposure*. The bar still has the original twenty-three-foot running water spittoon and basement jail cell. Today, it has live entertainment, bar grub, and of course, they are still pouring booze.

WYOMING

MINER'S AND STOCKMEN'S STEAKHOUSE (EST. 1862) | HARTVILLE

This is Wyoming's oldest bar and one of the last trading posts and copper mine structures still in existence. It once served as a hideout for bank robbers and outlaws. The bar was hand-carved in Germany in 1862, shipped to New York, transported by train to Cheyenne, and then delivered by horse and buggy. If you plan to visit, then drive slowly so you don't miss it, because the population of Hartville is sixty-five.

• • •

AROUND THE WORLD

CANADA

AUBERGE SAINT-GABRIEL (EST. 1754) | MONTREAL

This was the first auberge (inn) in North America to receive a liquor license. Today, it is a spacious fine-dining restaurant and bar with event spaces available.

MANSION TAVERN (EST. 1828) | ST. CATHARINES, ONTARIO

This is Canada's longest-running licensed bar and St. Catharines's oldest bar. Today, the tavern puts on live bands multiple nights a week with local and touring bands sharing the stage.

CUBA

FLORIDITA (EST. 1817) | HAVANA

Floridita in Havana, Cuba, is a historic restaurant and cocktail bar famous for its Daiquiris and a favorite hangout for Ernest Hemingway. © lembi / Shutterstock

This bar first opened under the name La Piña de Plata (Silver Pineapple) and one hundred years later, it changed to Bar la Florida (Floridita). In 1914, Constantino Ribalaigua Vert started tending bar here, then bought the bar four years later. It became famous for the Frozen Daiquiri. Ernest Hemingway lived in Cuba for twenty years, and this was his favorite bar. He mentioned the bar in his books, and if you visit today, you will see a Hemingway statue, a Hemingway barstool, and a Hemingway bust.

AMERICAN BAR AT THE SAVOY (EST. 1889) | LONDON

The Savoy was not only the first luxury hotel in London—it was the first in the United Kingdom. In the late 1800s and early 1900s America made the best cocktails and set the industry standard. The rest of the world was fascinated with American-style cocktails and soon "American Bars" began popping up. The American Bar at the Savoy Hotel is one of the most prestigious bars to work in. Many famous bartenders have worked here including Ada Coleman, Harry Craddock, Peter Dorelli, and Joe Gilmore. In 2012, the current multiple award-winning head bartender, Erik Lorincz, was asked to create a drink in a grand form for the celebration for Queen Elizabeth's Diamond Jubilee (sixty years being queen). Lorincz created the Diamond Jubilee Punch and poured 360 liters into the hotel fountain outside at the main entrance of the hotel.

THE SPANIARDS INN (EST. UNKNOWN) | LONDON

No one knows exactly when this bar opened, but it is agreed that it was in the seventeenth century sometime. It's claim to fame is that it was mentioned in Bram Stoker's 1897 *Dracula* and in 1837's *The Pickwick Papers* by Charles Dickens. Today, the pub provides a haven for book lovers who love dogs by offering a dog-friendly beer garden and a doggie bath area.

THE EAGLE AND CHILD (EST. NOT CERTAIN) | OXFORD

As far as we know, the first record found for this bar dates back to 1684, and the name has something to do with an aristocratic baby who was found in an eagle's nest. Since it has always been an Oxford college bar, it was often referred to as "Bird and Baby." Starting in 1933, the quartet literary enthusiast group—who called themselves "The Inklings"— met in the bar's private lounge (Rabbit Room) on Monday and Tuesdays. The group included the nontraditional college-aged patrons (they were in their thirties and forties) J. R. R. Tolkien, C. S. Lewis, Hugo Dyson, and Charles Williams. If those names do not ring a bell, then think *Lord of the Rings* or *Narnia*.

FRANCE

HARRY'S NEW YORK BAR (EST. 1911) | PARIS

Tod Sloan wanted to create an American bar in Paris, so he dismantled a New York City bar, shipped it to France, and named it New York Bar. Sloan hired Scottish bartender Harry MacElhone (1890–1958), who bought the bar in 1923 and changed the name to Harry's New York Bar. The bar has attracted many celebrities and tourists. In 1953, the bar was mentioned in Ian Fleming's first James Bond novel, *Casino Royale*, when Bond said it was the best place in Paris to get a solid drink. MacElhone published two classic cocktail recipe books and is credited with inventing the Sidecar, Monkey Gland, French 75, and White Lady. Some believe that the Bloody Mary was invented at the bar as well.

BAR HEMINGWAY AT THE RITZ (EST. 2016) | PARIS

This is where bartender Frank Meier created the Mimosa in 1923. It was named after frequent visitor Ernest Hemingway. Coco Chanel lived at this hotel, Cole Porter spent hours composing music here, F. Scott Fitzgerald had his favorite seat in the bar, and the list goes on.

Kennedy's (Est. 1850) | Dublin

In the beginning, this pub was a grocery store in the front and bar in the back. Its most famous employee was novelist Oscar Wilde. It was known as a hangout for many literary greats. Today, it is a stone's throw from Trinity College, so it is mostly visited by students and tourists, of course.

Sean's Bar (Est. 900) | Athlone

Sean's Bar has been researched thoroughly by the Guinness Book of Records and holds the record for the oldest pub in Ireland. During renovations in 1970, they learned that the original walls were made of wattle and daub, and old coins were found. The walls and the coins are on display in the National Museum, and one section remains on display in the pub.

ITALY

Harry's Bar (Est. 1931) | Venice

Bartender and bar owner Giuseppe Cipriani (1900–1980), created the Bellini here in 1931. When it first opened, Cipriani put out a guest book, and some names that appear in the book include Charlie Chaplin, Truman Capote, and Orson Welles.

Albrindisi (Est. 1100) | Ferrara

This bar has been around since 1100. In the 1400s, Italian painter Tiziano Vecelli and goldsmith, sculptor, and musician Benvenuto Cellini drank here, and in the 1500s, mathematician Nicolaus Copernicus lived above the bar while studying at Ferrara University.

JAMAICA

Rick's Cafe (Est. 1974) | Negril

The first public bar and restaurant of its kind on the West End cliffs of Negril. It is a perfect place to watch the sunset and is known for its cliff divers.

PUERTO RICO

Caribe Hilton (Est. 1949) | San Juan

This luxury hotel began as a design contest for five architectural firms. The San Juan firm Toro-Ferrer won. It is highly believed that Ramón "Monchito" Marrero Perez invented the Piña Colada we know today at the hotel's Beachcomber Bar on August 16, 1954. That is what makes this bar famous.

SINGAPORE

The Long Bar at Raffle Hotel (Est. 1887) | Singapore

This is where the Singapore Sling was said to have been created in 1915 by Chinese bartender Ngiam Tong Boon. It is said that they serve over one thousand a day. In 1991, the original Long Bar was relocated from the hotel lobby to double-level space in the new Shopping Arcade wing; however, they say it retains its original colonial-era decor and atmosphere.

CERVECERIA ALEMANA (EST. 1904) | MADRID

This bar is famous because Ernest Hemingway not only hung out there, he also mentioned the bar in his novel *The Sun Also Rises.*

Acknowledgments

This book is part of a thirty-eight-year collection of cocktail history and trivia. It started with me scribbling bar tricks and magic on cocktail napkins; it then quickly grew in the 1980s–1990s when I was able to meet thousands of tourists tending bar on a Caribbean cruise ship and at Walt Disney World. Its next growth spurt started when I was introduced to the internet via WebTV in 1998. So, I'd like to give a big thank you to all the people who shared their cocktail-related tricks, trivia, and history with me.

Cheers! To Brenda Knight, Yaddyra Peralta, Natasha Vera, and Morgane Leoni at Mango Publishing. A well-deserved toast to my agent, June Clark at FinePrint Literary Management and a Champagne tower of thanks to my gracious cocktail friends who emailed me images for this book. Thank you, John, "JB" Bandy, Paul Harrington, Darcy O'Neil, Jamie Boudreau, Jared Brown, Anistatia Miller, Ocean Organic Vodka, Sean Kenyon, Ted A. Breaux, Brian Huff, Adam Elmegirab, Sobelman's Pub & Grill, Eau de Vie Bar, Joseph Ambrose, Gläce Luxury Ice, Jeff "Beachbum" Berry, Bobby "Robert" Lozoff, Diana Lehman, Neal Murray, Patrick "Paddy" Mitten, Cheryl Cook, Gosling's Black Seal rum, Dennis Oda, Lisa Laird, Camper English, Dale and Jill DeGroff, Natalie Bovis, Anthony Joseph Filippone, Tony Abou-Ganim, Christian Delpech, David Wondrich, Employees Only, Christy Pope, Chad Solomon, Tobin Ellis, H. Joseph Ehrmann, and Doc Eason.

INDEX

A

Abou-Ganim, Charles Anthony "Tony": 1, 28, 31-32, 136, 159, 166-167, 171, 243

absinthe: 1, 5, 11-12, 14-15, 22, 29-32, 34, 46, 74-77, 100, 102, 104-106, 139, 143, 147, 161, 165, 167-168, 170-171, 189, 191-192, 198-199, 201-203, 205, 208-209, 211, 222, 224

Absolut: 22, 26-32, 48-50, 113-114, 116, 118-122, 137-138, 197, 220, 224-226

aguardiente de caña (rum): 8-9, 39, 126

AGWA (Amsterdam high-proof liqueur): 65

Akvavit: 18, 65

Alabama Slammer: 123, 148, 197

Albert, Bridget: 31, 167, 171

Alciatore, Jules: 20, 105

Alexander, Cato: 155

Alperin, Eric: 31, 166, 171, 186

Amaretto Disaronno: 8

Amaretto Sour: 64, 150

Amarula: 65

Ambrose, Joseph: 92-93, 243

Americano: 23, 71, 73-74, 133, 146, 149, 196

Ancho Reyes: 22, 34, 65

Angostura bitters: 19, 63, 78, 104, 126, 136, 143, 146-150

aperitifs: 5, 73-74

applejack (apple brandy): 11-13, 140, 157, 226

Appletini: 29, 64, 123, 204, 218, 224-225

Apricot Sour: 150

aqua vitae: 7-8, 36-40, 60

Armagnac: 7, 38, 74, 209, 217

Arnold, Dave: 169

arrack: 7, 12, 36-38, 100

Auberge Saint-Gabriel: 239

Aviation: 23, 44, 52, 64, 91, 130, 133, 157, 206

Azar, Joe: 105

B

Bacardi: 24, 28, 32-33, 35, 55-57, 68, 106, 124-126, 128, 133, 179, 193-194, 197, 202-203

Bacsik, Paul: 114, 117

Bahama Mama: 147

Baileys Irish Cream: 22, 26, 64-65

Bandy, John "JB":

Banshee: 135

Barbados Cosmopolitan: 111

Bar Magician: 230

bartender organizations: 162

bar tools: 5, 15, 31, 156, 171-172, 177, 179

bathtub gin: 41, 43

Baum, Joe: 158

Bay Breeze: 136, 203

Beachbum Berry's Grog Log: 167

Beachcomber, Don the: 24, 96-97, 150, 157-158, 230, 246 (*see also Gantt, Ernest Raymond Beaumont*)

Beattie, Scott: 31, 167, 171

Beaujolais: 71-72

Belcher, Edward: 208

Bellini: 24, 127-128, 133, 241

Bénédictine: 65, 71, 100, 104, 148-149

Bergeron, Klebert: 105

Bergeron, Victor Jules "Trader Vic": 24, 97, 142, 157

Bergeron, Walter: 24, 104-105, 150

Bermejo, Julio: 149, 165

Bernhardt, Earl: 26, 106

Berry, Jeff "Beachbum": 154

Bessan, Achilles Mehault "Mayo"

Between the Sheets: 41, 133-134, 179, 197

Beverage Alcohol Resource (BAR): 30, 170

Bezuidenhout, Jacques: 153, 166

bitters: 5, 11-12, 16-17, 19, 32, 63, 78-81, 85, 100, 104, 107, 126, 136, 142-143, 146-150, 159, 165, 169, 172, 180, 196, 208

T

U

V

W

Y

Z

CHERYL CHARMING

Cheryl Charming—a.k.a. Miss Charming™—began working in the food & beverage industry in 1976. At age sixteen, she took a job as a pizza waitress then quickly progressed to a cocktail waitress, barback, bartender, and head bartender. With a penchant for travel, Cheryl tended bar in nine American states, a cruise ship in the Caribbean, Walt Disney World, and Bourbon Street in New Orleans. While working at Walt Disney World, she became the bar trick and magic instructor for Disney's F&B training program, Quest for the Best.

Cheryl has hosted events for Tales of the Cocktail, studied graphic design at Ringling College of Art & Design, teaches cocktail classes, and for ten years designed cocktail menus for Brown-Forman. She is also the author of several books. *The Cocktail Companion* is her sixteenth.

Currently, Miss Charming lives in the French Quarter and is the bar director at the Bourbon "O" Jazz Bar on Bourbon Street. In 2015, she held the *New Orleans Magazine* title of "Mixologist of the Year." Her next adventure will be called Charming Wanderlist (Wanderlust + bucket list = Wanderlist). She will make America her backyard by living and exploring her country in a small RV. And yes, she will visit all the famous bars.